WHAT'S NEXT

★ ★ ★

WHAT'S NEXT

A Backstage Pass to *The West Wing*,
Its Cast and Crew,
and Its Enduring Legacy of Service

Melissa Fitzgerald
&
Mary McCormack

DUTTON

DUTTON

An imprint of Penguin Random House LLC

penguinrandomhouse.com

Copyright © 2024 by Melissa Fitzgerald and Mary McCormack
Penguin Random House supports copyright. Copyright fuels creativity,
encourages diverse voices, promotes free speech, and creates a vibrant culture.
Thank you for buying an authorized edition of this book and for complying
with copyright laws by not reproducing, scanning, or distributing any part of it
in any form without permission. You are supporting writers and allowing
Penguin Random House to continue to publish books for every reader.

DUTTON and the D colophon are registered trademarks of
Penguin Random House LLC.

Materials on pages 416 and 418 reprinted with permission of
Bradley Whitford and Richard Schiff.

LIBRARY OF CONGRESS CATALOGING-IN-PUBLICATION DATA
has been applied for.

ISBN 9780593184547 (hardcover)
ISBN 9780593184554 (ebook)

Printed in the United States of America
1st Printing

Interior art: Flag © OSORIOartist/Shutterstock.com

BOOK DESIGN BY KRISTIN DEL ROSARIO

While the authors have made every effort to provide accurate telephone numbers,
internet addresses, and other contact information at the time of publication,
neither the publisher nor the authors assume any responsibility for errors
or for changes that occur after publication. Further, the publisher does not have
any control over and does not assume any responsibility
for author or third-party websites or their content.

FROM MELISSA:
To my parents, Carol and Jim Fitzgerald.
You model what it is to live a life of meaning and service.
This—and everything—is for you.

FROM MARY:
To my mother, Norah McCormack,
who approached the world with joy, empathy,
and an unshakable sense of justice.
I miss you.
I think you would get a kick out of this book.

And to my father, Bill McCormack,
you led by example, in service as in everything.
Your final words will stay with me forever:
"The message is: To give as much as you can, everywhere you can,
for as long as you can. Keep your hand out. Keep giving."

FROM MELISSA AND MARY:
To our perennial Number One, Martin Sheen,
whose dedication to and joy in service
inspires and motivates us every day.
We love you.

And to Aaron Sorkin,
who sat alone in a room, staring at a blank page,
and conjured up the world of *The West Wing*:
You created a family. We are deeply grateful.

CONTENTS

FOREWORD

by Aaron Sorkin

My agent had asked me if I'd like to have lunch with John Wells. I'd never met John, but I knew him by reputation as the producer of high-end dramatic television, such as *E.R.* and *China Beach*. I wasn't sure why I was being asked to meet with him. I had a pretty good career writing movies, and I knew nothing about television. I liked television as much as anyone else, I just didn't know anything about it.

"He just wants to say hello," my agent told me.

I could do that. A lunch was scheduled for the following week.

As it happened, the night before the lunch I had some friends over for dinner. One of the friends was Akiva Goldsman, who'd not yet won his Academy Award for writing *A Beautiful Mind*. I mentioned the lunch I'd be having the next day, and he said he thought I'd like television.

"This is just a lunch to say hello. I'm not writing a television series."

Later that night, Akiva and I went off to sneak a cigarette in the small office I kept at home. He pointed at the wall to a poster for *The American President*, a romantic comedy I'd written a few years earlier.

"You know what would make a good series? That. If you made it about senior staffers at the White House."

"This is just a lunch to say hello," I said. "I'm not writing a television series."

The next day. Lunch. I walked into the restaurant and immediately saw that this was not just a lunch to say hello. John Wells was seated at a table with several executives from Warner Bros. Television. "So what do you want to do?" John said. At that moment, I could have said, "I'm sorry, there's been a mistake; I don't have anything to pitch."

Instead, I said, "I want to do a show about senior staffers at the White House." John reached his hand across the table and said, "We've got a deal."

I was terrified. I had to write a one-hour pilot. It never occurred to me that the pilot might get picked up to series and I'd also have to write Episode 2, Episode 3, and so on, until we were inevitably canceled after thirteen episodes. After all, there was no way a network was going to put this on the air. Shows about politics didn't work. Moreover, in popular culture our leaders are portrayed as either Machiavellian or complete dolts; but in this show, due to the romantic and idealistic style of my writing, our leaders would be as hyper-competent and dedicated as the doctors and nurses on hospital shows, the cops on police shows, and the lawyers on legal dramas. Would the audience really stand for that?

They did.

NBC ordered thirteen episodes. Then ordered the "back nine." Then a second season and, in the blink of an eye, a seventh. I wrote the first eighty-eight episodes of the series before stepping down at the end of season 4. And for that time, I had the best job in show business.

I'm grateful to Mary and Melissa for keeping all these memories alive and sharing them with fans of the show. Welcome to Warner Bros. Stage 23 and the set of *The West Wing*.

INTRODUCTION

by Allison Janney

Apparently, this all began at my house. Or at least my friend Ilana's house, because that's where my birthday party was in 2019, when Melissa Fitzgerald and Mary McCormack went to the table to get a piece of cake at the same time, and ten minutes later came back with not only cake (vanilla, chocolate frosting) but also an absolutely ludicrous plan to write this book. Ludicrous because it just seemed so . . . big. I think back on those *West Wing* years and it's an almost overwhelming confusion of memories, friendships, late nights, walk-and-talks, volunteering and advocating together, sharing so much with so many people. It was years, but it was over in an instant. How would they go about capturing all that? Where would they even begin, and where would they find the time? It was a fun conversation to have over a piece of cake at a birthday party, and they would both leave the party, resume their lives, and forget it ever happened.

Except, the one thing you don't do with Melissa Fitzgerald and Mary McCormack, you don't underestimate them. When they decide to do something, they get it done.

Both Mary and Melissa are activists who care passionately about their causes—Melissa cares so much that she left Hollywood and moved to Washington, DC, to dedicate herself to advocacy full time. When they first mentioned to me that they wanted to write an insider's book about *The West Wing* through the lens of service, it all started to come into focus for me. After all, the show itself was just that—stories of people in the East Wing of the West Wing, each of whom is there because of their own lifelong devotion to serving their country. Aaron's scripts always seemed full of that reverence for service, whether it was actively part of the dialogue or—more often—a feeling that was there under every scene.

But what they've done with the book that follows is something I couldn't have imagined they would be able to do so well: They've captured the feeling of what it was like to be part of this show. It's a stroll back through Soundstage 23 on the Warner Bros. lot. It's full of stories from on set and off, full of insights and anecdotes, and it's full of all the voices you know, and many you may not have met yet.

Somehow they brought those years back to life, and that is a profound gift to all of us who were part of it, and I hope for all of you who watched it. They call it a "backstage pass," and I can tell you, that's exactly what it is.

So, thank you, Mary and Melissa, for honoring this show we all love, and for setting down on paper so many memories from so many people. I thought I was big enough to resist the obvious joke, but dammit I'm not. This idea you had together at my birthday party years ago was certainly no piece of cake, and you almost bit off more than you could chew. But you did it. This introduction is really nothing more than the icing on . . . You know what? I'll stop.

—ALLISON JANNEY

A NOTE FROM THE AUTHORS

This book is about *The West Wing* and the army of dedicated people who created it, starred in it, watched it, and kept it moving forward for seven seasons. It's also about what the world of the show, and the characters who inhabited it, represented: a dedication to service. It was assembled from a number of sources, chief among which are more than a hundred interviews we conducted from 2021 to 2024 with members of the cast and crew, including actors, writers, directors, and producers; designers, technicians, executives, and casting directors; and even a handful of devoted (and in some cases, prominent) fans, aka "Wingnuts." (Note: Brackets are periodically used for clarity or to change the tense of a statement, and a full list of sources by chapter is available at the end of the book.)

Supplementing these primary-source Q and As, we were fortunate to have available to us the extensive archival material that living in the twenty-first century allows. These sources range from published articles, broadcast interviews, and DVD commentaries to websites, blogs, and podcasts. The abundance of this content has been particularly meaningful to us as it pertains to those now unavailable to share their stories, including and especially our dear friends—gone but never forgotten—John Spencer and Kathryn Joosten.

Finally, we are singularly indebted to *The West Wing Weekly* and its hosts, Josh Malina and Hrishikesh Hirway. Without this brilliant, insightful, enlightening podcast, we could not have painted as full a picture of the show as we hope to have done in the following pages.

We are deeply grateful to *all* of you.

WHAT'S NEXT

Up above a small, unmarked door leading to Soundstage 23 on the Warner Bros. lot, a red light sits mounted, silent and still. This is one of numerous so-called wig-wags, or red-eyes—some inside, some out—that alert cast and crew (and occasional stray visitors) that cameras are rolling. It warns them to stay out, steer clear, or at least keep mouse-level quiet, until someone somewhere inside yells, "Cut!," a loud bell rings, and the din of actors, artists, and operators suddenly fills the space inside like a collective exhale. Right now, though, that outside red light is off. Right now, it's just sitting there, waiting. Waiting for the next take to begin, waiting for the magic words that serve as the run-up to "Action!"—words like "on a bell . . ." and "rolling . . ." Waiting . . . for Martin Sheen.

It's safe to say most of us on set that day idolized Martin. Honestly, who wouldn't? An acclaimed star of countless venerated films—*Badlands, Apocalypse Now, Wall Street, The American President*, to name a few—he was also an icon in the realm of social justice. The patriarch of a famous acting family, Martin was a bona fide movie star, a widely respected member of the Hollywood community, and a consummate professional.

So, of course, it wasn't that Martin was late or missing. But, just before the director got ready to roll, you could see something happening, right over there, just steps away. That was Martin, walking around to every single background artist, the actors often referred to as "extras," despite their absolutely fundamental contribution. That was Martin, playing host to person after person, welcoming them into his "home," treating these new faces like old friends. That was Martin, this deeply kind and generous spirit, engaged in a genuine exchange with each one of them.

> "I'm Martin Sheen. Welcome. What's your name?"
> "Nice to meet you. Thank you for joining us today!"
> "Hi, I'm Martin. How you doin' today?"
> "Hi there—good to see you! So glad you're here!"

That was Martin.

Watching this time-consuming exercise, I stood there perplexed, wondering what was going on. "What is he *doing*?" And then it dawned on me: He was teaching us. He was showing everyone on set how this was all going to go down, today and for however long we would stay on the air. He was letting us know, from the beginning—even before the cameras rolled on him—that how we act off camera is just as important as how we act on camera. He was letting us know that every single person who was part of *The West Wing* would be treated with dignity, respect, and gratitude; that every single person had an important role to play and that every role would be valued. We were all a part of the team. That gesture, which he repeated without fail for each season that followed, established a culture and a simple, powerful set of values that we all treasure and carry with us to this day. "Watch," his unspoken lesson went. "This is how we treat each other."

(This is Melissa, by the way. Mary was hanging out on movie sets with Clint Eastwood at the time, I think . . . or Russell Crowe or Robert

Duvall. In any case, this seems like a good moment for us to welcome you to the book. For most of it you won't know which one of us is speaking—though, of course, you're welcome to guess. But a quick heads-up: every now and again we'll check in with thoughts, commentary, or insights that come specifically from one of us. With that, as they say, on with the show! Let's see . . . what's next? Oh yeah—"It was 1999 . . .")

It was 1999, just a handful of days into shooting a new, high-profile, big-budget series for NBC, and the stress level was, well . . . not, like, "through the roof" or anything, but we weren't exactly sipping mai tais on the beach either. It was somewhere between the two—closer to "roof" than "mai tais." That's what I'm *told*, anyway. (This is Mary. I show up in season 5. Maybe I would've been on sooner, but, according to some pilot casting notes we unearthed during the research for this book, I was apparently "not interested in series work." Great call, right? Career advice? I'm right here. Seriously—I'm the worst.)

Now, the first thing you need to understand about production is this: If cast and crew are new to each other—especially early on, like when shooting the first episode, aka the "pilot"—it can be exciting (of course), but it can be stressful as well (also of course). The second thing you need to understand about production is that every literal *minute* on set is expensive. Even back in the late '90s, where our story begins, we're talking thousands upon thousands of dollars a minute. So, naturally, no one likes to waste a single second. Especially the executives overseeing the show.

Yet there we were, standing around. No "on a bell . . ." no "rolling . . ." No "sound speed" and nothing even close to "Action!" And, still, no Martin. (SPOILER: He'd get on his mark once he finished with every single handshake.)

★ ★ ★

THERE'S a common saying in TV: "As Number One goes, so goes the show." This refers to the ranking of cast members on a call sheet.

Martin was Number One. (John Spencer, who played chief of staff Leo McGarry, was Number Two.) The idea is, the person with that top billing in the cast sets the tone for everyone else. As Melissa saw on day one, on this show Martin was our walking, talking primer. When "crew lunch" came and the background artists filed to their separate catering line—it's the norm for background artists to eat separately (different food, at different times, in a different area) from the rest of the cast— Martin wouldn't hear of it. "We're all going to eat together," he insisted. "We're a family. Families eat together." This moment above all instituted the cardinal rule of *The West Wing*: "Families eat together."

To the millions of people who tuned in to seven seasons of the series on NBC—and to those viewers who gave it new life on Bravo and Netflix and, now, the app formerly known as HBO Max—the characters on *The West Wing* seemed like a family. A family of smart, committed, but flawed patriots who cared deeply about America and the world beyond its borders. They watched as beloved (if occasionally boneheaded and arrogant) characters would hustle, cajole, flirt, lobby, joke, fight tooth and nail, and, more than anything, walk-and-talk— all in service to a higher calling, to a country they truly revered. Taking up critical issues of the day, Jed and Leo, C.J. and Toby, Josh and Donna and Charlie and the rest of the gang, aimed to solve problems big and small, to make life better, sweepingly or by degrees. And while they didn't always hit it out of the park, even when they failed, they went down swinging.

Who was the monk who wrote, "I don't always know the right thing to do, Lord, but I think the fact that I want to please you *pleases* you"?

—LEO TO PRESIDENT BARTLET, "POSSE COMITATUS"

From the start, a commitment to service was in the bones of *The West Wing*, in its DNA. It was the ethos of a show designed to be, in the words of creator Aaron Sorkin, "a love letter to public service." That said, you can't get people interested in service if they're not watching. As Aaron has told countless journalists countless times, it was an hour a week devoted to "telling good stories."

And Lord knows there were lots of good stories. But between the smart, interwoven narratives, the periodic flourishes of workplace romance, and the back-and-forth banter, Aaron also managed to offer up a weekly civics case study, one laced with inspiration, a robust sense of patriotic optimism, and a bold ambition too. On top of all that, his stories seemed to steer the conversation toward the better angels of our nature. But don't tell him that. After all, Aaron's the one who famously said, "It's important to remember that, first and foremost, if not only, this is entertainment. *The West Wing* isn't meant to be good for you."

You think I think that an artist's job is to speak
the truth. An artist's job is to captivate you for
however long we've asked for your attention.
If we stumble into truth, we got lucky.

—TABITHA FORTIS TO TOBY, "THE U.S. POET LAUREATE"

Not unlike the show, this book is about service as much as entertainment. Over the years, lending our voices to issues and causes we care about, the cast of *The West Wing* got involved and stayed involved. (That feeling, as Josh Lyman once famously told a wide-eyed Charlie Young, "it doesn't go away.")

Different causes are near and dear to different members of the *West Wing* family, but whenever someone sends out the bat signal, we all respond to the call. The cast text chain lights up with details about this cause or that, and what any or all of us can do to help. And then . . . we get to work. More often than not, the keeper of the signal (and to be clear, this is Mary talking now) is Melissa Fitzgerald, C.J.'s always sunny shadow, born smiling with a briefing book in her hand and trailing one step behind.

ALLISON JANNEY: I may have played Melissa's boss on *The West Wing*, but in real life, she's my boss, no doubt about it.

DULÉ HILL: If Mary asks you to do something—a book or whatever—there's no way to say no. If you need to negotiate a hostage situation, she's the one for the job.

LAWRENCE O'DONNELL: When you're growing up in a big family, you never know who's going to be the glue who holds the family together long after you've all gone your separate ways. In the *West Wing* family, that turned out to be Melissa and Mary. Melissa has something uncommon in the acting community and that is an organized mind. She organizes us in ways that no one on Earth could. Martin and Melissa are kind of the heart and soul of the place. And Mary is a force of nature. Give her an impossible task in support of a good cause and she has this uncanny ability to inspire others to jump on board without even realizing they've signed on to do it.

BRADLEY WHITFORD: Mary and Melissa are two of the bossiest people I've ever met. They said they're writing a book and that I had to participate. I was afraid to say no.

Here's the bottom line: Just as Aaron considered *The West Wing* a love letter to public service, we see *What's Next* as a love letter to *The West Wing*, the people who made it, and the fans who loved it and were inspired by it. This, of course, includes the superfans, aka the "Wing-nuts." On the off chance you aren't aware of this term, we'll be clear: If you're reading this book, odds are good you are one. We all are. Welcome.

Thanks to scores of interviews with members of our *West Wing* family—actors and writers, directors and designers, gaffers and grips—you're about to get a backstage pass to the Warner Bros. lot, to our stages and trailers, to best boys and prop masters, set dressers, script supervisors, and background actors. These are the army of artists who made the show go. In addition, we'll take a deep dive into how the series came together, from its inception to the final FADE OUT. We'll also dispel some popular *West Wing* rumors and, while we're at it, maybe start a few new ones. (Ask us about the time Josh Malina tried to break a hundred at a kids' lemonade stand.)

As we relive classic moments from *The West Wing*, as you virtually walk-and-talk with your favorite White House staffers, we'll periodically regale you with stories about *our* service journeys, like participating in campaigns and advocating for issues we care about. We hope you'll be inspired to learn more about those organizations (our own personal "Big Blocks of Cheese") that have kept us coming back to one another year after year.

This spirit—of continually working together, of seeking new and meaningful ways to deepen our connections and maybe do a little good along the way—is not unlike the one that guided *The West Wing*. It's the same spirit that went into this book. It is the spirit embodied by Jed Bartlet, the one captured in the rousing phrase he uttered so often across seven seasons of the show: "What's next?"

What's next? Turn the page.

PART I

★ ★ ★

RUNNING FOR OFFICE

Conceiving the Show

ORIGIN STORY

The *West Wing* Pilot

In 1998, Aaron Sorkin, acclaimed Broadway playwright and the writer of lauded films like *A Few Good Men*, *Malice*, and *The American President*, had never really considered writing for TV. But, as Aaron alludes to in his Foreword, on the advice of his agent, he had agreed to meet up with John Wells, a producer who had come off the critical darling *China Beach* to executive produce and write another critical darling, the ratings-monster hospital show *ER*. The night before the meeting, Aaron had been hosting some friends, among whom was screenwriter Akiva Goldsman. Just a few years later, Akiva would win the Academy Award for his feature screenplay *A Beautiful Mind*. On this night, though, he was slipping down to the basement to sneak a cigarette with his friend. Mid–smoke break, Goldsman turned to Aaron and said, "You know what would make a good television series? That." He was pointing at a poster of *The American President*. Akiva remarked that "there doesn't have to be a romance, just focus on a senior staffer." To Aaron this sounded like a good idea, but . . . "I'm not going to be doing a television series." That declaration lasted less than eighteen hours.

As Aaron would tell *The Hollywood Reporter* more than a decade later—as he's told members of the *West Wing* family over the years—his expectations for the meeting with John weren't remotely career oriented. He approached their get-together as more of a fan.

"I wanted to hear stories about *China Beach* and *ER*," but, the former musical theater major confessed, "I especially wanted to hear about his years as stage manager for *A Chorus Line*." The moment Aaron walked into the restaurant, though, he realized that the meeting was going to be something more than a "Hello, how are you?" affair. In what you might call a friendly sort of ambush, waiting there with John Wells were a pair of agents and some Warner Bros. studio executives.

"Right after I sat down, John said, 'So what do you want to do?' and instead of saying, 'I think there's been a misunderstanding, I don't have an idea for a television series,' which would've been honest, I said, 'I want to do a television series about senior staffers at the White House.' John just looked at me and said . . . 'You got a deal.'"

Years later, John reflected on the first of what would become myriad conversations about the project. "We talked about how Aaron had spent a lot of time preparing the script for *The American President* with the staffers who worked in the [actual] West Wing, and how he hadn't been able to write about them as much as he wanted to in the movie." (**MELISSA:** In *The American President* a recently widowed commander in chief, played by Michael Douglas, jockeys over matters of policy and politics, all while single parenting a teenage daughter and falling for an environmental lobbyist who bears an uncanny resemblance to Annette Bening. President Shepherd is supported by a team of hyper-articulate, passionate, overworked, and idealistic staffers—sensing a trend?—and a best friend–cum–chief of staff fans of *The West Wing* would find eerily familiar.)

Aaron was intrigued by the hallowed halls he'd gotten to know while working on the movie. He was interested in a political narrative that took place, as he has often put it, "during the two minutes before and after what we see on CNN." And it wasn't just that. "I like things that take place behind the scenes," he says, "whether it's behind the scenes at the White House, behind the scenes at a naval courtroom, or behind the scenes at a national cable sports show." Aaron had always been attracted to workplace shows, and this—the West Wing of the White House—was undeniably a glamorous workplace in which to plant his flag. "I thought I would tell a contemporary story of kings and palaces," he says. "It appealed to a sense of romanticism and idealism that I have."

Now it was just a matter of getting started, which, for Aaron, is always the hardest part. "If I'm writing a script, really ninety percent of it would be walking around, climbing the walls, just trying to put the idea together. The final ten percent would be writing it." Fortunately, his first draft of *The American President* had been extremely long. Typically, a screenplay runs anywhere from 90 to 120 pages. This one came in at 385 pages, about the length of *four* screenplays! Choosing from several "tiny shards of ideas" woven into those nearly four hundred first-draft pages, he landed on one involving Cuban refugees. From that kernel, Aaron began to sketch out the underpinnings of the pilot.

Selecting a handful of key senior White House jobs, starting with the president's chief of staff, press secretary, and communications director, Aaron looked to populate his "palace." To a harried, thriving, whirling-dervish ecosystem within these halls of power, he added a collection of well-intentioned if flawed deputies, assistants, and staffers and gave it all a propulsive verbal energy. This West Wing, Aaron knew from the start, would be marked by a collegial group of fast-talking, whip-smart, highly competent people, who would, as he put it, "lose as much as they win, but we're going to understand that they wake up every morning wanting to do good. That was really the spirit behind *The West Wing*."

The people that I have met have been
extraordinarily qualified, their intent is *good*.
Their commitment is true. They are righteous,
and they are patriots ... and I'm their lawyer.

—AINSLEY HAYES TO HER REPUBLICAN FRIENDS,
"IN THIS WHITE HOUSE"

Armed with a six-series deal at NBC, and excited by Aaron's idea, executive producer John Wells took it to the network, telling them he wanted to make the pilot as part of his deal. It didn't go well. "The American audience isn't interested in politics," Wells was told. Additionally, given the political climate at that time, the subject was, in the view of the executives, nothing short of toxic. Plus, Sunday mornings were wall-to-wall politics on all the major networks. Was there really an appetite for *more*? It was a fair question.

At that moment, the White House was mired in a sex scandal involving Bill Clinton and Monica Lewinsky. During the time Aaron was writing the pilot, every newspaper, magazine, and cable news show was breathlessly reporting the sordid "presidential intern" story around the clock. "It was hard, at least for Americans," Aaron says, "to look at the White House and think of anything but a punch line."

By early 1999, Aaron had finished writing the pilot and submitted it to Warner Bros. What happened next may constitute the most important step in the development of *The West Wing*. On February 22, 1999, veteran studio executive Peter Roth left his post at Fox and 20th Century Fox Television to become president of Warner Bros. Television. Given a stack of scripts representing the potential slate for the upcoming season, he pored through them all. He wasn't exactly wowed by most of what he read, but a silver lining came shining through. This one script—*The West Wing*—knocked him out.

"I thought, 'This is brilliant,'" Peter told us. "'This is as smart, as powerful, as well written as anything I have *ever* read!'" That was the weekend of February 22. That Monday, Peter picked up the phone and dialed the writer.

"Hey, Aaron," he said. "You don't know me—I'm the new guy. I just want you to know, I read your script and it may be one of the best scripts I've ever read. The only thing that I feel sort of compelled to tell you is that in the history of broadcast television, there has never been a successful series set in Washington, DC."

As a real student of television, Peter Roth believed he knew why. "People don't want the institution of the presidency to be sullied or to be ballyhooed. Whatever the reasons"—and this he said to Aaron— "Washington just hasn't worked." Aaron's near instantaneous response, according to Peter, went something along the lines of "Well, why the fuck should I care about *that*?" Today, Peter laughs at the memory with a sense of admiration. "I sat back in my chair," he told us, "and said, 'You know what, Aaron? I'm embarrassed. You're absolutely right. The fact that it's never worked doesn't mean that it *can't* work.'"

Setting aside Aaron's bravado and Peter's unbridled support, the project, it seemed, had its back against the wall. Luckily, the structure of John Wells's deal was such that NBC had to either make the show or give it back to him to set up someplace else. But between the subject matter's meager past performance and the current state of political affairs, an uphill battle was the best they could hope for. Ultimately, a deal was struck. NBC would make the show. There was just one catch—they wanted to wait a year.

In the meantime, Aaron had followed up his *West Wing* pilot by writing another fast-paced workplace show, the half-hour dramedy *Sports Night*. Set in the world of a fictionalized *SportsCenter* (ESPN's nightly highlights program), *Sports Night* aired on ABC for two critically acclaimed seasons. The success of that show was due in no small part to what would become one of TV's most celebrated dynamic duos—Aaron Sorkin and his new and trusted creative partner, producing director Tommy Schlamme. Tommy had come on board at the recommendation of John Wells, who had hired him years earlier as a director on *ER*.

To this day, Tommy looks back fondly on the evening of not-so-light reading that changed his life forever. "My agent sent me Aaron's scripts for both *The West Wing* and *Sports Night*. I read them the same night, called [my agent back] at, like, twelve thirty, and went, 'These are the two best scripts I've ever read!'"

Even two decades later, Tommy's effusiveness for the writing remains unbridled. "When I read his words, there was just energy, I would read standing up!" Even on a page with a big block of monologue, without another person talking, to Tommy both scripts still felt . . . almost musical. "I loved *Sports Night*, but everything I wanted to do was in the *West Wing* script, everything I wanted to say about America . . . about my immigrant parents coming to this country . . . my sense of patriotism . . . was there. I saw this show right away. It just was so clear to me."

To that point in his career, Tommy had been best known for directing in the half-hour space, so the timing—on *his* end anyway—couldn't have worked out better. Since *The West Wing* was delayed by the Clinton sex scandal, he started working on *Sports Night*, a show squarely in his dramedy wheelhouse.

With Tommy excited about being on board, Wells went to NBC with a compelling "dream team" pitch: "It'll be Aaron and Tommy and me. Aaron's going to write them, Tommy's going to direct them, and I'll produce. You told me if I signed this six-series deal with you, you were going to make stuff, I want to make it, so let's make it!"

And with that, the *West Wing* pilot got the green light.

★ ★ ★

LOOKING back, it's hard to fathom anyone seeing Aaron's initial pitch as anything but a dead-perfect fastball down the heart of the plate. A crew of quick-witted, passionate, unsung public servants sacrificing the prime of their lives for the betterment of their country? It's an idea so patriotic that it's practically romantic, and uniquely *American*. At the time, though, even after the project got the go-ahead, in the halls of NBC there was a lingering skepticism that this "dream team" could pull it off.

Aaron was Aaron, sure, and he'd teamed up with John and Tommy. Still, even if the series were flawlessly written, directed, acted, and produced, a nagging doubt persisted. Could a show about not-so-glamorous civil servants navigating cramped hallways and discussing policy minutiae command a large audience, let alone hold it week to week? And could a clarion call to public service, however rousing and romantic, compete with the sex, drugs, and rock and roll–scape prime-time viewers had come to expect?

They were fair questions. But while the "rock and roll" would have to wait, Aaron's pilot script came armed with a little "sex and drugs" up its sleeve. That was thanks to a certain dashing deputy communications director, who can wear the *hell* out of a suit but can't quite manage to keep his pants on or his pagers straight. Yes, God bless Sam and that mix-up with Laurie the call girl. Without them, we would've been robbed of his succinct—if hilariously desperate—sum-up of pretty much everything that went down in the pilot:

> Ms. O'Brien, I understand your feelings, but please
> believe me when I tell you that I am a nice guy having
> a bad day. I just found out the *Times* is publishing a
> poll that says that a considerable portion of Americans
> feel that the White House has lost energy and focus, a
> perception that's not likely to be altered by the video

footage of the President riding his bicycle into a tree.
As we speak, the Coast Guard are fishing Cubans out
of the Atlantic Ocean, while the governor of Florida
wants to blockade the port of Miami, a good friend of
mine is about to get fired for going on television and
making sense, and it turns out that I accidentally slept
with a prostitute last night!

—SAM SEABORN TO LEO'S DAUGHTER, MALLORY, "PILOT"

To sidestep the reality that *real* West Wing conversations typically take place in small offices with the doors closed, Tommy suggested setting the script's wide-ranging policy debates on the move. Winding in and out of hallways and offices, passing the baton from this character to that, and then to another . . . and another, Aaron and his director endowed the "world" of the show with a whirlwind feel. This stop-and-go-go-go choreography had the added benefit of showing off production designer Jon Hutman's breathtaking set, which actual West Wing staffers would later marvel "looked better than the real thing!"

If you go to the real West Wing it looks like
a boring law office. . . . The moulding is frayed,
the carpet is a little dirty. . . . By putting windows
in the Roosevelt Room . . . they created this
maze of rooms you can see through.
The bullpen has glass, where the writer's
bullpen in the real West Wing is on the bottom
floor and it looks like a series of closets.

—RICHARD SCHIFF, EMPIREONLINE

Despite all the pop of the dialogue, punctuated by soaring speeches, the pilot script—early on, anyway—still drew concerns at NBC. In a meeting with the network, Aaron got the distinct impression that they were having trouble following the various plot lines. There was, the executives suggested, "too much dialogue" and not enough time spent on each story. One pitched the alternative of a populist celebrity president, along the lines of Minnesota's then governor Jesse Ventura (the former pro wrestler turned Reform Party politician) or maybe "a . . . race car driver?" Another mused that perhaps instead of *talking* about the plight of the Cuban refugees, one White House staffer could rent a boat, jump in, and speed off to save the immigrants himself. The network note, according to Brad Whitford, lived somewhere in the vicinity of "We need to get Sam and Josh in the water."

"I honestly didn't know if I was being messed with or not," Aaron later recalled. "And I didn't want to insult the executive or appear to be difficult to work with. So I said, 'That's worth thinking about.'"

On the other hand, to anyone remotely familiar with the inner workings of the White House, the teleplay was nothing short of a masterpiece. Indeed, when the *West Wing* pilot script made its way to longtime Senate aide and seasoned politico Lawrence O'Donnell, it floored him. "I read it and I'm kind of stunned," the future MSNBC host (and *West Wing* writer-producer) remembers. "I've been in that room . . . the interior Oval Office . . . in a governing meeting. Aaron Sorkin never has. He's just imagining this stuff. How did he get this so *right*?"

Down the road, of course, the script would be praised as one of the great pilots of all time. Critics, historians, and film school professors would celebrate the groundbreaking ways in which it established character, braided storylines, and conveyed a palpable sense of stakes and urgency. This, despite the fact that President Bartlet wasn't an alum of NASCAR or the WWE, just an old-fashioned New England governor, and Josh didn't rescue fleeing Cuban refugees personally, he just relentlessly worked the levers of power to help make it happen.

A surrogate for President Biden's 2020 campaign, Kevin Walling is a leading Democratic voice on Fox News who often references *The West Wing* in his political analysis. (He's also these three things: a dear friend, a fan of the show since high school, and the first and most persistent voice pushing us to write this book.) "The story arcs of *The West Wing* were, for many of us now working in politics, our first introductions to public policy," he says. "Whether it involved serious issues like immigration, gun control, military interventions, or navigated the intricacies of a government shutdown, every episode provided a crash course in what governing could actually look like without ever having to dilute the complexity of each issue."

To Kathleen York (congresswoman Andrea Wyatt, aka Toby's ex-wife), that level of sophistication, and the level of trust *The West Wing* would show in its audience, stood out. "It was a broadcast network series that didn't spoon-feed information or emotional moments. That was really novel. In network television," Kathleen continued, "the note you always get is: clarify, explain . . . simplify, so no one's left out. But Aaron Sorkin is a rocket—you get on or you don't."

Before that rocket had a chance to take off, though, Aaron's script was put into the proverbial "graveyard drawer," alongside a depressingly large number of other unproduced pilots. And it may well have stayed there, if not for a change of network leadership. The new president of NBC West Coast, Scott Sassa, pulled the script out, read it, and called Aaron to say NBC was going to shoot the pilot. "I was inexperienced enough in that job," Sassa would tell *The Hollywood Reporter*, "that I didn't know why I should not like it, so we set it up."

To any writer almost anywhere on the planet, the president of the network issuing a pilot order for your script would be pretty big news. And we imagine it must have been for Aaron as well. But it also had to have posed a bit of a dilemma. By then, he and Tommy were hip-deep in production on *Sports Night* for ABC. Could Aaron handle the chaotic slog of writing *two* weekly series simultaneously? After all, a single

TV schedule turns a showrunner's life upside down. But two series, especially when you're doing the vast majority of the writing on both? Fortunately, Aaron was armed with support from Tommy and John, along with an impressive team of writers, consultants, and research assistants.

Act as if ye have faith and faith shall be given to you.
Put another way: Fake it 'til you make it.

—LEO TO GOVERNOR BARTLET,
"IN THE SHADOW OF TWO GUNMEN: PART I"

Even setting aside the *Sports Night* double duty of it all, when it came to getting the *West Wing* pilot on its feet, there were still countless details on the creative team's to-do list. Now that plans were falling into place for this "contemporary story of kings and palaces," now that this world of columns and corridors—of outer offices and busy bullpens—was under construction, now that Leo and Jed, Toby and Sam, C.J. and Josh and everyone else, had walk-and-talked their way onto the page . . . one to-do loomed larger than all the others:

Who the hell were they gonna get to play these guys?

TWO

CASTING, ABOUT

Casting director John Levey is an easygoing, ebullient gentleman with a million war stories, a disarming laugh, a lifetime achievement award, and two very special rosebushes in the back of his house. Thanks to his years of work with John Wells on *ER*, Levey and his colleague Kevin Scott were tasked with one of the great alchemist gigs in the history of television: mixing and matching the magic carousel of staffers who would spend the next seven-plus years walking-and-talking their way through the West Wing of *The West Wing*.

While Levey's presence continued through the first two seasons of the show, the work he and Kevin Scott and the rest of their team began in casting the pilot reverberated through the run of the series. That's due to the ongoing performance of the original series regulars, of course, as well as the countless guest stars who populated the show. But it's also thanks to the culture that Levey observed way back when *The West Wing* was just words on a page. What the script represented, and what the cast shared, was a hunger for *community* and an abiding sense—in the characters and in the actors themselves—of what Levey described to us as "intelligence, core values, and shared dreams."

To unearth a cast like that required a deliberate, if deceptively simple, strategy. "My feeling in casting," Aaron has said, "and it's shared by Tommy, is sort of like the NFL draft. Just take the best athletes available. Sometimes actors are right or wrong for parts, but mostly you're not gonna go wrong if you just have a real world-class actor in there. To wind up with John Spencer and Allison Janney, Richard Schiff and Rob Lowe and Brad Whitford, Martin and Dulé and Janel, is just wonderful."

Levey and his team agreed. In this collection of talent they recognized a community of individuals, all of whom led with intelligence and passion. That culture—the draw of community, of *family*, intelligence, and passion—was established from the top down, thanks to Aaron, Tommy, and John.

"All three," Levey told us, "were extremely confident, extremely experienced, extremely good at what they did. So it wasn't an absence of competitiveness. It was the *presence* of competitiveness." And yet those words—"community," "family," "core values"—those were things Aaron, Tommy, and John clearly believed in.

Here's the allure of television:
Working with the same group of people every week,
you develop as a team and as a family.

—AARON SORKIN, *THE WEST WING WEEKLY*,
"SPECIAL INTERIM SESSION (WITH AARON SORKIN)"

That was our experience, too. During season 1, Melissa and other original cast members experienced that 'round-the-campfire vibe, which was stoked by Martin, Aaron, Tommy, and John. I joined the show in its fifth season but had previously witnessed that side of John

Wells from my time on *ER*. The best way to sum up what Levey and others sensed from the early days of *The West Wing* is that John Wells is a true and fierce advocate for keeping his people—on camera and behind the scenes—feeling like a family. Happy and healthy and connected. As a showrunner, John Wells is a nurturer. He's a real "dad."

As Levey put it to us, "It soon became clear that John was busy. I think the two hundredth episode of *ER* came around the same time. So John . . . I think out of respect for Aaron and Tommy, [and] out of the fact that he had other fish to fry . . . took on a role that was different than his usual role. He wasn't in every casting session . . . or in every meeting that I was in with Tommy and Aaron. And so his leadership was more between the show and the studio . . . about things like budget and production and other elements of it. Also, because of his gift of *ER* to NBC, his relationship with the network was extraordinary. He had carte blanche. So when he spoke to the network on behalf of Aaron and Tommy he was able to accomplish things that, frankly, I don't think Aaron and Tommy would have been able to do on their own." Even in the pilot casting sessions, Aaron was eager to connect with the actors, exercising an unusual degree of involvement.

"One of the enormous differences working with Aaron," Levey notes, "is that he reads in auditions." (Typically, actors read their audition scenes opposite someone from the casting office.) For Levey, Aaron's participation required a serious adjustment and, frankly, took some getting used to. But as he did, he came to appreciate Aaron's partnership, even as he marveled at his penchant for multitasking. "I think the more Aaron can take control, the more he's alive in the moment of what he's working on, the better his judgment is." That said, for Levey it was weird at first, and a bit challenging to track. "[Aaron's] scenes, for the most part, play very fast, and he reads faster than that!"

On top of that, coming off *Sports Night*, Aaron and Tommy were really tight. And, thanks to a natural simpatico, along with a season's worth of creativity and its attendant crises, they'd developed a short-hand. And thank God for that, because *The West Wing* had been picked up quite late and was on a tight schedule. There wasn't a lot of time to get others up to speed. "They had a language," Levey recalls, "that, if you didn't speak it, you were pretty much left out."

When working on a pilot, casting directors are typically hired for ten weeks. By the time *The West Wing* order got picked up, and Levey's team got approved—first by Aaron and Tommy, then by Warner Bros., then by NBC—they had only four weeks to cast the show. That was a "hard out" because, from late winter into spring, the pilot had to be rehearsed, shot, edited, and scored—this included incorporating network and studio notes—in time for the mid-May upfronts in New York City. (The "upfronts" represent one of the key annual events in the world of broadcast television. Executives—along with some cast and other "creatives"—appear before critics, advertisers, and members of the press to present and promote programming for the upcoming season.) In some ways, according to Levey, the need for speed wasn't necessarily a bad development. "You don't wind up with everybody sitting around wondering if Meryl Streep wants to play C.J." Still, there were so many damn parts to cast, and ten times that many damn actors to see. And the damn clock was ticking.

★ ★ ★

SINCE the 1970s, casting notices in Hollywood have run through an integral resource known as Breakdown Services. Producers send out descriptions for various roles to talent reps, who, in turn, fire off the headshots, résumés, and reels of their clients to be considered for the parts. Today, this process plays out almost entirely online. Back in '98, though, it meant a flurry of messengers lining up at studio doors to deliver a bunch of big, bulging envelopes. This left Levey and his small team of casting ninjas with mountains of prospects to sift through.

I have traditionally done the breakdown.
If I did it, I certainly sent it to Aaron,
who then rewrote me fabulously and
probably wrote too much.

—CASTING DIRECTOR JOHN LEVEY,
INTERVIEW FOR *WHAT'S NEXT*

What this glut of product really comes down to is a little thing we call "basic economics." (**MARY:** I was a comparative arts major in college, which is a discipline I *made up*, deep into my sophomore year, so probably take "basic economics" with a grain of salt.) The bottom line is, there are just way more actors than parts. Always. Supply and demand and all that. Sometimes, though, the number of people you see for a particular role doesn't really matter. Because for some roles, there's only one choice. Which brings us back—as life so often does, for so many of us—to John Spencer.

THREE

"THESE WOMEN . . ."
AND A FEW GOOD MEN

Part I

LEO McGARRY

Grizzled veteran politico Leo McGarry was the former labor secretary–slash–Democratic Party bigwig and the president's best friend and chief of staff. In the Bartlet administration and, obviously, in many nonfiction ones too, the chief of staff is the person in whom POTUS enjoys undeniable, unwavering faith. Midway through season 1, President Bartlet outlined the key traits for that position with three simple questions and one definitive—and definitively moving—answer. (**MELISSA:** The fact that Leo overheard this moment is, in our humble opinion, a deeply underrated *West Wing* grace note.)

> You got a best friend? Is he smarter than you?
> Would you trust him with your life?
> That's your chief of staff.

—PRESIDENT BARTLET TO SECRETARY OF AGRICULTURE
ROGER TRIBBEY, "HE SHALL FROM TIME TO TIME . . ."

Several talented people auditioned for the role of Leo, including "obtuse" *Shawshank Redemption* warden Bob Gunton; veteran character actors Paul Dooley, Michael Lerner, and Alan Rosenberg; and actress CCH Pounder, who would later come within an Allison Janney of landing the role of C.J. Cregg. (More on that later!) One other potential chief of staff, Levey told us, brought a more comedic pedigree to the table. Jay Thomas—an alum from another iconic NBC show, *Cheers*—had the room in stitches. In the end, despite these excellent challengers stepping into the ring, it wasn't anything remotely like a fair fight. Because years earlier, this guy named John Spencer—an actor's actor from TV, film, and stage (on and off Broadway)—had done a series in New York for John Wells Productions. Thanks to *Trinity*, Wells and Levey were already enchanted by his work. (As were devotees of his smirky, scrap-tastic lawyer Tommy Mullaney on a third iconic NBC show, *L.A. Law*.) But when the role of Leo first came up, John Wells says, it was complicated by one fact: "We wanted Martin to play Bartlet."

See, in *The American President* Martin Sheen had played Andrew Shepherd's best friend and chief of staff, A.J. McInerney, aka the "Leo" part. "Who can we put into that part," John Wells wondered, "who's not going to interfere in Aaron's head with how *Martin* had played it in the movie?" As he put it to us, "It had to have a completely different kind of thing to it."

In early conversations about casting, members of the creative team typically throw out the names of actors who could be a good fit for the characters in the script, or who might, at the very least, serve as templates for them. For Leo McGarry, Aaron kept coming back to the same name, the perfect model for Jed Bartlet's closest friend and confidant. "I told Tommy and the casting directors, 'We need someone like John Spencer!'" In the first instance of what would become a common refrain during the show's early years, Tommy Schlamme chimed in with a question that was hiding right in plain sight. "What about John Spencer?"

Having grown up in New York and New Jersey, John Spencer had spent decades in close proximity to some of the country's finest filmmakers and theater professionals and had come to view acting as a high art. He knew well the power in making the audience truly *believe* something—in transporting them somewhere new—because he had experienced it himself countless times throughout his life. It helped, too, that, through quirk of fate, genetics, or geography, John had the look of a lifelong public servant—steely-eyed and competent, he naturally exuded a twinkly, smartass, streetwise optimism. And no one did *sincere* like John Spencer. When he smiled—and he smiled a lot—he had folds in his cheeks, which conveyed hard-won wisdom and true grit.

Leo's made out of leather.
His face has a map of the world on it.

—PRESIDENT BARTLET TO JOSH, "BARTLET FOR AMERICA"

According to Levey, when John came in and read for Leo, everybody in the room was kind of just blown away. "John was camera-ready for that part after the first sentence," the casting director says. "No one else on the planet had a single chance in hell after he finished. I mean, it was a *shootable* audition. If it wasn't for the picture of my son in the background, you could've just put it in the show."

When John ambled out of the room, Tommy told us, it was clear: "He's *got* to play this character," the director said, "or let's cast him as the manager of the Yankees." Growing up, Tommy had played a ton

of sports. John's take on Leo brought him right back to "those benevolent, brilliant coaches that I had, who just felt like . . . ya know, that
toast: *Never above you, never below you, right with you.*" The director
saw the Leo that John Spencer had just brought to life as the perfect
man to control the chaos of Jed Bartlet's West Wing.

In a 2002 conversation with CNN's David Daniel, John Spencer
himself reflected on that life-changing day. "I knew the audition was
good. I loved the material . . . I was obsessed with it. I learned all eight
scenes. So, when I read for Aaron and John Wells and Tommy, I had
it all memorized. Aaron said to me, 'You're not going to use your
book?' and I said, 'No, no, no, I want to put the book aside, so I can
act.' And he read with me. I said, 'You're going to read with me? How
are you going to watch me and read with me?' He said, 'That's the way
I do it.'

"So, Aaron and I acted those eight scenes together. It was thrilling.
I finished that audition on a high and I knew I had done my work.
And . . . as an actor, that's all you can do. Because the choice is somebody else's and the most control you have over the situation is to give
the best example of your craft as possible. Ultimately, that can get you
the job . . . and it may *not* get you the job. But I felt very positive about
it. By the time I drove back to my house, the offer was already on my
telephone machine."

If you think the casting of Leo McGarry represents the perfect
match of actor to role, you're in good company—so did John Spencer.

John connected with his *West Wing* counterpart in a personal way,
as both men were open about their battles with addiction. Each knew
well the costs associated with losing that battle, and each found solace
through service to others and in a devotion to his respective vocation.
"Like Leo," John told the Associated Press in 2000, "I've always been
a workaholic, too. Through good times and bad, acting has been my
escape, my joy, my nourishment. The drug for me, even better than
alcohol, was acting."

Indeed, for all of us who had the great good fortune to work with the great, good John Spencer, it is not hyperbole to say, as Mary has more than once, that the man was "touched with genius." We'll talk more about him later—here in the book and for the rest of our lives—but for now let's return to casting director John Levey's backyard.

Remember those very special rosebushes we mentioned earlier? They originally belonged to John Spencer. Transplanted from his home following his passing, they were gifted to Levey as a token of appreciation and affection from John Spencer's off-screen family. A constant and beautiful reminder of an actor, and a man, who was nothing if not constant and beautiful.

Sigh. Breathe. Okay. What's next?

JOSH LYMAN

Once the chief of staff is named, an incoming president—in consultation with his newly minted right-hand man—goes to work nominating cabinet secretaries, senior-level administrators, and envoys. *The West Wing*, though, was light on these kinds of officials. Its action, after all, centered on the White House, not the State Department or the office of the ambassador to the Federated States of Micronesia. An indispensable player in the Bartlet administration was deputy chief of staff (and resident political enforcer) Josh Lyman.

Levey brought in several actors to read for the part of Josh, but Brad Whitford had an edge. In 1990, he had appeared in Aaron's Broadway play *A Few Good Men*, which would eventually be adapted into the blockbuster film starring Tom Cruise, Demi Moore, and this one random Lakers fan. During the Broadway run, Brad played Lieutenant Jack Ross—aka "the Kevin Bacon part." Years later, Levey would recall that Aaron "wanted Brad somewhere on *The West Wing*—either Josh or Sam," but that they expected to see a bunch of guys who'd been in *A Few Good Men* or were just "in Aaron's world." Speaking of . . .

(**MELISSA FUN FACT:** Tim Busfield—*The West Wing*'s Danny Concannon, *Washington Post* columnist and C.J.'s de facto goldfish deliveryman—appeared in the Broadway play, too. Josh Malina was in the original cast and both he and William Duffy [the Larry half of "Ed and Larry"] did the national tour. Oh, and it appears Malina successfully pestered Aaron into putting him in the movie!) But back to Brad . . .

As the Broadway production of *A Few Good Men* went on, Brad and Aaron really hit it off. And, naturally, Brad had quickly fallen head over heels for Aaron's writing. But . . . the course of love never did run smooth. And the course of *this* love—of his friend, of a TV script, of a role, of a collaboration that would change his life—ran all the way back to New York City and a 490-seat theater on West Fifty-Sixth Street.

"I was doing *Three Days of Rain*—the Richard Greenberg play—at Manhattan Theatre Club," Brad told us.

At the time, Aaron was in New York, too, camping out at the Four Seasons while he put the finishing touches on the first draft of his *Sports Night* pilot. As Brad's brother, David Whitford, would reveal in his wide-ranging personal profile of Brad for *Esquire* magazine, the night Aaron finished writing the script, he found himself taking refuge from a rainstorm—and printing a copy of the script—at a local Kinko's. "The first place I took it," Aaron confessed, "was the stage door at Manhattan Theatre Club, because I wanted Brad to read it."

But, as fate would have it, Brad was already spoken for. With a baby on the way, and an ABC sitcom called *The Secret Lives of Men* (and its twelve-episode order) in hand, Brad broke it to Aaron that he couldn't do *Sports Night*. Saying no to his friend had been painful at the time, but in hindsight Brad considers it a fortuitous decision. After all, if he had landed on *Sports Night*, he wouldn't have been free to do *The West Wing*.

Ultimately, upon hearing about the cancelation of Brad's show—after just six episodes—Aaron phoned him, offering his condolences and, he hoped, something of a consolation prize. "I want you to play Josh on *The West Wing*." He sent over the script that afternoon.

It was a script—and a role—that seemed tailor-made for Brad. His own innate mix of playful and fiery was a perfect profile for Josh, who, more than any other staffer, would be called on to muscle through the president's agenda, like a bulldog with a backpack.

Right in the band gazebo, that's where
the President's going to drape his arm around
the shoulder of some assistant DA we like.
And you should have your camera with you.
You should get a picture of that, 'cause that's
gonna be the moment you're finished in
Democratic politics. President Bartlet's a good
man. He's got a good heart. He doesn't hold a
grudge. That's what he pays *me* for.

—JOSH TO CONGRESSMAN KATZENMOYER,
"FIVE VOTES DOWN"

"Reading the pilot," Brad told us, "I was blown away. It was this . . . stunning . . . beautiful piece of writing. I just thought, 'I love this character, I love this guy, I share his politics. We share a personality!'"

Obsessed with winning the part of Josh, he recognized that navigating the audition process would require next-level prep. "I had done *A Few Good Men*," he told us, "and I knew you've got to get the words *in* you, so you can forget them and just think the thoughts." So, for two weeks he'd walk up and down Beachwood Canyon and go over the material, to get it locked down.

"I remember thinking how pathetic it was. I'm alone up in a canyon . . . totally off book for days. I was trying to make it completely airtight," Brad explained to us, "because sometimes you walk into auditions and, like, frogs fall out of your mouth. I just over, over, over, over, over, over, *over*prepared." (**MELISSA:** Yep. Seven "overs." We checked the transcript, triple-counted.)

It's worth mentioning here that some brilliantly talented actors struggle with Aaron's language. As Levey told us, they come in to read "and their mouth and brain just don't function." And some of them really are gifted actors. Levey acknowledged how his team was able to whittle down that pile of submissions: "One of the ways in which it was easy to cast *The West Wing* was that, if you couldn't keep up with the pace, you were gone. There are many, many really talented people that just don't have that facility for language and pace."

This was not an issue for Brad Whitford.

"Early on we read Brad and confirmed Aaron's certainty that he belonged in the show," Levey said. "He understood the language, he could speak that speak, he could do it while he was walking and talking."

On the day of the audition, Brad landed at Levey's Warner Bros. casting office with his scenes memorized cold. He cut short any small talk with Aaron and Tommy—"Can I act now?"—and, for several minutes, just . . . channeled his inner Lyman. He raised his voice and raised his fists. He mixed a soft-spoken reverence for the president with a red-faced incredulity, turning to imaginary subordinates as if to say, "How am I the only one who *gets* this?!" He even strategically glanced down at the script to subtly convey that, "on the day," when the cameras rolled, he could go even further.

By the end of the session, the three men watching him were in such hysterics that Brad wasn't sure if he'd nailed the audition or pushed his performance into caricature. The confusion didn't last long. Walking him out, casting associate Kevin Scott gushed, "Nobody has done it like that! Wow! *Wow!*" Brad drove off the Warner Bros. lot on a high.

He arrived home to Aaron's voice on his answering machine. (**MELISSA:** "Answering machine"—aw . . .) Brad had, according to Aaron, "hit it out of the park." All that hard work, all those days in Beachwood Canyon overpreparing, all those frogs *not* falling out of his mouth, all of Aaron's effusive praise for the job he'd done—it felt amazing. Until it didn't.

"I was told Tommy and John Levey didn't think I was right."

Tommy remembers it differently. While Aaron seemed thrilled with the audition, Tommy was just a bit hesitant about casting Brad so quickly. "He's so funny, but Josh had to be the emotional center of the piece and I needed more than one audition to see that he had that too. It just felt a bit too fast, too quick." Meanwhile, the casting director, as Brad remembers it, told his agent that he lacked two qualities Warner Bros. considered essential for Josh. That's the nice way of putting it. Here's how Brad says it actually came out: "He's not funny. He's not sexy." (Years later it still stings, even as Brad laughs it off. "'Not funny, not sexy'—thaaaaanks. Okay, I got it—I GOT IT—I don't want the feedback!")

While he sees the humor in it now, at the time the unexpected reaction was a WTF moment for Brad. He knew well that audition curveballs are part and parcel of being an actor—*this is the business we have chosen* and all that—but he still felt blindsided. Even as Aaron assured him that he'd "try and figure something out," Brad knew his friend was in a tricky spot. Back then, he told us two decades later, he understood that Aaron didn't have the kind of clout he would later enjoy. He wasn't in a position to proclaim from on high whom he wanted for which part.

"I've been with my manager for a quarter century now," Brad says, "and it's because of this situation." Indeed, when it came to getting her client the role he felt truly destined to play, Brad's then agent, now manager, Adena Chawke, was like a dog with a bone. "I think she still has an email from John Levey that says, 'What do you not understand? *Bradley Whitford is not going to get this part!*'" Pushing back against conventional wisdom, Adena refused to take "not funny, not sexy" for an answer. "It took a while," Brad remembers, "but I got back into the mix."

At one point during the cajoling process, Brad got called in for what purported to be a "chemistry read" with actress Moira Kelly. Considering her for the role of White House media consultant Mandy Hampton, the powers that be wanted a sneak peek at the dynamic between a possible Josh and Mandy—his ex-girlfriend, foil, and potential love interest.

Brad arrived at the casting office that day under the impression that he was there essentially as a facilitator for Moira's audition. "I thought Aaron was shepherding me in and that I was just there, you know, kind of reading with her." When he got home later that day, the news was not exactly what he was looking for. "The response was, I am totally out of the running because Moira blew me off the screen. I thought—I mean—I thought it was *her* audition! I was like, C'MON!"

But Aaron kept working his magic. Brad kept keeping the faith. And Adena Chawke kept emailing John Levey. Eventually, and at long last . . . the winds changed. At a gas station in Santa Monica.

Adena called—"I had a car phone, which was exciting"—and said, "You got it. Call Aaron." So Brad called Aaron, who said, "'I have great news—you're in the show!'" (**MARY:** There was just this one thing.) "'But you're playing Sam.'" (**MELISSA:** *That.*) In other words, at least in Brad's mind, he was being cast as . . . *not Josh.* He honestly couldn't believe it, and he couldn't understand why. Aaron tried to placate him: "It doesn't matter who you are, I write for *you.* I'll be writing for you!"

Still, Brad made his case, assuring Aaron that none of this had a thing to do with vanity, money, or seniority in the food chain of the fictional White House. His heartfelt appeal came from a deep-seated conviction of character: "I was like, 'Look, I'm only going to play this card once: I'm not Sam, I'm not the guy with the hooker!'" Years later, it seems obvious—he wasn't a Seaborn, caught up with a call girl; he was a *Lyman*, the bully to Bartlet's pulpit, losing his shit and, as Brad put it to us, "chewing out the right-wing lady!"

Sitting at the gas station, Brad felt compelled to remind Aaron that Josh Lyman—that *particular* Josh Lyman—"is what you *wrote*, you told me you wrote it for me!" That said, as unsettled as he was, Brad had to acknowledge the absurdity of his objection. He'd just landed a plum role on a top show. This "Josh or Sam" conundrum was the epitome of a first world problem. "Of course," he added graciously, "I'll do whatever . . ." He trailed off.

That outburst might've played differently with another creator, possibly enough to take Brad out of the running for future projects. But based on their friendship, mutual respect, and understanding of each other's instincts and talent, Aaron said he'd consider it.

We'll get back to Brad and the "Josh or Sam" of it all in a bit (SPOILER: It's Josh) and to how this earliest *West Wing* conflict resolved itself, but for the time being—and in the spirit of the show— let's pass the baton over to the race for the would-be C.J. Cregg . . .

C.J. CREGG

The White House press secretary's primary function is to act as a spokesperson for the executive branch, especially as it pertains to the president and his or her senior aides and officers. At turns charming and informative, wily and discerning, she is often seen as the face of the administration and a key public voice for its policy positions. One of the most prominent noncabinet posts in government, the press secretary interacts on a daily basis with global media outlets—digital, print, and broadcast—as well as "the Socratic wonder," as Josh Lyman likes to call them, "that is the White House press corps." Sizable slices of the world see this most public-facing member of the Communications Office as a polarizing figure. On *The West Wing*, though, she is often positively enchanting, periodically yukking it up with fawning reporters from the *Washington Post* and getting gifted things like goldfish and—depending on the president's mood—compulsory Notre Dame baseball caps.

Oh, one more thing: Every now and then it falls on the press secretary to lead visiting children in song. This, despite her being (as C.J. will remind you) a National Merit Scholar who has "a *master's* degree from the University of California at Berkeley!" Yes, when C.J.'s not enjoying the home field advantage of the briefing room, there are times she's forced to navigate (and support!) the hindquarters of at least one pardoned Thanksgiving turkey. There are times when she has an emergency "woot canal" and Josh dupes her into trying to say "Foggy Bottom." And there are times she experiences stress-dream-level iffiness on the words to "We Gather Together." (Meanwhile, she's got "The Jackal"—an arguably more lyric-heavy song—down pat.) Somehow, though, C.J. always makes it work. That's due as much to the words on the page as to the woman who brought them to mesmerizing life on-screen.

Claudia Jean Cregg and the actress who would make her an international icon share many admirable traits. A mix of quirky, quixotic, and quick on her feet, each is professional and revered, and both could be—or have been—compared to a 1950s movie star. But beyond the supersonic talent, beyond a breathtaking range of skill set, heart, and intellect that would stop an animal in its tracks (even on a wolves-only highway), beyond all that is this: They both have an appeal that just won't quit. Ask anyone.

I like you. You're the one I like.

—ASSISTANT SECRETARY OF STATE ALBIE DUNCAN
TO C.J., "GAME ON"

This simple line, courtesy of Hal Holbrook's delightfully crotchety Albie Duncan, sums up C.J. Cregg as well as any eight words viewers of *The West Wing* ever heard.

To hear Martin tell it—like he did during a *West Wing* cast special on the talk show *Ellen*—Allison is everybody's number one. "From the get-go," he gushed to the program's host, "she was our favorite. We would all be asked privately in interviews, 'Well, who do you *really* like working with?'" According to Martin, each member of the ensemble would offer up a version of "Well, don't tell anyone else"—they didn't want to offend the others—"but she was always our favorite." (On *Ellen* that day, the laughter and nods affirming Martin's press-junket gossip suggested something like unanimous consent.)

But while perpetually winsome, Allison back then and Allison right now are, like the rest of us, different people. And now, thanks to her 2017 turn as LaVona Golden, the hot-mess mother in *I, Tonya*, she's also an Academy Award–winning actress.

That said, even back in 1998, Allison enjoyed quite a following. During this period, her professional identity resided in the comfortable space between New York theater community cult hero and the moderate, manageable stardom of "What's her name again? She should be in *everything*!" So, really, all these years later the acclaim hasn't changed, in intensity or persistence. All that's different is the crowd size. Point being, the moment *The West Wing* hit Allison's doorstep, her star had already begun streaking across the sky.

"I was out in LA, shooting *American Beauty* and *Nurse Betty*, the

Neil LaBute movie. Then I got a call about this pilot that Aaron Sorkin
had written."

Here's the thing: Allison wasn't looking to do television. (**MELISSA:**
Until around the mid-'90s, the cross-pollination we see now—actors
doing a feature here, then signing up for a limited television series
there—didn't really exist. Allison, at that time, was in the features
camp.) Her eyes were fixed, understandably, on the road ahead, a road
that was clearly rising to meet her and leading to what she hoped would
be "a big movie career." But, as she told us, "then I heard it was Aaron
Sorkin, and that stopped me short."

She was, of course, fully aware of Aaron from the New York theater
scene, and she knew and admired what she refers to as "his pedigree." Add
to that the presence of white-hot TV vets like John Wells and Tommy
Schlamme, and Allison's agents were right on the money when they told
her, "If you're going to do television, this is the kind of television to do."

For Allison, minutes into sitting down with the pilot, it was love at
first press brief. "Reading the part of C.J. as she talked to the media
about the president having *ridden his bicycle into a tree*, I was in. I just
thought it was hilarious." The allure of playing a character that typically delivered serious news—at times dead-serious news—alongside
stories about "one of the most inane, stupid things a president could
do, *ever*" was irresistible. "I just loved the humor . . . that fine line of
being serious and knowing it was hilarious. Not funny . . . but *funny*."

He rode his bicycle into a tree, C.J. What do you
want me—"The President, while riding his
bicycle on his vacation in Jackson Hole,
came to a sudden arboreal stop."

—LEO TO C.J., "PILOT"

The impact of the pilot script on Allison is especially remarkable, given the fact that she wasn't naturally drawn to its subject matter. Having come of age during the Watergate era, raised in a family that discussed politics rarely, if at all, she didn't trust politicians and never considered herself savvy when it came to the world in which they operated.

In addition to the cynicism with which she tended to view government, when she read the pilot, political scandal in the US appeared to have reached its most toxic depths. (If only.) It says something about the script, then, or maybe something about Allison, that she saw *The West Wing* as a harbinger of hope. Could this "palace" Aaron had put on the page give civil service an extreme makeover? As she said to us, "It seemed like a terrific way to put politics back in a good light. The staffers genuinely wanted to do the right thing. They just seemed to have their priorities straight."

According to John Levey, Allison had come to the attention of the Warner Bros. casting department along the same route Dulé would travel months later during *The West Wing*'s search for Charlie Young. "My colleague and friend Kevin Scott brought in a demo reel of a tall and elegant, smart and funny woman who I didn't know from Adam, for the role of C.J. Cregg. Her name was Allison Janney."

At that time, as second chair to Levey, Kevin Scott regularly logged countless hours poring over video of actors the studio was not yet aware of, always on the lookout for undiscovered gems. "I had watched Allison in her various film roles," Kevin told us. "They could have been roles where she had five lines. It didn't matter who was talking—she didn't have to say a word—your eye would automatically go to her. I was like, Oh my God, this woman is so damn intriguing, and so odd. And yet . . . beautiful-looking." Yep, Kevin was hooked. And he wasn't alone.

"She was so damn funny," Levey still marvels to this day, "and so smart." But it wasn't just the funny, and it wasn't just the smart. When it comes to Aaron and Tommy, the actor also needs to be *fast*. "Allison," John Levey is quick to point out, "had all three."

And then there was that celebrated banister moment from *Primary Colors*. In that memorable scene, Allison performs a perfect, and perfectly goofy, pratfall *up* a flight of stairs, a maneuver that risks coming across as cheesy and dangerous if not executed with exacting precision. Aaron was quite taken with this very particular set of skills because the early pages of the pilot just so happened to feature C.J. on a treadmill. In the midst of some inane, flirty chitchat at the gym, her beeper starts bleating. Flustered, she picks it up, fumbles a bit, trips . . . and goes flying off the belt.

Allison arrived for the first pilot audition of her life, in the words of Kevin Scott, "a nervous wreck." Back then, Warner Bros. ran casting out of a single building, Building 140. There were twenty-plus casting directors working on numerous projects for the studio, which meant there were dozens of actors in the waiting room when Allison walked in. "She didn't know what those people were waiting for," Kevin says. "She may have thought they were all waiting for *The West Wing*!"

Despite her rising star, the burgeoning film work, and extensive theater experience, Allison came in and . . . freaked. "Her eyes were, like, bugged out. I had to hold her hand and calm her down in the waiting room: 'It's gonna be fine, it's gonna be fine . . .'" To help slow her pulse, Kevin set the scene and Allison's expectations for what she was about to confront. "You're gonna go into the room and see John Wells," he said. "You're gonna see Aaron Sorkin, you're gonna see Tommy Schlamme." Only half listening, Allison nodded, took a deep breath, and, when her name was called, got up and headed in.

Looking back—20/20 hindsight and all that—Allison's perspective on the way her audition went down is pretty comical. When we think about how uniquely perfect she was for the role, to the point that it seems now to have been written for her, it's hard to fathom the bout of insecurity she experienced in the audition's aftermath. Heading in to read for Aaron, Tommy, and John, Allison remembers, she felt nervous, of course, but also excited. Walking out, she recalls feeling . . . less so. "I was pretty sure they hated me."

Now, to the uninitiated, the following may seem counterintuitive, but: When you audition for a role, you *want* the casting people, the director, the producers, to give you notes. If they ask you to perform it a different way, that's not remotely a bad thing. In fact, what you really *don't* want is for them to say, "Okay, great! Thanks!" (Translation: "Next!") When the people in the room *like* what you did, they tend to give you an "adjustment," to gauge your ability to "take a note," in other words, to deliver the material with some contrast. Sure, sometimes you've utterly missed the point of the scene, and the generous (and smart) directors offer up a second swing at it. But most of the time, being "given direction" is undeniably a *good* sign. And, as Allison told us, "I don't remember them giving me *any* direction or letting me know that they liked it—at all."

It wasn't just a lack of direction; it was a lack of . . . basic social norms. As Allison remembers it, neither Aaron nor Tommy made the usual small talk with her. "They didn't ask me a single thing about myself, or what I was doing!" She laughs.

This is one of those Rashomon effect situations. We can attest as actors that sometimes you look at an audition through a very particular misery lens. The glass isn't just half-empty; there was never anything in it in the first place. Allison remembers no one asking her a single thing . . . but Tommy is about the friendliest person in the world. He loves actors, is married to an actress, and is famously generous in auditions. "Allison was pretty nervous," he told us, "I could see it. So she may not remember our conversation, but I sure do!"

Back in AJ's version of events, when she finished reading C.J., it didn't get much better. "They just said, 'Okay, thanks.'" Allison walked out a bit bewildered—grateful for the opportunity, but, as she put it to us, "definitely feeling like, 'Yikes! Not gettin' that part!'"

Then she got a callback.

Flying back to LA from her home base in New York, Allison arrived feeling . . . cautiously optimistic, based on the fact that "this is the kind of part I love to play—strong women who are not without . . . *awareness* of humor. Smart, strong, funny women." It was, as she said to us, "in my wheelhouse. I knew it was mine to lose."

Oddly, though, even when she came back in to read for Aaron, Tommy, and the others, she remembers not a hint of shooting the breeze, no "Tell us about yourself," no nothing. "And no notes on what I did!" she remembers now, with a still-puzzled incredulity. (**MARY:** Tommy weighed in on this too. "There weren't a ton of adjustments to give her," he says, "because Allison was so damn good.") Sure, the role of C.J. Cregg was squarely in her strike zone, but in that moment Allison couldn't help thinking, "I don't know what these people want from me! Why do they keep bringing me in?!"

For whatever reason, they did indeed keep bringing her in. And when she returned to test for the network "in front of [Warner Bros. head of TV production] Peter Roth and the 'ups' at NBC," as she calls them, there was an additional layer of stakes, one that came with serious career implications and a long-term commitment. Just like all the other series regulars—including Richard Schiff, who, more than any of them, was driven bonkers by the "business" end of show business—Allison had to put her cards on the table *before* the test. Because on the off chance a show gets picked up to series—actually . . . we'll let her paint the picture: "You're sitting in a room and you have to sign a contract in advance of the audition. So if you get it, bang—you're committed for five years." Bottom line, though, despite locking herself in for half a decade in the midst of a budding film career, Allison badly wanted to land this part. "I was afraid to admit how much I wanted it."

Waiting to go in, Allison took note of her C.J. competition, as well as several candidates vying to make up the balance of Bartlet's senior staff. The collection of actors milling outside the audition room represented a veritable murderers' row of talent. "I thought to myself, 'Okay, this is just a learning experience. I've got to go through this—like a trial, like something to be *endured*.'" Luckily, and right on cue, a familiar face rounded the corner with some encouraging words. It was her future co-star, in to test for Toby Ziegler.

"Richard came up and . . . I remember him being so nice to me. I think he said, 'Well, if *you're* here, I'm glad *I'm* here,' which I took as high praise."

In the end, the competition for C.J. came down to two distinct, equally formidable talents: Allison and CCH Pounder, an Emmy-nominated actress with approximately one billion credits, who was well-known to Warner Bros. and John Wells, thanks to her revelatory work on *ER*. (CCH would eventually join *The West Wing* cast as Deborah O'Leary, President Bartlet's outspoken, controversial secretary of housing and urban development. It was a powerful and stunning performance, which appears to be the only kind she gives.)

As for Allison, to this day she remains convinced that she landed the role due in no small part to that *Primary Colors* pratfall every single one of you should've long since gone to check out on YouTube. "Aaron," Allison says, "loves Mike Nichols and he *loved* that movie, and my first scene in the pilot I do a pratfall!"

Regardless of Allison's theory, in comments to *The Hollywood Reporter* in 2014, Aaron made it crystal clear that, while choosing her may have begun with the facility she'd once exhibited for falling on her ass, it didn't end there. "The only thing I'd ever seen Allison in was *Primary Colors*. She'd made an immediate impression on me with a simple trip on a flight of stairs. Pounder's auditions were great, but looking back, it would be hard to argue we made the wrong decision casting Allison, who became the heartbeat of the show."

"The heartbeat of the show." Talk about high praise. And it kind of hits the bull's-eye, right? Allison's C.J. Cregg always came across as . . . steady. Dependable. The ever-constant big sister or favorite daughter everyone could count on—for a kind word, a kick in the pants, or an outlier view on a bump in the polls. But there was also this: While every one of the show's main characters—and every series regular who played them—delivered his or her share of emotional life-blood, in terms of sweeping, iconic "heartbeat" moments, we defy any-one to top C.J. for frequency or impact. And we don't just mean the romantic fireworks and grapevine fodder of her will-they-or-won't-they with Danny Concannon. She had poignant emotional moments with *everyone*. Hell, she even had them with *herself.*

Sobbing alone on a bench after Simon Donovan's death, in the middle of Times Square and Jeff Buckley's "Hallelujah."

Lambasting Nancy McNally with her fiery, full-throated support for the women of Qumar. "They're beating the women, Nancy!"

Quietly confessing to Sam that she knew he was the one who pushed her out of harm's way during the assassination attempt in Rosslyn. "Sam . . . I think you have my necklace."

Assuaging Josh's guilt over the NSC card that he got—and that she (and Sam and Toby) didn't—to secure him in the event of a nuclear attack: "You really are very sweet sometimes."

Gently offering Toby a towel, some ice, and a sympathetic ear as he mourned the suicide of his brother . . . and lamented the fistfight he'd just had with Josh, his once and future comrade-in-arms.

And, of course . . . breaking the news to President Bartlet about the sudden, shocking death of his dearest friend and confidant, Leo McGarry.

MELISSA: Everyone always asks what it was like to work with Allison Janney, and the answer is . . . even better than you could imagine. It was a Friday night during season 2. We were filming the follow-up to "Noël," an episode called "The Leadership Breakfast," and there was one scene left to shoot. I had one line—as usual, Allison had the bulk of them—so I was enjoying a light workload. We went in for rehearsal, and Aaron stopped by, which always made me a bit nervous. You always want to do extra well when he's in the room. But again, it was only one line. We ran through the scene, and it went fine, but just as we finished, Aaron said, "Yeah, I just don't feel like C.J. would say all of that. We're going to have Carol say this part."

All of a sudden, my light workload on a Friday night just got a little less light! As we were walking out to our trailers to get into wardrobe, Allison clearly sensed my anxiety level. She leaned over to me and said, "Don't be nervous. Get changed fast and come to my trailer. We'll run it—you'll be great." That's what it was like to work with Allison. Like a dream—and like a master class on every single take. (Oh, FUN FACT: That night when we filmed the scene, Aaron wound up not coming to set because he got called to the hospital for the birth of his daughter Roxie!) But back to AJ's West Wing test . . .

When everything was said and done, Allison left the room (and the Warner Bros. lot) feeling all kinds of positive and some level of serene. She had stood tall and done her job the best she knew how. The rest of it, now, was out of her hands. "I remember going back to my hotel, and just . . . letting it go." "Whatever happens," she thought to herself, "happens."

What happened is that the next day, Allison heard a knock on her hotel room door. She got up and opened it to a special delivery, a stunning bouquet of flowers. Not long after—as if it were scripted—the phone rang. It was Aaron. With a smile in his voice, he uttered the words she'd been hoping to hear:

"Welcome to The West Wing."

In that moment, the soon-to-be "heartbeat of the show" skipped a few. From that directionless first read . . . to the chitchat-free callback . . . to the final test for the NBC "ups," Allison had been putting one foot in front of the other and focusing on the task at hand: to breathe life into the wonderful words in ink on the page, to lift them up and show the powers that be her undeniable vision for an unforgettable C.J. Cregg. Then, at the sound of Aaron's proverbial rolling out of the red carpet, reality began to sink in—fast.

"Oh shit," she realized. "I gotta *do* this now."

★ ★ ★

POSTSCRIPT: *When the* West Wing *pilot was being cast, there wasn't enough material in the script for the actors reading Toby and C.J. to really show what they could do. Tommy approached Aaron, asking him to write an audition scene, any audition scene, featuring those two characters. He promised Aaron, "No one's ever going to see this, we're never going to do the scene. I'm never going to point a camera at the scene." But a few episodes into the series, Tommy came to Aaron again, saying, "You know that scene you wrote for casting . . ." That scene—the one Tommy promised he would never point a camera at—wound up in "The Crackpots and These Women." (C.J. tries to talk Toby down from feeling insecure about his place in POTUS's pecking order.)*

                              C.J.
          Since when do you need help talking
          to the President?

                              TOBY
          Since all of a sudden I became the
          kid in the class with his hand
          raised that nobody wants the
          teacher to call on.

★ ★ ★

A SERVICE STORY

Allison Janney

Like the character she portrayed on *The West Wing*, Allison Janney is a team player. Maybe it's her humble Midwest upbringing, but the woman believes in sharing the credit, almost to a fault, in shining the spotlight outward. When it comes to activism, she tends to downplay her role, but the fact is, among the *West Wing* crowd, it'd be hard to name a more supportive voice than the one coming from behind C.J.'s podium. She'll often say things like, "All I do is show up and get the word out!" But having her "show up and get the word out" is what takes the work of advocacy into an entirely different stratosphere. We can organize and advocate all we want, but it's hard to overstate what an impact it makes when a magnetic figure like Allison Janney comes in, right on cue, draws a crowd, and picks up the bullhorn.

Since we first met in year one of *The West Wing*, Allison has been incredibly supportive of everything I've done, from theater-based youth programs to my work at All Rise. One memory that sticks out is the day we both spoke at the "Unite to Face Addiction" rally on the National Mall in Washington, DC. For Allison, the issue of addiction and recovery will always hit painfully close to home. And not just because of the character she played on CBS for eight seasons.

ALLISON JANNEY: I am among the tens of millions of Americans whose lives have been touched by the tragedy of opioid addiction. Addiction rips through so many families and mine is no exception. In 2011, my brother Hal lost his battle with this disease. He was one of my favorite people on this planet. He was incredibly charming and quick-witted, kind and generous, smart and quick to laugh. I miss him every day. This is a big part of what attracted me to playing Bonnie on *Mom*. It felt like playing someone in recovery was a way to honor him. This has also fueled my support of some of the incredible work being done around addiction and recovery and my work as an All Rise ambassador.

Family is deeply important to Allison. One of the values she grew up around was a love of animals. "We were surrounded by them!" she told us. That presence made an impact on Allison and continues today. Over the years, she has rescued many dogs—Dutch, Sippy, and Henry are her latest—and supported a number of animal rescue organizations. "My connection with animals," she says, "is unlike any I've ever experienced." Recently, her connection to animals (and to her family) received an extra jolt of inspiration . . .

ALLISON JANNEY: My niece, Petra Janney, is one of the coolest women I know. I am a serious animal lover, but Petra has taken that to a new level. In 2019 she joined forces with a pilot named Dean Heistad to co-found this organization, Amelia Air. These people are amazing. They fly around, rescuing pets from overcrowded kill shelters, often in more rural areas with less dense population centers, and taking them to more populated areas, where it's a bit easier to place them in "forever homes." It's an extraordinary organization.

While helping with the legwork to get Amelia Air off the ground, Petra studied to get her pilot's license. Once she did, she was wheels up and off to the rescue!

ALLISON JANNEY: Petra will wake up on a Sunday, get a call about a rescue in, wherever, and she'll get up, hop in her plane, and jet off to rescue a dog! She's awesome.

Amelia Air relies entirely on donations, so, obviously, the flights need to be orchestrated in a cost-effective way. The magic number Amelia Air has come up with is right around a hundred dollars per animal. Keeping the cost per animal to a minimum maximizes the number of animals that can be rescued. Every now and again, Allison lends a helping fundraising hand, thanks to her passion for the work and her ability to shine a light.

ALLISON JANNEY: Whether it's in television interviews or via other media outlets, I just love to spread the word of this incredible mission and my incredible niece.

Petra serves as a real inspiration to Allison—not just because she loves her niece (and her canines) and not just because the mission of Amelia Air is so admirable.

ALLISON JANNEY: I've always been terrified to fly, so I think Petra is courageous to fly *at all*. Add in the reason she got her license in the first place—getting in this Cessna, flying off to rescue shelter animals—she's, like, my hero!

Another of Allison's heroes is her mother, Macy Janney.

ALLISON JANNEY: As a board member of Planned Parenthood of Miami Valley (Ohio), my mom spent decades advocating for family planning education. She later did so as that chapter's president.

But it didn't start with Macy Janney. Support of women's health education and services appears to run in Allison's family . . .

ALLISON JANNEY: My grandmother also worked with Planned Parenthood, and my great-grandmother, Frances Ackerman, worked with Margaret Sanger, the pioneering birth-control activist who established what became Planned Parenthood.

With the Supreme Court's recent overturning of *Roe v. Wade* and the subsequent political and legislative attacks on women's health and choice, Allison's commitment to the cause has only grown.

ALLISON JANNEY: This is a vitally important time to support Planned Parenthood and other organizations that protect and support women in making their personal health decisions. I am deeply proud to do so.

AMELIA AIR

Amelia Air is a tax-exempt rescue organization staffed by volunteers dedicated to saving animals from high-kill shelters and flying them to rescues that have the resources to find them loving families. They are a small but mighty group of volunteers committed to one goal: save five hundred animals each year by flying them off death row to rescues that place them with loving forever families.

www.ameliaair.org

PLANNED PARENTHOOD

Planned Parenthood's mission is to ensure all people have access to the care and resources they need to make informed decisions about their bodies, their lives, and their futures. Founded in 1916, Planned Parenthood is a trusted healthcare provider, educator, and passionate advocate in the US as well as a strong partner to health and rights organizations around the world. Each year, Planned Parenthood delivers vital sexual and reproductive healthcare, sex education, and information to millions of people.

www.plannedparenthood.org

★ ★ ★

TOBY ZIEGLER

White House Communications Director Toby Ziegler was the president's chief speechwriter and the guardian of his better angels. Arguably the soul of the West Wing staff, Toby was undeniably its conscience. Alternately preachy and taciturn, gloomy and strident, he was a passionate idealist and the closest thing this White House had to a true believer. And however prickly he could get—and he could get prickly—Toby always seemed to find ways, subtle or otherwise, to wear his bleeding heart on his rolled-up sleeve.

We're running away from ourselves. And I know we can score points that way—I was a principal architect of that campaign strategy, right along with you, Josh. But we're *here* now. Tomorrow night we do an immense thing. We have to say what we feel. That government, no matter what its failures in the past—and in times to come, for that matter—government can be a place where people come together and where no one gets left behind. No one . . . gets left behind. An instrument of good.

—TOBY TO PRESIDENT BARTLET AND JOSH,
"HE SHALL FROM TIME TO TIME . . ."

Scanning the internet for ways to describe Toby, one lands on a laundry list of quasi synonyms for . . . "difficult":

Moody
Arrogant

Uncompromising
Self-righteous
Irascible
Contrarian
Prickly (see above)
Simmering
Mournful
Stubborn
Curmudgeonly

What follows, then, is a testament to the true greatness of both the character and the actor who would come to portray him: At the core of the messy jumble of humanity that is Toby Ziegler, one descriptor stands above all the others.

Lovable

But we're getting ahead of ourselves. Let's go back a bit, to this irrefutable fact: Richard Schiff didn't really want to do TV.

★ ★ ★

THE year before *The West Wing* came calling, Richard had successfully auditioned for four different shows. Successfully enough, that is, to have been asked to "test" for them. Testing, we'll remind you, is when you audition again—like an advanced callback—except this time the actor performs the material not only for the creative team, but also for the studio and network executives. This part of the process is nobody's favorite. Certainly not Richard's. "There's a torturous nature to auditions. And I allowed myself the freedom to play it moment by moment and decide at the last minute whether I'm going to go in or not." This tended not to endear him to casting directors and nearly got him blacklisted by NBC. To this day, Richard defends his tendency to pull himself out of the running at the midnight hour, especially as it pertains to reading for studio and network bigwigs.

"Their job is not to evaluate talent," Richard argues. "It's to evaluate what talent will sell advertising for them, and I'm not at the top of that list. So, it's always been a fight."

So, yes, more often than you'd think, Richard just . . . wouldn't show up. That happened on multiple projects he'd nearly booked the year before. On the days leading up to the test, he'd listened to the voice in his head telling him, "I don't want to do this show," and it was . . . game over.

Perhaps it goes without saying, but this pattern didn't sit well with Richard's representatives, who—after one missed network test—tried to convey the dire consequences their client would likely face. "They will be fucking *furious*," they told him. "If you don't go in, you will never work for NBC again!" Sure enough, Richard recounted to us, "they were fucking furious, screaming bloody murder. They wanted heads to roll." (A year later, of course, he was hired by NBC for *The West Wing*.) To be clear, none of this is a matter of Richard not caring enough about the work. If anything, he cares too much—about the art of it, the truth of it—to do work that fails to meet that standard.

When the opportunity to play Toby Ziegler came up, Richard was, as usual and rather fittingly, a bit tortured about it. Because, while all actors audition and want to get jobs, at that particular time what Richard *really* wanted was to do movies. (Wanting to do movies was, of course, *also* true for all actors—that is, until shows like *The West Wing*, *The Sopranos*, *The Wire*, and myriad other acclaimed and beloved programs came along, featuring film-worthy roles on "prestige TV.")

Thanks to an exceptional script, and the fact that Tommy Schlamme was shepherding it along, Richard was intrigued. "He

wanted to see me. We had worked together a couple of times before."
Prepping for the audition, Richard recognized the level of the material,
as well as its potential to run for multiple terms of a single presidency.
He recognized something else too. All things considered, he had a decent shot at landing the role of Toby, especially given his familiarity
with Tommy and Tommy's familiarity with him.

So, he went in for the first audition. The main "Toby" scene saw him
dressing down Josh for his "smug, taunting, you know . . . calamitous
performance on *Capital Beat*!" Diving into the confrontation, with
Aaron reading Josh, Richard had no idea about what would become
one of the cardinal rules of *The West Wing*. So, he did his "normal
thing," which was to "change stuff" and "improvise a little." (**MARY
AND MELISSA:** Uh-oh.) "I found out later Aaron was furious that I
had the audacity to do that." Turns out, it wasn't disqualifying.

"We read a lot of people for Toby, and it was a great part," John
Levey told us. "Toby was like the *Peanuts* character Pig-Pen, but followed around by *worry*, instead of a cloud of dust." A key to Toby, it
seemed to Levey, was his tremendous capacity to see everything from
both sides. "He understood a multitude of points of view," which was,
of course, a blessing and a curse. Luckily for Richard, the messy business of emotional and intellectual complexity is, to borrow a well-worn
Sorkinism, "where this man eats."

"Talk about being right for a part," Levey marveled about Richard.
"He is the embodiment of ambivalence. And that was perfect for Toby,
just perfect."

There's a story Brad Whitford likes to tell—by which we mean he
LOVES to tell (by which we mean he can't stop telling)—that came up
one time in, of all places, a memorial service for John Spencer. Brad
got up to deliver a message from Richard. He said, "Richard sends his
regards. He's in New York doing a one-man show. And he hates everyone in the cast."

There's literally no one in the world that
I don't hate right now.

—TOBY TO SAM, C.J., MANDY, AND LEO,
"FIVE VOTES DOWN"

You know the old adage "Nobody picks on my brother but me"? That's why Brad can get away with saying stuff like that. In a very real way, just like their *West Wing* counterparts, Brad and Richard are almost like siblings. In fact, they first met thanks to Richard's actual brother Paul Schiff, a film and TV producer who, back in his undergrad days, happened to be Brad's roommate at Wesleyan University.

"He and my brother took care of my dog for six months," Richard recalls. "So I was forever indebted to Brad for that." (**MELISSA:** The dog's name was Lyle and was, as Richard puts it, "a Manhattan mutt that got into a thousand fights and didn't win one.")

Given his long history with Brad, it had to have felt like kismet for Richard—a "sign," even—when, upon entering the room for his callback, he spotted his old dog-sitter. "I walk in and there he is," Richard would recall years later. "And he's playing Josh! I just started giggling, it was so weird." Indeed. As another famous *West Wing* Josh (Malina) points out, "Giggling is not something you would normally associate with Toby Ziegler."

Despite the "church laughter" and the resulting fits and starts it caused both actors, Richard got through the callback relatively unscathed. He had come into this phase of the process—reading for the Warner Bros. executives—with Tommy's assurance that it was "just a formality," and had taken that mostly to heart.

When it was over, Tommy led him out of the room, reminding his future Toby that "tomorrow's the test." He added, "We hope to see you there."

"Well, just so you know," Richard replied, "I might not show up."

Tommy nodded at this, not unkindly, but with a knowing smile. "Yeah, I've heard."

"And if by any chance I do show up," Richard volleyed back awkwardly, ". . . I'm going to be really bad."

Tommy chuckled. "I've heard that too."

What Tommy did next made a real difference to Richard and went a long way toward putting him "at ease," or at least as close to at ease as Richard manages to get. It would also effectively set the course for the next several years of their work together. Tommy put a hand on Richard's shoulder, looked in his eyes, and said, "I really hope you come tomorrow."

"There was such love in that gesture," Richard told us, "such an appreciation, a *genuine* appreciation for how crazy we all are—and no judgment. He must've been thinking, 'You're outta your mind! This is, like, the best show that's come along—you're not gonna show up?!' But he didn't do that. He just said, 'I hope you do show up.'"

This would be the first of many times during the run of *The West Wing* that Tommy was able to do that for him, "to kind of disarm all of my neuroses and psychoses," Richard would later reveal. It was quite a moment. But the moment wasn't over. Walking out, Richard turned the corner to find a bunch of women mentally prepping for their auditions. "This," he thought, "is for C.J." Looking around, he spotted the brilliant actress CCH Pounder and, sitting nearby, another familiar face.

Allison Janney.

At the time, Richard didn't know Allison all that well. He'd met her one night after a show in New York—"a little off-off-off-Broadway thing"—and remembered how great she'd been. "Then I saw her in *Primary Colors*." Allison's standout turn as a goofy, vaguely flighty adult literacy teacher (who would wind up having a "quickie" with John Travolta's philandering presidential candidate) had wowed him that night and established the actress in Richard's mind as truly special.

A year or so later, there she was, outside the audition, waiting to test for Claudia Jean Cregg. In that moment, Richard had a classic Richard thought: "I went, 'Oh God, these guys will *never* hire her, they're not that smart.'" Then again, he thought, "If they're serious about her . . . they really know what they're doing." Allison's presence that day was one more piece—along with the sky-high quality of Aaron's script, Brad's coincidental involvement, Tommy's kindhearted insight—that contributed to Richard's burgeoning excitement about the project and his chance to be a part of it. And, of course, we know he did indeed show up for the test.

As he remembers it, the audition for the NBC executives took place in a cramped little room, where everybody sat in rows, stacked up narrowly behind a single desk. "Like an album cover of suits." Richard says he was "so bad, I started laughing in the middle of it and said, 'I'm sorry, this really sucks. I suck today. Let me start again.'" But an hour later, walking across the lot to his car, a decidedly un-Richard thought came to mind: "I think I got this thing."

A few years into Richard's stint on *The West Wing*, at "one of three parties I ever went to in Los Angeles," he was approached by a well-regarded performer whose talent he knew and loved. "I don't know if you're aware of this," the gentleman said to Richard, "but I was the other actor that was up for Toby the day you tested, and I was one hundred percent sure that I got the part."

When Richard asked him why, he was told, "Because I put my ear against the door when you auditioned and I couldn't hear a fuckin' word you said."

That actor was Eugene Levy. (Given the staying power of Eugene's career since the early days of SCTV, readers may know him as the *Best in Show* character who "wasn't the class clown, but sat *next* to the class clown, and studied him" or the father in the *American Pie* series or, most recently, the dad on *Schitt's Creek*. In any case, he's tough to beat.)

As Aaron told *The Hollywood Reporter* in 2014, "Levy was fantastic—strong and sad and very compelling"—but for Tommy, casting Toby came down to, among other things, a matter of music. "Richard," as he put it to us, "just played a different instrument."

Still, according to John Levey, Eugene's read of Toby Ziegler was truly remarkable. He calls it "the single funniest audition I've ever seen that didn't get the job. He made the executives in that room at NBC laugh out loud eight or ten times!"

The problem—for Eugene, anyway—was twofold. First was the character's intrinsic grumpiness, a quality that Richard Schiff has in spades and that Aaron had always seen as quintessentially Toby. Eugene Levy may have played the role brilliantly and with great humor, but Richard *embodied* it. Second, the creative team believed they could divine comedy out of other cast members—not Brad, of course, he was too busy not being sexy to bother not being funny—which meant they didn't necessarily need Toby for comic relief. (Thanks to Richard, they would get it from him anyway, and more often than expected.) What they needed out of Toby, John Levey has rightly acknowledged over the years, "was cynicism and worry—and that was Richard's corner of the market."

Which brings us back to "lovable." It's difficult to pinpoint precisely what it is that drew so many of us—cast and crew and viewers alike—to the rumpled, cranky, brilliant humanity of Richard Schiff's Toby Ziegler. Maybe it's just too hard to choose. His tumultuous inner life forever simmering just below the surface, or his raw, steadfast affection for a woman named Andy. His occasionally volcanic insistence on speaking truth to stupid, or his quietly joyful epiphany that "babies come with hats." His indefatigably brooding genius, or the fact that bouncing a pink Spaldeen against his office wall was the best way he knew to harness it. Maybe it's just our sense that, more than any other character, Toby Ziegler seemed like the stand-in for *The West Wing*'s creator, its own "chief speechwriter," Aaron Sorkin.

Whatever the case, one thing's for sure: Tortured as he may have been at the prospect of "testing" for *The West Wing*, it's a good thing Richard took Tommy's words to heart and appeared at that callback. As Toby would later say, "The things we do in our lives—many of them are not voluntary." This one, Richard, *was* voluntary. We're really glad you showed up.

SAM SEABORN

"Deputy White House communications director" is something of a mouthful. Then again, "Toby Ziegler's number two" doesn't quite do the role justice and also sounds like the worst band name of all time. The deputy in the comms office operates as more than an additional voice in the room and on the page. He or she is a key political sounding board, a trusted counselor—around the West Wing and, at times, inside the Oval—and a true partner to the person in charge of the executive branch's messaging apparatus.

Anyone who watched even half an episode of *The West Wing* saw Sam Seaborn as far more than just a dreamboat "Robin" to Toby's brooding "Batman." Aaron's North Star muse for poetry and inspiration, Sam was the gleaming, unabashed romantic of *The West Wing*, its signature blend of innocent cockeyed optimist and charming quasi–golden boy. And if he got himself into trouble—by way of his mouth, his ego, a misplaced pager, or plain old hubris—odds were Aaron would bring his starry-eyed hero down to earth with a little comeuppance, like having his ex-girlfriend sleep with a professional hockey player or getting outdebated by Ainsley Hayes on a popular Beltway news program. Stuff like that.

MARK

The House is expected to vote next
week on President Bartlet's one
point five billion dollar education
package. Sam Seaborn: Why is this
bill better than its Republican
counterpart that the President
vetoed last year?

SAM

Because it buys things that
teachers need. Like textbooks. In a
fairly comprehensive study that was
done, an alarmingly high number of
teachers—forty percent of the
teachers in Kirkwood, Oregon, for
instance, and Kirkwood, Oregon,
being a fair model for public
school districts across the
country—forty percent of the
teachers in Kirkwood, Oregon,
report not having sufficient
textbooks for their students. The
package offered by the Republican-
controlled Congress offered a grand
total of zero dollars for new
textbooks.

Moments later . . .

AINSLEY

The bill contained plenty of money
for textbooks, Mark, and anyone who
says otherwise is flat-out lying.
And we should tell the truth about
this. Textbooks are important, if
for no other reason than they'd
accurately place the town of

Kirkwood in California and not
Oregon.

—"In This White House"

As Toby's second-in-command, Sam served as a subordinate but somehow equal member of the speechwriting staff and, eventually, as a senior advisor to President Bartlet. He also represented one of the public "faces" of the administration. And when it comes to faces, you could do a lot worse than trotting out Sam's galactically handsome one to appear on shows like *Capital Beat*, no matter how bad he got his ass kicked that time. I mean, seriously. Say it out loud: "Sam Seaborn." He even *sounds* good-looking!

Yes, "Seaborn" is a wonderfully evocative character name and brings to mind the metaphor John Levey has often used to describe the process of casting a pilot. He says it's like putting together a mobile at the beach. The kind where you hang a seashell from an old piece of driftwood, and then you find another shell of equal-ish weight, and another, and another, or maybe a piece or two of blue-green sea glass, to balance it out on the other end. Suddenly all those shells and the sparkling sea glass, in orbit around the dried-out driftwood, don't just look like they "go" together; they look like they need one another, like they complement one another—they look like they *belong* together.

"It's why working on pilots is exciting," Levey says. "Because, when one piece falls into place, when you get John Spencer, you get all the gravitas, all that realness, that sort of . . . unmade-bed-ness." Then Rob Lowe walks in and, Levey explains, "he's a completely made bed. His shirt is tucked in and his tie is well tied and always in place. He's a real leading man." For casting directors, those jigsaw puzzle moments feel like more than just magic. They feel truly—actually—*creative*.

Hard as it is to believe now, given the last twenty-plus years of his résumé, before joining the cast of *The West Wing*, Rob Lowe had never done a TV series before. His Sam Seaborn origin story began the day a junior agent at United Talent Agency sent him a copy of the pilot script with what felt, to Rob Lowe, like something less than high praise.

"She literally just said, 'Read this.' Not 'It's good,' not anything, no backstory, no nothing." In fact, when the actor saw the words "*The West Wing*" on the cover page, he genuinely thought it was the script for a spin-off of a popular syndicated show called *Pensacola: Wings of Gold*. "I thought it was gonna be about a fighter squadron!"

But then, just below the title he saw "written by Aaron Sorkin." His eyes lit up. "Ohhh," he thought to himself, "that guy." His mind instantly went not to *The American President* or *A Few Good Men*, but to a lesser-known Sorkin work, credited to both Aaron and Scott Frank, the neo-noir medical thriller *Malice*. (This film was perhaps an early predictor of Josh Malina's keen ability to enlist his friend Aaron's help in landing acting jobs. In this case, he played the no-doubt pivotal role of "Resident.")

As for the *West Wing* script, from the moment Rob sank his teeth into it, he was hooked. The first scene, set in a dimly lit DC bar, featured a journalist fishing for inside-the-Beltway gossip from the character Rob would eventually come to play for eighty episodes.

"Nobody had told me what part to think about when I read it," Rob explained on *The West Wing Weekly*, but by the end of that first scene, he had his eyes—and his heart—set on Seaborn. "Maybe 'cause Sam was the first character, and that opening scene at the bar is so interesting. Maybe it was that I liked the name. '*Sam Seaborn*,'" Rob rightly points out, "had a nice ring to it." Later in the script some guy called Josh Lyman showed up, which, Rob suggests, was another role he could've been right for. But there was something about Sam—his unbridled passion perhaps, a Kennedyesque penchant for soaring idealism and great hair—that he connected with, instantly and on a visceral level.

Education is the silver bullet. Education is
everything. We don't need little changes,
we need gigantic, monumental changes.
Schools should be *palaces*. The competition for
the best teachers should be fierce. They should
be making six-figure salaries. Schools should be
incredibly expensive for government and
absolutely free of charge to its citizens,
just like national defense. That's my position.
I just haven't figured out how to do it yet.

—SAM TO MALLORY, "SIX MEETINGS BEFORE LUNCH"

For perhaps the only time in his career, Rob couldn't help thinking he was the only person in the world who could play the part. "It wasn't like, 'How am I gonna play it, what could I do with it, this could be interesting, wow what an opportunity!'—it was literally 'This is my part and I'm just gonna go in and blow the doors off it for these guys.'" That was the idea, anyway, and Rob Lowe had the capacity to sell it. But here's the thing: One of "these guys" wasn't sold on Rob Lowe.

★ ★ ★

WITH production on the pilot looming, some believed that the *West Wing* cast could still use a jolt of star power. While any number of the actors already on board possessed sufficient talent and charisma to carry a show, NBC still had concerns. An hour-long drama about public service—and public servants—remained a tough sell in any climate, let alone one as toxic as American politics in 1999. Adding another big name was a tried-and-true way of attracting eyeballs and keeping them on the network week after week.

Aaron saw things differently. To him the foundation of the show was the *team*—a story centered on a staff of hardworking civil servants, none of whom shone brighter than any of the rest.

Just north of thirty years old at the time, Rob had already enjoyed a long, successful, and high-profile career. He was a full-fledged movie star. He'd appeared in many popular films, ranging from *The Outsiders* and *St. Elmo's Fire* to lighter fare, including *Youngblood, Wayne's World,* and *About Last Night.* He'd acted opposite the likes of Patrick Swayze and Jodie Foster, as well as Martin's son—and Rob's fellow "Brat Pack" member—Emilio Estevez.

I grew up a few houses down from the Sheens.
If you look back on your childhood, there's always that one house you went to after school. For me, that was the Sheens'. Martin was like my second dad. He was the guy who let me bum cigarettes and steal his ice cream. Plus, I was this kid who wanted to be an actor and Martin was this acting giant.

—ROB LOWE, INTERVIEW FOR *WHAT'S NEXT*

Given that résumé, plus a pair of Golden Globe nominations to his credit, Rob Lowe was undeniably a star. But that was the problem. As Aaron would later reveal in *The Hollywood Reporter*'s piece "*West Wing* Uncensored," he had no idea Rob was even coming in, at least at first. And even after learning that Rob's manager, Bernie Brillstein, had convinced Kevin Scott to let his client read for the role, Aaron was determined not to cast him. "Tommy, John, and I were putting together an ensemble, and while it was all right with me that the president was being played by a movie star, I thought having one play Sam would throw the balance of the cast out of whack."

Having fallen in love with the material, though, Rob was not to be denied. He still raves about that pilot script. "It's amazing. And it's every bit as good in its written form as it is in its completed form." Truly enchanted by the Seaborn character, when it came time to respond to the creative team, Rob and his reps didn't play coy about his level of interest. "I was like, 'I'm in, I wanna be a part of this!'"

But in a moment of "not so fast," he was informed that he'd have to come in and read for the part. "Everybody," Rob was told, "is auditioning for this." To his credit, rather than play the "I'm offer-only" card, Rob didn't blink. He actually likes to come in and read. "I always feel like, 'Wait a minute, I actually get to compete with the other people?!' When I'm given the ammo to kill in the room, I'm all about it."

The day Rob drove through the gates at Warner Bros. to read for *The West Wing* was, in his words, "rainy" and "horrendous." Adding to the gloom, Bernie Brillstein had laid down the law for Aaron, Tommy, John Wells, and anyone else who cared to listen: Rob would read only once—and never again. As Levey put it to us, "He wouldn't do chemistry readings with any other actors, wouldn't test at the studio, wouldn't test at the network . . ." What Brillstein was offering, the casting director explained, was a good old-fashioned Hollywood "go fuck yourself."

Rob, on the other hand, was charm personified. Walking into a room packed with people he didn't know, he introduced himself to Aaron—who, of course, would be reading opposite him, first as Leo McGarry's daughter, Mallory. That scene involved a White House tour Sam was meant to give to "Leo's daughter's fourth-grade class" and climaxed in his big speech about having accidentally slept with a prostitute. Rob had the whole thing down cold but held the script because "you never want to have them think that they're getting the absolute best. You want 'em to think there's still more to come."

Talking to us about his audition more than two decades later, Rob was still starry-eyed. "I loved auditioning with Aaron," he told us. "I couldn't wait to do it. He and I immediately—I honestly don't think it's an overstatement to say—fell in love." As for Aaron . . . Remember how he initially pushed back against the idea of another movie star coming in and upsetting the delicate balance of his foundational *West Wing* ensemble? It took less than a page for that to go out the window.

"He read the first of three scenes he'd prepared," Aaron says. "I don't remember the second or the third because he'd already gotten the part a page into the first, and I was thinking of stories for a character who has no idea he looks like Rob Lowe." (**MELISSA:** Just want to flag that Aaron's dialogue in real life is as entertaining as the stuff he puts on the page.)

That scene, by the way, ends with Sam basically begging Mallory to "please, in the name of compassion, tell me which one of those kids is my boss's daughter!" Mallory, of course, hits him with a deadpan "That would be me." In the audition, as Rob landed on that moment, and on the scene's last line—"Well, this is bad on so *many* levels!"— everyone in the room laughed. Hard. Then, as Rob tells it, "Everybody looked around at each other and it got really quiet. Nobody said anything."

Then Aaron turned to John Wells and said, "See, I *told* you the scene was funny!" Moments later, Aaron said something else, something that sounded like surrender. A happy, sweet surrender: "Pay him whatever he wants."

Of course, it wasn't that simple—nothing ever is in Hollywood . . .

★ ★ ★

A SERVICE STORY

Rob Lowe

To many of us it feels like Rob Lowe's been appearing on-screen forever. Between *The Outsiders* and *St. Elmo's Fire*, *The West Wing*, *Parks and Recreation*, and *9-1-1: Lone Star*, it almost seems easier just to name the projects he *hasn't* been in. But there's one show you may not recall his having done: *Family Feud*. It is on that long-running game show that I still remember Rob (and a number of his loved ones) waiting to buzz in and shout out Top Ten answers to "Name something you always find two of!" or "Name things your lips are good for!" It was touching. Sweet. Hilarious. I loved watching it. But what I loved even more is the cause he was there to amplify and win money for: the Wounded Warrior Project.

ROB LOWE: I have deep respect for the men and women who have served our country and continue to enable us to have the freedoms and privileges America was built on. Wounded Warrior helps men and women who have served our country and been disabled and need our help. Not just them, but the families that they come home to. It's a great, great charity. I work with another group, White Heart. With White Heart, you can literally go online, pick your wounded warrior, see what kind of prosthetic they need, and help pay for it.

I also do a lot of work for various charities in the breast cancer world. Susan G. Komen is an organization I work with a lot. Working on *West Wing* that first year, I was the first-ever male spokesperson for Breast Cancer Awareness. I was very proud to do that, in honor of my mom, my grandma, and my great-grandma—all of whom died of breast cancer.

———

WOUNDED WARRIOR PROJECT

Every warrior has a next mission. We know that the transition to civilian life is a journey. And for every warrior, family member, and caregiver, that journey looks different. We are here for their first step, and each step that follows. Because we believe that every warrior should have a positive future to look forward to. There's always another goal to achieve, another mission to discover. We are their partner in that mission.

www.woundedwarriorproject.org

SUSAN G. KOMEN

In 1980, Nancy G. Brinker promised her dying sister, Susan, that she would do everything in her power to end breast cancer forever. In 1982, that promise became the Susan G. Komen organization and the beginning of a global movement. Their efforts helped reduce deaths from breast cancer by 40 percent between 1989 and 2016 and they promise that they won't stop until their promise is fulfilled.

www.komen.org

★ ★ ★

JOSH/SAM

Nostalgia is a marvelous thing. In terms of painting pretty pictures, regardless of the factual landscape, it's undefeated. When it comes to puzzling together the who's who of *The West Wing*, as clean a sweep as it may seem to have been, the messy business of casting the show really came down to the wire. Less than seventy-two hours before filming was set to commence on the pilot, Aaron informed Tommy, John Wells, and Warner Bros. that Brad *had* to play Josh Lyman, end of story. And the rest, as they say . . . is neither funny nor sexy.

Looking back at Brad's heartfelt Santa Monica gas station moment, pleading his case to play Josh, it's hard to miss the fitting seren-dipity at work in the casting of Jed Bartlet's deputy chief of staff. While perhaps lacking in diplomacy, Brad Whitford, like Josh Lyman, stood his ground and raised his voice, proving himself the pitch-perfect man for the job. That impulsive, impassioned outburst perfectly captured the go-for-it spirit of the character, and of the actor who felt called to play him; a spirit articulated by Donna Moss, the woman who would come to know him best . . . the one who always loved him most: "Gather ye rosebuds, Josh!" (Plus, did you not see him hungover in Sam's yellow foul-weather gear?! Come on, Tommy—if that's not sexy, we don't know what is.) As for the man who would be Sam . . .

Following Rob Lowe's audition—his one and only read—in the time it took him to walk to his car, drive off the lot, and steer his way over to Lankershim Boulevard, the powers that be had called and of-fered him the part. Isn't that a nice ending? It's positively Sorkinian. Or it would be, anyway, except it wasn't the end. For that, we'll hand the reins to Rob himself. After all, he's not *actually* a deputy commu-nications director . . . but he plays one on TV:

"They famously couldn't make my deal, so I took a giant pay cut to be in it, and we still weren't anywhere near close to making a deal. When asked, they were like, 'Well, we don't want any stars. We don't care about stars, we just want people who are great for the parts.' So I cut half my price, they did not cut *any* of their price, and we agreed to disagree."

(**MELISSA:** Just jumping in to say this—Rob told us that despite the public negotiations and the ongoing search for the perfect Sam Seaborn, privately he and Aaron were in back-channel communica-tions throughout. **MARY:** They mainly connected via phone, though there was that time they spotted each other across the proverbial crowded room, having coincidentally reserved tables at one of LA's hot-spot steak houses.) But back to Rob . . .

"I saw Aaron at the Palm as I was hearing through the grapevine that they were literally reading every member of the Screen Actors Guild—'so-and-so read for Sam Seaborn, so-and-so read for Sam Seaborn'—and I was dreaming about the part every single night. At the Palm, we both practically had tears in our eyes, hoping that the bean counters could figure it out. Because at the end of the day, the only two people who mattered were already in love—the guy making the show and the actor playing the part!

"Finally, forty-eight hours before they were ready to start shooting, they came back to me. As I had met them halfway, they then met me halfway . . . and we made the deal. I signed my deal in front of Tommy Schlamme in Lyn Paolo's wardrobe department, trying on my suits.

"I was fitted at five o'clock on a Sunday afternoon, and Monday morning—I'll never forget—we were downtown at the Biltmore, shooting the very first scene of the pilot. In the bar. We shot that scene and the sun hadn't even come up yet when we were done."

How's *that* for an ending?! Shooting the first-ever scene of *The West Wing* in a downtown hotel bar before the sun comes up? Good, right? Okay. Who's up? Ooh—Janel!

DONNA MOSS

"Welcome to the White House. My name is Donnatella Moss. I work here in the West Wing as an assistant to Deputy Chief of Staff Joshua Lyman. Which I guess makes me Deputy-*Deputy* Chief of Staff." (CRICKETS. Then . . . a lone, awkward, hilariously muffled cough.)

—DONNA TO WHITE HOUSE GUESTS,
"AND IT'S SURELY TO THEIR CREDIT"

Months before her ascent to the self-proclaimed position of "deputy-deputy," Donna Moss had joined the Bartlet for America campaign as Josh Lyman's new assistant. ("When I said I was assigned to you . . . I may have been overstating it a little.") Back then, Donna was an almost college graduate in shaky possession of roughly five majors, two minors, and one deadbeat med student ex-boyfriend, aka "Dr. Free Ride." By the time the action in the pilot kicked off, she'd risen to "senior" assistant to the deputy chief of staff and, perhaps more notably, had established herself as one half of *The West Wing*'s Olympic gold medal winner, "Fan Favorite Couple" Division.

Donna was, of course, more than just the sum of her not-so-subtle swoonings over Josh and whatever it was he inscribed in the book he gave her for Christmas that time (Beckengruber's *On the Art and Artistry of Alpine Skiing*, for those scoring at home). She was an assistant of such fierce loyalty that she'd venture out into the frigid night to call up small-town New England voters and beg them to pull the lever for Bartlet; a junior staffer willing to *perjure* herself before Congress in service to a decent man she deeply admired; a former student so devoted to her twelfth-grade English teacher that she tried to get the man in the Oval to issue a *presidential proclamation* on the occasion of the woman's retirement. (**MELISSA FUN FACT:** The educator in question, "Mrs. Morello," was named in honor of *West Wing* writer Eli Attie's real-life social studies teacher at Hunter College High School.)

To be clear: Donna's love for her boss was hardly unrequited. Who can forget Josh's periodic feignings toward dismissiveness when it came to his loyal assistant's social life?

> **JOSH**
> Can we clear up a few things about
> my level of interest in the revolving
> door of local Gomers that you see in
> the free time you create by not
> working very hard at your job?

Over the years, in addition to proving herself an invaluable West Wing staffer (and, ultimately, rising up the chain to become chief of staff to first lady Helen Santos), Janel's delightful, layered Donna was far more than a budding love interest. Representing the Bartlet administration, she found her way from DC to fifty percent of the Dakotas and also took an ill-fated trip to Gaza. (Speaking of, if you ever doubt Josh Lyman's heartfelt pining for his beloved assistant, we'll direct you to the overseas beeline he made to her bedside the second word came down that she'd been blown up by a roadside IED.)

The years-long arc of Donatella Moss is indelible for lots of reasons. Her sweet, funny, complicated dynamic with her boss was one, to be sure. And if you called her the heart and soul of the bullpen, we wouldn't argue. But she was its eyes and ears too. Donna and Josh didn't just flirt; they bickered—about each other, about social issues, fiscal policy . . . about the electoral nobility of swapping votes with a Ritchie supporter. And, because of that, more than any *West Wing* character, Donna was the wide-eyed, faithful stand-in for viewers across all seven seasons of the show.

But yes, our memory of this blond-haired, doe-eyed underdog will always be most closely tied to the "crush"-ing sentiment she could never quite contain for her boss. She managed to convey these feelings with the tiniest of gestures, the fleeting-est of looks; as much through the words she uttered as through the things she left unsaid.

The most idolized of Donna's outspoken/unspoken love for Josh came in season 2's "17 People," in which she reveals the whys and wherefores of her bygone breakup with Dr. Free Ride. (Upon learning that Donna had been in a car accident, the guy headed over to the hospital to see her but stopped off along the way for a drink with some friends.) Appalled, Josh tells Donna, "I'm just sayin', if you were in an accident, I wouldn't stop for a beer." Donna replies, . . . "If *you* were in an accident, I wouldn't stop for red lights."

I mean . . . *come on.* That's the exchange you put in the Donna-Josh time capsule. But it takes more than just a special sort of actor to make these moments shine. Sometimes it takes the exact right *person*. And that exact right person was Janel Moloney. A root-able mix of sassy and sincere, her Donna Moss comes across as simultaneously vulnerable and plucky: outspoken, with a built-in, inescapable charm. As for her *West Wing* origin story, it goes back a ways—to a hostess stand, a psychic, and an assistant wardrobe supervisor (who is not to be trifled with) on a Sorkin joint called *Sports Night*.

★ ★ ★

IN 1998, ABC viewers got their one and only look at Monica Brazelton, another fiercely loyal fictional underling, this one from the wardrobe department at a cable network called Continental Sports Channel. Helping outfit the on-camera talent for the ESPN-ish sports highlights show, Monica takes a moment to confront one of the anchors, Casey McCall, for failing to credit her boss during a promotional appearance. The assistant's plaintive, empathetic speech was delivered by a little-known actress named Janel Moloney and showcased some of the bedrock values *West Wing* fans would come to know by heart: standing up for the little guy; giving credit where it's due; speaking truth to power. These themes, which dotted the *Sports Night* landscape, would be easy to spot in any and every episode of the Sorkin show that would follow on its heels. Rewatching that scene now, and the actress who broke our hearts in it, you can't help noticing a whisper of Donna Moss in Monica Brazelton. Which, eighteen months later, was good news for Janel, who would be called in to read for *The West Wing*. But there was one little problem.

"I had just quit acting."

Back in 1999, Janel had been trying for more than a decade—deep into her twenties—to land more steady work in film and TV. She'd waited tables in twenty restaurants and been fired from fifteen. "I don't know what was not right with me as an auditioner, as an actor," she

lamented to us, "but I worked so hard and I got so few jobs. I was bust-
ing my hump, buying a pair of sale shoes once a year . . . and I was like,
'I'm almost thirty. I can't be an out-of-work actress and an out-of-work
waitress. I've got to do something more valuable with my life!'"

The problem, at least as Janel identifies it, was frustratingly typical
for Hollywood, as wholly unoriginal as it was patently false. "Not pretty
enough." "Can't play that girl." "Not famous enough." "Not sexy enough."
Nevertheless, thanks to her memorable turn on *Sports Night*, and because she knew John Wells and John Levey, both of whom she had
auditioned for "a million times," Janel found herself—in what she described to us as "the last gasp of my acting career"—walking onto the
Warner Bros. lot to audition for the role of C.J. Cregg.

Oh yeah—for *C.J.*! Weird, right? Not really. It isn't uncommon for
actors to wind up in a different role from the one they were originally
called in for. That said, Janel approached the audition with her expectations scrupulously well managed. "They asked me to come in and
read for Allison's part. And I felt not quite . . . substantial enough, as
a presence. There was something about that character that needed a
bigger personality. It just needed *Allison*, really." Which is not to say
Janel didn't do a good job in the audition. She did. Just ask the guy
who read opposite her.

"Aaron was reading with me . . . and he stopped me in the middle.
And I think, 'Oh, I'm *bad*.' He said, 'I just want to tell you, you're doing great.' Literally in the middle of the line! I mean, who does that?!"
As Janel (and common sense) suggests, when you're auditioning and
it's going well, the last thing you want is for someone to stop you. "Because," as she says, "it's really hard to do well!" After a moment, she
looked at Aaron and asked, "Um . . . do I keep going?"

"Yes," he replied. "Please. Go on." So, she did. And it went fine.
Better than fine. Everyone in the room—Aaron and Tommy and John,
the Warner Bros. casting folks—they all liked her work plenty. She
even got a callback. Except . . .

"The casting director told my agents at the time that they wanted me to read for a smaller part . . . a 'secretary' . . . and there was no show commitment, just a one-off." Still, they all hoped Janel would be willing to come in.

Okay, quick time-out for a key piece of the puzzle: As Janel told us, and as we can certainly confirm, that period in Hollywood was extremely teenager-heavy. "I went through two pilot seasons with barely any auditions because there were no *adults* in any of the shows!" So, a role written for a grown-up? And a chance to work again with Aaron and Tommy? (**MELISSA FUN FACT:** Tommy Schlamme was so moved by Janel's *Sports Night* audition that he actually cried.) For Janel, it all added up to "What do I have to lose?"

So she went back in to read for this smaller, one-off role of some "secretary" called Donna Moss and . . . "I really loved the part. I *really* loved it. It was petite . . . but complete." What she loved about Donna is what we all came to love about Donna: "There was sass and empathy, devotion and intelligence and bravery. She was," as Janel put it to us, "completely there." Which is another example of what she calls (what we all call) "the genius of Aaron." As the old adage goes, "There are no small parts." "You could have this part that they themselves may have thought, 'Oh, this is not substantial.' But it was the part that was meant for me because *I* felt it was very substantial."

When she went back in to read, this time for Donna, Janel found the same array of faces as the last time. Due to the size of the role—the size they had originally *thought* the role would be, anyway—she didn't have to jump through a bunch of hoops for network suits. There was no test. She just had to read Donna's pilot scenes for Aaron, Tommy, and John, along with the casting team at Warner Bros.

"I still remember exactly what I wore. These really cute tweed slacks—like a nubby gray, tweedy wool—and a black turtleneck, and I had my hair long and down and, ya know, I looked like . . . Donna!"

One standout memory from her callback is that she did "this really superdorky thing." The audition, she told us, included "this little scene with Josh in his office, where I'm . . . basically empowering him." From the pilot you may recall the guy needed some empowering. Representing the administration on one of the Sunday morning news shows, Josh had gone after Mary Marsh, a hot-tempered, high-profile evangelical with an axe to grind. As a result, for most of the episode it appears that President Bartlet might actually fire Josh. Wearing *fiercely loyal* on her sleeve, Donna seethes: "You *won* that election for him! You and Leo and C.J. and Sam!"

"There's a little bit of emotion," Janel told us, "so before I did that scene, I turned my back on them to center myself and breathe." As John Levey revealed on the podcast, while Janel was familiar to all of them, from *Sports Night* and otherwise, casting her came down to simple competition: "She just *won* that part."

Which is not to suggest there wasn't luck involved—or, we should say, good fortune. As Janel concedes, "If my part had been the part that it *became*, I would never have gotten it." Heck, if from the get-go Donna Moss had been, you know, *Donna Moss*, she "may never have been called in at all." Oh, and speaking of good fortune, wasn't there something about a *psychic*?

Ohhhhhh yes. Yes, there was. Right around the time Janel had decided to quit acting, she went to see the sister of her friend, actor Hank Azaria. "Hank's sister is an amazing astrologer," Janel told us, "she's the real thing." (**MELISSA:** 'Kay . . .) "She's also a little bit psychic." At this point in our interview Janel said, "You're gonna think it's a lie, but I literally have this on tape." (She does.)

At the reading, Hank Azaria's possibly-somewhat-psychic astrologer sister said, "I'm looking at your chart and you're just about to have this opening." She then gave Janel a fourteen-day window—between this date and that date—saying, "Because you're an actress . . . it's probably an audition. It's going to change your life. It's gonna be political . . . and it's gonna be . . . huge. It's going to affect people in a really deep way. It's *important*."

Given the diligence Janel has always exhibited, the place where she learned she'd been cast as Donna Moss is hardly surprising. "I was hostessing at Il Pastaio in Beverly Hills. I checked my voicemail from the hostess stand."

Looking back, even Janel has to admit, the psychic story sounds like "total bullshit." And it does, right? Until you realize that the day she got called in to read for *The West Wing* fell between the exact two weeks the astrologer had given her three months before.

Let's make one thing perfectly clear, though. Janel got cast as Donna Moss not because it was "in the cards" but because she'd proven herself to be right for the part, thanks to having done a bang-up job in the audition *and* in another role for the same creative team a year or so before. She got it because she's *good* and because all those days and nights splitting time between auditioning and working at the hostess stand paid off. There's nothing remotely "meant to be" about it. Except . . .

Remember when Aaron wanted Brad to be in that half-hour he'd just written called *Sports Night*? Guess which character Brad was going to play. Casey McCall. Yes, one way or another, come hell or high water, Janel Moloney was going to get her chance to chastise Brad Whitford on-screen. These two were inexorably drawn toward each other, and nothing—not rain or snow or time or space—was going to stop them. Not even red lights.

FOUR

MOVING MOUNTAINS AND SCRUBBING FLOORS

The West Wing and Service

> In this day and age of 24-hour cable crap devoted
> to feeding the voyeuristic gluttony of an American
> public hooked on a bad soap opera that's passing
> itself off as important . . . How do we end the cycle?
> "Be subject to one another."
>
> —JED TO ABIGAIL, "WAR CRIMES"

The pro-environment slogan "Think globally, act locally" may be the best example of snappy, effective "bumper-sticker-wisdom" messaging the world (and its collection of 1970s VW buses) has ever seen. Progressive voters everywhere likely wish the DNC could replicate a version of that memorable über-motto for a whole host of issues close to their bleeding hearts. But regardless of the issue or the message, it's important to keep in mind that public service is not a one-size-fits-all proposition. There's not a threshold to meet or some magic formula that spits out exactly what constitutes an adequate level of "pitching in" or "giving back." In every single community—yours,

ours, or the ones on the other side of the country—there's plenty for us to do. That goes for *The West Wing* community too.

From a lifelong devotion to the great causes of our time, of *any* time—social justice, religious freedom, civil rights—to microscale efforts like sprucing up a children's waiting room at the local police precinct . . . there's so much we can do. And so much to be done. You don't have to get arrested at a nuclear power plant to feel rooted in a sense of civic duty.

When we get bogged down in just how much *need* there is out there, it's easy to get overwhelmed. It's also easy, when skimming an op-ed or catching half an hour of your favorite cable news, to throw up your hands and surrender to that nagging sense of "What difference will it make?" But here's the thing: It'll make a *world* of difference. To a family. To a kid. To a grandma in a snowstorm who needs her sidewalk cleared.

One of the canniest takes on this subject came from, of all people, a writer who goes by the name of Aaron Sorkin. He didn't write it for a president to say, or a first lady, a press secretary or a chief of staff. He wrote it for a single-dad sports anchor, who said it to his periodically neurotic co-anchor, a charitably minded guy struggling with how best to do his part in an increasingly needy world.

Can I say something? You're not gonna solve everybody's problems. In fact, you're not gonna solve anybody's problems. So, you know what you should do? Anything. As much of it, and as often as you can.

—CASEY McCALL TO DAN RYDELL, "THE QUALITY OF MERCY AT 29K," *SPORTS NIGHT*

A related expression of civic-mindedness can be found in wisdom of an altogether different sort—the ancient Chinese proverb kind. This one, along with many variations, is common across countless cultural and family traditions but also exists in internet memes and—according to our semi-exhaustive online recon—numerous Pinterest user groups. It goes like this: "The man who removes a mountain begins by carrying away small stones."

Now, we don't know what to make of the following—perhaps our old friend is deeper into online craftiness than we ever would have imagined—but this lovely idea has been espoused quite often in recent years by Dulé Hill.

"I always say, as I'm going through life, if I come to a mountain that seems overwhelming to me—to scale it, to go around it, to move it out of the way—what I can do is pick up a stone. I could chip a little piece of it, and pick it up, then move it out of the way. Now, if I could pick up a stone, and get *you* to pick up a stone, get Melissa to pick up a stone, and then *you* all get people, the domino effect—that ripple effect—can make a big difference. I can't pick up a million stones, I can't pick up a billion stones. But I can get a million people or a billion people to pick up a stone . . . and then we can move the mountain."

Sure, you may be thinking, Allison or Richard or Rob, Janel or Brad or Martin, come to their causes armed with the power of visibility and the access celebrity affords. Of course *they* can "move mountains," but what on Earth am I supposed to do? We get it.

One of my most vivid memories of *The West Wing* came early in season 5. I had recently joined the show as Kate Harper. Like at any other job, Monday mornings saw us standing around, engaging in your typical watercooler talk. The main difference being that, when filming a TV show, the "So, Mary, what'd *you* do this weekend?" part occurs during downtime in hair and makeup or while various departments set up the next shot.

That morning, before rehearsal in the Oval Office, some of us were talking about how we'd spent the last couple of days. As usual, filming the previous Friday had blown past midnight and deep into Saturday morning—aka, "Fraturday night"—so more than one of us said, "I just slept!" There were, of course, more exciting answers too—someone had tickets to a Dodgers game, a few crew members went to hear a band at House of Blues, Allison had attended a premiere, and some poor soul had a kid's birthday party in Topanga. Then Martin said, all casual, "I got arrested." I did a double take, like . . . "Whaaat?!"

Martin, turns out, had been at a protest—I don't recall what he was protesting that time; this would happen more than once during my run on the show—and, for him, sometimes a part of protesting was . . . getting arrested. That's how committed he was, and is, to the causes he believes in. But, while I was taken aback, particularly at how blasé he was about *going to jail*, nobody else in the room was remotely shocked. They didn't even flinch. To the rest of them, and to me soon enough, that was just Martin being Martin.

Again, though, you don't have to spend a night in the clink to show commitment. You don't even have to go to a protest. And your version of public service almost certainly won't entail leaving your job and moving to DC to advocate for veterans, the climate, or anything else. You don't have to put together a massive fundraising event at Warner Bros. to make a massive difference in your corner of the world. Like Dulé said, all you have to do, really, is pick up a stone. Set small, achievable goals and build on them. You can do it on your own or . . . rope others into doing it with you, like our friend Chris Misiano does.

Chris was a director and producer on *The West Wing* for all seven of its seasons, directing nearly three dozen episodes, including a ton of your all-time favorites: "Mr. Willis of Ohio." "The Black Vera Wang." "Celestial Navigation." And the series finale, "Tomorrow." He has engaged in some of his service opportunities locally and has done so with his family. All it took was convincing them to go along with it. And PS, when you get your *kids* to do it—out of the kindness of their hearts or to earn back iPad privileges—boom, just like that, you've increased your service footprint exponentially! Here's the Misiano story, short and you won't believe how sweet.

"My family and I got into doing a thing where we would go to the local police precinct on a weekly or biweekly basis. We would scrub and clean the children's holding room . . . because people would be brought in and arrested while their children were in the house. The kids had to play someplace, they had to do *something*, and the station had this kind of ratty little room, so we would try and decorate that and bring toys."

That's it, that's all, that's the story. And it's . . . *fantastic*. This seemingly small-scale, low-key project, something they did "just every now and then," makes a deeply personal impact on the lives of people in their immediate community. On the lives of folks they may not even know, but who *need* it. Parents at rock bottom. Children who are suddenly scared and sad and confused, their heads and hearts spinning, wondering what comes next. The Misiano family did that because, well, that's something they could do. It's a stone they could pick up, a mountain they could help move. To quote *Sports Night* again—to paraphrase it, anyway—there oughta be congressional medals for families like that.

The "families" that formed within the cast and crew during *The West Wing* have continued their commitment to service since the series wrapped up. Maybe the show (and the people who worked on it) left a mark on them, encouraging them to remain involved in those sorts of endeavors. Maybe people came to the project already hardwired for civic engagement. Whatever the case, the spectrum of commitment and the diversity of the causes inspire both of us to this day. And, as with a lot of things *West Wing*, it started at the top of the call sheet.

FIVE

A SERVICE STORY

Martin Sheen

The Irish tell a story of a man who arrives at the
gates of heaven and asks to be let in. St. Peter says,
"Of course, just show us your scars." The man says,
"I have no scars." St. Peter says, "What a pity.
Was there nothing worth fighting for?"

—MARTIN SHEEN

For as long as he's been a public figure, and long before that, Martin
Sheen has been a tireless champion for social justice. His go-the-
extra-mile commitment to service has inspired countless people around
the globe, including his *West Wing* family.

MELISSA: Martin and I met before *The West Wing*. That was, in
fact, the *second* project we worked on together. The first was a
1998 film called *Monument Ave.* that starred Denis Leary and
was directed by Ted Demme. I remember Ted saying that he told
Martin, 'This is a low-budget movie. You can't get arrested because we can't afford to change the schedule!'"

MARTIN SHEEN: I was doing a movie with the British film director John Borman and I had a day off. I did some demonstration over in New York and got arrested. Borman heard about it Monday morning and he said, "I shall have no more of this arrest rubbish! You finish the film before you begin that nonsense again!"

So, when Martin signs on the line, "that nonsense" is part of the package.

MARTIN SHEEN: During the war in El Salvador, I joined an organization in Los Angeles with the laity and the religious concerned. We had this Wednesday morning coalition. We'd gather at La Placida for a prayer circle, then march on the federal building and shut it down. In those days, they let you get away with a lot. We'd chain ourselves to the door and stop business for the day. It's very effective. We'd get booked and told to come back for a court appearance and so forth. I was there for a week, so by the time I had to appear in court to deal with all this, it was up to thirteen arrests. My lawyer and dear friend Joe Cosgrove came up.

(**MELISSA FUN FACT:** Joe played one of the defense lawyers in the death penalty episode "Take This Sabbath Day" and played a key role in securing permission for production to film on the steps of the US Supreme Court.)

MARTIN SHEEN: So, Joe's defending me and we drew a very interesting judge. I don't know what level of the federal bench, but it was in the same building I'd been shutting down. She looked at the record and says to me, "Ramón"—every time I'm arrested, the only ID I have is under my real name, Ramón Antonio Gerardo Estévez—"I'm looking at this series of offenses and . . . you're just going to start this again. I don't think it's going to do any good to send you to jail for a while, is it?" She's actually talking to me like a human being.

I say, "Probably not, under the circumstances. I mean, Your Honor, you know what's going on in Central America . . ." She says, "Oh, I do. Will you do community service?" I said, "I will." She sentenced me to 150 hours of community service. I got sent to Bread and Roses in Venice, California. The Sisters of St. Joseph had a soup kitchen. I had to work off 150 hours, which I did in short order. I stayed for another ten years. I didn't leave until *West Wing*.

Of course, I went back and volunteered, and my son Ramón joined up as a short-order cook. When he was in high school, my grandson Taylor would come during days off and we'd serve the homeless. It was a wonderful experience.

Somebody asked me the other day, "What's your favorite gospel quote? What advice do you take from the scriptures?" I said, "There's only one." It's a long verse, but it's a very short line. It's Matthew, I think it's 25 or 26. "Lord, when did we see you hungry?" That's it. It's like the character Emilio played in the film *The Way*. To that character, kindness is an instinct. Service can become an instinct. Where you cannot *not* do it and be yourself.

Martin has supported numerous causes over the years, but when asked which ones he would like to highlight, he shared these two.

MARTIN SHEEN: Since my early adulthood, the Catholic Worker has been an organization I support. Dorothy Day founded it. Because they oppose so much government activity, particularly military, you don't get any tax deductions. There's a wonderful one here, the Los Angeles Catholic Worker. They feed the homeless, they have a soup kitchen, and they're always in jail, protesting something, God love 'em.

As a young actor in New York, I used to go there to eat. It

was the only place that you could get a nice meal every night, a hot meal without having to pay. They were on Chrystie Street at that time. I was at the Living Theatre. (The Living Theatre is the oldest experimental theater group in the United States. It was founded by an actress named Judith Malina—no relation to Josh; we checked—and an artist and poet named Julian Beck.)

Julian Beck and Judith Malina would say they "had this great friend down there on Chrystie Street . . ." I went there for months and months. One day I said, "I'm here all the time, eating, and I never get a chance to pay you guys. What can I do?" He said, "Come and help us fold the paper." I said, "You guys got a paper?!" That was the *Catholic Worker* paper. It all started on May Day, I think, in 1933. Now they're all over the country, God bless 'em.

MELISSA: Martin is the person who got me involved in advocacy for treatment courts more than a decade ago. (Treatment courts are alternatives to incarceration that provide lifesaving treatment to people with substance use and mental health disorders.) His passion for the work was undeniably infectious, and still is. Over the last thirty-plus years, Martin has given speeches and testimony at a variety of conferences, rallies, media appearances, and other gatherings—including before the US Congress—in support of treatment courts. Like his character on *The West Wing*, the man knows his way around an inspiring speech. Having heard many of the following remarks in person, I can attest that it's hard not to drop everything and join Martin in his fight for this cause. Here are just a few examples from Martin's three decades of treatment court advocacy:

> "[Treatment courts represent] the most realistic, the
> most innovative and the most productive program to
> emerge from the justice system regarding drug and
> alcohol abuse in our nation's history."

"I come to my support of drug [treatment] court through my work with social justice. My first exposure to them opened my eyes to the miraculous recovery of people that, before drug [treatment] court, were just thrown away and added to an already overcrowded and tragic prison population."

"Now you're talking about courage. Now you're talking about change. Now you're talking about possibility. Now you're talking about drug [treatment] court. In the end, we are made worthy of the long-promised blessings reserved for those who do justice and show mercy. Keep going forward. There's enough people following you and history is going to be the judge of what you did. Stick to it like a stamp, and remember: Fear is useless. Faith is necessary. Love is everything."

THE CATHOLIC WORKER MOVEMENT

Catholic Workers live a simple lifestyle in community, serve the poor, and resist war and social injustice. Most are grounded in the gospel, prayer, and the Catholic faith, although some houses are interfaith. There are 159 Catholic Worker communities across the United States and 28 Catholic Worker communities abroad.

www.catholicworker.org

ALL RISE

All Rise is a national nonprofit championing justice system reform for people impacted by substance use and mental health disorders by promoting treatment instead of incarceration. All Rise leads the establishment of treatment courts, the most successful intervention in our nation's history for leading people living with substance use and mental health disorders out of the justice system and into lives of recovery and stability.

www.allrise.org

SIX

"THESE WOMEN . . ."
AND A FEW GOOD MEN

Part II

CHARLIE YOUNG

According to the good folks at PoliticalDictionary.com, the "personal aide to the president"—formerly referred to as the "body man" or "body woman"—coordinates with the president's political advisors, administrative staff, and family members to manage the president's schedule. In addition to that, they stay with POTUS at all times except for particularly sensitive meetings—like, say, consulting with Leo and the Joint Chiefs in the Situation Room.

In order to ensure strict confidentiality, in the real-life White House this position is typically selected from a pool of trusted insiders from the campaign or a previously held office. But in the world of *The West Wing*, he came to the job at the recommendation of an alpaca farmer hopped up on antianxiety meds who may or may not have had a minor gambling problem. "A Proportional Response"—the third episode in the *West Wing* saga—gave viewers their first look at a wide-eyed old soul named Dulé Hill. This new kid on the block played the new kid on the block, Charlie Young . . . the body man with the baby face.

It's a very sensitive job. It's also a very hard job.
Twenty-hour days aren't uncommon, long trips
at the last minute, a lot of wait and hurry up.
Moreover, there'll be times when you'll have to
make yourself invisible in plain sight, as well as
an undeniable force in front of those who want
more time than we want to give. Sometimes the
people I'm talking about will be kings and
prime ministers. You understand so far?

—JOSH VETTING CHARLIE, "A PROPORTIONAL RESPONSE"

Eighteen months earlier, before he'd ever heard of *The West Wing*, Dulé auditioned for a Warner Bros. pilot that had been cast by one of his early champions, Kevin Scott—second chair to the studio's head of casting, John Levey. On that particular project, Dulé didn't make it as far as the network test. But a year and a half later, Kevin Scott still remembered him and thought enough of Dulé to call him in for the role that would turn his life upside down in the good way. Dulé was twenty-three and almost broke, to the point he was even considering moving back home to New Jersey. But his luck was about to change . . .

Kevin had mentioned him to John Levey, who'd only known Dulé from his starring turn in the tap dance–heavy Broadway phenomenon *Bring in 'da Noise, Bring in 'da Funk*. (**MARY:** Dulé remains one of the most esteemed tap dancers of his, or any, generation. When he was ten, he performed on the muscular dystrophy telethon for Jerry Lewis and the millions of viewers watching at home. **MELISSA:** Almost a decade later, as a student at Seton Hall, Dulé landed a featured role in that production of "*Noise/Funk*," alongside Savion Glover and Jeffrey Wright. Every so often, we were lucky enough to watch him tap-dance on set and it was a "pinch me" moment each time, including when he improvised with cellist Yo-Yo Ma during the filming of "Noël.")

Yo-Yo Ma's sitting there playing around with his cello, and Dulé walked up to him and said, "Can you play that thing you were playing earlier?" And Yo-Yo Ma goes, "Sure." He starts playing, and Dulé starts to try to tap along a little bit to this classical piece. And Yo-Yo is like, "This is cool." He starts playing, and before you know it . . . Dulé is shuffling along to Yo-Yo Ma. It was one of the most beautiful moments I've ever seen anywhere.

—RICHARD SCHIFF, *THE WEST WING WEEKLY,*
"*WEST WING* REUNION (LIVE FROM ATX)"

So, yes, while Dulé was already an acclaimed dancer in 1999, Levey "didn't know anything about his range as an actor." Luckily for John and Dulé—for all of us, really—Kevin Scott had a more holistic sense of him as a performer. "When the role of Charlie came up," Dulé told us, "Kevin searched me out because I'd left my old agency—or, I should say . . . they left *me*." Around the time he got called in for Charlie, Dulé was a twenty-three-year-old going out for teen movies and TV shows that were, in his view, "not anywhere near the caliber of artistry" of *The West Wing*. In fact, shortly before he got dropped as a client, Dulé met with his soon-to-be-ex-agents and told them "the reason I'm not booking is that the material I'm being offered is not good.

You give me something that's good, I guarantee you I will do a lot better on the audition."

Fortunately, Kevin Scott put in the effort to track him down, connecting with Dulé's longtime manager, Kathy Atkinson (and his new agents), to discuss bringing him in to read for *The West Wing*. It should be noted that they didn't have to sell Dulé too hard on this latest endeavor. Twenty-plus years later, he still recalls his immediate reaction: "Aaron Sorkin? And it's about the White House? That's all I need to know."

Since he was auditioning to play a character who wouldn't be joining until the show's third episode, Dulé was able to do more than just read Aaron's original pilot script. He got to watch a copy of the produced pilot itself. (**MELISSA FUN FACT:** He watched it on a VHS tape that his agency had passed along to him, thanks to another of their clients, some guy named Bradley Whitford.) Alone in his Studio City apartment on Bluffside Drive—a place that didn't have a couch but did have a big-screen TV—Dulé stuck in the tape and pressed play. For the young actor it was a thrilling and unforgettable experience, the first of many as it related to *The West Wing*.

"When I saw the pilot," Dulé remembers, "I went back to my manager, my agent, and said, 'If they can do that, week in and week out, this will be one of the greatest shows ever put on television. The question is, Can they do *this* show every time?'"

What struck him as especially remarkable, he told us, "was the interaction between the cast members, how it *moved*, how it really 'caught' conversation between people, and how they interjected the cinematic experience that Tommy Schlamme put together." To take a world often considered drab in appearance, and dull in every other way, and make it truly *captivating* was, in Dulé's view, an astonishing achievement. "It was the type of thing," he says, "that made me *lean in*. And I stayed leaning in all the way 'til the end."

What really got his attention was the moment Bartlet finally shows up. "It was like, Wow, there's a president and he has such a calming force, and has something profound to say, to share. I was impressed that you could take a subject like government and make it interesting, make me wait to see what's next. I know that became one of the themes of the show, but even in that episode I was waiting to see . . . what's next. It made it hip and cool and sexy. And suspenseful."

The morning of his audition Dulé was at home, prepping for what would become one of the most consequential days of his twenty-three years. Armed with little more than a nervous version of his talent, the abiding faith of casting director Kevin Scott, and a marked-up script, he was hours away from a truly life-changing event. He had a chance to be a part of something special, something *rare*. Standing alone in his spartan apartment on Bluffside, there remained one major question to address:

Which shirt should he wear?

★ ★ ★

DULÉ arrived at Warner Bros. casting for the audition in what he remembers as "a dark blue, collared Mossimo shirt." Kevin Scott ushered him back into his office for some last-minute coaching. He took the young actor through the preferred pace of the dialogue ("up-tempo"), stressing the critical importance of sticking to the script, word-for-word and down to the letter. It was basically a 101 cram session on "How Aaron Does It." Dulé, though, was plenty familiar with Aaron's work and respectful of the writer's professional MO. He had no plans to deviate from the text. As he put it to us, "Why would I? I mean, the man wrote 'You can't handle the truth!'"

As if there were any doubt that he was meant for this role—for this writer, for this *show*—in the run-up to the audition Dulé's focus had been on the only thing that mattered. The words. "You don't need to do much prep beyond Aaron Sorkin's words," he recognized. "You just deliver the words as they are."

Indeed, in his view, the nuts and bolts of Charlie Young were laid out on the page. "He's a kid who's lost his mother, trying to handle business for his sister. He lives just on the outside of 'Camelot'—in DC. He can *see* the castle but can never go in the castle. And now, all of a sudden, he's right at the center of the castle. It was," as Dulé tells it, "like Dorothy landing in Oz, like, 'What the heck is going on here?!' All of a sudden I'm in the Oval Office talking to the president of the United States!"

According to Dulé, for the audition . . . it was all about the awe-struck. And, at that moment, on the cusp of reading for Aaron and Tommy, "awestruck" was in plentiful supply.

Asked what he most recalls from the minutes leading up to his read for Charlie, Dulé didn't hesitate: "I remember being nervous." To settle himself, he and Kevin did a quick final run-through of the material, which came directly from the latest draft of season 1, episode 3, "A Proportional Response." (**MARY FUN FACT:** Aaron famously borrowed from his *American President* screenplay for President Bartlet's multi-scene tirade in this episode.)

Someday, someone's going to have to explain to
me the virtue of a proportional response.

—PRESIDENT ANDREW SHEPHERD,
THE AMERICAN PRESIDENT

What is the virtue of a proportional response?
Why's it good? They hit an airplane,
so we hit a transmitter, right?
That's a proportional response!

—PRESIDENT JOSIAH BARTLET,
"A PROPORTIONAL RESPONSE"

"My audition scenes were the two in the Roosevelt Room with Brad," including the part, Dulé says, "where Rob comes in." Despite running lines with the casting director, despite having them down cold and word-for-word, Dulé remained not altogether . . . all together. As luck would have it, though, the character he was reading for felt pretty much the same way.

"The character's supposed to be nervous," Dulé says. "At first I was trying to calm my nerves . . . and then I remembered my acting teacher Bill Esper saying to us, 'Use what's there. Whatever is inside of you . . . use it. That's what keeps you *alive*.' This is a scene where Charlie is nervous. So, what, I'm going to try to get *rid* of my nerves, then manufacture some nerves to then *act* like I'm nervous? If you're nervous, just *be* nervous. And that's exactly what I did. I just . . . let the nerves live and have their way inside of me."

Walking into the room, he spotted Tommy and Aaron alongside Marc Buckland, the director of the upcoming episode. Just as Dulé had found all he needed to know about Charlie right there on the page, the decision makers found all they needed to know about Dulé right there in the room.

Tommy, it turns out, had been pretty well convinced even before that moment, based on the tape of Dulé's "pre-read" for the role. Before this, having watched six young actors, *The West Wing*'s producing director had begun to panic: "Fuck! We're never gonna find this kid!" Then he put on the tape of the seventh prospective Charlie and his pulse slowed. *Ohhhh*, he realized thankfully, *we found the kid*. "It was just so charming and innocent . . . but really deep eyes. It was," as Tommy described it to us, "like a *slap*."

When Dulé began to read, John Levey says, "it was one of the things that's great about working on something so specific, where the qualities are so well-defined. You're either right . . . or you're wrong." Dulé's Charlie, it goes without saying, was right, but just for fun . . . let us count the ways: nervous but sincere, with off-the-charts smarts alongside a lingering tragic history, self-possessed but unassuming to a fault. He was, truly, everything Aaron had put into the script, and then some. Given all that, you'd think the casting of Dulé Hill as Charlie Young would've gone off without a hitch, right? Well . . . yeah. It kinda did.

And it seems appropriate that this would be the most straightforward casting story, right? Of all the characters on *The West Wing*, the one who hardly ever lost his cool, the one whose true emotional "outbursts" you could count on barely half a hand, was this kid, the president's body man. Think about the swirl of tragedy, tumult, and violence that marked Charlie's life—losing his mother to a cop-killer bullet, raising a little sister all on his own, dating the youngest daughter of the leader of the free world and watching white supremacists nearly assassinate the president because of it, because of *you*. Despite all that—*surrounded* by all of it—Dulé Hill's Charlie Young walked through the West Wing with a relative lack of drama.

And yet, as smoothly as the process may have run, in casting Dulé Hill the creative team managed to square the circle for what is a deceptively challenging role. For Charlie they had to find an actor buyable as a true "outsider"—a proxy for the viewers, a fresh set of eyes getting a peek behind the curtain—*and* as a member of Bartlet's inner circle, a new face that somehow felt of a piece with the others. Dulé executed this magic trick, one with a high degree of difficulty, and he made it look easy. (No wonder they gave him the knife.)

Charlie, my father gave this to me,
and his father gave it to him,
and now I'm giving it to you. . . .

—PRESIDENT BARTLET TO CHARLIE, "SHIBBOLETH"

For Dulé, the honor bestowed by that fictional gift, and what it represented—both to Charlie and to his surrogate father, Josiah Bartlet—has to feel impossible to match. But we think we may have found a real-life equivalent that at least comes close. It came in the form of a compliment dished out by the show's creator, Aaron Sorkin, while speaking on a panel at the 2016 ATX Television Festival in Austin, Texas.

"We managed to cast eight actors, all of whom could be carrying their own show. And now I was faced with a very glamorous problem, which is, I have eight mouths to feed. How do you not give every scene to Dulé Hill?"

★ ★ ★

A SERVICE STORY

DULÉ HILL

When Dulé Hill landed on the set of *The West Wing*, he was in his early twenties. He wasn't just the youngest member of the cast; he was one of the only "young" people on the show at all. Like a lot of younger people, and unlike many series regulars on the show, Dulé didn't arrive with a white-hot passion for politics and public service. He loved the pilot—we've covered that—but for him, the day-to-day mechanics of governance hadn't sparked an interest . . . yet.

DULÉ HILL: For myself, a young, coming-of-age man at that time, politics was: "Please—they're just a bunch of con men pulling the wool over our eyes, trying to speak out one side of their mouth while doing some funny business. I'm gonna *vote*, but I know this is all a big game."

Dubious of politicians and their habitual "funny business," he saddled up for the show with little interest in getting roped into the political corral. That reluctance didn't last.

DULÉ HILL: The first time I campaigned for anybody started off with . . . Martin stopping by my trailer—I was changing!—to ask what I was doing that Saturday. I said, "Nothing." He said, "Great! You're going out with me and we're campaigning for Al Gore!"

We ended up flying around—myself, Rob Reiner, Alfre Woodard . . . Ben Affleck . . . Helen Hunt, I believe, and Julia Louis-Dreyfus, too. . . . We went to about four different states . . . just hopped around . . . from one place to another and did these rallies. That was the first time I really got to see democracy at work. I went from being unemployed and almost broke in the summer of 1999 to going out and giving speeches in the summer and fall of 2000. All I could think was, This is crazy, this is great!

But his newfound passion for politics wasn't just about jetting off to swing states. It was the downtime spent with folks who were, to borrow a phrase, "fired up and ready to go."

DULÉ HILL: Being on that set every day with Martin and John, Brad and Richard and Rob, Aaron and Tommy—these different political points of view, that was a part of their daily conversation. Those conversations started to change how I looked at government.

These days, in addition to campaigning for politicians whose policy positions he believes in, Dulé supports a number of causes near and dear to his heart and soul.

DULÉ HILL: Everybody Dance exposes children in underserved communities to the arts, especially dance. I first came to know about the organization thanks to my guiding mentor, Gregory Hines, who had been deeply involved with them.

In 2004, a year after Gregory Hines passed away, Everybody Dance introduced the Gregory Hines Humanitarian Award. Dulé was their first honoree.

DULÉ HILL: I was incredibly humbled to receive that award, and from there I got to know more about Everybody Dance. I just fell in love with what they were doing. In the years since, I've taught classes to the students there and done whatever I can to help out.

The core mission at Everybody Dance appeals to Dulé, whose passion for that art form has been with him through a long career as a dancer, and which he tapped into early on.

DULÉ HILL: I began going to dance school at the age of three. Ever since, dance has been a real gateway for my life and my career. Everybody Dance does a similar thing, opening up pathways for children to find a voice within themselves, understand artistic expression, and really grasp onto their power. I just love this organization.

Over the years, Dulé has devoted himself to the Make-A-Wish Foundation as well.

DULÉ HILL: Working with Make-A-Wish over the last two decades, there were a lot of people whose wish was to simply meet me or meet the cast of *Psych*. That's so humbling and such a privilege. It always amazes me how a little effort can make such a huge impact on somebody else. To bring a little joy to children who are facing a terminal illness, to bring some light into their lives during such a challenging time . . . that is a beautiful thing to get to do. Make-A-Wish really ties into how I hope to live my life. Focusing on others more than ourselves. I feel if we can do that as individuals, if we can do that as a community, if we can do that as a nation, then we could really make this world a better place, a much more peaceful place, a much more joyful place.

EVERYBODY DANCE LA!

Everybody Dance LA! began as an after-school program in 2000 in an affordable housing project near downtown Los Angeles. Today, the program serves 2,400 students, ages four to twenty-one, and is the leading provider of high-quality, low-cost dance instruction in the city's impacted, underserved communities.

www.everybodydance.org

MAKE-A-WISH FOUNDATION

The Make-A-Wish Foundation creates life-changing wishes for children with critical illnesses.

www.wish.org

★ ★ ★

ABIGAIL BARTLET

Okay, let's just say it. FLOTUS is not the most appealing acronym. No one—certainly not a board-certified thoracic surgeon—aspires to be called something that sounds vaguely gross or, well . . . cold medicine–adjacent. But, on *The West Wing* or otherwise, what it stands for (first lady of the United States) has always been something your typical citizen-slash–audience member feels like they truly understand—and we mean beyond just . . . "POTUS's wife." Her role, for some, carries a real majesty and her presence is a subtly impactful one—on the campaign trail, in photo ops, behind the scenes, or right up front, staking her claim.

Having served as the first female press secretary in US history—in the first term of the Clinton White House—*West Wing* consultant Dee Dee Myers got a close-up look at how FLOTUSes (**MARY:** "FLOTAE? FLOTI?") operate, before ever even setting foot in Aaron's inaugural writers room. Speaking on a featurette for the show's season 4 DVD, she underscored the unique level of access and influence first ladies have historically enjoyed. "She's there when he wakes up in the morning, she's there when he goes to bed at night. I don't care if it was Martha Washington or Dolley Madison or Nancy Reagan or Hillary Clinton or Laura Bush, they're *powerful*. They play a role, they have an influence, and they affect the culture of the White House."

Late in the series, as prospective chief of staff to Helen Santos (*West Wing*'s FLOTUS 2.0), Donna Moss drew in broad strokes the distinction between two varieties of first lady: "There's the activist model, with your own policy agenda and objectives . . . or a more traditional, chiefly ceremonial presence, representing the country as kind of a hostess/goodwill ambassador without any particular policy focus." Donna presumed Mrs. Santos would opt "to chart some middle course," just like the show's original first lady had.

A feisty force of nature, an intoxicating blend of confident, savvy and erudite . . . with a sly side of flirty, Dr. Abigail Bartlet was wholly credible, both as a medical doctor and as a traditional (but not) Daughter of the American Revolution. While few would contest the wry intellect that lived in her eyes—a keen, sarcastic quip forever lurking around the bend—fewer still would deny the capacity she possessed for matters of the heart. At the bedrock, Abbey Bartlet exhibited a loyal, protective mama-bear ferocity—to her husband, to her family, to the scores of people in their vast inner circle . . . even to her own integrity.

> There are fourteen people in the world who know
> this, including the vice-president, the chief of staff,
> and the chairman of the joint chiefs. You're going to
> be the fifteenth. Seven years ago my husband was
> diagnosed with a relapsing remitting course of MS.
> When all this is over, tell the press, don't tell the
> press. It's entirely up to you.
>
> —ABIGAIL TO DR. LEE,
> "IN THE SHADOW OF TWO GUNMEN: PART I"

This is not to say that she was pure or uncomplicated. Abbey Bartlet would prove to be ambitious, at times contentiously so, carrying political priorities (and a political staff) that periodically clashed with those of her spouse. Tracking down someone who could play all that, and do so with a preternatural effortlessness—all while exuding a distinct sense of style and glamour—was a seriously tall order. The creative team needed to find an actress who could stand on equal footing with, and be an equal partner to, Martin Sheen's Jed Bartlet, a figure who, much to Abbey's eye-rolling chagrin, once claimed to be "like Gatsby . . . but without the problems." Oh, one more thing: They needed to find her *fast*.

According to John Levey, Aaron's inspiration to introduce the role was more sudden spark than slow burn. "Literally, Aaron emerged from his office and said, 'The first lady is in the next episode!'" Boom, just like that, as Dee Dee remembers it, she and the other writers were sitting around a conference table, watching Aaron pass out a list of actresses to play President Bartlet's wife.

As they talked about the character, who she was, and who she might become, the trio in charge found themselves singing a familiar refrain. It was the one they'd initially given voice to when seeking the ideal Leo McGarry. "We need someone like John Spencer," you'll recall Aaron insisted back then. Now the team's wish casting went like this: "We need someone like Stockard Channing!" Tommy's counsel was nothing if not predictable: "Well . . . let's ask Stockard Channing!"

From that moment forward, things started moving fast, though the journey was not without its peaks and valleys. As Stockard would recall years later in a conversation with the Screen Actors Guild Foundation, she was in Canada filming a movie. Her agents reached out to discuss an opportunity that had come across their desk. According to Stockard, "This part in *West Wing* . . ." was all she needed to hear. "I'd just seen the pilot on television in the hotel room." She came away from that initial viewing hooked—"Well, that's a *great* show!"—but, in her view, the script introducing the first lady left something to be desired.

"She was just in and out," Stockard remembers, as opposed to anything substantive. She couldn't help thinking, "Well, that's a waste of chalk." Script concerns aside, she honestly didn't believe they could navigate the logistics of shooting in LA around production on the Canadian film. And anyway, to Stockard it was no big deal if it didn't pan out—she was busy. "I had six days off from this movie. I was going hiking in Canada!" Seriously. She was. Until she wasn't.

As she told us, she was "all decked out in full-on hiking gear" and waiting to change planes at the Calgary airport. As Stockard stood with the guide who'd be leading her into the mountains, something kept nagging at her. She held up her cell and leveled with her guide. "I know this is really sort of show biz–y, but . . . can I just see if I have a message?" Off his shrug, she took to the phone and listened to the voicemail.

"Don't move!" she heard her agent's voice say. "We think we can work it out!" She grabbed a seat in this "little airport" while they tried to hammer out her deal. Four hours later, Stockard had her marching orders: "Don't get on the plane! Get on the *other* plane!"

So . . . she headed directly to "the other plane" and flew home. "I arrived in ninety-five-degree heat in Los Angeles in my hiking boots and duffle coat." (**MELISSA:** Tricky look. *Boss* move.) From there, a car picked her up and whisked her over to the Warner Bros. wardrobe department, where, as Stockard tells it, she was "poured into an evening dress." She spent the rest of the day (and into the night) preparing to transform into arguably the most famous fictional first lady in the history of television.

I always remember Tommy saying you can't just slap a pair of glasses on someone and call them smart. They have to *be* smart, and Stockard is just enormously smart.

—JOHN LEVEY, *WEST WING* DVD FEATURETTE, "BEHIND EVERY GOOD MAN IS THE FIRST LADY"

Stockard woke up the next morning—"quite cranky" in ninety-degree heat—feeling frustrated. "I didn't know anything about the character . . . who I was supposed to be. I remember I had to refer to Allison as 'Babe.' Who calls someone 'Babe'?" (When Stockard gets nervous, she explained to us, "I get very literal. I really hold on to the details.")

Once Stockard got settled on the Warner Bros. lot, Tommy and Aaron came to her trailer, approaching her with what she remembers as "patient affability." But she wasn't biting. She had questions about Abbey. And she needed answers. "Who is she?" she asked them. "How old is she? Where'd she come from? What's the *background*?" Aaron, she recalls, just looked at her and said, "I don't work like that." Stockard's heart sank. "I said, '*Wh-what?* What do you mean? Why am I here?!' I think Aaron said, 'Because you're so talented.' And I said, '*I don't have time for flattery now!*'"

Twenty-plus years later, she can't help laughing at the memory of that exchange in her trailer. She told us her theory about that moment, what it showed Aaron, and what it led to: "I put some pieces together and realized . . . *that* was Abigail! That's where he got Abigail Bartlet! 'Cause that's how he works, how his brain works. As he gets to know the actors, he *writes* to them. . . . I thought, 'Oh my God.'" Yes, in retrospect, it's hard to miss the intense levels of "Stockard" Aaron must have drawn from that moment and injected into the strong-willed Dr. Bartlet viewers came to know through the run of the show.

Calm in the eye of the whirlwind, later that first *West Wing* morning Stockard found herself all glammed up and scripted to mingle through the state dinner her first lady was hosting. She recalls spotting Martin "in white tie and tails, sneaking a cigarette behind the set." Then, only moments before the director called "Action!"—with dozens of background artists milling about and dressed to the nines—the actors who breathed enchanting life into Abigail and Jed Bartlet greeted each other for the very first time. Stockard extended a hand. "Hi, we've never met, but I think we've been married for about fifty million years."

That was the start of what would become a paradigm, one of the more authentic marriages ever portrayed on television. Dee Dee Myers summed it up well: "I think we see a marriage that feels *real* to us, in an incredibly high-pressure situation, where they have their strengths and their weaknesses . . . their places where they are in sync and places where they probably always had a little friction."

High-pressure situations. In sync. A little friction. Those elements of the Bartlet marriage were on full display in Stockard's first episode, which featured significantly more dialogue for Abigail than had existed in the initial iteration of Aaron's script. In addition to hosting the White House state dinner, FLOTUS was doing far more than just flitting "in and out." Now there was a sweet moment of tough-love truth telling, a speech that saw Aaron at his soaring, romantic best,

introducing and underscoring the tiny little intimate connections between these larger-than-life characters.

As her husband juggled an FBI hostage standoff gone wrong, an
aircraft carrier group sitting smack in the path of a Class 4 hurricane,
and a potentially economy-crippling truckers' strike, Abbey pulled the
president aside. In just a handful of lines, she set him straight and, with
the core of who she was, got to the core of who *he* was, to the core of
who *they* were: "You know, one of the things that happens when I stay
away too long is that you forget that you don't have the power to fix
everything. You have a big brain and a good heart . . . and an ego the
size of Montana. You do, Jed. You *don't* have the power to fix everything. But . . ." she added with a charmed, heartfelt, and sympathetic
smile, "I do like watching you try."

Abigail Bartlet's introduction to the series would also mark the
beginning of one of the more unusual romantic triangles ever drawn
on TV. As John Spencer revealed in a season 4 interview, the cast
would often jokingly refer to Abbey and Leo as "the two Mrs. Bartlets." Armed with his own unique perspective, and that trademark
impish smirk, John described their respective points in the POTUS
triangle as "the man behind the man and the *woman* behind the man,"
going on to explain that "I'm giving him the advice and holding him
up in the Oval and the Sit Room . . . and she's doing it in the residence."

When it came down to the brass tacks of the first lady, longtime
West Wing writer Eli Attie may have hit the nail most squarely on the
head. He defined Stockard's Abigail not just in terms of who she is as
an individual, but in terms of her true value to the show, the presidency, and the man she stood beside: "There's got to be somebody who
can pop the bubble, stand up to the president and remind him to be
humble, remind him who he is. There's got to be somebody at the end
of the day who can take a pair of scissors and cut the president's tie off."
That moment—when Abbey looked to give her husband a jolt of

adrenaline by snipping off his necktie just *seconds* before he would take the stage for a presidential debate—perfectly captures what made Dr. Bartlet who she was, and why we *loved* who she was. At the same time, it perfectly captures the actress behind that moment, one skilled enough to glide naturally between a seriousness of purpose, a depth of marital connection, and a playful sense of mischief.

Audacious and instinctive, Abigail Bartlet was a thoroughly modern woman with an abiding faith in the man she loved; a formal first lady with a fun and winky sultriness and a keen ability to rise to the moment. Stockard brought all of that to the part . . . from the earliest meeting of the first lady—helping her husband weather a literal storm—to the day we said goodbye, as their storybook romance took to the skies. The cooler-than-cool pro, whose *West Wing* journey began bundled up amid the freezing climes of a Calgary airport, closed out her turn as Abigail Bartlet, side by side with her unofficial prince of New England—flying off, happily ever after . . . and on toward the sun.

MRS. LANDINGHAM

Quick—name five personal secretaries to the president (real or fictional) more famous than Delores Landingham. Obviously, there's Rose Mary Woods—of the "'missing-18.5-minutes-of-the-Nixon-tapes" Woodses. Then there's the whole "Lincoln had a secretary named Kennedy and Kennedy had a secretary named Lincoln!" thing. Then there's, um . . . who? Betty Currie from the Clinton administration? Much respect to Betty Currie, but please. Mrs. Landingham is *obviously* next, which puts her squarely in the top five. (For the record, next in line is, hands down, Lily Tomlin's brilliant, unforgettable, über-quirky Debbie Fiderer.)

The president's personal secretary needs to possess elite

organizational skills and endless stores of patience. During each (extremely long) workday, from a perch just outside the Oval, she or he oversees and coordinates the president's daily appointments, including myriad high-level, high-pressure meetings and phone calls. But there are times when the personal secretary has to do other stuff like, you know, withhold cookies from Toby Ziegler or mentor-slash-chide her boss about rudimentary modes of communication.

Maybe after the ceremony you can get one of
the fourth graders to come in and show you how
to use the intercom.

—MRS. LANDINGHAM TO PRESIDENT BARTLET,
"SHIBBOLETH"

Moments like that exemplify not just what viewers adored about Mrs. Landingham, but what made her unique and essential to *The West Wing*. Of the president's entourage—including the first lady and Leo—who shared the breadth of history with Jed Bartlet that Delores Landingham did? And who, thanks to that shared history, could so consistently put the leader of the free world in his place with total immunity?

The casting of this role involved a sneaky, complex bit of alchemy that spanned decades and called on multiple sets of actors. In "Two Cathedrals," one of the show's all-time tear-jerker episodes, audiences time-traveled via flashback to what appeared to be the set of *Dead Poets Society* to meet up with Young Jed Bartlet and Young Delores Landingham. (**MELISSA FUN FACT:** *West Wing* writer-producer / future MSNBC host Lawrence O'Donnell played Jed's not-so-warm-and-fuzzy father—the *first* "Dr. Bartlet" in his life.) Expertly executed by Jason Widener and Kirsten Nelson, the performances of Young Jed and

Young Delores felt authentic, *lived-in*. That's a tribute, of course, to those two actors, who had their future counterparts down pat, and to the creatives who helped write and direct them there. But it's also thanks to a depth of characterization and chemistry established by Martin and a former nurse and community theater actress who, until the age of fifty-three, had never before been on television.

We lost our friend Kathryn Joosten in 2012 and we are so grateful to be able to memorialize her, and the role she played, within these pages. Kathryn was an actress born to play no-nonsense—or, we should say, born to underplay it. As comfortable in her skin as anyone you'll ever meet, and with the driest delivery this side of the Sahara, Kathryn knew who she was, and she infused Mrs. Landingham with that same degree of certitude. And, like a lot of things with this show, she first came to its attention thanks to Aaron Sorkin's inherent sense of loyalty and family.

As Aaron's longtime friend and former roommate Tim Davis-Reed told us, they reconnected in Los Angeles around the time the film version of *A Few Good Men* was underway. Having heard the early rumblings of what would become *The West Wing*, Tim sent his old pal a promotional postcard for a show he was in. It read: "I'm doing this play and the character's very similar to a political operative—hint, hint."

The next weekend, Tim got a phone call just before curtain. It was Aaron, saying he'd be coming to see the play that night! "I think when he saw that show, he remembered, 'Oh yeah, Tim wasn't just my roommate. He's an actor.'" (Indeed he was. Tim went on to play reporter Mark O'Donnell for six seasons on *The West Wing*.)

That night Aaron saw something else, too: a wonderful performer by the name of Kathy Joosten. "It was an evening of one-acts," Tim recalled to us, "and she was in one of the other one-acts, a very Mrs. Landingham kind of character."

Warner Bros. casting director John Levey said of Kathy, "I think she moved to California and started acting after her husband passed away." In that rarest of Hollywood turns, Kathryn's age actually played to her advantage. For the president's personal secretary, Aaron and the rest of the creative team landed on someone with greater life experience, both to set her apart from the junior staffers and to convey a measure of calm and wisdom around the president. In addition, a challenging and even irreverent approach to her interactions with President Bartlet would contrast nicely with the rest of the staff's starry-eyed esteem.

You know, if you don't want to run again,
I respect that. But if you don't run 'cause you think
it's gonna be too hard or you think you're gonna
lose—well, God, Jed, I don't even want to know you.

—MRS. LANDINGHAM TO PRESIDENT BARTLET,
"TWO CATHEDRALS"

On the day of the audition, Kathryn entered the casting room at Warner Bros. with her uniquely brash style, which gave the men inside something of a start. It would be easy to see Kathryn's brusque manner as a subtle strategy, pitching herself as the abrupt, blunter-than-thou Mrs. Landingham. But any resemblance to the character, however beneficial or apt, was more like a happy accident. Honestly, that's just how the woman operated.

As she shared in her *Emmy TV Legends* interview for the Archive of American Television, when it came to auditioning, Kathryn didn't mess around: "If it's men, they all start to pop up [out of their seats], so I say, 'Sit down, sit down, you're gonna do that all day.' And then I immediately say, 'Who'm I reading with?' In other words, I *take* the room. I don't wait." (**MELISSA:** My hero.)

Once those not-so-pleasantries were out of the way, she would get right to it. "I don't chat, I just do the audition." But . . . what if they want to, you know, get to know her a little? "If they want to chat after . . . eh, a little bit, but then I leave, I get out of the room." Huh. Okay. What else?

"I always want to be the first person in the room because I think it's important that the writers hear their words from *me* first. Because, in spite of themselves, they're going to compare everybody else to what I did first. I don't think 'Go last and show them something different' is valid. I don't want to show them something different, I want to show them something they want to *buy.*"

With this uncanny assurance, Kathryn entered the Warner Bros. session to vie for a part she would later describe as "more or less a Jiminy Cricket figure" in Jed Bartlet's story. Prepping for her audition, she had drawn on her own life experience. "I had at that point a cater-waiter job . . . There was an executive secretary there. I would watch how she dealt with *her* boss, and I used that as a template for how I'd deal with my boss."

In the end, Kathryn took the room, performed the audition, then abruptly got up and walked out—no-nonsense incarnate. And if no-nonsense was all Kathryn brought to the part, that might've been enough. She was that good an actress, that natural a comedienne. But there was much more than that to Kathryn Joosten, just as there was much more to Mrs. Landingham. A weary, Yankee steadfastness. A survivor's pride in having seen a life of heartbreak and lived to tell the tale. These were qualities Kathryn could play, too; qualities that would emerge most notably in a moving speech her Mrs. Landingham delivered to Charlie in an all-time great *West Wing* episode called "In Excelsis Deo." Rob Lowe calls the speech "probably my single favorite *West Wing* moment." Richard refers to it as "a master class in acting." As for us, it's exhibit A for what Aaron shared with *Entertainment Weekly* in the summer of 2020: "Kathryn . . . lent her humanity to the show."

In the coming pages, we'll have more to say about that episode, and that speech, and the remarkable story of how it came to be. For now, though, we'll end on the memory of our friend Kathryn, a woman who knew how to make a joke and take the room; a woman who came to acting late, only to wind up with a meaningful place on the *West Wing* mantle, as well as two Emmys on her shelf; a woman who would want us to shut up now, so we'll follow her lead, cut short the chitchat . . . and go.

CAROL FITZPATRICK

Disclaimer: Mary here. It's obviously a bit awkward when you come to the part(s) in the book that involve the people <u>writing</u> *the book. So, please know that, while we've been passing the baton back and forth 'til now, I'm anchoring this leg of the race. It's hard to express how mortified Melissa would feel if a single reader thought she was writing a single word, so outside of providing background information (and a fact check), she's sidelined.*

IT should come as no surprise to any of us that the actress behind Carol Fitzpatrick happens to be the sister of a professional football coach. Because Carol is the epitome of a locker room "glue guy." She's a "circle the wagons" type. Whether serving as C.J.'s dutiful and constant shadow, matching her stride for stride (briefing papers forever at the ready), or as a steady leader by example for the real-life West Wing cast, a "Carol"—or, in this case, a Melissa—majors in dependable, holds a master's in the power of positive thinking, and never, ever, *ever* quits. Case in point, Melissa stayed on through the entire run of the show—until the very last day—before leaving LA for DC to pursue a career in advocacy.

That Melissa became a consistent presence on a program known for celebrating (and spurring on) civic engagement could be seen as a "happy accident," but that feels like selling it short. Honestly, reflecting on where she came from and where life has since taken her, even "fitting" doesn't quite suffice. No, her connection to *The West Wing* feels like . . . destiny. (And not just because her character name, Carol Fitzpatrick, so closely resembles her mother's name, Carol Fitzgerald.) Before, during, and, most notably, *after* her seven-year stint on the show, Melissa Fitzgerald dedicated herself and her career to service. That's not just a fundamental part of who she is; it's practically the family business.

For most of Melissa's life, her father has worked in the world of criminal justice. An assistant district attorney during Melissa's childhood, James J. Fitzgerald III went on to become a judge, eventually serving on the Supreme Court of Pennsylvania. "My dad was among the people who established the first mental health court in Philadelphia," Melissa told me with no small measure of pride. (More on that later, both the story about the court and the pride!) As for her mother . . .

Carol McCullough Fitzgerald is what her daughter calls "a real force." In 2000, Carol was hired by Philadelphia's then mayor, Democratic Party heavyweight Ed Rendell, to produce PoliticalFest during the Republican National Convention. "She took over the Pennsylvania Convention Center and produced a celebration of the history of politics in America for more than 100,000 people." As if that wasn't enough, one fictional staffer from NBC's hit new show *The West Wing* agreed to conduct a Q and A. (Apparently, Carol Fitzgerald had an "in" with the actress playing Carol Fitzpatrick.)

Considering who raised them, it's no wonder Melissa and her brothers, Jamie and Craig, spent much of their childhoods volunteering for campaigns, stuffing envelopes, and going door-to-door for candidates and causes. All of this is to say that it seems like Melissa

Fitzgerald was destined to follow the path she took to *and* from her work on *The West Wing*.

As keen observers of the show have surely noted, Aaron loves few things more than a good sports metaphor. In that spirit, we'll just say that, when it came to casting—series regulars, background talent, and everything in between—*The West Wing* had a pretty deep bench. And there may be no better example of that than Melissa Fitzgerald.

Melissa took her first steps toward her future boss back when she was an acting student at the Neighborhood Playhouse School of the Theatre (where Allison had also been a student a few years before) in the heart of New York City. At drama school, free tickets to shows often find their way onto a hallway corkboard. One day in the fall of 1989, Melissa spotted some for a Broadway production about a military trial. The play, in "previews" just days before its official opening night, was *A Few Good Men*.

Settling into her seat at the famed Music Box Theatre in Times Square, Melissa flipped through the *Playbill*, scanning the credits and headshots of people who, a decade or so later, would wind up among her castmates on *The West Wing*. Long before joining the MCU's *Agents of S.H.I.E.L.D.* as Agent Phil Coulson, and before he appeared as FBI Special Agent Mike Casper on *The West Wing*, Clark Gregg originated the role of Lieutenant Jack Ross in that very first production of Aaron's play. Other future *West Wing*–ers Melissa saw onstage that night included Josh Malina and Ron Ostrow. Looking back on that production, Melissa still can't shake the astonishment: "I thought it was spectacular."

A few years after that magical evening at the Music Box, Melissa was in New York, doing an off-Broadway play called *North Shore Fish*. One night, Aaron came to the show and, not long after, cast her in a reading of his play *Hidden in This Picture*, at the Bay Street Theater in the Hamptons. Those would not be the last plays Aaron saw her do.

Years later, Melissa appeared in Graham Reid's drama *Remembrance*, at the Odyssey theater in Los Angeles. The play was co-produced by Sean Penn and starred the Oscar-winning actor's parents, along with a veteran of stage and screen whose most celebrated work was right around the corner. His name was James Gandolfini. Before they started rehearsal, "Jimmy" had to fly back east for a week or two. As he put it to Melissa, "I gotta go shoot a mob thing in New Jersey." (Little did they know, *The West Wing* and HBO's *The Sopranos* would spend the better part of the next decade battling it out for Emmys and Golden Globes, setting the stage for what would become the Golden Era of "prestige TV.")

Gandolfini's loutishness gives off a charge of
deep woundedness, and Fitzgerald makes
Deirdre's fiery frustration at her husbandless,
child-worried lot viscerally affecting.

—CHARLES ISHERWOOD, REVIEW OF *REMEMBRANCE*,
VARIETY, OCTOBER 1997

Following a performance one night, Melissa came out of her dressing room to find Aaron, whom she'd invited to see the show. They chatted some about the play and then Aaron said, "I'm working on something you might be right for."

Not long after that, Melissa found herself staring at a copy of two pilot scripts: a half-hour called *Sports Night* and a drama called . . . well, you know this tune by now. Just like Busfield before her (and Tommy before *him*), Melissa tore through them. Holding both scripts in her hand, she gushed to a friend, "*Sports Night* is going to be the best show on TV. *The West Wing* is going to be the best show *ever* on TV."

Once Melissa had gotten her hands on that *West Wing* pilot, with its tailor-made aspirational call to public service, she was determined to find a way onto the project. "In addition to being one of the best scripts I've ever read, it's just rare to read something that makes you think, 'This could actually put some good out into the world.' I didn't care so much about the size of the role, I just really wanted to be a part of it."

As her initial audition approached, Melissa ran the scenes she'd been told to prepare. For an as-yet-unnamed lower-level staffer, who had only a single line in the pilot, Melissa was given a "Donna" scene, as well as one in which Leo's daughter, Mallory, tells off a beleaguered (but somehow still cocky) Sam Seaborn.

The day of the callback, less than an hour before her audition, Melissa stood in her apartment, dressed in a blouse, black tights, and a black skirt, ready to go. Until, that is, her longtime friend Anne Tower remarked, "You know, because of the light, when you stand right in front of that window you can kinda see through your skirt." This was, of course, nothing major. After all, Melissa had on black tights, right? Plus, as she told Anne, "I don't really have time to change—and it's not like I'm gonna have to stand in front of a window or anything."

Okay, so she gets there. She heads into the callback to find what feels like a lot of people in the room, among them John Levey; his associate, Kevin Scott; Aaron Sorkin; and Tommy Schlamme. Oh—also in the room? A floor-to-ceiling window.

"I walked in," Melissa remembers, "and got settled into a chair. After a few minutes of chitchat, it was time to read with Aaron. Then somebody said, 'Would you mind standing?' The only place to stand was— you guessed it—right in front of the floor-to-ceiling window!! So, still sitting, I said, 'Actually, I'm really comfortable right here.' Silence. I tried to look as comfortable as I could, sitting on a metal folding chair in the middle of the room. Then I awkwardly repeated, 'I really am comfortable right here.' (Best piece of acting I did all day.) They must have thought I was the biggest weirdo or super high-maintenance, but I didn't want to be anywhere near that window! 'I'm really comfortable right here'? What was I thinking?"

Melissa ran through the first scene—the one with Mallory flirt-bickering with Sam Seaborn outside the Roosevelt Room. When she and Aaron finished, it seemed clear that it had gone well. In fact, when Melissa looked to move on—"I prepared the Donna scene too"—Aaron cut her off. "Nope, it was great, Melissa. Melissa—it was great."

In that moment, she remembers sensing Aaron's signal to quit while she was ahead. "It felt like, 'Get going, kid. Good job. Get outta here before we change our minds.'"

Days later, Melissa's friend Anne—of the "I can see through your skirt" Annes—took her to lunch at King's Road Café. You see, Anne worked at the agency repping Melissa and had asked if she could be the one to break the good news. And so she did—over a Nicoise salad and a zucchini muffin. (**MELISSA:** You're not gonna get this kind of inside information just anywhere.)

From the pilot onward, Melissa's character evolved from unnamed "staffer number something" with barely any dialogue . . . to C.J.'s ever-present and loyal assistant, Carol Fitzpatrick. "Eventually I got a first name. Then I got a desk. Then I got little moments with C.J. or Danny, and every now and then an exchange with President Bartlet. And each time it was *really* exciting. I had originally thought it would be a one-off, that I'd just be a part of the pilot. Even if all I said was, 'If you all would walk this way, please . . .' I didn't care. I was hired episode-to-episode for all seven years, and I considered each one a gift."

Melissa likes to joke that, when your lines are so few and far between, "there's no real way to shine . . . but you *can* screw it up." The simple truth is, it's extra challenging to make an impact when you have less to work with. But that's what makes her portrayal of Carol Fitzpatrick remarkable. She managed to infuse her moments, spoken and otherwise, with authenticity and detail and with a grounded and true sense of character. Her blending of a seriousness of purpose with a subtle, wry sense of humor, her chemistry with Allison, and the palpable sense of history between them—these are the work of an exceptional actor. This is, I think, why her presence on the show is so indelible and so full.

During our interview with Allison Janney, Melissa reflected on Carol's development into a more defined presence in the world of *The West Wing*. This was, as Melissa reminded her, *before* she had officially (if subtly) become C.J.'s assistant. "You and I had a scene with Tim Busfield," she told Allison, "just a passing bit in a hallway. Tim turned to me and said, 'You guys are really good together. I bet they're gonna make you her assistant!' I remember thinking, Oh, I hope so, that would be the best if I could be her assistant! That would be so fun!" Whether Aaron came up with the idea on his own or Busfield planted it in his head, *Inception*-style, we are eternally grateful. Because without our Carol, there's a real chance the *West Wing* cast would not have remained as close as we have for as long as we have. (Melissa, I can feel you cringe reading that, but those are the facts. So keep your cringe to yourself.)

You see, more often than you might think, one of us—it's most often Melissa—sends out that bat signal to the others. The cast text chain lights up with details about this cause or that, and what any or all of us can do to help, and then . . . we get to work. More than anyone, Melissa is the keeper of the signal. That sense of dedication goes back to James and Carol Fitzgerald, who instilled in their daughter the idea that "you never regret showing up for your friends." Melissa Fitzgerald is that kind of loyal and she reminds us, by example, of all the good there is to do in the world. The spirit behind that bat signal and, come to think of it, behind the way she deploys it, can be summed up in one classic Carol phrase:

"If you all would walk this way, please . . ."

∗ ∗ ∗

A SERVICE STORY

MELISSA FITZGERALD

Hey. Still Mary here. Melissa, pipe down a little bit longer.

Every team, they say, needs a captain. When it comes to service and the cast of *The West Wing*, Melissa's often the one in the center of the photo with the ball in her hand and the *C* on her jersey. And while we're on the topic of photos, picture this . . .

Standing at a podium bearing the presidential seal, Allison Janney commands a jam-packed room. Melissa stands a step or two behind, just off to the side. It's like many scenes we've filmed on the Warner Bros. lot . . . but today something is a little different. Today, the people filling the seats aren't actors playing reporters. Today, the reporters filling the seats are . . . reporters. Real ones.

Situated among the reporters are some familiar faces: Chuck Noland, William Duffy, Dulé Hill, Richard Schiff, and Brad Whitford (I'm there, too). So, what's going on here? 'Cause a quick sweep of the place reveals the presence of Peter Roth, chairman and CEO of Warner Bros. Television, and Dee Dee Myers. Once upon a time a key member of the *West Wing* writers room, not long before this day Dee Dee landed at Warner Bros. as an executive vice president at the studio.

Despite appearances, we aren't gathered here to film a scene. We are the guests of Warner Bros. Just moments ago, Peter and Dee Dee, the gracious hosts of this event, welcomed everyone to the official launch of a Justice for Vets public service video in support of veterans treatment courts. Dee Dee looks right at home behind a podium with a presidential seal. And that's no surprise. She was, as we've mentioned, the first female White House press secretary in US history. Expressing genuine enthusiasm for the cause we're all there to champion—and for her old colleagues on *The West Wing*—she introduces Allison.

As Allison channels C.J., delivering rousing remarks about the work of Justice for Vets and the PSA, it's like we've been transported back in time. "Veterans treatment courts," she says, "ensure that, when our veterans struggle with the transition home and become involved with the justice system, they receive the structure, treatment, and mentoring they need to get their lives back on track, returning to our communities where they are needed most." Watching Allison at the podium, Melissa is struck by how lucky she is to be part of this stellar *West Wing* family.

But this service story doesn't start here. It starts back in 2011. . . .

MELISSA: A dear friend who had been struggling with addiction for years had recently died by suicide. Martin Sheen reached out and asked if I would like to join him in Washington, DC, to speak at the national treatment court conference. Supporting treatment court programs was, Martin said, an opportunity to advocate for those struggling with addiction and mental health disorders. Martin has been a passionate champion of treatment courts for over thirty years—even before people knew this was a thing. And if Martin was asking, I was going. I joined him at the conference and on Capitol Hill, and it truly changed my life.

While I was at the conference, I learned about All Rise's newly launched veterans treatment court division, Justice for Vets. At that time, I happened to be working on a documentary called *Halfway Home*, which profiled several veterans who were struggling with the transition home. I quickly became an All Rise supporter. About two years later, when we finished the film, I asked All Rise if they'd like to screen it at their annual conference. They said yes and, on top of that, mentioned that they were looking for a new senior director of Justice for Vets. I leapt at the opportunity. When asked when I could start—it was October—I said, "How about January?" They said, "How about Monday?" Three days later, I packed a bag, left Hollywood, and boarded a plane for DC.

But let's back up a moment. What exactly are "treatment courts"?

MELISSA: Essentially, treatment courts are evidence-based alternatives to incarceration that provide lifesaving treatment and recovery support to people with substance use and mental health disorders. Treatment courts save lives, put families back together, and make our communities safer. They are proven to reduce drug use and crime, and research shows they also improve employment, housing stability, and family reunification. I believe everyone deserves the opportunity to get the help they need to turn their lives around. In these courtrooms I see the incredible capacity of human beings to change. I see individuals mired in the deepest depths of addiction find hope and empowerment. They rise up from those depths. I have seen it—over and over again.

After working on behalf of veterans treatment courts for a number of years at All Rise (formerly known as the National Association of Drug Court Professionals), Melissa has expanded her work to include treatment courts for civilians as well. But her memories of attending the first treatment court conference resonate with her to this day.

MELISSA: What I saw at that conference with Martin were thousands of individuals who had dedicated their lives to transforming the justice system's response to addiction and mental health disorders from one of strictly punishment to one of healing, compassion, and mutual accountability. Across four hot days in July, I spoke with judges, court staff, treatment providers, law enforcement, prosecutors, and defense counsel. To a person, the sentiment was the same: "Working in treatment court has been the high point of my career in criminal justice for one simple reason: In treatment courts, people get better."

In the years since arriving in Washington, Melissa has heard a variation on that story countless times.

MELISSA: At one of the first treatment courts I visited as a member of All Rise, the judge invited everyone back to his chambers to celebrate the treatment court participants. Surrounding them were the judge, court staff, treatment providers, parole officers—even the arresting officers were there—asking about each other's families, work, sharing photos of their children. It was hard to believe we were in a courthouse.

As you'll recall, when it comes to courthouses and judges . . . Melissa knows whereof she speaks.

MELISSA: Days before I began working at All Rise, my dad was being honored for judicial excellence for his career in criminal justice. During his speech, he said something that has stayed with me. "How are we, as a nation, going to take care of the most vulnerable among us? Will we make room for them in our hearts or will we make room for them in our prisons?" This is the question at the center of justice reform.

As a judge in Pennsylvania, Melissa's father, James, had seen firsthand the devastation mental health disorders had on individuals who got caught up in the justice system. He knew there had to be a better way, so he helped establish the city's first mental health (treatment) court.

MELISSA: I remember the first time I asked my dad what he thought about treatment courts. He said, "Melissa, anyone who knows anything about treatment courts is *for* them, and they're for them because they <u>work</u>." He was right; they do work. Treatment courts are the most successful intervention in our nation's history for leading people living with substance use and mental health disorders out of the justice system and into lives of recovery and stability. Each year, treatment courts connect approximately 150,000 people to treatment and recovery support. In treatment court they are given another chance to live life, to repair relationships, to spend time with their families and contribute to our communities.

Melissa was raised by a mother and father who believe deeply in giving back (and showing up for your friends), and her history of service not only instilled a sense of purpose in her, but cultivated many of the friendships she cherishes most from grade school and into adulthood.

MELISSA: Since I was young—long before *The West Wing*— I've been drawn to storytelling as a medium for social change. It's one of the reasons I love acting so much. Sharing stories— stories that otherwise might not be heard—is a powerful way to connect with people and share the experience of what it is to be human.

In 1995, Melissa put that idea into action with Voices in Harmony, a mentoring program that used theater to work with teens from historically underserved communities in Los Angeles. Then, in 2007, Melissa helped bring a version of that program to work with former abducted child soldiers and other teens displaced by the brutal rebel war in Northern Uganda and made a documentary about that experience—*After Kony: Staging Hope.*

MELISSA: We couldn't have made the film without our *West Wing* community, including two of the executive producers on the film, Martin Sheen and Dulé Hill.

That's what it always comes down to for Melissa, whether it's in a theater in LA, in a war zone in Uganda, on the set of *The West Wing*, or in Washington, DC, working on behalf of treatment courts—community.

It's no surprise, then, that members of our West Wing community and the Warner Bros. community gathered as Allison stood at the podium, reprising her role as C.J. to champion treatment courts that day.

MELISSA: When Allison finished her remarks, she called me to the podium to sing the praises of Justice for Vets / All Rise. I spoke about the veterans I've met whose lives have been saved by treatment courts. I told them that you'd be hard-pressed to find any family that hasn't been impacted by substance use / mental health disorders. I shared that in treatment court, we believe in the enduring, absolute value of every human being, their potential and their humanity.

You're the only person I know who,

when you cry about your job,

it's because you love it so much.

—JANEL MOLONEY, INTERVIEW FOR *WHAT'S NEXT*

The convergence of communities that day was an example of the ripple effect that service can generate.

MELISSA: The program culminated with the unveiling of our new treatment courts public service announcement. *West Wing* writer (now Academy Award winner) Josh Singer helped with the script. The video featured a number of cast members: Martin, Allison, Mary, Dulé, Richard, Janel, Brad, and me. Comcast donated millions of dollars in the form of valuable airtime, allowing us to broadcast the PSA nationwide.

Spreading the word about the value of treatment courts is not just important to Melissa, and it's not just her job. It's a mission. And it's personal.

MELISSA: The best part of my job is attending treatment court graduations around the country and hearing the stories of graduates who have worked so hard, faced their demons head-on, and rebuilt their lives—and their families. Graduates like . . . Carlos Gonzales:

Carlos's addiction had led him to commit serious crimes. When he was arrested, he was charged with five felony offenses and was facing decades behind bars. He told me the only thing he felt was hopelessness. But, instead of being sent to prison, Carlos was sent to the Santa Fe, New Mexico, treatment court. He remained in his community for treatment, and the program helped him secure housing and employment and reunify with his family. The program was strict but expressed compassion and the sincere desire to see him succeed.

CARLOS GONZALES: Almost everyone in my life had given up on me. I gave up on me. But the court team didn't give up on me. They treated me like a human being, and I will work every day to give to others what was so freely given to me.

MELISSA: In June 2020, Carlos received a pardon. Today, he is a statewide program manager in charge of alumni and peer initiatives for fifty-nine treatment courts. Carlos is a family man, an asset to his country, and someone I am proud and lucky to call a dear friend.

Carlos isn't the only one. Far from it. Take Abby Frutchey.

MELISSA: Abby grew up in a small New England town. After being exposed to alcoholism in her family, she began experimenting with substance use at a young age. She graduated in the top ten of her high school class and was a member of the National Honor Society, all while her drug use continued to increase.

Over the next several years, Abby's life began to fall apart as she became addicted to opioids. In 2004, shortly after giving birth to her son, she was arrested for selling OxyContin in Maine. Rather than face incarceration, she was given the chance to enter the Washington County adult treatment court, where she would begin her journey to recovery.

Over fourteen months, Abby participated in treatment and, with support from the treatment court team, began planning for her future. The program helped Abby rebuild her relationship with her son and encouraged her to enroll in school. She participated in AmeriCorps and graduated from college, ultimately becoming the treatment provider for the very treatment court that saved her life.

Today she is married, a mother, and a vital member of the community, helping people who struggle just as she once did. In 2014, she applied for and received a pardon from the governor of Maine. And, in 2020, Abby joined the All Rise board of directors!

While these stories are exceptional, Abby and Carlos are not the exceptions. I have met so many treatment court graduates across the country who are committed to giving back, to making sure others receive the same opportunities they did. That motivates me every day.

Graduates and their families prove that these programs are badly needed and deeply worth fighting for. They are our parents, our children, our friends and neighbors. Their lives—and their contributions to their families and to our communities—are worth saving.

As for Melissa's West Wing family, that support did not end with the PSA launch.

MELISSA: I often say, I've never done anything of value by myself. As was the case in *The West Wing*, any success I've enjoyed has always come as part of a team, and All Rise is no exception. I am fortunate to be part of a dedicated and talented team of people, whose support I have enjoyed in the work that we do together and, I should mention, in the process of writing this book. While deeply appreciated, this is not new to me. As recently as the fall of 2023, Dulé appeared on *Celebrity Jeopardy!*—and won! His charity of choice? All Rise. The support of Warner Bros. and *The West Wing* has been invaluable and constant, and that includes our family of *West Wing* fans. Your engagement has touched me and helped us do the valuable work we feel called to do.

It is not lost on anyone here how fortunate we are to have the full support from the *West Wing* community, which includes having Melissa working on this issue from within. It has not always been easy to engage the general public around issues of justice reform for people with substance use and mental health disorders. The cast of *The West Wing* has been instrumental in helping us do this.

—ALL RISE COMMUNICATIONS DIRECTOR CHRIS DEUTSCH

Oh, one more thing: I absolutely love that our organization is called All Rise. Of course, we all know that when a judge enters the courtroom, the bailiff says, "All rise!" It is meant to instill awe and respect for the proceedings. We envision a justice system in which the words "all rise" signify a promise that individuals will be treated with dignity and humanity; where success is measured in lives saved, families put back together, and communities made safer, because when one person rises above adversity and finds hope and healing, *we all rise.*

ALL RISE

All Rise is a national nonprofit championing justice system reform for people impacted by substance use and mental health disorders by promoting treatment instead of incarceration. All Rise leads the establishment of treatment

courts, the most successful intervention in our nation's history for leading
people living with substance use and mental health disorders out of the
justice system and into lives of recovery and stability.

www.allrise.org

JUSTICE FOR VETS

Justice for Vets is a division of All Rise that transforms the way the justice system
identifies, assesses, and treats our veterans. Justice for Vets provides training and
technical assistance to bring together local, state, and federal resources to directly
serve justice-involved veterans, including specific training and resources for
veterans treatment courts. Justice for Vets keeps veterans out of jail and prison
and connects them to the benefits and healthcare they have earned.

www.allrise.org/jfv

★ ★ ★

MARGARET HOOPER

Senior assistant to the chief of staff Margaret Hooper is something of
an odd bird. A mishmash of eccentricities and off-beat quirk, she
boasts next-level competence and a recall so total it borders on disorienting. But once you get to know her deep down, beyond the all-world
flakiness playing on the surface, it's hard to dismiss the value of a walking, talking precursor to Siri, a loyal staffer able to call up institutional
minutiae at the drop of a hat. And if she risks the occasional coup
d'etat by forging POTUS's John Hancock—"I have it down pretty
good!"—well, that's the price of freedom in the Bartlet White House.

> We've got separation of powers, checks and
> balances, and *Margaret*—vetoing things and
> sending them back to the Hill!
>
> —LEO TO C.J., "IN THE SHADOW OF TWO GUNMEN: PART II"

It's no surprise, then, that the actress Tommy, Aaron, and John chose to walk in her shoes possessed a bit of a quirky soul. Before *The West Wing* came calling, NiCole Robinson had originally been spotted in an acting class by a member of the Warner Bros. casting department. Jeff Roth recognized something special in NiCole, particularly as it pertained to her comedic talent, eventually bringing her in to audition eleven times for, among other shows, the smash-hit sitcom *Friends* and the John Wells brainchild, *ER*. For the Idaho native, the twelfth time was the charm. She booked the first pilot she'd ever read for and, in Margaret, created an unforgettable character who would last the length of the series.

But while the run of the show was long, NiCole's audition was anything but. "This is going to be the shortest audition of your life." That's what Aaron said when she walked in to read. It's also what she'd sort of assumed, since the one page she'd been given included the one line of dialogue her character had in the episode. And that was fine with NiCole, who, in an interview for *TV Guide*'s "Watercooler" column, would later admit to having felt somewhat daunted by the lineup of Hollywood power players in the room that day. "There was John Wells, Tommy Schlamme, two of the biggest casting people in the business—John Levey and Kevin Scott—and the person I'm going to be reading with is Aaron Sorkin!"

Now, there are two ways of looking at an audition where you're armed with only *one line*. First, what are the odds you're gonna mess up? Chances are pretty good you're not going to forget your one line. On the other hand, there's a hell of a lot riding on that one line. Oh— and how on earth are you meant to separate yourself from the competition?

If you're NiCole Robinson, you harken back to what your acting teacher, Don Richardson, told you: "Think of what everyone else is going to do, and then . . . do something different." If other potential Margarets were going to do "actively funny," NiCole would do the opposite. That idea—"if you want to be funny, don't *try* to be funny"—is well illustrated in the following exchange from Aaron's *West Wing* follow-up, *Studio 60 on the Sunset Strip*:

> HARRIET
> I got a laugh at the table read
> when I asked for the butter in the
> dinner sketch. I didn't get it at
> the dress. What did I do wrong?
>
> MATT
> That's one laugh out of thirty
> you're going to get tonight.
>
> HARRIET
> What did I do wrong?
>
> MATT
> You asked for the laugh.
>
> HARRIET
> What did I do at the table read?
>
> MATT
> You asked for the butter.

NiCole's instincts told her that the obvious choice, the one most of her competition would likely make, was to lean in to the old-school sassiness of the line. Zigging where the others would zag, the actress with the comedy background opted to play it straight. In the hysterically earnest voice of Leo's devoted, dutiful assistant, NiCole found the key she would use to unlock the funny of Margaret Hooper for seven seasons to come.

```
                    LEO
      Margaret, call the editor of
      The New York Times crossword
      and tell him that "Khaddafi" is
      spelled with an "H" and two "D's"
      and isn't a seven-letter word for
      anything.

                  MARGARET
      Is this for real or is this just
      funny?

                    LEO
      Apparently, it's neither.
```

In that "shortest audition of her life"—in that *one* line—NiCole managed to perfectly capture one of the key tenets to the spirit of *The West Wing*. Smart is good. Subtle is great. Ask for the butter.

★ ★ ★

A SERVICE STORY

Emily Procter

Emily Procter's lasting presence as everyone's favorite Republican on *The West Wing* is remarkable, given the fact that she appears in only twelve episodes of the series. Her sincere, hyper-patriotic outsider turned team player Ainsley Hayes left such a mark on *The West Wing* that it feels like she never really left. And, in a parallel universe, it's possible she didn't. I mean, if you put yourself in the right headspace, and jiggle the rabbit ears on your TV set, you can get a nice, clear picture of her down in the Steam Pipe Trunk Distribution Venue. Maybe she's drafting another brilliant legal argument to rankle Sam one last time or puttering around in a bathrobe, chomping on a comically large muffin. Maybe she's just chugging a Fresca (or, failing that, a ginger ale) while dancing to the bossa nova or Gilbert and Sullivan.

> I said to Aaron, "How will I know when I'm
> leaving?" He said, "You'll know because the
> last words you say will be, 'I'll be in the basement.'"
> And those were the last words I ever spoke
> on the show. "I'll be in the basement."
>
> —EMILY PROCTER, INTERVIEW FOR *WHAT'S NEXT*,
> ON HER DEPARTURE FROM THE SERIES

But as impactful as Ainsley Hayes was in the fictional realm of *The West Wing*, it's nothing compared to what Emily has done in the real world.

EMILY PROCTER: We tend to think that we grow and become this thing . . . or we grow up and decide what we want to do. But, really, our experiences are all outcroppings of what we've been trying all along. I got really lucky to trip and fall into acting. If I had been a better student in college, and really paid attention—enough to go see my advisor—I think I would have chosen to become a behavioral scientist. Acting was like the cheap and easy version of that.

Community service is something I've always enjoyed. In college, I helped initiate an after-school children's program, and then post moving to Los Angeles, I worked at a soup kitchen. I found at the soup kitchen I was most helpful just sitting with people and talking. It was easier for me to gauge mental states and what people needed by visiting with them, as opposed to serving food. And, of course, if I sit with someone at lunch, I'm gonna eat! Being a volunteer, we weren't allowed to get a plate, so I ate off everyone else's. I would ask, "Ya gonna eat your rice?!" What happened was . . . we shared, and that action that is normally very intimate created a connection. When someone says to you, "I'm willing to eat off of your plate," they're saying, "I'm not worried about all your stuff." And it helped to forge relationships. At that soup kitchen, I met one of the greatest friends of my life, Jim Fadely.

In recent years, Emily was inspired to form her own nonprofit.

EMILY PROCTER: I went with a friend of mine to a Defy Ventures workshop inside Kern Valley State Prison. Trying to find common ground with people, I asked if they had children. Almost every single person I talked with was a parent and I couldn't stop thinking about how incarceration was affecting the lives of their children. Prison visitation is understandably very specific, but not having access to a parent is damaging to the family structure in a way we're just now starting to understand and talk about. Being inside the prison gave me perspective. I walked away from that day learning the importance of a post-release business plan, but also realizing how deeply important it was to have an *emotional* plan as well.

So I started the Ground Breakers Inc. Our program provides social/emotional and conflict management education and language to the currently incarcerated community. Parenting is hard no matter what; being in healthy relationships is hard no matter what. People are more productive and react better when operating from a place of security. Providing a way to talk through experiences—how one got there, why one got there, and what it could look like to reenter society well—has been incredibly rewarding. Programming in this space also allowed me to form a wonderful relationship with Concordance, an organization doing amazing work with people post-release.

Reflecting on how her time on *The West Wing* connects to her life of service now, Emily expressed a retroactive word to the wise.

EMILY PROCTER: I wish I had understood when I was working as an actor how much my support could mean. Lending voice, lending funds, lending time, to small nonprofits out there . . . I wish I had done *more*. I just didn't know. So if anyone reading the book is thinking about helping, go for it! If we all pitched in . . . we'd all be working in the West Wing, and I believe that's what "united we stand" is really all about.

THE GROUND

The Ground is a social and emotional language awareness program designed to combat negative personal narratives and support peaceful conflict resolution. The goal of the Ground is to recognize what we share, celebrate what makes us unique, and support the ability to build healthy community everywhere.

www.emilyprocter.com/the-ground

★ ★ ★

DANNY CONCANNON

Most of our generation became familiar with Tim Busfield long before his stint representing the fourth estate on *The West Wing*. Many associate him with Elliot Weston, the yuppie graphic designer from the zeitgeisty baby boomer program *Thirtysomething*. Fans of *Field of Dreams* got to know Tim as Kevin Costner's unlikable-until-the-last-few-minutes, farm-foreclosing brother-in-law. Older fans recall him as J.T. McIntyre, the medical intern on *Trapper John, M.D.* (**MELISSA:** For our fresher-faced Wingnuts, imagine a mid-'80s *Grey's Anatomy* with no voice-over, no Space Needle, no McDreamy, and—I think we can safely assume—profoundly crappier music.) But if *Trapper John* is too deep a cut for you, perhaps the classic character name "Arnold Poindexter"—from a totally different mid-'80's project—will ring a bell.

In 1984, *Revenge of the Nerds* helped transform "Poindexter" into a culture-defining symbol of supersized geek. (**MELISSA FUN FACT:** The dorktastic box office bonanza also included at least four future cast members of *The West Wing*. Along with Busfield, *Revenge of the Nerds* vets included James Cromwell, Ted McGinley, and John Goodman. Brad Whitford wouldn't arrive in the Nerdiverse until the sequel, *Revenge of the Nerds II: Nerds in Paradise*.) Back when that film was released, the White House correspondent we would come to know as the future "Mr. C.J. Cregg" didn't yet exist, and Tim Busfield was just a wild-haired violinist in jelly-jar glasses. But by the time his Danny Concannon showed up in C.J.'s office with nothing but a byline, a goldfish, and a dream, the die was cast. The long and winding road Danny and C.J. took to their version of domestic bliss felt, if not quite predestined, then unfailingly cute and—as Carol kept trying to tell her—mutually beneficial. And even though the reporter's wooing of C.J. fell short of a full-court press, his low-key pursuit was truly relentless. The result was a feel-good coupling that everybody (outside the Oval) could root for.

                         C.J.
          When you flirt with me, are you
          doing it to get a story?

                         DANNY
          No.

                         C.J.
          Then why are you doing it?

                         DANNY
          I'm doing it to flirt with you.

                                —C.J. and Danny, "The State Dinner"

As tied-up loose ends go, this press office romance constitutes one of *The West Wing*'s most anticipated and satisfying happy endings. (**MELISSA:** Sorry if that's a spoiler. You should watch the show. It's pretty good.) As for the *beginning* of this story, we have to go back thirty-plus years to an ex-Amadeus, a famous Music Box, and an audition room in NYC.

★ ★ ★

IN 1990 the Broadway production of Aaron's hit play, *A Few Good Men*, was shopping for a brand-new Daniel Kaffee. With Oscar-nominated actor Tom Hulce set to leave the show, and a certain other "Tom" two years away from playing the part in the film version, Tim Busfield and numerous other actors were champing at the bit to step into the lead role. Preparing for the audition, Tim sat down for his first go-through of Aaron's stage play with no idea it would be a life-changing read. That realization came ninety seconds in.

"I knew on page two that I knew how to say Aaron's words. They weren't a struggle for me, there was just that thing we go through as actors when you read a script, you immediately know how to say every line." That sense of connection, of familiarity—of *fluency*—stirred up an unusual reaction in Tim. "I sort of broke out in a sweat."

"By page five," he told us, his eyes positively dancing at the memory, "I was ripping through pages, going, 'This is mine! This is me, I know how to do this!'"

Walking around Times Square in the days leading up to the audition, Tim avoided looking at the Music Box Theatre marquee, doing his best not to get romantic about *A Few Good Men*, all up in lights. Once he was reading for the part, though, the scenario that played out was as romantic as it gets, and every actor's dream. "I got the part in the room." There was just one problem. Fortunately for Tim, the problem wasn't his. "Jon Cryer was waiting outside."

Inside, Broadway producer Robert Whitehead had seen and heard enough out of Tim. "You got it," he said. "When can you start?" Feeling a little bit stunned and more than a little bit awkward, Tim whispered, "Jon Cryer's right outside. Maybe you should wait 'til you see Jon read, and then decide." On the other hand, Tim made it clear that he'd go into the show the day after Tom Hulce left if that's what the producers truly wanted. (It was.)

Walking out of the room, Tim remembers exuding "that euphoria of just *killing*." He also remembers sensing that Cryer had heard everything that happened. "He had that look on his face, like . . . 'I'm fucked.'" All these years later, Tim still sympathizes. He's been on the other side of that door, the other side of that casting call, multiple times. (**MARY:** I've been that person, too. I've been that person a lot.) That said, we're guessing Jon Cryer can live with the memory of that disappointing afternoon, given the ludicrous success he's had—with Martin's son Charlie—since falling just short of *A Few Good Men*.

During that Broadway run, Tim and Aaron quickly became close friends. Over the next eight years, they stayed that way. "I was in his wedding, we'd vacation together . . ." He and Aaron had built up a deep friendship; they'd built up trust. And, of course, part of what went into that trust was regular sneak previews of Aaron's scripts.

Tim loved this perk of their friendship, but he respected it as well. Aaron sent him the pilots for both *Sports Night* and *The West Wing*, and Tim tore through them. Finished, he called Aaron and said, "*Sports Night*'s great." He then added, ". . . *The West Wing*'s maybe the best script I've ever read." Wow. Aaron must've been over the moon, right? Yeah . . . not exactly.

"He got mad at me." Hold on, Busfield. Seriously?

Seriously. "Aaron was mad that I didn't like *Sports Night* as much as I liked *The West Wing*!" Laughing at the memory (and still a bit incredulous) more than two decades later, Tim continues to defend his reaction to the *Sports Night* script. He remembers saying to his friend, "I don't know what to tell you. It's great. I didn't say it was bad, I said it's *great*. But this one [*The West Wing*] is *magic*."

Indeed, when it comes to that magic *West Wing* pilot script, as Tim put it to us, "you turn every page and fairy dust kicks off."

Somehow, despite Tim's unforgivable downgrade of the *Sports Night* pilot to merely "great," Aaron found it in his heart to call his friend in for a part on *The West Wing* pilot. So Tim went in—"it was a Saturday at Warner Bros."—to read for Toby Ziegler. Oh! Cool. For Toby. "Allison"—there reading for C.J., Tim says—"was in the outer area."

Clocking the other actors outside the audition room, Tim settled in a few seats from Allison. "I wasn't familiar with her work at that point," Tim told us. "Looking back, it's kind of funny—Allison would eventually become my future on *The West Wing*. In that moment, though, it was just two actors sitting in a waiting room, exchanging friendly smiles." Then there was Tim's dynamic with the director . . .

"I went in and got the same face from Tommy Schlamme that I got whenever I read for him . . . sort of a deep hatred is what I was picking up on." (A little bit he's joking, a little bit he's not.) Over the years—during and after *The West Wing*—these two have enjoyed a fun and prickly, brotherly give-and-take. For the record, though, Tommy has hired Tim as an actor more than once *and* guided him toward becoming a sought-after veteran director himself.

Okay, quick primer: Sometimes when you audition, you're not psyched with how it's going—or how it just went—so you ask to "go again." Most of the time, people in the room are cool and say, "Sure, go ahead." But sometimes—this is what happened with Tommy and Tim that day—they just say, "No, that's okay . . . we got it." It's the *worst*. According to Tim, Tommy had done that to him before, on a couple other pilots. But, given his tight friendship with Aaron, and given that this audition was for a show his friend had created, Tim found Tommy's curtness a little weird. "I still don't think he likes me," he says, laughing with a somewhat bemused incredulity, "and he's my *mentor*!"

So, yes, Tim went in to read for Toby, got "that same face" from Tommy, and didn't *get* the role. I mean, obviously he didn't get it, Richard did. What he meant was, he didn't "get" it, couldn't solve the puzzle of playing Toby. "You just know when it's not for you. And that part wasn't for me."

During one of our sit-downs, Tim elaborated on this idea. "There's a lot of roles that, having an ear for Aaron's stuff, I could've played—we all could sort of . . . sing his music, the parts become interchangeable. I couldn't play Marty's role and I couldn't play Allison's role, but . . . just about every other role in the script, I thought, 'Well, I can probably pull that off.'" But there was something about Toby that he couldn't quite crack. He knew it, and that was . . . okay. "I walked out and I was like, 'Cool. No big deal.'"

Months later, long after the pilot had been shot and the series had been picked up, Tim was sitting in his Sacramento home when he got a call from Aaron. The *West Wing* cast and crew were shooting their second episode, and Aaron was writing the third one. (**MELISSA:** Episode 3—"A Proportional Response"—introduced Charlie Young *and*

Danny Concannon! **MARY:** And Admiral Fitzwallace!) Over the phone, Aaron told his old pal Tim, "I need you. I need your heart on this show." Explaining that he'd just written the part of a reporter as a possible love interest for C.J., Aaron asked if he could send Tim the script.

Without missing a beat, his friend replied, "I'm in, whenever you want me, of course I'm in. I'm family, I'll do whatever you want." (In a moment of inspiration, and the best kind of sentimentality, Aaron named Busfield's character "Danny" after Daniel Kaffee in *A Few Good Men*, the role that had brought them together in the first place.)

Going through the script for "A Proportional Response," Tim responded to Danny with near-instant understanding. "This is easy," he remembers thinking as he read the reporter's first scenes. "It's gonna be *easy*." He certainly made it look that way. From second one, Tim knew how to play the character, despite having nothing close to a firm grasp on the seasoned politico's area of expertise. "I wasn't well-read. I didn't understand any of the politics, I didn't know *anything*—I didn't know what a 'lame duck' was!"

What he did know was what every actor always hopes and ultimately needs to know. In this episode, in this scene, in this *moment*, what does your character *want*? For Tim, the answer to that question had come in the phone call with Aaron. As he readied himself for the role, grappling with who this Danny guy was, he remembers thinking, "Aaron said 'love interest,' he said he wanted my heart, so . . . I'm just gonna be in love with C.J. That's all I'm gonna play." And that was that. Except, there was this one thing . . .

On his first day of shooting, Tim got into wardrobe and went down to set. But in those earliest moments—in his very first scene—it became clear that there was one key player to whom Aaron had neglected to reveal Danny's overriding motivation. "I could tell he didn't let Allison in on the fact that I was a possible love interest because she was looking at me across the desk like, '"The fuck is *this* guy doing?!'" (SPOILER: Eventually, she found out.)

We're both about to fall off a cliff . . . and I don't know
what I'm gonna do with the rest of my life—except I
know what I don't want to do. And on inauguration
day you're gonna be released from that glorious
prison on Pennsylvania Avenue. . . . So if I'm gonna
jump off the cliff, and you're gonna get pushed off the
cliff . . . why don't we hold hands on the way down?

—DANNY TO C.J., "INTERNAL DISPLACEMENT"

In the end and against all odds, Danny and his epic long game
convinced C.J. that he'd help her learn to "share a life," that they were
"gonna get good at new things," that they'd "figure it out—all of it."
And, somehow, this kindhearted puppy dog of a middle-aged man
convinced her he was the one to hold hands with on the way off the
cliff. Talk about revenge of the nerds.

★ ★ ★

HEY. It's Melissa. (Hope you're enjoying the book.) Remember this
classic Leo sequence from season 1?

                    LEO
        Andrew Jackson, in the main foyer
        of his White House, had a big block
        of cheese. . . . The block of
        cheese was huge—over two tons. And
        it was there for any and all who
        might be hungry. Jackson wanted the
        White House to belong to the
        people, so from time to time, he
        opened his doors to those who

```
wished an audience. . . . It is in
the spirit of Andrew Jackson that
I, from time to time, ask senior
staff to have face-to-face meetings
with those people representing
organizations who have a difficult
time getting our attention. I know
the more jaded among you see this
as something rather beneath you.
But I assure you that listening to
the voices of passionate Americans
is beneath no one, and surely not
the people's servants.
```

—Leo to the senior staff, "The Crackpots and These Women"

Just as Leo wanted to shine a light on some smaller worthy causes, we'll be periodically sharing little gems that we couldn't live without having in the book. And since we just finished off the Danny Concannon section, this seems like a good time to talk about goldfish. (Not the crackers.)

★ ★ ★ BIG BLOCK OF CHEESE STORY ★ ★ ★

Tales from Gail's Fishbowl

Blanche Sindelar was *The West Wing*'s property master, the person in charge of, among a ton of other things, taking care of C.J.'s goldfish, Gail, and decorating Gail's fishbowl. You may have noticed the fun Blanche and her team had with the objects in the fishbowl over the years: a mini ballot box for an Election Day episode, a couple of pandas as a tribute to a recently deceased fictional bear named Lum Lum, and a herd of bovine as a subtle reference to a mad cow subplot. For "Galileo," Blanche added red gravel with a miniature spacecraft and a Mars Rover, and when Ainsley Hayes got hired, she opted for a tiny elephant, as a nod to the GOP. Oh, and lest we forget: One storyline in "Six Meetings Before Lunch" centers on Abbey and Jed and their shared desire to steal away for a little "alone time" together. So, naturally, the props department scored Gail a pink bed and a bit of company in the form of a second goldfish playing a "gentleman caller." Bravo, props department. Bravo.

In all, Blanche tells us, there were somewhere in the ballpark of "fifty or sixty" different fishbowl themes, "but not all were seen on-screen and some I used more than once." One that wasn't on-screen was this, an absolute work of art: "After Bartlet got shot, for the season 2 premiere I put a small figurine of the White House in the bowl and made the gravel red again. Then I got the special effects team to make a bullet hole through the tank, as if there was a shooting at the White House. I don't think that was ever shown."

One that *was* shown—in fact, the last one ever shown—appeared in the series finale, "Tomorrow." In this episode, Blanche offered viewers a final, fleeting look at Gail's glass habitat, which includes a sign bearing the old Looney Tunes motto, "That's All Folks!"

SEVEN

FOURTH FOUNDING FATHER

The Origin Story of Josiah Bartlet

Mr. President? Sir, your absence in the other room is
conspicuous.

—MANDY TO PRESIDENT BARTLET, "IN EXCELSIS DEO"

You didn't actually think we'd forget President Bartlet, did you?
We were just saving him—you know, as an homage to his
eleventh-hour introduction in the pilot.

Let's start with a quick reminder. Making President Bartlet the
centerpiece of the series wasn't always the plan. True, *The West Wing*
focused on his administration, but its spotlight—in the early stages of
the show's conception, anyway—was meant to shine on the Rosen-
crantzes and Guildensterns of this world more than the Hamlets and
Ophelias. Still, regardless of the number of scenes featuring the commander in chief, regardless of the degree to which his presence trickled
down to impact staffers and storylines, there could not have been a
more pivotal piece of the puzzle.

Now, defining what exactly makes a person "presidential" has always been a tricky and subjective endeavor. To paraphrase Justice

Potter Stewart's famous take on obscenity, it's one of those "we know it when we see it" kinda things. This *West Wing*'s POTUS would constitute a blend of attributes from a trio of twentieth-century presidents. The inspirational vision and rhetoric of JFK . . . mixed with the outsize heart and abiding religious faith of Jimmy Carter . . . underscored by Bill Clinton's relentless intellect, savvy, and charm. As Martin put it, "Those three men covered all of the territory that Bartlet would inhabit."

As long as Aaron was creating this "mosaic" president, there was room for other creative liberties that could help free the show from the conventional confines of real life circa 1998. One of the most intriguing of these was the notion of a Black president, which, in a pre-Obama era, stretched the imaginations of even the wildest "Hollywood liberal" fantasy. According to Tommy Schlamme, early discussions heard the name James Earl Jones pop up. The key collaborators also kicked around the idea of a female President Bartlet. (**MARY:** While writing the book, we were lucky enough to get our hands on casting notes that included an initial brainstorming list. Many of the names on the list for female President Bartlet jumped out at us: Helen Mirren, Blythe Danner, CCH Pounder, Glenn Close, Alfre Woodard, Stockard Channing, Jessica Lange, and Jane Fonda.) In the end, though, they went—as the saying goes—in another direction.

Since the president was initially expected to be less prominently featured, showing up in just a handful of episodes, the casting of the role had a sneaky-tough needle to thread: finding an actor who could exude strong moral resolve and inspirational gravitas, who could serve as a beacon of sorts . . . without overshadowing the rest of the cast.

One of the best-known early ideas the team had for President Bartlet was Sidney Poitier, the Oscar-winning Hollywood elder statesman, who would bring instant star power to the ensemble. Talks with Poitier's reps, according to Aaron, "didn't get far." Another brilliant actor on the short list, Jason Robards, was more than qualified, having delivered acclaimed TV and film portrayals of Abraham Lincoln, Ulysses S. Grant, and FDR. Robards knew his way around DC, too, given his Oscar-winning work as *Washington Post* executive editor Ben Bradlee in the classic Watergate biopic, *All the President's Men*. Unfortunately, at seventy-six, Robards was in poor health and likely not up to the rigors of a network TV drama, even for only a few episodes each season. (Sadly, the world lost the great Jason Robards not long into *The West Wing*'s run, in 2000. His son Sam Robards ended up playing reporter Greg Brock in eight episodes of *The West Wing*.)

Another actor vying for the role of Jed Bartlet was Tony Award–winning actor John Cullum, best known to TV audiences as the dry, oddball barkeep on CBS's *Northern Exposure*. Describing him as a "grandfatherly figure," the casting principals were, it seems, big fans of Cullum's audition, with one of them commenting, "Don't let him get away." Others on an early "brainstorm list" ranged from esteemed actors Jack Lemmon, Bruce Dern, and Donald Sutherland to outside-the-box choices like Colin Powell, Johnny Carson, and New York Yankees owner George Steinbrenner. (**MELISSA:** Can you imagine an alternate universe with Steinbrenner as President Bartlet? He *definitely* would've fired Josh in the pilot. And then rehired him for episode 3. And then fired him again.) How about these other names on the "ideas list"—a Clint Eastwood President Bartlet. Sally Field in the Oval. Carol Burnett. Tom Brokaw. Walter Cronkite. (Near the top of the Bartlet wish list was future cast member Alan Alda, who told us, "I wasn't interested in doing a series on the West Coast because I lived on the East Coast, and I had already done that. I didn't want to fly back and forth every week again. I was flattered [to be asked] and it would've been wonderful. . . . But the guy who did it was great." Of course, seven years later, Alan would come within a few electoral votes of succeeding Bartlet on *The West Wing*.) Then there was Hal Holbrook . . .

When the steely-gazed Holbrook read for the part, it appears his audition went rather well because he came out of it cast as President Bartlet. Yes, you read that right—Hal Holbrook was originally offered the role of POTUS. As Tommy would inform us two decades later, the legendary actor perhaps best known for his stirring stage portrayal of Mark Twain (or his compelling turn as "Deep Throat" in *All the President's Men*), had been tapped to play the president. "He had come in," Tommy told us, "we'd cast him. Then . . . later that night, both Aaron and I woke up with the same thought: 'It shouldn't be Hal Holbrook.'"

While no contracts had been signed, the offer had been made. "He was a wonderful actor," Tommy says, "but it wasn't right for the show. We realized . . . we have to take it back." So, the next day John Wells had the unenviable task of calling the actor up and walking the offer back. "It was," as Tommy described it to us, "really messy . . . terrible." Or it could've been, anyway. Except, to nobody's surprise, Holbrook handled the situation like a true gentleman. "He was," as Tommy remembers it, "nothing but gracious and wonderful."

Down the road, Holbrook would delight viewers with his multiple turns as cranky-charming Assistant Secretary of State Albie Duncan. (**MELISSA:** If you're a fan of this performance—and how could you not be?—pour yourself a Schweppes Bitter Lemon in tribute. Or C.J. will have an attractive aide bring it over. Either way.) While countless actors gave terrific auditions for the role of the president, a number of the early contenders were pushing seventy, if not blowing right past it, and possessed a quality more evocative of Ronald Reagan than the JFK type the team would ultimately land on.

One day, John Wells asked Aaron, "What about Martin Sheen?" Fifty-eight years old at the time, Martin was a brilliant, universally respected actor who was well-known for being uncommonly down-to-earth and widely liked. Off set he was famous for his fervent social justice activism. For this potential Jed Bartlet, activism was more than a hobby; it was a way of life. (**MELISSA:** Pssst . . . it still is.)

> I have no conscious memory of ever not being
> an actor, but while acting is what I do to make a
> living . . . activism is what I do to stay alive.
>
> —MARTIN SHEEN, "WE DAY" RALLY, VANCOUVER, 2010

Martin was pretty easy to picture in the Oval, given his experience in projects set at 1600 Pennsylvania Avenue. In a 1974 TV miniseries called *The Missiles of October*, he played President Kennedy's brother and primary advisor, Attorney General Robert F. Kennedy. Nine years later, in another Camelot-era miniseries—cleverly titled *Kennedy*—Martin played JFK himself, opposite Blair Brown's Jackie. (**MELISSA FUN FACT:** Martin's wife, Janet, was also in *Kennedy*. **MARY FUN FACT:** Martin's son Emilio wrote and directed the feature film *Bobby*, based on RFK.) A made-for-TV movie called *Medusa's Child* followed in 1997 and featured Martin as a fictional commander in chief staring down a potential global catastrophe. Of course, most relevant to *The West Wing* was Martin's work in Aaron's film *The American President*, where he played Andrew Shepherd's chief of staff—his "Leo," if you will. Upon reflection, it's hard not to see tapping him for President Bartlet as sort of meant to be.

> Martin never had to read for the
> role because, you know, throw *Badlands* up
> on the screen or *Apocalypse Now*, and you
> know what Martin can do.
>
> —AARON SORKIN ON *CHARLIE ROSE*, MAY 15, 2001

Given that Martin was a world-class actor–slash–movie star, it's not surprising that Aaron considered their odds of landing him for Bartlet somewhere between slim and none. Nevertheless, they sent over the script . . . only to have it wind up on a transatlantic flight.

"My son Ramón and I had a trip planned in the spring of '99," Martin told us. "I got a call from my agent saying that Aaron Sorkin had written this new series and that there was a part, but . . . it wasn't a very big part, and he only came in in the last scene of the pilot." Asked if he'd consider it, Martin said, "Absolutely, please send me the script. But get it here quickly because I'm leaving tomorrow for Ireland!" As Martin recounted it to us, "They sent it out by messenger and I read it on the plane. By the time we landed, I talked to my agent and said, 'I want to do this part!'" While in the Emerald Isle, he and Aaron set up a time to discuss the possibility of his doing the show. As their overseas call connected, Martin remembers with a laugh, "I said 'Yes' before Aaron even answered!"

What Martin loved about the Bartlet character is that he shone through as a true public servant, rather than a predictable careerist politician. He also appreciated that woven into the script was a celebration of public service in a broader sense, and that the show's central focus was to illuminate the people who serve, unknown and unnamed, in the federal government. In terms of actor and project, it really was an ideal match.

I can sense civic duty a mile away.

—PRESIDENT BARTLET TO LEO, "IN THIS WHITE HOUSE"

And speaking of ideal matches . . . let's speak about Martin's wife, Janet Sheen, and the role *she* played in the role he played. "Janet," Martin told us, "was a big reason I said yes to *The West Wing*. She read the script too and said, 'You've got to do this and there's no discussion!'" "This series," Janet predicted, "will be far more important than any series on television." (**MELISSA:** Martin told us that, months later, there was a screening of the pilot. "As soon as it ended, Janet turned to me and said, '*See?!*'" Janet's the best. Everyone needs a Janet.)

Once Martin had agreed to do the pilot, the creative team let him know the deal, or at least what they had presumed the deal would be. "The show," he was told, "is not about the president or the first family. You may be called upon to do one out of every four or five episodes, so that's four or five in the year. Are you all right with that?" Martin didn't bat an eye. "Absolutely."

"The only condition they had," Martin told us, "is that I could never play another president while the show was in production." He laughed. "What are the chances?"

As for making things official, the business of it all—the contract, the money, the schedule—had come to a quick and happy agreement. "I wasn't so much concerned with the dough as I was with the quality of the program," Martin says. "I invested in the show. It had such enormous possibility." But Bartlet inspired something else in the man who would bring him to life, something beyond "possibility" . . . inevitability.

"I had a strong feeling that, once the NBC executives saw the pilot," Martin told us, "they would be asking themselves, 'Who works in *that* office?' I figured they were going to call me back in as a series regular, and that is exactly what happened."

After the pilot was completed, Aaron and the actors began to dig more deeply into the characters that inhabited the world of *The West Wing*—their respective backstories, foibles, and idiosyncrasies. Martin had a pair of suggestions that would come to define President Bartlet. "I asked if he could be a Catholic . . . and if he could be a graduate of Notre Dame."

As Hollywood requests go, both were relatively benign and entirely reasonable. Also, character-wise, his ideas were spot-on. Establishing the moral underpinnings of a figure millions would come to know and love, those two seemingly minor details formed the bedrock of a man whom everyone, from focus groups to the executives at NBC, wanted to see more of. Thanks to *The West Wing*'s four founding fathers— Aaron, Tommy, John Wells, and, now, Martin—those groups (focus and otherwise) were about to get their wish.

Yes, President Josiah Bartlet—favorite son of New Hampshire and unofficial prince of New England, devout Catholic and die-hard fan of the Fighting Irish—was ready for his close-up. If only they'd told him to steer clear of that bicycle (and that tree).

PART II

★ ★ ★

LIFE IN THE OVAL

The Sorkin-Schlamme-Wells Administration

EIGHT

THE TABLE READ AND
THE WAR ROOM

Okay. Let's talk about table reads. Also known as "read-throughs," table reads are when the cast, director, writers, producers, ADs (assistant directors), and department heads gather around a big table, usually during lunch, to read the script aloud before shooting begins. What's special about table reads is that, for the one time during the production of that episode, everyone is in the same room at the same time. It creates a sense of a "company." Table reads aren't mandatory and, on some shows, series regulars don't always attend the table reads, but on *The West Wing* no one ever wanted to miss it. They were there every time—and they came to play.

The West Wing table reads were held in the Roosevelt Room and attracted intense interest from pretty much all corners—cast and crew and everyone in between. Tim Davis-Reed played Mark, one of the credentialed reporters in C.J.'s briefing room. He remembers waiting at the table read sometimes because the scripts were still being printed. "Then they would come in, in a big box, they were still warm. And you realize, 'I am gonna be the first person who hears this out loud!'"

Ask director Chris Misiano about the table reads and he gets positively misty. "When you would sit down at that read-through with a new Aaron script, there was an excitement to know what was gonna happen. Where was this gonna go? How was he going to tie the story together? This thing was woven so beautifully, and to hear each of the actors and their voices . . . they were magical. That roundtable in the Roosevelt Room was one of my favorite moments of the whole process."

So many of us feel that way. Now a producer, Julie DeJoie worked tirelessly as Tommy's assistant back in the *West Wing* days. You couldn't keep her away from the table reads, even when Aaron's then assistant, producer Lauren Lohman, threatened to make her read a line or two. But Julie and her stage fright—"Please, *please* don't make me read!!"—didn't stand a chance against the magnetic draw of the *West Wing* read-through. "People would come at crew lunch," Julie remembers. "They just wanted to sit for this forty-five-minute play. Those table reads were like a little piece of art."

★ ★ ★

"DON'T kill the messenger, Leo!"

That's the first line a staffer ever uttered on *The West Wing*, and it came courtesy of Bonnie, a regular presence in the communications bullpen. Even before the read-through, the woman who played her, Devika Parikh, couldn't believe her good luck. "I was like, 'Oh my God, I get to go to the table read?!'"

A bit cowed when she first walked in—"There's all these seats, it's all the actors, the producers, the writers, it's everybody!"—she didn't see her name anywhere. She thought maybe they'd forgotten to assign her a place to sit but figured, no big deal, she could just stand. Then somebody said, "No, no, your seat's right up here, next to John Spencer."

"At the main table?" Devika asked. "With one line?!" Quickly gathering herself, she took a shot at playing it cool with a few rounds of chill professionalism—"Hi, how are you? Nice to meet you!" Then came a quiet confession: "I can't believe I'm here, this is *awesome*."

In that moment, Devika's attempt to keep calm met the irrepressible passion of John Spencer refusing to do so. "Yeah," he gushed, "this is really great! I have to pinch myself 'cause I can't believe I'm here!"

"Literally, I almost started crying," Devika told us. She turned to John, a mix of exhilarated and relieved, and said, "Oh my God, me too! I thought the same thing!" There she was, trying so hard to be so cool while taking in a sea of famous faces. "As soon as John said that, it was like a release. I could just be honest." For Devika, that moment revealed two of John's finest qualities: his unabashed love of acting, and his humility. "He was just the best of the best."

Devika wasn't the only cast member feeling anxious that day. "Table reads were valuable for everybody else," Richard Schiff told us, "but I hated them. I was just so nervous." It may not have helped his nerves that on day one he was sitting across the table from an actor he'd long admired but had never met, Martin Sheen. To that point, Richard hadn't known what to think of the man who would be Bartlet, beyond the fact that Martin had been in so many projects he loved and was "such an interesting actor." But, with *Badlands* and *Apocalypse Now* deposited in his memory bank, Richard says, he was totally unprepared to deal with Martin's rare combination of "humanity" and "clowniness." Richard, not exactly known for his exuberance, must've felt like Martin landed from another planet. . . . "He was quite overwhelming with how happy he was to be there . . . and how happy to meet me."

Also quite overwhelming that day? The presence of one Tommy Schlamme. From the moment the director walked into the Roosevelt Room, Allison Janney noticed—he was kind of hard to miss. "I was sitting next to Brad. Tommy was at the head of the table. As soon as he started talking, I turned to Brad and whispered, 'He's *really* loud!' I just started laughing. Brad did too. I'd never heard someone talk so loudly before! Tommy, God love him, is just . . . boisterous . . . he's capital-*L* LOUD!"

That day, Allison experienced her first fit of *West Wing* church laughter, the most memorable example of which came years later in response to a famously hysterical introduction: "I'M MARION COTESWORTH-HAY!!!" (Of Marblehead.) For the record, that instance of unbound laughter occurred *on-screen*, which is a different sort of fox hunt altogether (and definitely worth checking out on YouTube). But back to the table read . . .

Brad, too, remembers that moment, along with the four years of moments with Tommy that followed. "I used to tell him that, when his kids were in therapy in their twenties, their epiphany would be that Daddy wasn't mad at them, he just talked too loud." Brad laughs at the recollection. "Being directed by Tommy was always just . . . loud and . . . coming in at you and there's always some shit going on with his glasses . . ." Once, while filming an episode, Brad yelled at Tommy, "Jesus, it's like a 3D horror movie!" That said, at that first-ever table read, Brad took a measure of comfort from the director's ability to command the room, and so did Allison.

"I was like, 'Okay, this guy is in charge,'" she remarked to us, "'he is *in charge* of this show. This is a man who knows what he's doing.'" There was a lot of that going around that day, Allison revealed, and in the ones to come too. "I felt like I was with a lot of people who knew what they were doing. And that was exciting."

In terms of her performance at the table read, and what was bubbling just under the surface, Allison was "incredibly nervous and also kind of thrilled." She went into the read-through with a healthy confidence. "Frankly, I felt like it was a good part for me," Allison recalls. "I loved feeling I could make everyone believe I'm the smartest woman in the room because, I can promise you, I was not." Sitting around that big conference table, in those early *West Wing* minutes, is something she'll never forget. "Everyone was just so good so immediately— Martin and John and Brad and Rob and Richard and everyone else— it was just . . . electric."

Richard's memory tells him the same thing. The electricity—on the page and in the room—was palpable. It tells him a couple of other things too: that he felt a nearly instant connection with Allison . . . and that the snacks were top-notch. "I remember the food. There were a lot of bagels and a lot of really good food. I was just like, 'Ohhh, this is what happens when you're on a real TV show!'" (**MARY:** Actors are so used to being poor. On a flight, I will still wake up for the free meal. I'm not hungry, I don't like it, I'm *allergic* to it—the poor kid in me is still like, "I am gonna eat that meal.")

What Melissa remembers from her first table read is what she felt at pretty much every one that followed. The talent level—from a regular like John Spencer to a supporting player like Devika—was impressively high. "There was a commitment to excellence at every position. Looking around the room, I remember thinking, 'Man. What a deep bench . . .' Also this: 'Melissa, you only have one line . . . don't mess it up!'"

Meanwhile, absorbing the performance at the head of the table, the man who started it all was blown away as much by the acting skill around the Roosevelt Room as by his own good fortune. "Boy, did we luck out with the casting of the show," Aaron says. "Not only was it an ensemble of wonderful actors, but wonderful people. To use a basketball metaphor, it was a group that liked to pass as much as they liked to shoot."

Those of us in the room where it happened that day could not have foreseen the wild successes around the bend. But even from those first steps—even in those less than fifty minutes—we sensed something special about the path.

★ ★ ★

PILOT read-throughs are, naturally, where a lot of actors first meet one another. In the race to production, though, most of the *West Wing* cast had gotten a serious head start. "I had already rehearsed for almost two weeks," Tommy told us, "which I try to do with pilots." The early stages of rehearsal involved, of course, the actors going over the scenes together—Richard called them "mini table reads"—but Tommy felt it was equally critical for the ensemble to establish a common history.

This gave him an idea. Screening real-life stories of real-life staffers for their soon-to-be *West Wing* counterparts might be an effective way to cram two years of shared history into two weeks of rehearsal time. So, he sat the cast down, turned off the lights, and fired up documentaries like 1993's *The War Room*. Following Bill Clinton's first successful run for president, *The War Room* features Southern-fried political guru James Carville, aka "the Ragin' Cajun," and made stars out of the campaign's trio of Young Turks, Paul Begala, George Stephanopoulos, and future *West Wing* contributor Dee Dee Myers.

But it wasn't just watching *The War Room*. And it wasn't just going over the script and running the scenes. They also broke bread together. Yes, for Tommy, a key to the cast's burgeoning affinity came down to one simple fact: "We always had lunch together." The point was for the cast to get to know one another—for real—to get a sense of everybody's rhythms, a sense of the connections between them. "You guys have already been together for two years," Tommy reminded them. Come the first day of shooting, he pointed out, you don't want it to read like a rushed, half-baked "Oh, by the way, we've known each other forever!"

The goal was to make clear—to actors and audience alike—that, from the first beat of the pilot, these people have been in the trenches together through the two-year-long slog of a presidential campaign; that Leo, Josh, Toby, Sam, and C.J. have seen, shoulder to shoulder, their fair share of battles and, as Tommy put it, "already know each other's habits." What resulted was a dynamic energy ideally suited to Aaron's dialogue. They bantered back and forth, talked over one another, cut each other off.

During rehearsals, Tommy informed the cast that, when it came time to shoot the pilot, "everybody would be called every day" and could expect to be put into scenes even when they didn't have lines. "If you look at the pilot," Tommy points out, "they're *all* background artists. Deep behind the scene we're watching, you'll catch a flash of Allison crossing to her office, Richard talking to an unnamed staffer back by a copy machine. Everybody had to be there all the time." That's very unusual. On most TV shows, production focuses a lot on getting the stars home for the night. Here the emphasis was on establishing an unspoken culture—within both the world of the show and the world of *making* the show. This would signal to viewers that these devoted public servants work ungodly hours, that they never go home, that they're there, like Tommy says, "*all* the time."

The West Wing was a very demanding, often scary set to be on, but mostly always in service of trying to be great. How we never settled for second best, how we demanded that everyone be prepared—that was fostered from the beginning. Every set I go on I try to emulate what we had on *The West Wing*. So the show lives on in how we conduct ourselves and what we demand from people we work with.

—ANDREW BERNSTEIN, FIRST ASSISTANT DIRECTOR/ DIRECTOR, *THE WEST WING*

In a subtler way, it suggested that series regulars were not the stars of every scene. Sometimes they were, but sometimes they would just be handing off a piece of paper to an actor in an office toward the back. How these indefatigable staffers would work in the trenches of the White House was not unlike how Tommy saw this "company of actors" working in the trenches of a network TV show. As Allison put it to us, "The fact that we were all in scenes together, even when we weren't the focus—when we did a cross, when we didn't even have a line—made me feel connected. To Richard or Brad or Melissa, to our background actors. That started there, with Tommy, in the pilot."

A week or so into rehearsal, Tommy told Aaron he could see the chemistry getting there, that it was really going to work. "They all have this *relationship!*" Thank God for that, because not every aspect of the show was going according to plan.

"We had a party at John Wells's house not long before we started shooting," Tommy says, "and the president still wasn't cast. Time was running out." With the clock ticking, John contacted Martin to more officially gauge his interest. After that, Aaron talked to Martin. As they chatted, each grew excited by the notion of this potential collaboration.

A few days later, the deal was struck. That weekend, Martin came in to rehearse with Tommy. "It was," the director told us, "the first time any of us had heard him read it." In the run-up to Martin's arrival, Tommy remembers feeling nervous and "a little overwhelmed." His mind's eye had him expecting the burned-out operative from *Apocalypse Now*. His mind's eye was wrong. "All of a sudden," Tommy said, laughing, "in walks the sweetest guy in the world!"

From there, they had a memorable, spirited rehearsal, with ideas flying back and forth. What struck Tommy then surprises none of us now. On that first day of rehearsal, as on every day that followed, Martin acted like he always did, which is to say with humility uncommon in a star of his stature, with exceeding good humor and unwavering commitment.

And so it was. Their president now "sworn in," their war room officially complete, the ensemble of *The West Wing* was ready to continue into the fray with their full complement of troops. Ready to drink from the keg of glory and blow through red lights. Ready to do what is hard and achieve what is great. This was a time for American heroes, and they reached for the stars. They were ready, at last, to make the pilot.

THE FIRST STEPS TOWARD TOMORROW

Making the *West Wing* Pilot

N ightmarish."

That's how costume designer Lyn Paolo describes the week before *The West Wing* started filming. It all stemmed from this one problem. "We didn't have any cast."

This is not to say the roles hadn't been filled. They largely had been. But several of the deals hadn't yet closed, and there were hundreds of other details to attend to before anyone came anywhere near yelling "Action!" Then . . . in the five days leading up to principal photography, a sudden flurry of fittings overtook the wardrobe department.

The last of these would mark the *i*-dotting, *t*-crossing end of that very public negotiation we mentioned earlier. It would involve Warner Bros., NBC, a trio of *West Wing* heavy hitters . . . and Sodapop from *The Outsiders*. Which is how it would come to be that, the night before filming the pilot's very first scene, Lyn Paolo's fitting room was getting a little crowded.

Standing together, Aaron Sorkin and Tommy Schlamme watched Rob Lowe as their last-minute, newly minted Sam Seaborn tried on suits while officially signing his contract, just hours before the next day's five a.m. call time. It was crazy, if not totally unprecedented, for Rob to be trying on suits and shoes—and a shirt he'd soon be taking off—before the ink had even dried, but . . . better late than never.

Days earlier, another cast member had entered the wardrobe department's inner sanctum. Sam Seaborn's boss, Toby Ziegler, was a bit older, more than a bit less sunny, and played by an actor Lyn Paolo loves, one whose first impression she won't soon forget. "Richard walks in—one of those big fitting rooms at Warner Bros., we had nine or ten racks of clothes for him—and I was like, 'Nice to meet you, come on in!' He glanced around and said, 'Yeah, I don't see anything in this room that's gonna work for Toby.'"

"I love him for that!" Lyn told us with an affectionate laugh. "So I said, 'Why don't you sit down for a minute, let's just talk about who you think Toby is, and maybe we can figure out a way to move forward just for the first episode.' We were there for a couple of hours. He finally put stuff on and walked out and goes, 'This was great. I love everything!'"

Looking back, this had to have been one of the earliest examples of *The West Wing*'s culture of respect for process. As Lyn put it to us, "I think with actors, it has to be a dialogue. It's my job to hear them and to let them *know* that they've been heard."

When it came to making the pilot, Tommy had exactly thirteen days and at least one guiding principle: "I wanted to shoot the beginning in order, and try to shoot the pilot in sequence as much we possibly could." Due to typical production restraints, that wasn't entirely doable, but the director hoped to shoot the *introductions* of the characters prior to their appearing in the White House. This is how Rob Lowe went from signing his contract while trying on suits to sitting slumped in a makeup chair just hours later. His first two scenes were the first ones up.

When we chatted with Rob, it seemed like he could still feel the shudder of that first *West Wing* wake-up. "Whoa . . . so early," he said, wide-eyed. "It sounds insane to say now, but I had never done a TV series." And it was an *hour-long* TV series, which is extra brutal on the sleep schedule. For the first scene shot—in the bar at the Biltmore Hotel—Rob set his alarm for four a.m. As someone used to acting in movies, that had to be a real shock to the system. (**MARY:** You know what TV actors call a four a.m. wake-up? "Monday morning.")

Per Tommy's pilot hopes and dreams—and since Sam Seaborn had not yet arrived at the White House—Rob's introduction sequence continued apace, including the "company move" (when the entire crew moves to a new location) to Laurie's bedroom. That's where viewers woke up with Sam and his call girl–slash–law student date from the bar, where they first heard the word "POTUS," and, as Rob put it to us, "where I took my shirt off for the first and only time in the history of *The West Wing*—just enough to get the show on the air."

From the hotel bar to Laurie's bedroom and on through the rest of the pilot, Aaron was on set the entire time, never leaving Tommy's side. He was there for Leo's complaints about the spelling of "Khaddafi" in the *New York Times* crossword puzzle, for Josh waking up (groggy and drooling) with his head on his desk, for Toby kvetching on the airplane about having to turn off his cell . . . and, of course, for C.J.'s much-anticipated treadmill pratfall.

```
              C.J. CREGG
        See, it's all about budgeting your
        time. This time, this hour, this is
        my time. Five a.m. to six a.m. I
        can work out, as you see. I can
        think about personal matters. I
        can . . . meet an interesting man.
```

(Soon her beeper goes off and, well, you know the rest . . .)
Over the next thirteen days, Tommy and Aaron oversaw what cast

and crew recall as an exceptionally professional, impressive beginning. Rob Lowe describes the production of the pilot as "smooth from start to finish. It was heaven on earth." That said, "smooth" does not always mean easy. Take that opening walk-and-talk . . .

The inspiration for this introductory scene did not originate on the *West Wing* soundstage. While some may point to the on-the-move Steadicam sequences that John Wells and Tommy used on *ER*—or that Aaron and Tommy employed to such stellar effect on *Sports Night*—the seed of that first walk-and-talk had been planted years before.

Prior to *The West Wing*, the director and his family had enjoyed a Lincoln Bedroom stay at the Clinton White House. Outside the Oval, while waiting to speak to the president, Tommy witnessed a moment that would come to define what he calls "the movement of the show."

"I remember the doors opening up and Stephanopoulos and other staffers coming out, talking to each other, some going this way, some going that way." To Tommy, as that Oval Office meeting ended, it felt like another was still going on. "It never stops, they're constantly juggling, there was never downtime." Reflecting on that moment years later, he hoped to create that same energy for *The West Wing*, a sense of "this world that was all continuous."

Wisely, Tommy and Aaron and John Wells had stacked the cast with theater actors. For folks like Allison Janney, Richard Schiff, Brad Whitford, and John Spencer, these long, involved takes, which often included dense, fast-paced dialogue and intricate, ranging choreography, were right up their alley.

As John Spencer revealed in a 2002 interview with CNN's David Daniel, when it came to his opening sequence on *The West Wing*, he was deep in his comfort zone. "As written, they were eight separate scenes. Tommy came to me the first or the second day of rehearsal and said, 'I have an idea. I would like to put those eight scenes together in a walk-and-talk and have you sort of geographically show us the West

Wing. It's going to be our first vision of this workplace.'" Taking eight mini-scenes and combining them into one long nonstop scene? For an actor who'd spent the first two decades of his career onstage, it was like Christmas morning.

Seeing the sequence on its feet a handful of times was enough for the director to realize they were onto something. "We figured out a visual way to shoot it," Tommy says, "as well as a performance and a level of energy." After rehearsal, he *knew*—and he didn't want to know it alone.

"I was in my office a couple of days before shooting on the pilot started," Aaron remembers. "Tommy popped his head in and asked me to come to the set so he could show me something. Tommy with an idea is like a kid who's just learned a new card trick. As originally written, the pilot opened with each staff member learning that POTUS had injured himself while on vacation. (The opening depended entirely on the audience not knowing what the acronym POTUS stood for, which, when the show premiered, they did not.) After that opening," Aaron says, "we go to the White House for the first time and follow Leo down a corridor and into Josh's office, where the rest of the scene is played, after which we cut to Leo's office. Tommy—taking out his 'deck of cards'—said, 'What if instead of cutting to Leo's office, the scene was continuous and we walked there?' He took me on the route he was pitching—Leo enters the lobby, walks through what we called 'Josh's Bullpen,' went into Josh's office, then back into the lobby, past the communications bullpen, into Mrs. Landingham's office, through the Oval . . . and into his own office. No cuts. I'd write dialogue to cover the whole shot. Tommy had just invented the shooting style of the show."

One bit of dialogue from this opening includes a memory that Tommy still cherishes. Turning to Aaron at a *West Wing* reunion panel at the ATX TV Festival in 2016, he said, "I remember shooting this . . . asking you to include my three children's names."

```
                              LEO
           Hey, Emma.


                              EMMA
           Morning.


                              LEO
           Wilson.


                              WILSON
           Hey, Leo.


                              LEO
           Joe.
```

"I can't believe Aaron did that," Tommy said. "It was so loving."

It took just under twenty tries to film that entire introduction to the West Wing, and while that may sound like a lot, it was more or less par for the course. For any walk-and-talk, all it takes is one actor to flub a line, one Steadicam operator to slightly stumble, one boom mic to dip into frame, and it's—to quote a thousand exasperated ADs— "back to one!"

But, in John Spencer's hands, one of the most ambitious sequences in the show's history (and the heaviest lift of the pilot) seemed like just another day at the office. "That charge of being able to do eight scenes back-to-back without stopping," John would tell David Daniel, "is sort of like a stage performance. It's *thrilling.*"

Tommy shared John's excitement. "To have this group of mostly theater actors who could do that felt like everything came together for me right at that moment."

Now, if you're going to walk-and-talk your way through a world, you have to have somewhere to walk and talk. And it's worth noting that the world in which Leo and the others were walking-and-talking represented a sizable investment by the studio, in terms of dollars *and* faith in the project. The financial outlay to the production budget spared no expense and imbued the show with both a sense of grandeur and an uncommon focus on the tiniest details. The piles of carpeting were thick, the flowers in and around the offices were real and fresh, the portraits of former presidents were accurate down to the last detail, and the Oval Office was an exact replica.

They're beautiful sets, they're the most beautiful sets I've ever worked on. The detail is exquisite. I remember the first time I walked into the Oval Office, it just took my breath away.

—ALLISON JANNEY, "INAUGURATION,"
BEHIND-THE-SCENES DVD FEATURETTE

As unusual as the number of dollars invested may have been, it made sense to the key creatives in charge. "It's the world we live in," Tommy recounted to us matter-of-factly. "It's the most important office building in the world. These are big-ticket items."

It wasn't just the richness of the detail and the overall opulence of the set; it was the size and scope of it all. As Aaron acknowledges, "Warner Bros. made a gigantic commitment . . . before it was ever picked up for series . . . by building the biggest set, by a wide margin, ever built for a pilot."

The massive set included more than that exact replica of the Oval. It was the residence, the kitchen, the Mural Room, the Roosevelt Room, the press briefing room, and the bustling communications bullpen; the offices of the chief of staff, the press secretary, and their assistants . . . and the countless hallways that connected them all. The set was, in fact, so vast that, for the first season, it had to be divided between two adjacent television soundstages. In the pilot, one walk-and-talk has Leo and Josh crossing a lobby and through a set of double doors, then continuing seamlessly down a corridor. "That continuation happened in a different building on a different day," Aaron says. "That's how we were doing the show. People would walk through one door on a Tuesday, walk out the other side on a Thursday in a different building."

Luckily for all involved, starting in season 2 the studio moved production to a larger soundstage typically used for feature films. Having the entire set in one spot made sequences like the one with Leo and Josh far more manageable.

The stages weren't the only aspect of *The West Wing* that changed from the pilot to the second season. Take Donna, for instance. Aaron had initially envisioned the character as relatively minor, just one amid the buzzing beehive of junior West Wing staffers. Then Janel Moloney showed up.

"She was a day player on the pilot who came in as my assistant," Brad says. "But I remember her being absolutely luminous. After the first Josh-Donna bit—we have a sort of smartass exchange—I went up to Aaron at the monitors and said, 'Oh my God, I *love* her!'" Aaron was right there with him.

"Janel Moloney was a revelation," Aaron says. "She had one little scene . . . with a couple of lines. She came in and did beautifully. When we finally got the pilot in the can, we were a couple of minutes short. I needed to add a little scene . . ."

                    DONNA
        Put it on.

                    JOSH
        No.

                    DONNA
        You've been wearing the same
        clothes for 31 hours now, Josh.

Susan Massin, her brother (director Tommy Schlamme), Brad Whitford, and producer Llewellyn Wells on location in Washington, DC, in season 2. *Courtesy of Julie DeJoie*

Allison Janney and John Spencer on a break outside the Oval Office set on the Warner Bros. lot. *Courtesy of Allison Janney*

(File 1113p01-kf) L N
(O. 1112p02-rh)
JOHN WELLS PRODUCTIONS / WBTV
"THE WEST WING"
PILOT / NBC
DRAFT: 2/6/98

Executive Producers: John Wells, Aaron Sorkin
Producer: Kristin Harms
Director: TBA   DELIVERED NOV 1 6 1998
Writer: Aaron Sorkin
Sr. V.P. of Casting: Barbara Miller
Casting Directors: John Levey / Kevin Scott
Sr. Casting Coordinator: Cheryl Kloner
Casting Coordinator: Maxine Harris
Start Date: Approx. 2/1/99
Location: Pilot TBD; Series L.A.

WRITTEN SUBMISSIONS ONLY TO:

JOHN LEVEY / KEVIN SCOTT
300 TELEVISION PLAZA
BUILDING 140, FIRST FLOOR
BURBANK, CA 91505

SCRIPTS AVAILABLE: 11/18

NOTE: DIRECT ALL SUBMISSIONS AND INQUIRIES TO KEVIN SCOTT'S OFFICE.

DUPLICATE SUBMISSIONS (COVER LETTERS ONLY) TO BARBARA MILLER AT THE ABOVE ADDRESS.

[SAM SEABORN] Early 30s, Sam is the Deputy Communications Director at the White House. The subordinate to Toby Ziegler, Sam works closely with Leo, Josh, Toby and C.J., planning the appropriate Presidential response to the events of the day. Not the most well-read guy in the world, Sam works in the White House, but is a strictly political animal, knowing nothing of the history of the White House, and under the mistaken impression that FDR is the 16th President of the United States. While the rest of the staff wrestles with the main events of the day (the President's broken ankle, the Cuban refugees headed towards Florida, and Joshua's major gaffe on yesterday's "Meet The Press"), Sam deals with a little personal problem all his own. The woman he met and went to bed with last night is not just cheerful and attracted to him--she's also a part-time hooker, the kind of faux pas that can ruin an ambitious man's career for good...SERIES REGULAR (1)

[JOSHUA LYMAN] A youthful man in his 30s, Josh is the Deputy Chief of Staff, working directly beneath Leo Jacobi, and is a highly regarded brain. Josh helped elect President Bartlet, and during the campaign, had an affair with gifted political consultant Mandy Hampton. He broke up with Mandy after he was tapped to go to the White House and she was let go, but he's clearly still very much attracted to her. A very liberal Democrat who has nothing but contempt for the Religious Right, Josh is in the doghouse after a disastrous appearance on "Meet The Press," during which he smugly denounced Mary Marsh, a spokesperson for Christian Family Values. Believed to be on the verge of losing his job, Josh is on tenterhooks throughout the day, and even agrees to apologize to Mary Marsh for his thoughtless sarcasm. Delighted to learn that Mandy is back in town (and not so delighted to find she's working for the opposition), Josh gets a surprise when the President shows up unexpectedly to back him during a conference with Mary Marsh and Reverend Al Caldwell...SERIES REGULAR (8)

DOUBLE - SIDED

ABOVE AND FACING PAGE (TOP):

These original character breakdown descriptions for casting were written by Aaron Sorkin, or at least rewritten by him. A rare glimpse into how Aaron originally imagined the characters. C.J. as "compact and athletic." Sam as "not the most well-read guy in the world." The man we'd come to love as Leo McGarry described as "55 and professorial"—and named Leo JACOBI.

FACING PAGE (BOTTOM):

Pilot casting list for the role of "Mandy." And proof that Mary is very capable of making poor decisions.

Courtesy of John Levey

BREAKDOWN SERVICES, LTD.
Los Angeles (310) 276-9166
New York (212) 869-2003
Vancouver (604) 460-0444
London (01) 459-2781
www.breakdownservices.com   The Link: www.submitlink.com

The information contained in this document is the exclusive property of Breakdown Services, Ltd. Any unauthorized reproduction, duplication, copying or use of the information contained herein, without prior written consent of Breakdown Services, Ltd., is strictly prohibited.

JOHN WELLS PRODUCTIONS / WBTV
"THE WEST WING"
PILOT / NBC   PAGE TWO...

[TOBY ZIEGLER] In his 40s, a rumpled and sleepless Communications Director at the White House, Toby is Sam's boss, and he works closely on a day-to-day basis with Leo, Sam, and C.J. A man with a cynical sense of humor, Toby worries about the political implications of every decision, and is very peeved with Joshua for his uncalled-for remarks on "Meet The Press." After raking Josh over the coals for having vastly exceeded the parameters of his instructions, Toby tries to preserve Josh's job by arranging a peace meeting. But when Toby attends the pow-wow with Mary Marsh and Reverend Caldwell, he blows his own stack when he thinks Mary is making anti-Semitic cracks about Josh and himself...SERIES REGULAR (13)

[MADELINE "MANDY" HAMPTON] A fine looking, instantly likeable woman in her mid to late 30s, Mandy is a top political consultant, who had an affair with Josh during Bartlet's Presidential campaign. Intelligent and ambitious but sometimes a bit scattered, Mandy did not go to the White House along with everyone else; Josh got tapped for his slot, and Mandy went off to a $650,000 per year consulting job. However, Mandy has just returned to Washington with a new job, as political consultant for her lover, Senator Lloyd Russell. Intrigued to be back in the same town with Josh, Mandy intends to stage-manage Russell's bid for the Presidency, and hopes to be fighting toe-to-toe against Josh all the way. Quite pleased to have lunch with Josh, she lets him know that their new relationship will be personally friendly but professionally adversarial...SERIES REGULAR (30)

[LEO JACOBI] 55 years old and professorial, Leo is the President's Chief of Staff. A stickler when it comes to his crossword puzzles, Leo knows the President quite well, and regards him as a klutz and a spaz. Leo is furious with Joshua for having behaved foolishly on "Meet The Press," and chews Josh out royally, but appears to have no intention of firing him. None too thrilled with the lack of solid intelligence about the Cuban refugees, Leo clearly keeps a careful watch on the pulse of the nation, despite the fact that no two economists can agree on anything. A man with a dryly sarcastic sense of humor, he hits the ground running when Josh brings him evidence that Senator Lloyd Russell is running for President against Bartlet...SERIES REGULAR (2) PLEASE SUBMIT ACTORS OF ALL RACES AND ETHNICITIES.

[C.J. GREGG] In her 30s, compact and athletic and quite coolly competent, she lives in Georgetown, and is the White House Press Secretary. Used to working closely with Toby and Joshua, C.J. is in charge of briefing the press, conducting press conferences, and deflecting their awkward questions with grace and skill. She spends most of the day evading questions about Joshua's gaffe, and fears that the press are bloodhounds on Joshua's scent. She tries to moderate the tempers during the conference with Caldwell and his supporters...SERIES REGULAR (3) PLEASE SUBMIT ACTORS OF ALL RACES AND ETHNICITIES.

[PRESIDENT JOSIAH (JED) BARTLET] The President of the United States, Bartlet is a Democrat from New Hampshire, and is a descendant of one of the original signers of the Declaration of Independence. "Looking every bit the country lawyer, you wouldn't immediately guess that he's brilliant, which he is. While the left hand is lulling you with folksy charm, you don't even hear the right hook coming." Regarded by his staff (especially Leo) as a klutz, Bartlet has just added to his reputation by riding a bicycle into a tree and spraining his ankle. When he returns to the White House, he reveals why: he was in a rage because an anti-abortion movement called Lambs Of Christ has sent his 13 year old daughter a Raggedy Ann doll with a knife stuck n its throat. Still furious but under control, he wastes no time in kicking Reverend Al Caldwell out of the White House and ordering him to denounce the LOC publicly. He demands that his staff re-focus their attention on the real problem: the Cuban refugees...SERIES REGULAR (60)

****

ROLE OF "MANDY" - NOT AVAILABLE/NOT INTERESTED:

MARY McCORMACK (GERSH)	NOT INTERESTED IN SERIES WORK
KIM DICKENS (GERSH)	NOT INTERESTED IN SERIES WORK
CARA SEYMOUR (ICM)	PASSING
VERA FARMIGA (INN)	PASSING
HOPE DAVIS (W&A)	NOT INTERESTED IN SERIES WORK
LAURA LINNEY (ICM)	NOT INTERESTED IN SERIES WORK
DIANE VENORA (INN)	NOT AVAILABLE – IN TONGUE OF A BIRD AT MARK TAPER THEATRE UNTIL 2/7 – THEN IT MOVES TO THE PUBLIC THEATRE, NY, FROM 2/16 – 4/18

While it appears that Dulé has just accepted Brad's proposal of marriage, in fact they had simply won a foosball game against Tommy and Allison. Also featured: our gaffer, Jeff Butters. *Courtesy of Brad Whitford*

There was always more than a little magic in the passion and artistry of Dulé's tap dancing—here, outside the real White House, in Washington, DC. *Courtesy of Brad Whitford*

Brad Whitford and John Spencer between takes.
Courtesy of Brad Whitford

Allison at her desk, with her feet out of frame.
Courtesy of Allison Janney

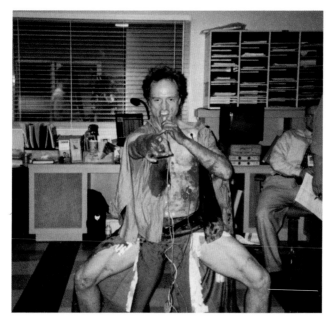

Brad between takes on the set of the season 2 premiere, "In the Shadow of Two Gunmen."
Courtesy of Brad Whitford

On location at the National Cathedral in Washington, DC, during the filming of the season 2 finale, "Two Cathedrals," in the spring of 2001. (L-TO-R: Rob Lowe, Dulé Hill, Melissa Fitzgerald, NiCole Robinson, Brad Whitford, Janel Moloney, Richard Schiff, and Allison Janney) *Courtesy of Melissa Fitzgerald*

"Five-Dollar-Friday" drawings with cast and crew typically took place deep into a "Fraturday night." (L-TO-R: Chris Misiano, Janel Moloney, utility sound technician Yervant Hagopian [seated], Tommy Schlamme, Allison Janney, and Brad Whitford) *Courtesy of Julie DeJoie*

Minutes after a tea ceremony in the Rose Garden, Melissa makes herself at home at her counterpart's desk in the actual West Wing.
Courtesy of Melissa Fitzgerald

SET DESCRIPTION	SCENE NO./CAST NO.	D/N	PAGES	LOCATION
INT. W.H.-HALL/McGARRY'S OFFICE (LEO TELLS JOSH IT WAS STUPID)	#6 PT.3 - 2,3,5,6,11 (7A)	DAY	1 4/8	
INT. W.H. OUTER OVAL OFFICE (7A) (LANDINGHAM ASKS LEO NOT TO CALL PRES. 'GEEK') (7A)	#7 PT - 2,3,4,5, 8,9,11,15	DAY	1 2/8	WARNER BROS STAGE 18
INT. W.H.-WESTWING CORRIDOR (CATHY SEES REV., PASSES KIDS)	#A26 - 10,12,17,18,20,38	DAY	3/8	
INT. W.H.-HALLWAY (4P) (CATHY IS ON A MISSION)	#26 PT.1 - 12	DAY	1/8	
INT. W.H.-HALL/ROOSEVELT RM (4P) (CATHY DOESN'T KNOW LEO'S DAUGHTER)	#27 PT.1 - 4,5,6,10,12	DAY	4/8	
INT. W.H.-ROOSEVELT RM (4P) (SAM DOESN'T KNOW HIS HISTORY)	#27 PT.2 - 4,5,6,10	DAY	1 3/8	
			5 5/8 TOTAL PAGES	

NO.	ACTOR		CHARACTER	MAKEUP CALL	SET
1	MARTIN SHEEN	—	JED BARTLET	—	—
2	JOHN SPENCER	W	LEO McGARRY	9³⁰am	RPT TO ST. 18 (ENTER GATE ?
3	BRAD WHITFORD	W	JOSH LYMAN	9³⁰am	
4	ROB LOWE	W	SAM SEABORN	8³⁰am	
5	RICHARD SCHIFF	W	TOBY ZIEGLER	8³⁰am	
6	ALLISON JANNEY	W	CJ CREGG	7³⁰am	
7	MOIRA KELLY	H	MANDY HAMPTON	—	—
8	KATHRYN JOOSTEN	W	MRS. LANDINGHAM	9³⁰am	RPT TO LOT 'W' (ENTER GATE7
9	NICOLE ROBINSON	W	MARGARET	9am	
10	ALLISON SMITH	SW	MALLORY O'BRIEN	10A	
11	JANEL MOLONEY	W	DONNA MOSS	8am	
12	SUZY NAKAMURA	W	CATHY	7³⁰am	
15	DEVIKA PARIKH	W	BONNIE THE AIDE	9³⁰am	
17	ANNIE CORLEY	SW	MARY MARSH	10A	
18	F. WILLIAM PARKER	SW	REV. AL CALDWELL	11A	
20	DAVID SAGE	SW	JOHN VAN DYKE	11A	
38	MELISSA FITZGERALD	SWF	STAFFER (Sc. A26)	10A	

SPECIAL INSTRUCTIONS:
PROPS - OFFICE PROPS

TV PLAYBACK & RECORD - CAMERA SYNC BOX; CNN & C-SPAN TAPES;
COMPUTER FEED; TV PLAYBACK

ATMOSPHERE & STANDINS	
2 SI (M) @ 8³⁰A	2 UNIFORMED SECRET SERVICE @ 8³⁰A
2 SI (F) @ 8³⁰A	40 STAFF/AIDES @ 8³⁰A
15 KIDS @ 11³⁰A	1 PRIEST @ 11³⁰A (Recycle)
2 PARENTS @ 11³⁰A	4 RIGHT WINGISTS (2M/2F) @ 11³⁰A (Recycle)
WELFARE WORKER: 2 @ 11³⁰A	*ALL D.G. PARK IN GATE 8/RPT TO GATE 7/TAKE WARNER SHUTTLE

ADVANCE SCHEDULE	
MONDAY, APRIL 12, 1999 SHOOT DAY # 11	MONDAY, TUESDAY, APRIL 13, 14, 1999 SHOOT DAYS 12 & 13 TO STAGE 19
Sc. 28 INT. W.H.-HALLWAY #4,5,6,10	Sc. 30, 30A INT. W.H.-MAP ROOM #1,2,3,4,5,6, 8,9,11,12,17,18,20
Sc. 29 INT. W.H.-HALLWAY #3,5,6,11	
Sc. 4 INT. GEORGETOWN-HEALTH CLUB #6,33,37	
STAGE #18	STAGE #18

1st A.D.: Tony Adler
2nd A.D.: Brian Bettwy

"C" CASTING MUST CALL

Unit Production Manager: Jean Higgins

Call sheet from day 10 of the pilot. Martin Sheen is number 1. Number 38 is an unnamed "Staffer" played by Melissa Fitzgerald, who would go on to be named Carol Fitzpatrick, and who would appear in 102 episodes of the show.
Courtesy of John Levey

To Whom It May Concern:

"THE WEST WING"

ADDITIONAL IDEAS FOR "POTUS"
AS OF 2/18/99

ALAN ALDA (ICM) WILL MEET WITH OFFER- DOING "ART" IN L.A.
TOM ALDRDEDGE
ALAN ARKIN (WMA) OFFER ONLY WITH OWNERSHIP
JOHN BADHAM
HAROLD BECKER
PETER BOGDANOVICH
ROBERT BORK
ED BRADLEY
DAVID BRINKLEY
TOM BROKAW
BOB BUTLER (WMA) N/A CBS PILOT
JAMES CAMERON
JOHN CARPENTER
JOHNNY CARSON
JAMES CARVILLE
SHIRLEY CHILSOM
WES CRAVEN
WALTER CRONKITE
JAMES CROMWELL (SDB) N/A "RKO 281" IN LONDON 3/25 (4 WKS)
OSSIE DAVIS (TAA)   AVAIL NY BASED
RON DELLUMS (DIRECT) WILL READ
BOB DOLE
SAM DONALDSON
TOM DONNELLY
MIKE DOUGLAS
RICHARD DREYFUSS (ICM) NO INTEREST IN TV
CLINT EASTWOOD
WALTER FAUNTLEROY

Handwritten notes:
short list
Ronny Cox
Bob Newhart
Eli Wallach
Richard Cienna
HAL HOLBROOK
OF fenway — SIDNEY Poitier
MAKE OFFER — M. Emmett Walsh
Philip Bosco
June Alexander
Olympia DUKAKIs
Stockard Channing
Diane Ladd
Alfre Woodard
Blythe Danner

FRANCIS FORD COPPOLA
JOHN FRANKENHEIMER
BILL GATES
FRANK GIFFORD
NEWT GINGRICH
JOHN GLENN
DANNY GLOVER
ANDY GRIFFITH
JOHN GRISHAM
TOM HAYDEN
*HAL HOLBROOK (ABRAMS) OFFER ONLY
LEE IACOCCA
MAYNARD JACKSON
JESSE JACKSON
PHIL JACKSON
PETER JENNINGS
C. EVERETT KOOP
TED KOPPEL
KRIS KRISTOFFERSON
F. LEE BAILEY
KARL MALDEN
DELBERT MANN
JOHN McLAUGHLIN
AL MICHAELS
ROBERT MORSE
DAN PETRIE
SIDNEY POITIER- (CAA)- MAKE OFFER
MAURY POVICH
COLIN POWELL
HARVE PRESNELL (S/M/S) WILL READ
ANNE RICHARDS
RICHARD RIERDAN
JASON ROBARDS (ICM) POSSIBLE INTEREST AS GUEST
ANTHONY ROBBINS
KENNY ROGERS
ANDY ROONEY
NORMAN SCHWARZKOFF
GEORGE C. SCOTT- (wma) "Inherit the Wind"-muv 4-nbc 3/1 (4-5 wks.)Poss. Avail. Sending mgr. Script.
TOM SNYDER
GEORGE STEINBRENNER

An early-stage casting department brainstorming list for the role of President Bartlet. It's wild to consider how different the show would have been with Stockard Channing in the role, or Sidney Poitier, or George Steinbrenner!
Courtesy of John Levey

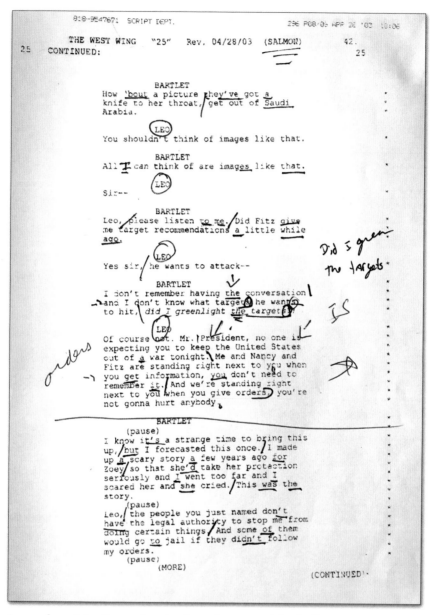

                    BARTLET
        How 'bout a picture they've got a
        knife to her throat, get out of Saudi
        Arabia.
                    LEO
        You shouldn't think of images like that.

                    BARTLET
        All I can think of are images like that.

                    LEO
        Sir--

                    BARTLET
        Leo, please listen to me. Did Fitz give
        me target recommendations a little while
        ago.

                    LEO
        Yes sir, he wants to attack--

                    BARTLET
        I don't remember having the conversation
        and I don't know what targets he wants
        to hit, did I greenlight the targets?

                    LEO
        Of course not. Mr. President, no one is
        expecting you to keep the United States
        out of a war tonight. Me and Nancy and
        Fitz are standing right next to you when
        you get information, you don't need to
        remember it. And we're standing right
        next to you when you give orders, you're
        not gonna hurt anybody.

                    BARTLET
                (pause)
        I know it's a strange time to bring this
        up, but I forecasted this once. I made
        up a scary story a few years ago for
        Zoey so that she'd take her protection
        seriously and I went too far and I
        scared her and she cried. This was the
        story.
                (pause)
        Leo, the people you just named don't
        have the legal authority to stop me from
        doing certain things. And some of them
        would go to jail if they didn't follow
        my orders.
                (pause)
                (MORE)

                                        (CONTINUED)

Handwritten notes in margins: Did I green / the targets · / IS

Handwritten note left margin: orders

A page from John Spencer's script from the season 4 finale, "Twenty Five." John's rigorous, detailed preparation is captured here in his special rhythm markings and handwritten scene notes. *Courtesy of Christopher Misiano*

This Emmy party gathering included five key figures* from Aaron Sorkin's original Broadway production of *A Few Good Men*. (L-TO-R: Ron Silver, Brad Whitford,* Stockard Channing, Aaron Sorkin,* Timothy Busfield,* Josh Malina,* and Ron Ostrow*) *Courtesy of Ron Ostrow*

Three and a half cast members on set. *Courtesy of Allison Janney*

Vacationing together during summer hiatus, 2003. Here Allison, Melissa, and Janel are having cocktails in Positano, Italy. *Courtesy of Melissa Fitzgerald*

Martin Sheen, Dulé Hill, and Lily Tomlin between takes on the season 5 lockdown episode, "No Exit." *Courtesy of Dulé Hill*

(L-TO-R) Mary, much-loved production assistant Holli Strickland, Allison Janney, Alex Graves, and Janel Moloney celebrate season 6.
Courtesy of Mary McCormack

Allison Janney and Brad Whitford just outside the White House gates along Pennsylvania Avenue. Some of our best times on *The West Wing* came when we'd fly to DC to shoot exteriors on location. *Courtesy of Allison Janney*

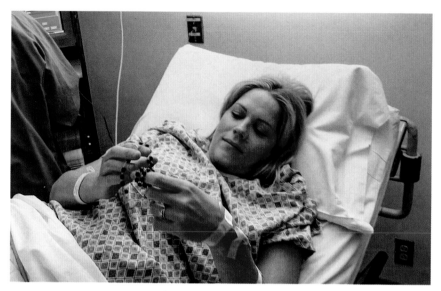

Mary in Cedars-Sinai hospital moments before the birth of her first child, Margaret, holding a rosary given to her by Martin Sheen. Martin would give her a rosary for the births of Rose and Lillian as well. You knew you were really in the *West Wing* family when you got a rosary from Martin.
Photograph by Michael Morris

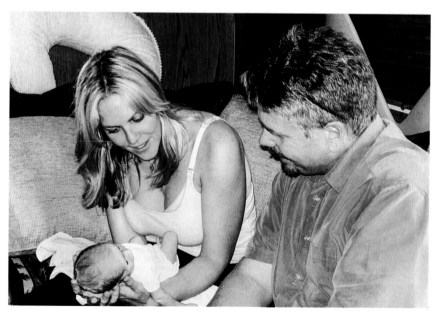

Executive producer John Wells visits Mary and newborn Margaret Morris in Mary's trailer. Due to production complications, Mary started back at work a week after giving birth. *Courtesy of Mary McCormack*

Martin Sheen with baby Margaret Morris on set. As executive producer John Wells put it to Mary, "This show is a real family. We've got tons of babies!"
Courtesy of Mary McCormack

São Paulo, Brazil, summer 2010: Janel Moloney, her son Julian, and Julian's godmother, Melissa Fitzgerald. "Melissa and I have always been family," Janel says. "I just codified it by making her godmother to Julian."
Courtesy of Melissa Fitzgerald

10.17.2005 05:01

John Spencer kisses his beloved dog, Zoey. We were filming a formal scene that day, which is why he is wearing a tux shirt and cuff links. This was the last photo ever taken of John.

Photograph by Holli Strickland

JOSH (OFF-SCREEN)
I am not getting spruced up for
these people, Donna.

DONNA
All the girls think you look really
hot in this shirt.

From off-screen, Josh grabs the shirt and tie. Donna walks
out of the office.

That was the first in a long-running series of flirtations that, much further down the road, would drive these two into each other's arms. Aaron couldn't help noticing. "This thing started developing between the two of them," he says, "so in the second episode I had her back, and then the third . . . She did all twenty-two that first season. The second season we made her what she already was—a series regular."

Allison Janney, of course, came in as a series regular, and from her very first scene—side-eye chatting up that "interesting man" at the gym—she hit the ground running (so to speak). To prep for the role of press secretary, Allison sought out someone who knew the lay of that particular land, former White House press secretary Dee Dee Myers. Now a member of Aaron's writing staff, Dee Dee was happy to help Allison get her arms around what it was like for a real-life C.J.

"Over dinner," Allison says, "Dee Dee and I talked about the challenges that come with being one of the few women in the often male-dominated inner sanctum of DC. It's a challenge wherever, even now, but it was far more pronounced back then. The 'boys club' dynamic can be . . . persistent," she told us. "Finding a way to assimilate isn't easy."

What John Wells appreciated about Allison from day one was the seemingly effortless fluency she brought to the material—material, the actress will tell you, that she sometimes barely understood. "It's not enough to simply have the lines memorized," John points out. "It's much closer to doing Shakespeare—you really have to understand the subtext." Allison's ability to execute that degree of verbal dexterity *and* convincingly fall on her face was there from the moment they began filming the pilot, and it never went away.

Tommy Schlamme summed up Allison best. "Her whole thing is, 'I've got to perform this. That's my job. I will keep working until I can figure out a way to make it truthful,' which is why I've never, ever, seen her lie. I used to always go to Allison and ask her to do another take, and the only reason was, I just loved watching her. It was fine, I don't have a note, but just . . . go do it again. For nothing more than my entertainment!"

Speaking of "entertainment," let's talk about Richard Schiff and his first two weeks rehearsing then shooting the pilot. There's a bunch of stories we could tell, but we've narrowed it down to two. First up . . .

THE JUDAH BUTTON

Toward the end of the pilot, we arrive at the Mural Room scene where Josh has to offer a bow-and-scrape apology to evangelical battle-axe Mary Marsh, for insulting her on TV. ("Lady, the god you pray to is too busy being indicted for tax fraud!") With Toby and C.J. by his side—and the Reverend Al Caldwell and a flock of religious Right figures on hers—Josh digs deep for the humility and contrition that will, he hopes and prays, keep President Bartlet from showing him the door. Problem was, to one actor anyway, a certain part of the scene didn't quite make sense.

"It's when Toby turns on Mary Marsh," Richard told us. "I got Josh there to apologize and then Mary Marsh makes a comment about 'that New York sense of humor.' And that was supposed to turn Toby and all of a sudden I go after her."

TOBY
She meant Jewish. When she said
"New York sense of humor," she was
talking about you and me.

"I said to Tommy and Aaron, 'Why am I turning? There's no reason for me to make this turn.' And Tommy goes, 'You've got a Judah button!' I'm like, 'What's a Judah button?' He goes, 'He's got radar—he can tell that somebody is antisemitic. He can just, you know . . . smell it out.' And I said, 'No, no, no, no, no. This guy has been around the world, he's been around antisemitism all his life. He's gotta have a *reason* to make this turn. Because we're at a disadvantage, our tails are between our legs, and now she's just made this heinous revelation with her comment on Jews. She's got to want to take *advantage* and turn Josh's misstep on television into a bargaining chip. That's when my hackles go up.'"

After a lengthy discussion with Aaron, Brad, and Tommy, Richard remembers, Aaron came up with the line that connected the dots. "Mary Marsh turns to me and goes, 'What do we get?' I say, 'I'm sorry?' And she goes, 'What do we *get?*' This woman is trying to take political advantage of Josh's faux pas, trying to turn it into a negotiation. As soon as he hears that, Toby turns."

For Richard, working through the scene with Aaron and Tommy was a defining moment. It meant a lot to him "as a *participant* with these two brilliant men." It was also a defining moment for Toby. "Her blatant opportunism is what gets my dander up, not a Judah Button. He's instantly like . . . *That's not how you negotiate in my room.*"

This part of our conversation really hit home. The instinct for an actor—for anyone, really—to "go along to get along," to "God, just *do* it"—can be hard to suppress. Richard's insistence may have meant the task at hand took a little longer, but aspiring to that granular level of detail isn't a vice; it's a *virtue.* Just ask seven seasons of Toby Ziegler.

MARTIN AND THE CHICKEN WINGS

This same scene—the apology meeting with the Christian Right—was among the last ones shot and was filmed over the final days of production. "The first time I met Martin, other than the read-through," Richard says, "was the first scene he did. 'I am the Lord your God.' That big entrance."

> VAN DYKE
>
> The First Commandment says, "Honor thy Father."

> TOBY
>
> No it doesn't.

> JOSH
>
> Toby—

> TOBY
>
> It doesn't!

> JOSH
>
> Listen—

> TOBY
>
> No—if I am gonna make you sit through this preposterous exercise, we're gonna get the names of the damn commandments right!

> MARY
>
> O-kay, here we go.

> TOBY
>
> "Honor thy Father" is the Third Commandment!

```
                    VAN DYKE
         Then what's the First Commandment?
```

A booming voice comes from off-screen. The camera moves to show . . .

```
                PRESIDENT BARTLET
         "I am the Lord your God. Thou shalt
         worship no other God before me."
         Boy, those were the days, huh?
```

"Every time we shot that big entrance," Richard remembers, "[Martin] would go over to crafty for chicken wings. And he'd come back—full of life and goodwill, and humor—with two gigantic cheeks filled with chicken, and grease all over his face. We'd start rehearsing the next shot with his mouth full, and he'd crack me up. I couldn't stop laughing. This was the thing with Martin—once he fucked up, he did something that set me off . . . and I'd be gone for forty minutes."

We can confirm this with one hundred percent certainty, based on personal experience. Through seven seasons of *The West Wing*, there may have been no greater threat to the smooth run of production than Richard Schiff with an uncontrollable case of the giggles. In moments like this, Richard was forced to deploy an unconventional acting strategy.

"Martin comes in—'I am the Lord your God!'—and there's this long loop [around the room] that he does. I would hold in my laughter . . . muscularly hold it still . . . feel the camera come off of me and run to the Oval Office and start laughing, trying to catch my breath, laughing and slapping my face and kind of . . . sensing the timing. Then I'd run back to my spot as the camera was coming back in, and be there for when he landed back in his spot. I had to do that, like, fifteen times."

THE END OF THE BEGINNING

On a rewatch of the pilot for the season 1 DVD commentary track, Tommy revealed that, as initially scripted, the end of the episode took place entirely in the Mural Room. Not just Josh's apology, the botched negotiation, and Bartlet's deus ex machina moment, but POTUS's closing remarks to his staff as well. "All of what occurred . . . in the Oval," he says, "[originally] took place in that same room where they met with the Christian Right." What made more sense to Tommy was to get the evangelicals out of Bartlet's White House, then bring the staff into what the director referred to as "the sanctuary" of the Oval Office. Aaron agreed.

There, standing behind the Resolute desk, President Bartlet delivers the first ever of too-many-to-count inspirational speeches. Tommy still remembers the first time he came across that uplifting address. "Sitting on the couch in my living room . . . about two in the morning . . . reading the *West Wing* pilot script." He was overwhelmed.

> **PRESIDENT BARTLET**
> Naval Intelligence reports
> approximately 1200 Cubans left
> Havana this morning. Approximately
> 700 turned back due to severe
> weather, some 350 are missing and
> presumed dead. 137 have been taken
> into custody in Miami and are
> seeking asylum. With the clothes on
> their back they came through a
> storm, and the ones that didn't die
> want a better life, and they want
> it here. Talk about impressive.

Closing the script, Tommy couldn't wait to meet Aaron. "My parents are immigrants and he wrote this beautiful speech . . . the essence of what you hope that our leaders feel. In shooting it, you just sort of keep your fingers crossed that you do service to what he wrote."

FAMOUS LAST WORDS

"What's next?" These two words are by now iconic as the final line of the *West Wing* pilot, to the point where we can't imagine it ending any other way. But, as initially scripted, the episode closed quite differently.

```
                     BARTLET
          Josh. "Too busy being indicted for
          tax fraud?" Don't ever do it again.

                      JOSH
          Yes sir.

     Josh exits. The door closes. Blackout.
```

"It was written," Tommy says, "that the curtain would drop as Josh closes the door. That would have been great onstage. It *wouldn't* have been great on a television show, where you're going to go to a car commercial right after." Tommy's vision for this moment leaned toward expanding the scope of the world, as opposed to making it meditative and internal.

As Aaron put it, "Tommy wanted a . . . 'and the world goes on' ending . . . so we could see this is just another day doing business in the White House. He asked me, 'Can we not have the abrupt ending? Can we pull back?' So I said okay and right after Josh goes, I had [Bartlet] shout, 'Mrs. Landingham—what's next?'"

It's kind of a perfect phrase, right? This idea—that there's always another problem to solve, that every day we get up and try to do better, that the work goes on, the cause endures, the hope still lives, and the dream shall never die—embodies the aspirational beauty of politics and service. On the other hand . . .

"He just had to come up with the line," Tommy says with a laugh, "because God forbid someone's not talking for a while."

Aaron, for his part, couldn't have been happier with the way the pilot turned out. "It was incredibly exciting," he said, "for all of us. Especially as you watch all the layers go in. You're there, obviously, during shooting, so you're seeing the performances, and then you're seeing the performances cut together, and then Snuffy Walden's laying down his incredible score and that's fantastic. And suddenly . . . it looks like a TV show."

What had started out as a smoke break in Aaron Sorkin's basement, an idea based on a movie poster pointed out by a friend, had suddenly become a thing in the world. Whether it would be seen as a worthy piece of entertainment—whether it would be seen at all—hundreds of people working thousands of hours had taken one man's inspired words and transformed them into a living, breathing, walking, talking universe.

The questions, then, were these: Who on earth was going to watch this perhaps too-fast-paced show about the slow grind of politics . . . and would they even like it? The answers would come soon enough—fast and not so furious, in fact—from a man named Peter Roth.

TEN

AND IT'S SURELY
TO THEIR CREDIT

I f you love television," Peter Roth says, "you have to love the people that *make* television." And it's true. But sometimes it takes a little effort. Sometimes scripts are late and days are long, sometimes budgets go over or production asks for a crane or a helicopter that you're not entirely sure they need. So, these people that make television, you don't always love 'em . . . but you have to. The former chairman and CEO of Warner Bros. Television Studios, Peter Roth, is passionate and optimistic. Blessed with a keen eye and a kind heart, Peter Roth is one of the good guys.

As the recently tapped president of Warner Bros. TV, Peter had been as closely involved in the pilot as a studio chief gets. Every second of the show's development—from keeping tabs on production to voraciously watching dailies in his office—only increased his love for the project. One might argue, in fact, that Peter Roth was the original "Wingnut." And now . . . the pilot was done. Kinda.

"I remember watching the rough cut with John, Tommy, and Aaron," Peter says. "There was a couch and a fairly large small-screen. We sat there together, the four of us, watching that opening tracking shot of the first walk-and-talk. I remember leaping out of my seat and going, 'Holy shit! This is one of the best things I have ever seen!'"

Asked what about the pilot comes to mind two decades later, Peter didn't blink. "I remember being particularly impressed with Allison Janney," he says. "And that Martin was barely in the pilot . . . just that cameo. I remember watching his entrance and thinking, 'Oh, my God.' So much weight. John Spencer is just extraordinary. It was that perfect combination: a brilliantly written script outstandingly well directed and perfectly cast."

Throughout the screening, Peter's running list of superlatives never slowed to a jog. By the time they reached the finish line, he was legitimately overjoyed, overwhelmed, and . . . conflicted. "Here's the problem, guys," he told Aaron, Tommy, and John. "NBC will never buy this show. It's too fucking good. It's just beyond network. It's too smart . . . there's moral ambiguity left and right . . ." The good news was, Peter Roth had a plan. "I'm going to call Chris Albrecht."

At the time, Chris Albrecht was running HBO, which at that point had only recently begun to dive headfirst into original television programming. In Peter's view, *The West Wing*—with its nuance and complexity, all that "moral ambiguity"—was more in the category of an HBO drama that had premiered earlier that year and would soon take American pop culture by storm. *The Sopranos* centered on New Jersey–based crime boss Tony Soprano and his psychological and emotional struggles with both his family and his, um, "family." It was a project Peter knew well.

"When I was at Fox," Peter told us, "I passed on *The Sopranos*." (**MELISSA:** Wait. Don't judge him yet.) "I love [*Sopranos* creator] David Chase. He was a protégé of my former boss Stephen Cannell, and I know he's brilliant. But I passed because I thought we would eviscerate it on broadcast television. The nudity, the violence, the heart . . . the *brilliance* of it." (**MELISSA:** Passing on *The Sopranos* because it's *too good* is the only sane reason to do it.)

So yes, Peter Roth, defender of all things *West Wing*, grabbed the phone and called up his friend and colleague Chris Albrecht at HBO. "I said, 'Here's the deal. I got this pilot, it's one of the best things I've ever seen. I don't think NBC is going to buy it. Would you take a look?' He said, 'Send it over.'"

Peter then called Garth Ancier, who was president of NBC Entertainment at the time, and said, "Garth, this may be the best pilot I've ever seen. I love it. I don't know that you're going to feel that it's appropriate for broadcast network television. So the only thing I'm going to ask before I send it over is that . . . if you choose not to buy it . . . you consider releasing it so we can position it on a pay cable system, which is not competitive to you, but will enable the audience to see such an incredible piece of work." That was on a Friday.

The following Monday, Peter was in his office at eight o'clock in the morning when his phone rang. "My assistant says, 'Garth Ancier's on the phone.' I remember thinking to myself an old adage of television, of *life*: 'Good news travels quickly. Bad news comes slow.'" Then Peter picked up the phone.

"How dare you insult me like this?" A bit thrown by what he'd just heard, the head of Warner Bros. Television quickly recognized this as one of those rare times when a question like that signals *good* news. "This," Ancier preached to the Peter Roth choir, "is fantastic." Thrilled that NBC apparently wanted to be in the *West Wing* business, Peter graciously replied, "You're absolutely right, Garth. I am so impressed. I knew you'd *like* it, I just wasn't sure you were going to be able to program it."

As soon as he hung up, Peter called Aaron, Tommy, and John to deliver the good news. But somehow, caught up in the whirlwind of that early-morning phone call, it slipped Peter's mind that there was another shoe to drop. Late that night—after eleven p.m.—"I said to my assistant, 'Have we heard from Chris Albrecht?' She says no. So I call Chris, get him on the phone." Albrecht, turns out, offered a muted "Thanks but no thanks."

Peter found it interesting, and frankly a bit surprising, that HBO would pass on *The West Wing*. Ancier, meanwhile, proved to be positively visionary. As Peter put it to us, "Garth had the foresight, the wherewithal, and the taste to realize that *The West Wing* would change the course of broadcast television."

Weeks later, Peter watched the pilot again, this time not as a "rough cut" but in its final form. "In one of the most exciting moments of my career, I screened it with what I call 'the three captains of the ship'—Aaron, Tommy, and John. That was a joyful, joyful moment in my life."

Peter wasn't the only early *West Wing* fan at the studio. One of the most ardent ones was right there in his office. "I remember fighting my extraordinary assistant—and eventual Warner Bros. senior vice president—Jennifer Littlehales, whenever the newest *West Wing* script would come in. We would fight over who could get it that night to read."

As for Jennifer, she weighed in too. "Peter not only watched every episode when the cuts came in; he also raced home every Wednesday night to watch it live, with his wife, Andrea."

The weekly delivery of the *West Wing* script is one of Melissa's favorite memories as well. "Back then, the scripts were hand-delivered in a sealed envelope marked, 'If this seal is broken, contact Warner Bros.' I would go into my bedroom, close the door, and turn off the phone. I wanted to read it start to finish without interruption. I didn't even go through and look for my lines! I'm so grateful I had the sense, even back then, that that was special. The *joy* of it. I still remember the sound of that clunk outside the door. The script is here!"

Now, we should warn you, in putting together this book, we came to understand that not everyone is going to remember things the same way, especially twenty years later. There's bound to be instances of the Rashomon effect. For example, Peter recalls the pilot "testing through the roof" with focus groups, whereas Aaron Sorkin has said, "The pilot did not test through the roof." (So, yeah, there's a bit of daylight there.)

What matters more—and what everyone's memory agrees on—is that, when it came to making sure Peter Roth's favorite new show had a chance to become *your* favorite new show, the studio got creative. Traditional demographics—then and now—are based on gender, age, marital status, income level, etc. . . . The coveted consumer "demo" for studio and TV skews younger, as in "the 18 to 34s" because that group has more disposable income and less brand loyalty. Historically, if your show doesn't perform well in the "key demo" you're off the air before you can change out of your costume. However, as Aaron recalled on the ATX *West Wing* reunion panel, "Warner Bros. very smartly . . . decided to invent four new demographics that had never been used in television before: households earning more than $75,000 a year; households with at least one college graduate; households where they subscribe to the *New York Times*; and finally—this is 1999, this was the most important one—households with internet access."

As Aaron reminded listeners, internet access was not the norm back then. And in 1999—aka "the middle of the dot-com boom"—dot-coms needed platforms on which to advertise. "That's what got us on the air," Aaron says. "Well over half of our ad buys were for dot-coms." So, when your mind wanders to, say, Josh and Toby throwing a hissy fit about Indiana time-zone quirks . . . or C.J.'s inability to brief due to a last-minute "woot canal," be sure to thank the internet for helping get *The West Wing* on the air.

And be sure to thank Peter Roth and Warner Bros. as well. While the marathon haul of a seven-season run would lead to moments of shared triumph, and times of conflict, too, there's no denying the impact of Peter's early and abiding belief in the show. Over the years, that faith would extend beyond the stages of the Warner Bros. lot to many of our causes from the early days and on through the publication of this book. Peter Roth and his former colleagues at Warner Bros. don't have to do that. Supporting *The West Wing* is no longer their job. But they do it anyway. And it's surely to their credit.

★ ★ ★

A SERVICE STORY

Peter Roth

When we talked with Peter about his forays into causes he cares most about, the name he kept returning to was Ava DuVernay. Fans may know Ava best as the creative force behind the critically acclaimed Netflix miniseries *When They See Us*, about the falsely accused New York City teens known now as the Exonerated Five, or from her 2023 film, *Origin*.

PETER ROTH: If you're committed toward making great television, you're constantly on the lookout for the next generation, the next voice, the next opportunity for updated variations on familiar themes. [Filmmaker] J. J. Abrams said to me, "You gotta meet Ava DuVernay." I met her with Oprah, actually, when I was begging them to allow Warner Bros. to become the studio for *Queen Sugar*. Ava is an extraordinary woman, a brilliant leader, a great writer and director. She opened my eyes to the world of the African American experience in a way I had never really seen, never experienced. She taught me things. I went on a rampage in the last two years of my career at Warner Bros. making many, many deals with people of color. My theory was that we've got to bring in alternative points of view here. We've got to open up.

Peter proudly supports Ava's work through her organization, ARRAY, where he sits on the board. Broadening the audience for inclusive, forward-leaning entertainment for film and television, on streaming platforms and in audio as well, ARRAY makes a global impact by producing, distributing, and amplifying the work of Black artists, filmmakers of color, and women of every background.

———

ARRAY

Founded in 2011 by filmmaker Ava DuVernay, ARRAY is a multi-platform arts and social-impact collective dedicated to narrative change. The organization catalyzes its work through a quartet of mission-driven entities: the film distribution arm ARRAY Releasing, the content company ARRAY Filmworks, the programming and production hub ARRAY Creative Campus, and the nonprofit group ARRAY Alliance.

www.arraynow.com

ELEVEN

PROCESS STORIES

Writing *The West Wing*

When it comes to politics, the Zieglers and Seaborns of the world prefer to steer clear of "process stories." Keeping the spotlight on policy, rather than the process behind setting it, is the hallmark of any effective communications team and is best achieved by "controlling the narrative" and maintaining "message discipline." When the focus winds up on the backstage machinations of how the policy gets made, it distracts—and detracts—from the political outcome itself. Then the comms team gets all pissy, and who wants that?

Well, as it turns out . . . *we* do—we love a process story! While political operatives might see only a downside to process stories, we believe there's good reason to dig up a little "inside baseball" dirt on the uncommon way the *West Wing* sausage got made.

There are two things in the world you never
want to let people see how you make 'em:
laws and sausages.

—LEO TO MANDY, "FIVE VOTES DOWN"

In Hollywood—where Ben Franklin's old adage "Time is money" truly came into its own—the concept of "process" is often seen as something to be endured. But a key element in the magic of this show, and the wellspring of some of its greatest challenges, involved a bedrock-level respect for the artistic process. Yes, process was arguably *The West Wing*'s greatest superpower and, at times, its kryptonite.

Kevin Falls is another of those *Sports Night* / *West Wing* crossovers, having served as a writer and co–executive producer on both shows. We asked him how Aaron and his room of writers and consultants worked. "Like no other," he told us.

Most writers rooms comprise a staff whose first job is to pitch ideas to the showrunner. The team then takes whichever stories most appeal to the person at the top and begins a deeper dive into them (all while sitting around a conference table awash in salty snacks, free lunches, and unlimited Fresca or whatever). Eventually, they "break the story," which is writer lingo for coming up with—and mapping out—the twists and turns of the episode's plot, scenes, themes, and so on. Once the story makes its way onto a wall of color-coded index cards (or up on a whiteboard), the episode writer heads off to start typing. Got it? Good. Now forget it. Because that's not how it worked on *The West Wing* . . . not for the first four seasons, anyway.

As Kevin told us, "Aaron wrote every teleplay and came up with many of the stories, but he relied on the writers and consultants to come up with the other storylines in the episode." These, Kevin explained, took the form of writers room–generated memos that would map out a path "with pro and con arguments for any political or governing issues. Oftentimes Aaron came up with his own story, or took it a different way than we laid out."

To get things as close to "right" as possible, Aaron and his team relied on political consultants from both sides of the aisle (folks like Dee Dee Myers, Pat Caddell, Gene Sperling, Marlin Fitzwater, and Peggy Noonan, to name an über-overqualified handful). "Everyone would send in their ideas . . . in memos," Dee Dee told us. "Then Aaron would write the cold open and fax it! We would gather around the fax machine: 'Oh, okay, so that's where he's going . . .' Then he'd want stuff for act one . . ." Knowing what she knows now, Dee Dee laughs. "I didn't have any experience, but I suspected that wasn't how every writers room worked." Because some members of the *West Wing* writing staff had contacts in and around the nation's capital, the room was dialed in to what writer Eli Attie called "a ton of super-smart DC people." As Eli remembers it, "Everyone in political Washington was watching the show and usually quite happy to hop on the phone and offer little plot twists or bits of detail." An impressive list of would-be luminaries included [former Biden chief of staff] Ron Klain (when he was at a law firm after the Gore recount in 2000), [U.S. Secretary of State] Tony Blinken (when he was at a think tank and then on Capitol Hill), and [SCOTUS Justice] Elena Kagan, who was just a lowly Harvard Law professor back then. "One time during season six," Eli told us, "my old pal Jay Carney [then a political reporter, later Obama's White House Press Secretary] dropped in on a production meeting and found himself answering questions about everything from props to set dressing."

The writing inspired an entire generation of political operatives, including me, to go into campaigns and public service. We didn't just want to chart our own paths: We wanted to grow up to be Jed Bartlet, Josh Lyman, C.J. Cregg, Ainsley Hayes. In those characters, we saw firsthand that politics didn't have to be about the loudest voice. It could be about competence, compassion, and selfless service to the country.

—KEVIN WALLING, INTERVIEW FOR *WHAT'S NEXT*

Of course, Aaron's staff wasn't just about Beltway insiders and paid consultants; it was also stocked with accomplished writers whose ability to generate narrative was well-established coming in.

"Paul Redford," for instance, was a "story savant," according to Kevin. "He was the first person you had to get your pitch past." Another member of the staff, Peter Parnell, was—and is—a respected Broadway playwright. Writers Allison Abner and Laura Glasser were eagle-eyed and dogged when it came to mining obscure government legislation (like, say, abolishing the penny) for narratives or quirky mini-arcs, aka "runners." Among the longest-serving writers on the *West Wing*, Eli Attie and Lawrence O'Donnell were what Kevin called "double threats" since they had worked in the actual White House and Senate, respectively, "and were great storytellers, too." Debora Cahn joined the staff deeper into Aaron's tenure, stayed on through the John Wells era, and was described by more than a few folks we chatted with as a "star writer." This list of top-drawer talent, we can promise you, goes on and on and on. So, yeah, it was a damn good staff.

And it was a damn good thing it was a damn good staff because back then, as Kevin tells it, "*The West Wing* burned through as many as five stories per episode." Given that an average *West Wing* season included twenty-plus episodes, that's a whole lot of narrative firewood to burn—and that's just the ones that made it on air. "For every story Aaron liked, ten were rejected. Make no mistake," Kevin revealed, "he was a demanding boss. Sometimes difficult. We had our moments. But great storytelling *should* be hard, and Aaron strived for every episode to be great, not just very good."

While Kevin believes that that constant push for greatness took its toll, the show's MO was the show's MO. "Only when Aaron fell behind did John have some of us write backup scripts. But Aaron rewrote them all." (It's fun to imagine a dusty shelf in some forgotten old back-lot office, on which there exists a bygone multiverse of unproduced *West Wing* scripts . . .) "That was his process and we all understood it."

Felicia Willson certainly did. Felicia was a production assistant who later landed in the writers room, thanks to her talent, a gift for being proactive, and the culture of support that she experienced on *The West Wing*. "It was just this wonderful incubator where people got to learn and grow, where there was a sense of loyalty and mentorship." One person Felicia saw as a mentor was Aaron Sorkin, who collaborated with the fledgling writer in season 2. "At the read-through," Felicia told us, "Aaron would always introduce the episode. On that one, he said, 'For this episode, I'm very proud to be sharing a credit with Felicia Willson.' One second I'm getting coffee, the next I'm getting credit from the most respected writer in television."

Aaron's writing process, for the lucky few who got to experience it firsthand, was a sight to see. Ask director Alex Graves about it, and one image in particular floods back. "I remember going into Aaron's office. He was curled up on his couch under a blanket. I said, 'Hey, what are you doing?' From under the blanket I heard, 'I'm writing.'"

Brad Whitford highlighted another aspect of Aaron's creative process, tying it to what motivates his longtime friend. "Aaron writes like he's on a first date and he really wants to impress. He's gonna throw the kitchen sink at it: 'We're gonna have a really complicated plot and there's gonna be some really funny characters—surprisingly funny, even in very serious situations. And there's gonna be some slapstick. But I don't *just* want to be funny, I will definitely make you cry. And hopefully we're gonna dazzle you so much with that kitchen sink technique that you'll come back next week for a *second* date.' For all his confidence, part of Aaron's brilliance is that underneath it there's this desperate fear of it not working on *every level*." Cultivating, or maybe just surviving, that signature blend of confidence and insecurity drove Aaron Sorkin to deliver, timelines be damned.

Ah, yes. Timelines. The elephant in the room.

Aaron may have no greater champion than his old creative partner, director Tommy Schlamme, who, predictably, leapt to his defense.

"Scripts were late. [But] they weren't late because Aaron was playing golf somewhere. He'd be there in the morning, pacing, trying to figure it out . . . lying on his couch and not knowing what to do!"

And, as Alex Graves points out, it was worth the wait. "I'd go to the Directors Guild and they'd say, '*West Wing* has late scripts, late scripts are terrible!' I was always like, 'I think late scripts are terrible, but if it's Aaron I don't care because when you finally get it, you get . . . Aaron!' And by the time it made it to the table read, nothing would need to change. He'd wrestle with it, wrestle the dragon alone in his office . . . and only then share it with us."

Okay, but when he was in that office, pacing the floor or huddled under a blanket, what exactly went into "wrestling the dragon"? In other words, as Devika Parikh ("Bonnie") once asked Aaron, "How do you write?"

"I write to the sound of the rhythm," he told her. "I hear the music."

This is not terribly surprising. Aaron has a degree in musical theater; his work includes frequent allusions to Broadway and hums along with an often melodic cadence. Throughout our research, so many people brought up the "music" of Aaron's writing.

Words, when spoken out loud for the sake of performance, are music. They have rhythm, and pitch, and timbre, and volume. These are the properties of music, and music has the ability to find us and move us, and lift us up in ways that literal meaning can't.

—PRESIDENT BARTLET, "WAR CRIMES"

Fluently delivering Aaron's language—making it "sing," so to speak—required a mastery of technical jargon and soaring rhetoric and called for steadfast preparation. It also required a bit of natural-born luck. Because, as we've mentioned, there are some phenomenally talented actors who simply couldn't do it.

> **JOHN WELLS:** With the complexity of the dialogue, and the difficulty with the language that's inherent in all of Aaron's work, we knew we needed theatrically trained actors who were going to be able to do it. It's really like putting together a Shakespearean company. You just don't go out and get people who don't do Elizabethan dialogue. We had a lot of actors . . . suggested for different roles . . . where my response, and Tommy's and Aaron's, was just, "They're lovely, they're talented, they can't do this." They can't step into this ensemble where you've got John and Brad and Richard and Allison. We cannot put somebody in there. They'll freeze, they'll feel in over their heads . . .

> **MARY:** I know really wonderful actors . . . some of my favorite actors . . . that don't have that verbal dexterity, and they're *so* talented. It's just not for everyone. You'd see people come in to rehearse and, honestly, ninety percent of the time you were like, "Oh, great, they get it. They have the *West Wing* mouth." But once in a while you'd see someone and, not even two minutes in, you were like, "Oh boy." Deer in the headlights.

> **TIM DAVIS-REED (REPORTER MARK):** My job was to make sure they didn't have to do another take 'cause I couldn't say "Mogadishu."

The dedication required to master the "music" of *The West Wing* is no joke. And not just for *The West Wing*. Jeff Daniels, who played cable news anchor Will McAvoy on Aaron's HBO show, *The Newsroom*, talked about it on the *SmartLess* podcast in 2021.

JEFF DANIELS: I had to work so hard on the first season of *Newsroom*. Harder than I've ever worked. You have to memorize mountains of dialogue and then you gotta spit it out at a hundred miles an hour. . . . You can't learn it in the makeup chair, you just can't. I've seen day players come in on *Newsroom* and they're trying to learn three pages of Sorkin in the makeup chair, and the flop sweat hits 'em. I've never seen it anywhere else. We all go through it, I went through it on episode 5. I got in and I just couldn't keep a word of it in my head anymore. The computer's overloaded and I literally took a knee in the middle of the newsroom and I said, "Gimme the line again." She gave it to me three times. Couldn't say it. They sent me home. We call it getting "Sorkin-ized."

KRISTIN CHENOWETH: One time we were in the airport hangar and I'm talking to sergeants and generals and all, and nobody—in the audience, I mean—expected this girl to be smart because I sound like Betty Boop. I have a three-pager and about the middle of page two, I blanked. And I panicked. But I was not about to let anybody wait on me. So we did it again and . . . same spot—I blanked. You know how you get a block?

MELISSA: Yep, then you start to panic, you get in your head: "Here comes that spot . . ."

KRISTIN CHENOWETH: Here it comes. And *West Wing* dialogue has to be not just fast, but in your mouth and *meaningful*. I was horrified. Then John Wells pulled me aside, and he said . . .

JOHN WELLS: "This has happened to every single person on the set. It's happened to *Allison*. Don't panic. If we have to cut, we will cut."

There's comfort in knowing that you're not alone, that it "happens to Allison." It's not everything, but it helps. John Goodman will tell you that. He was cast as Glen Allen Walken, the GOP Speaker of the House who ascends to the presidency when Bartlet steps down in the wake of Zoey's abduction. One of John's episodes felt like a convention of the show's most stressful elements: a long day, a late night, chunks of dialogue, and a bear of a scene with a ton of actors for the camera to cover. Welcome to *The West Wing*.

JOHN GOODMAN: I had a long speech, might've been a page and a half, two pages. By the time we covered it, it was getting to be two thirty in the morning.

CHRIS MISIANO: I had eight other people in the room, I could cut away and come back, and it would be okay. He'd disappear behind the set between takes and I heard him getting frustrated. I went back to him and said, "John, I just want you to know . . . we're good, I have it." Even for John Goodman, coming to *The West Wing* was this incredible challenge. And then, of course, his performance wound up being *great*.

JOHN GOODMAN: "If you don't do this, you're gonna look really stupid" was great motivation. By the time we wrapped, it was four in the morning. I remember getting to my speech and the coverage was on me—John Amos was there, Martin, Billy Devane—and Bill had his back to the camera. When he got to his speech, he started saying, "Scrambled eggs, scrambled eggs, scrambled eggs . . ." I finally realized that he couldn't remember his lines, but he didn't want us to have to stop filming. Best damn thing I've ever seen.

For Goodman, it was a tough night, in a tough scene, surrounded by actors he admired. And while he pointed to them for making a hard time easier, he reserved most of the credit for the words on the page.

JOHN GOODMAN: The thing that got me through it was the dialogue. The cadence of what I had to say, it was so actor-friendly. It was a brilliant speech. It just felt . . . important, like I was actually *saying* something. That's probably the only reason I could memorize it.

Another widely respected guest star, Oliver Platt, had his own "Welcome to *The West Wing*" moment. And Stockard Channing was there for it.

STOCKARD CHANNING: Aaron had that music in his head, the specificity of the dialogue. You couldn't change a word or anything, which is basically terrifying. It was always interesting when a new person would arrive to do a guest spot, not realizing how stringent the situation was. Oliver Platt—I'll never forget this—they'd flown him in and I guess on the plane he sat there— he's a very brilliant guy—and went, "Okay, I'll change that, I'll change that." And he had a script that had these notes in it. Well, I guess Oliver had had a chat with Aaron in makeup [because when we got to our scenes] he looked ashen. We had a little break and he told me, "Oh-my-God-oh-my-God-oh-my-God! I just took that script I'd marked up and threw it in the garbage!"

OLIVER PLATT: When I finally talked to Aaron, he said, "Just make it your own. I really want you to make it your own." I was coming a little bit more from the movie world, where scripts are a lot more fluid. I'm flying in on the plane . . . sort of crossing stuff out and going, "You know what, I'll probably say this instead." We get to the rehearsal . . . and everybody's arrayed around this table and, you know, Aaron's just very kindly introducing me, and then he's reading logistical notes. Marty, who I'm sitting next to, raises his hand, just stops everybody out of the blue—he very clearly had a question about the script—and Aaron walks slowly back around, looks over his shoulder, and Martin literally says, "You know, I really think that this is"—and I'm not exaggerating here—"I think this is a 'but,' not an 'and.'" Aaron looked down at the page . . . it was probably only for about fifteen seconds, but it felt like an hour . . . and then he finally said . . . "Let me think about that," and then he slowly walked out. My flippin' blood froze because I had eleven pages of dialogue the next day that I had sort of like very loosely committed to memory. It was sort of poetic justice that my character was supposed to be incredibly tired in that first scene, having stayed up all night because, in fact, I had.

Dialogue coach Hilary Griffiths often found herself in the role of "verbatim police."

HILARY GRIFFITHS: Often, guest actors would come in and they had been told by Aaron to "make it your own." Then, during the first rehearsal they'd realize, "Oh, when he said 'make it your own,' he didn't mean the dialogue, he meant the character." So, a lot of them were kind of unprepared, and they'd look at me, horrified.

ROB LOWE: There's so many different actors of stature who have worked with Aaron. I don't think everybody can do it. You can have all the Oscars you want, it doesn't mean you can do Sorkin.

To try and bring a unique, alternative way to it is kind of a fool's errand . . . unless you're Richard Schiff.

TOMMY SCHLAMME: Brad Whitford and Josh Malina are built for Aaron Sorkin. They just are. Other people—Richard Schiff is not built for Aaron Sorkin, but he's brilliant at doing it.

MARY: Richard Schiff is that actor who does the line reading and you're like, "Oh no, that's not how it's supposed to go!" And then he finishes and you're like, 'Oh crap, I wish I'd thought of that.' He changes the music and somehow it's *better*!"

MELISSA: Some actors aren't used to such rigidity and struggle with it. They prefer to play around with the dialogue, in hopes of making it feel more "natural" to them. And that's fine. It's just not how it was done on this show. That wasn't the process.

ROB LOWE: I get it. It's very fulfilling to find it, to make it your own. But on *The West Wing*, there was the fun and fulfillment of executing a *strategy*. Like a wide receiver in the NFL. You know what the routes are, it's not backyard touch football. You take discipline and pride in running a perfect route.

Speaking of the "perfect route," let's talk walk-and-talks . . .

TIM BUSFIELD: It wasn't just style. It was, the scripts are long, but they're *great*, how are we gonna get all the words in? We're gonna put it on the move and the second someone finishes a line, the actors have to speak. Aaron wanted to hear his words, but he's a team player. He lets his producers produce and his directors direct. That's how those walk-and-talks really happened. Not just because Tommy was trying to do something cool. The walk-and-talks became the best way for us to get shows on time.

MIKE HISSRICH (PRODUCER): God bless the Steadicam, because without it and the walk-and-talks to keep that thing on the move while you're telling people how the census works, how would you ever have made that show?

DAVE CHAMEIDES (STEADICAM OPERATOR): When you can sit three feet in front of John Spencer with your eye on an eyepiece and watch him chew up a scene and be so unbelievably natural and talented—it's a gift. Steadicam-wise, they always used to joke that we danced together, but there was a reality to that.

KATHLEEN YORK: I remember one of my first days on the job doing a walk-and-talk down the hall to the press room . . . and being told that "there are no pauses in dialogue allowed after a comma in a sentence . . . only after a period." Richard then nodded to me—"Get ready." I realized, *Holy hell*, I'm going to have to deliver all of this involved dialogue while moving down miles of corridors <u>and</u> not pause for half a second? GEAR UP, brain.

ALLISON JANNEY: I loved the walk-and-talks because they were very much like doing a play. It was just so exciting, knowing you were on a good team. You had people who could throw the ball, catch it, and toss it back. I had never had an experience like that with so many people coming to set totally with their A game.

TIM BUSFIELD: Tommy would rejigger the logistics of it—"Come out of the Oval Office, go in here, Rob'll flow in, Brad will pick it up, we'll dump off to Spencer, then Richard, he hands off to C.J., C.J. to Danny . . ."—then Aaron would rewrite to those specifications.

ALLISON JANNEY: There were only so many hallways you could turn down. This one time we had a particularly long walk-

and-talk, so we had to turn to go down the same corridor again. The set-dec people would pop in and quick-change a photo so when we came back around, it would look like a different hallway!

TIM BUSFIELD: C.J.'s office would often be at the end of walk-and-talks . . .

MELISSA: And Danny would often be in C.J.'s office.

TIM BUSFIELD: . . . and being at the end of one of the walk-and-talks is the *worst*.

MARY: Yes! Because it's yours to blow! It's like being a kicker in football, I don't want that pressure! I *hated* Kate Harper showing up at the end of a walk-and-talk. If you screw it up—

TIM BUSFIELD: If you screw it up, you'd hear it all the way back at one: "WHO WAS IT?!"

MARY: I remember facing my first *West Wing* walk-and-talk. It was horrible. I mean, I have a decent memory and I also come from theater and I come prepared. I wasn't gonna show up in the Situation Room with Martin Sheen and John Spencer and not know my words. But the walk-and-talks, even if you knew it, when you joined it last and everyone was nailing it, the pressure just mounted.

AARON SORKIN: We would always root for Allison to screw it up.

ALLISON JANNEY: Are you serious?!

AARON SORKIN: Yeah, because we're three rooms away with headphones on, and you would just have the best reactions to that moment when you just tripped over a word.

ALLISON JANNEY: I'd be all "arrrghhhh!!!"

AARON SORKIN: And then you would say, "Aaron, is there any chance the word is *actually* pronounced that way?"

Given how stressful these sequences were for series regulars, the pressure they put on guest cast had to have been immense. Casting director Tony Sepulveda remembers a situation with fan-favorite *West Wing* guest star Mark Harmon.

TONY SEPULVEDA: When I cast Mark, I went to visit him in his trailer and he was nervous—the walk-and-talk was his first scene. It became infamous in the circles of actors . . . because the cast could do it in their sleep.

Could they, though? Well . . . maybe one of 'em.

KRISTIN CHENOWETH: The walk-and-talks, that's where I'd thrive because it's like theater.

MELISSA: It's choreography, right, you're sticking it. It's like the high-wire act of theater: Everything is riding on it and there's nowhere to hide. Which is why having a stage background—like Kristin did, and Dulé, Allison, Richard, really everyone, from the top down with Aaron—was especially helpful.

DULÉ HILL: In the beginning, once I knew it was about the pace and I saw the show and looked at the dialogue, I heard the *song*, that Aaron's music is written as a song.

KATHLEEN YORK: If I could make a music analogy, Aaron writes in a six/eight time signature when television audiences were used to four/four.

DULÉ HILL: In life, there's very few times that people are just continuously talking, where there's no interjections, no breaks, no stutters or stumbles. Aaron's great at catching all that, the rhythms of life. If we take the time to listen, it is all music, it is all rhythm. It really is a big orchestration. It's a cacophony of sound . . . and then it all comes together. "C.J." "Josh?" "Yes, Mr. President." "Charlie, will you get this?" "Yes, sir." It's all rhythm.

MARTIN SHEEN: With Aaron, part of my motivation was to honor him because there was no one else—there is no one since—writing like that. I wanted him to know how much we valued that. John Spencer felt this way too . . . we all did. We loved him, we loved his work, and we were going to do the very, very best we could with his lines. We wanted to make sure he knew how seriously we took his work and how much we wanted him to *know* we loved it.

The "music" of *The West Wing*—the sound of Sorkin—could be challenging, for everyone from core cast to guest stars. Be it a walk-and-talk or a soaring rhetorical address, the lush language required focus and practice and painstaking work. Then again . . .

"Art," as Broadway's late, great Stephen Sondheim famously wrote, "isn't easy." But for folks like him and a certain musical theater major named Aaron, there is no other way. What's been said about Sondheim has been said about Sorkin too: that an exacting sense of "down to the last detail," while difficult, is actually kind of simplifying. 'Cause everything you need to know—the words, the notes, and how they sound—is right there on the page.

The Wrap on Casting

The impact that casting had on *The West Wing* is hard to over-sell. It was not an easy show to populate. The series regulars were one thing. But to consistently uncover guest artists who could hit the ground running and handle the language without missing a beat was a weekly triumph of creativity and vision. From John Levey and Kevin Scott to Tony Sepulveda to Laura Schiff, the show's casting directors demonstrated how critical a component their creativity was to *The West Wing*. Because it's not just about choosing the perfect piece to fit seamlessly in with the rest of the puzzle. Sometimes it's about choosing the right shoes.

Josh Einsohn was a full-on Wingnut when he joined Laura Schiff's team at the start of season 5. (Then a casting associate, he went on to become the casting director for this teeny-tiny NBC show called *This Is Us*.) Working with Laura, Josh quickly learned that, when it comes to casting, thinking a bit outside the box can play as dramatic a role as finding the perfect match. Case in point . . . Annabeth Schott.

Ultimately, the role of Annabeth came down to Kristin Chenoweth and a well-known dramatic actor, both of whom, Josh told us, could absolutely handle the inherent challenges of the show's dialogue. "One would fit in exactly like you'd think on *The West Wing* . . . and then there was Kristin." When Laura returned from the meeting where the decision was finally made, Josh could hardly contain himself. "So . . . ?"

The people in the room, Laura told him, had gone back and forth . . . until she had started thinking out loud. "Sometimes I'll go shopping and see the cutest black shoes. 'Oh my God, those are gonna go with everything I own!' And I love 'em, so I grab 'em and take 'em home. And they *do*—they go with everything I own. But they're kind of like all my other black shoes, and I think, 'You know what? I should've bought the pink shoes.'"

"That's how Kristin Chenoweth was cast on *The West Wing*," Josh told us. "She was the pink shoes."

TWELVE

BREAK TIME

Okay, time to press pause. We're going to go full Bartlet on you, look you square in the eye, and break the bad news: We will not be covering every single episode of *The West Wing* in this book. Or even every "iconic" one. Or even every so-called classic moment. There are not nearly enough pages in this book to dig down into all the hopeful-moving-dramatic-funny-romantic-bantery-big-block-of-cheese moments that were served up over seven seasons.

We're not going to do a deep dive into the fact that C.J.'s too sexy for her shirt, her skirt, or the other things . . . or that Charlie will always put his body between danger and Zoey when out at a Georgetown bar. We won't be delving into what gave President Bartlet the poker-faced guts to "shut it down" or how Leo wound up in Cuba, face-to-face with Fidel. We will be unable to accommodate your desire to get more than ankle-deep into Toby's various crushes on the Andy Wyatts and poets laureate of the world . . . or why we fell for the gender-neutral-name bait-and-switch—Joey Lucas . . . Ricky Rafferty— every time. Similarly, we regret that we cannot punch your ticket to

the Donna Moss v. Amy Gardner bout or devote more than the scant-
est of seconds to Sam Seaborn quotes both silly . . .

> Well over three and a half centuries ago, strengthened
> by faith and bound by a common desire for liberty, a
> small band of pilgrims sought out a place in the New
> World, where they could worship according to their
> own beliefs—and solve crimes.
>
> —SAM SEABORN, "SHIBBOLETH"

. . . and sublime:

> 'Cause it's next! 'Cause we came out of the cave and
> we looked over the hill and we saw fire. And we
> crossed the ocean. And we pioneered the West. And
> we took to the sky. The history of man is hung on a
> timeline of exploration, and this is what's next!
>
> —SAM TO MALLORY, "GALILEO"

You're not going to find any paragraphs here exploring Josh's secret
plan to fight inflation, Toby's solution to save Social Security, or Kate
Harper's proposal for peace in the Middle East. (**MARY FUN FACT:** *The
Jewish Journal of Greater Los Angeles* got on board with that proposal,
suggesting real-world politicians embrace its central tenets and referring to it as "the Harper Plan." Swear to God. I remember where I
was—the grocery store, actually—when I saw that cover story. It's the
rare show whose storylines are endorsed as a viable peace plan, and the
importance of it was not lost on me. Kudos to John Wells and his staff
for writing *The West Wing* into the leading edge of political discourse.
I'm still stunned that it's possible to write that sentence.)

Finally, if you're hoping to find within these pages genuinely so-phisticated analyses of the nighttime basketball game from season 1 or the daytime hoops from that Camp David summit episode, we're sorry to say it, but you're out of luck. On the other hand, we won't be going into Zoey dating that Jean-Paul guy, so there's an upside too.

We're happy for the trees saved by not having written a ten-thousand-page book, and we hope you'll enjoy the upcoming deep dives into what we consider some stellar "key episodes." For the record, we'd love to have written more—and who knows, maybe there's a sequel in our future. After all, a wise man once said, "Every time we think we've measured our capacity to meet a challenge, we look up and we're reminded that that capacity may well be limitless."

Okay. Break's over. Let's unlock our first "key episode" . . .

THIRTEEN

KEY EPISODE

"In Excelsis Deo"

Collaboration is essential to making television. It's essential to making a whole host of things. Policy. A family. A functional PTA. With the possible exception of stand-ups and golf pros, nearly every person reading this works in a field that requires a measure of collaboration. It's unavoidable. But it isn't always easy.

Richard Schiff calls "In Excelsis Deo" one of the greatest episodes of *The West Wing.* He's not alone. The show's tenth effort ultimately saw Aaron Sorkin and Rick Cleveland walk off with the Emmy for Best Writing in a Drama Series. It saw Richard leave the Shrine Auditorium stage clutching a statuette for Best Supporting Actor. And while the road to getting there was among the rockiest the series ever saw, the fits and starts that led to that triumphal September night make for one hell of a story. Actually, *more* than one.

The first of what would become a string of beloved *West Wing* Christmas episodes, "In Excelsis Deo" wove together a handful of narratives, including a yuletide shopping jaunt to a rare-book store; a well-intentioned (if ill-advised) visit to everyone's favorite call girl–slash–law student; a press secretary grappling with what she considers her "ridiculous" Secret Service code name, and, of course, one man's tire-less attempt to provide a deceased unhoused veteran with the venerable military burial he deserves. (Add to that a glorious rendition of "Little Drummer Boy" and this one was destined to be a classic.)

The unhoused veteran storyline constitutes the heart and soul of the episode and was inspired by Rick Cleveland's father. On *The West Wing Weekly* podcast, Richard Schiff aptly described the former play-wright as "a great writer . . . who has gone on to have a wonderful ca-reer." (With credits ranging from *The West Wing* to *Mad Men*, *Six Feet Under*, and *House of Cards*, the great Rick Cleveland's résumé speaks for itself.) But in the days leading up to filming "In Excelsis Deo," there was a lot going on within the overall production of *The West Wing*, which was still in its infancy.

While Aaron was locked away writing episode 8 ("Enemies"), Chris Misiano was editing his *West Wing* directorial debut, "Mr. Wil-lis of Ohio." Tommy, meanwhile, was hip-deep in putting finishing touches on the early episodes of season 1. So, when Alex Graves showed up to prep "In Excelsis Deo," it's only mildly surprising that he was told, "Yeah, we can't talk about your thing now." It was a bit of a whirl-wind. Then came the table read.

"This was the first time we ever read a script that Aaron didn't finish first," Richard told us. With production working on multiple episodes, and Aaron hunkering down with other scripts, the team was looking to speed up the writing process. That meant "In Excelsis Deo" made it to the read-through before, as Richard says, "Aaron got a chance to okay it."

Richard felt it was "a lovely story." He respected the place it came from and championed the issues it supported—the plight of homeless-ness and the way veterans ought to be treated and so rarely are. The problem, in his view, was that the perspective from which the story was initially written didn't line up with who Toby was at his core.

The Toby in that first draft—called to the scene by police who'd found his business card in the dead man's secondhand coat—came across as reluctant to get involved. He didn't exude the reverence Richard instinctively felt the situation demanded. The script even had him cracking jokes. It didn't make sense to him. "I know that Toby was . . . from the get-go . . . a little harsh in his opinions and not the most open person in the world," Richard says, "but I thought I was creating a character that felt things very, very deeply, and who cared extraordinarily about things."

As Richard recounted it to us, after the read-through a van drove the cast from the set to the other side of the lot. He was unusually quiet. Looking to break the tension, Allison turned to him and said, "This is a really great episode for you!" Richard looked up at her and, as he put it to us, "just kind of went off" about the script. While it was undeniably a major showcase for his character, it bothered him that Toby was so blasé about something so profound. Frankly, it offended him. That's what he told Allison, if in less polite terms. "Then, clearly Allison must have told Tommy because . . .

"Tommy came over to the trailers," Richard remembers, "and he said, 'I hear you're upset.' And I just started crying." Turning to Tommy, Richard asked, "Is this what America is seeing from my character?" Deploying the soft touch he'd exhibited after the actor's initial audition, Tommy calmed him down. "Listen," he said, "we're going to work on it; it's going to be fine." This dynamic would play itself out regularly throughout the early seasons of the series.

As Richard admitted to us, "Tommy and I would get into real healthy fights." The good news, according to Richard, is that those temporary conflicts always resulted in a better understanding of the story and the character of Toby. For both of them. It's part of why Richard considers Tommy not just a phenomenal director, but a remarkable person. "He can see what's happening in the human being that's creating the role. It's not a puppet show for him." After his heart-to-heart with Tommy, Richard regained his composure. Then Aaron showed up.

"I started crying again. And he says, 'We're gonna fix this.'" What Aaron recognized in Richard's reaction to the material, and what he appreciated about this deep-feeling actor, is a desire to dig down past the language to find what Richard calls "the stuff underneath." Aaron took the grace notes of Rick's beautiful story and made them sing in a key that felt right to both the character of Toby and the actor who played him.

"He wrote something very simple," Richard would reflect years later. "It's really only four or five scenes that I'm in . . . but it was from the correct perspective." That said, while Aaron retooled the essence of the original story, Richard's quick to point to Cleveland as the one who put the ball in play. "Someone comes up with a great idea and gets it going, they deserve credit."

What started out as a moment of crisis for Richard turned into what he calls one of the most satisfying creative experiences of his seven-year *West Wing* run. "It was problem solving, from all collaborators, from all sides."

> PRESIDENT BARTLET
> Toby, if we start pulling strings
> like this, you don't think every
> homeless veteran will come out of
> the woodwork?
>
> TOBY
> I can only hope, sir.

This episode is special to us for a number of reasons, but at the top of the list is the simple fact that it involves a community both of us revere and have spent time working with. "In Excelsis Deo" shines a light on veterans and a number of issues that impact them—and their families—in a very real way. One of those people was guest star Tom Quinn.

Tom Quinn's *West Wing* turn as the unassuming veteran running a VA-sponsored kiosk on the National Mall was brief but powerful. His humble heart-and-soul performance reminded Richard of a segment of society he's often empathized with—"people who have not been heard, not been paid attention to. I loved that actor. I absolutely loved him."

In addition to being an actor Richard loves, Tom Quinn was a military veteran. Richard knew because he asked him, but he also says, "You could see it. He blew me away . . . the simplicity and depth he had, just in his face." (**MELISSA:** If you pay extra-close attention to this scene, you can spot the unspoken "Thank you for your service" embedded in Richard's "Merry Christmas." **MARY:** A lot of *West Wing* episodes warrant a rewatch, but you'd be hard-pressed to find a scene more compelling, or more moving, than the one that features Tom Quinn.)

And you'd be hard-pressed to find an actor more comfortable playing *uncomfortable* than Richard Schiff. Never has that discomfort been more plainly on display than in the classic *West Wing* scene he shared with Paul Austin. It's a scene Richard says helped him unlock who Toby was. That's thanks, in no small part, to Austin's portrayal of George Hufnagel, the brother of the deceased veteran. "Shooting that episode," Richard says, "I connected to the homelessness storyline, to the idea of not being seen, not being respected. And I was so affected by him. He just captured the problem of communicating so, so beautifully." Let us set the stage . . .

Under an overpass, dozens of unhoused men have taken refuge against the bitter winter cold. Toby's seeking someone—anyone—who may have known the deceased vet who wound up dead on a bench in his old overcoat. Pointed in the direction of a man—"He's all right and everything, he's just a little slow," we're told—the White House head of communications struggles to communicate to Mr. Hufnagel that his brother, Walter, has died. Eventually, Toby manages to say, "I'm an influential . . . person, I'm a very . . . powerful person." But he can barely get it out. He's embarrassed by the words, by the idea of saying them out loud. As he looks away, his twitchy fingers graze his down-turned face.

"I remember putting my hand to my head," Richard told us. "That gesture . . . it just happened. Then I repeated it from all eighty-nine angles Alex shot. I wanted to make sure that that moment lived every time because it defined Toby. He was someone who's embarrassed by the fact that he's a powerful man, and who understands how useless that can be."

Tommy Schlamme loved this moment of generosity that Richard and director Alex Graves captured on-screen. In an appearance on *The West Wing Weekly*, Tommy found his way into the head of Toby Ziegler: "It costs me everything to have to tell you . . . that I'm impor-tant. That's not something I do. But, somehow, I need to do that for you." In describing what he considers simply "an amazing piece of acting," Tommy pointed out the paradox of what Aaron and Richard and Alex managed to so beautifully communicate: The act of saying something that, ninety-nine percent of the time, would be construed as all about ego was, for Toby, the ultimate act of humility.

If forced to pick just one more story to cap off the chapter on this iconic *West Wing* episode, there are a number of paths we could take. We might explore the fact that Alex Graves, in his very first time di-recting the show, was "terrified of actors," or that he consulted with the Arlington National Cemetery official who oversaw all the funerals and answered every one of the young director's questions. ("What happens after they fold the flag?" "When do they fire the salute?") We could dive into Gail's goldfish bowl to shout out set decoration (Ellen Totle-ben) and props (Blanche Sindelar) for their first-ever thematic nod: a tiny Christmas tree set in snow-white gravel, a miniature poinsettia perched on top. God knows we could dedicate a few pages to the earliest explicit reference to the romantic feelings between Josh and Donna. (It's Alex's lingering shot of Josh peeking out his office door as Donna rereads the inscription he wrote in the alpine skiing book.) But we're not going to do any of those things. You know why?

Because of the Mrs. Landingham speech, that's why! Alex? Take it away . . .

ALEX GRAVES: "In Excelsis Deo" was short. So, Aaron wrote the scene where Mrs. Landingham talks about how her sons were killed in Vietnam. We were filming and the ADs came to set and handed out the scene. I remember seeing the dolly grip standing there—guy's fifty years old, big guy, sweetheart of a guy. All of a sudden he starts crying. Then somebody in the Mural Room starts crying. Somebody starts crying in the hallway. Because they're reading the scene.

The scene, if you don't remember, has Charlie and Mrs. Landingham in her office just outside the Oval, talking about Christmas and the sons he never knew she had. In a beautiful, halting piece of acting from Dulé, Charlie asks why the twins—Andrew and Simon—didn't get a deferment from Vietnam to finish medical school. Then Kathryn Joosten breaks our hearts:

```
            MRS. LANDINGHAM
    They didn't want one. Their father
    and I begged them, but they wanted
    to go where people needed doctors.
    Their father and I begged them,
    but you can't tell kids anything.
    So they joined up as medics, and
    four months later they were pinned
```

down during a fight in Da Nang, and
were killed by enemy fire. That was
Christmas Eve, 1970. You know, they
were so young, Charlie. They were
your age. It's hard when that
happens so far away, you know,
because with the noises and the
shooting, they had to be so scared.
It's hard not to think that, right
then, they needed their mother.
Anyway . . . I miss my boys.

No wonder the dolly grip was crying. In singing Aaron's praises, Alex put it to us well: "This guy, when tasked with writing an extra scene, would step back and go, 'How do I elevate the whole thing in a page or two? How do I go to the next level, how do I climb even higher, just because I've got a little issue, like the episode is short?'"

And that kind of says it all. What felt special to us about working on *The West Wing* is captured in that level of commitment. No matter the size of your role or the length of your service, if the people in charge constantly go the extra mile, you can't help but ask yourself, *What can I do to make this work? How can I be fearless in the face of fits and starts to make this better?* The answer, as we see it, is . . . by matching that commitment. By doing what you can to elevate whatever it is you're working on. And, when in doubt, by looking for the wisest person in the room . . . and giving her something to say.

FOURTEEN

A SERVICE STORY

Richard Schiff

R ichard Schiff wants you to know something. He's not an activist.

RICHARD SCHIFF: I'm very moved and impressed by people
who I consider to be genuine activists. Like you two and Martin
and other people I've met along the way. Activism is something I
really respect, and I don't have. I'm a recluse, I don't like going
out into the world. When I do, I'm being pulled by people I love,
who expect something from me. So, I don't consider myself a real
activist even though other people might look at some of the
things I've done and define me as such. I know activists, I'm not
one of them. It's like, I know baseball players and I play
baseball . . . but I'm not a baseball player.

That said, veterans' causes, represented so movingly in "In Excelsis
Deo," reside close to Richard's heart and, as he puts it, "entered into
my psyche, so to speak, from a very young age."

RICHARD SCHIFF: "In Excelsis Deo" had a very profound effect on me. Growing up, I was really antiwar. I went to Washington and marched when I was thirteen or fourteen. Got my first joint on the train. I remember feeling for the servicemen, the veterans coming back from Vietnam would be spat at, heckled, and yelled at. I didn't understand the vitriol. If we are against the war and don't want to go to war ourselves, why are we aiming our venom at the person who had nothing to do with it, who was drafted?

When we spoke to Richard about his experience with service, he deflected and underplayed his role. But the fact is, his affinity for the men and women of the military, captured so beautifully in "In Excelsis Deo," has been a part of who he is for decades. From his teenage years protesting the war in Vietnam to his continuing work as a Justice for Vets / All Rise ambassador, Richard's commitment to separating the war from the warrior, and his support for military personnel and their families, is unwavering. Our conversation continually wound up in the neighborhood of one of the most important things any public figure can bring to an issue he cares about. Exposure.

Exposure is something Richard brings to another cause close to his heart—the American Civil Liberties Union. (Close observers can spot an ACLU poster on the wall in Toby's office.) Asked what appeals to him most about the mission of the ACLU, Richard points to its commitment to bipartisanship.

RICHARD SCHIFF: I've always been impressed with the fact that they really shouldn't take—and they mostly have not, as far as I know—political sides in defending the Bill of Rights and due process for whomever. Going back to the Nazis' right to march in Skokie [Illinois]. You have to be completely on the side of the Constitution and what it stands for, regardless of whether you like the message or not.

My stepfather was a civil rights leader and a lawyer for Martin Luther King. He was on the negotiating committee at Attica. And he [spent time] defending Mafia people and drug dealers. At one point, I said, "How can you defend these people?" and he goes, "Because when due process is violated, that is the end of freedom. As soon as Miranda is violated, as soon as your rights under the law are violated, it's over." I never forgot that.

For Richard, as complicated as issues of crime and punishment often are, his belief in the mission of the ACLU, and his appreciation for that mission, is simple and clear.

RICHARD SCHIFF: Whoever is in a trial under this justice system has to be awarded those rights. The ACLU is the only organization that protects them . . . and takes on causes that are not very easy. What they protect—due process and the Bill of Rights—is foundational to who we are.

(Toby Ziegler—and that poster in his office—would be proud.)
A few years ago, Richard found a unique way to put his passion for the ACLU into action when he met Meegan Lee Ochs, the artist relations manager at the ACLU of Southern California.

RICHARD SCHIFF: I approached Meegan at an ACLU dinner and said, "I've always thought that I could make money for someone signing pink Spaldeen balls."

Yep. The Spaldeens Toby would bounce off his communications office walls. And if you ever wondered how that came to be . . .

RICHARD SCHIFF: I once said to Aaron, "If you ever need Toby trying to figure a thing out; a confounding puzzle or some thing where the dots didn't connect—have him bouncing a Spaldeen in his office." A Spaldeen was the ball the kids in Brooklyn used for handball, stickball, stoop ball, et al. It was the inside of a faulty Spaulding tennis ball we'd buy for a nickel from a bin in the candy store. I said to Aaron it would be an ode to Steve Mc-Queen bouncing a baseball in the prison cell in *The Great Escape.* Aaron loved that movie. And the idea. It came to fruition many episodes later with "17 People."

Who knew, years later, after appearing on *The West Wing Weekly* podcast, I would have people sending me a ball to sign. So I offered that up to Meegan as a way to raise some money.

Meegan loved the idea, and Richard soon grabbed his Sharpie and he's been signing Spaldeens ever since. (Some of you may already have one, but if you don't, go here: www.aclusocal.co/spaldeen.)

The Spaldeen isn't the only *West Wing* element with staying power. We hear all the time that, two decades later, *The West Wing* is still relevant, thanks to certain policy-driven storylines.

RICHARD SCHIFF: There are issues today that of course remain colossal and overwhelming, even more so than they did back in the day of *The West Wing.* There are some things that Toby, the realist and practical tactician, could have tolerated in the hope of incremental change for the better over time. And then there are those issues to which Toby would have erupted in fury at the stupidity and rigidity of those blocking real and effective change. I too am—to use a Toby-ism—flummoxed by it all.

As we speak, the world is in crisis after crisis, and in a constant state of insufficient preparation for and response to a barrage of emergencies: out-of-control fires, hurricanes, tornadoes, floods. I would *ask* what Toby would <u>scream</u>: "What in the hell is the end-game strategy of those denying and preventing action?

What is going on in their brains? And how will their grandchildren regard them as the world falls deeper into chaos from mass migration as food sources shift and deserts expand and coastal cities are under the level of the sea?" I don't get it.

Is global warming a real environmental condition, or merely a temporary anomaly? Is it a global threat, or the exaggerated claim of alarmists? The time for such debate is over. As of today, it shall be the unequivocal position of the United States government that global warming constitutes a clear and present danger to the health and future well-being of this planet and all its inhabitants.

—SAM TO GINGER AND BONNIE, "THE DROP IN"

RICHARD SCHIFF: What would get Toby even more riled is that now that the world has begun the slow process of moving to alternate energy sources, why doesn't corporate America dive into that opportunity and dominate the market before it's too late? It makes sense from a strategic business perspective. You can make a fortune and save the planet as a bonus!

I believe, in this moment, that it's critical to go all in and support organizations like EDF, the Environmental Defense Fund. They focus on pollution reduction, energy transition, and establishing sustainable food and water supplies, among other things, and their reach is around the globe. I think Toby would approve.

While Richard can appreciate the value of shining a light on this cause or that, doing so "feels like not enough after a while." But he forgets the seismic impact of that. He forgets this: The light is crucial. It's how we get people to pay attention to and care about an issue. "Attention" can mean raising awareness in our own communities, via word of mouth or social media. By organizing, getting creative, and raising our voice. By shining the light on where the story is. You can be active . . . even if you're not an activist.

THE ACLU

The American Civil Liberties Union was founded in 1920 and is the United States' guardian of liberty. The ACLU works in the courts, legislatures, and communities to defend and preserve the individual rights and liberties guaranteed to all people in the United States by the Constitution and laws of the United States.

www.aclu.org

ENVIRONMENTAL DEFENSE FUND

Guided by science and economics, and committed to climate justice, the Environmental Defense Fund works in the places, on the projects, and with the people who can make the biggest difference.

www.edf.org

FIFTEEN

THE GOSPEL ACCORDING TO SNUFFY

S top off at any gas station or convenience store in the American South and you'll be sure to spot the name "Levi Garrett & Sons." It's everywhere. As far back as the 1950s, Levi Garrett was already a major manufacturer of powdered tobacco, more commonly known as "snuff," which is how the musician who went on to compose some of television's most heralded scores came to be known as W.G. "Snuffy" Walden.

William Garrett Walden inherited the nickname from his mom (and her dad), both of whom had been called "Levi" or "Snuffy," thanks to their surname, Garrett. The Snuffy that *we* know, the one whose majestic theme marked seven seasons of *The West Wing* and whose lush scoring provides connective emotional tissue throughout every single episode, remembers seeing "those little snuff cans" in old stores in Texas. He also remembers when he came to carry on the traditional family nickname.

"I picked it up because my parents sent me and my brother off to a camp every summer." The first day there he was told, "Well, we can't call you Garrett, that's too formal. We'll call you Snuffy." He was five years old.

More than four decades later, he had cemented himself in the rock-and-roll world as W.G. "Snuffy" Walden. Having spent a chunk of his life spinning vinyl on underground radio and playing guitar in strip joints, he eventually found a home, touring onstage and recording in studio alongside the likes of Stevie Wonder, Donna Summer, and Chaka Khan. But after years of that long, strange road trip, he landed on a new path and embraced what would become the two guiding forces of his life: sobriety and service.

"I was in Sydney, Australia—Christmas 1981. I looked in the mirror and realized I was an alcoholic. That's the last drink I ever took." At home three weeks later, Snuffy got a call to go back on the road. "I knew if I went, I would die. So I had to choose life over music. I put music down. I never intended to play again."

From there, Snuffy devoted himself to recovery—going to meetings, working the program, being of service—and to helping himself by helping others. After a while, he was able to get back to his music, but it wasn't easy, and he didn't expect it to be. "The first time I had to go fill in for somebody, I took my sponsor with me. Ten minutes before I went on, he thought I was in the bathroom doing blow. He found me in front of the urinal, praying."

Snuffy may have given up on music for a spell, but music hadn't given up on him. That's the thing about a calling. It keeps calling back. "Five years into sobriety, I didn't even know scoring TV and film was really a job. I was a rock-and-roll guitar player gunslinger." But as soon as he began writing music for the screen, it became evident that Snuffy Walden had the Midas touch.

He composed scores for high-profile project after high-profile project, from the paradigm-shifting *Thirtysomething* to the coming-of-age hit *The Wonder Years*. "I went from zero—not even knowing what the job was—to doing the two top shows on television."

It was these successes, and a string of follow-ups, that led Snuffy to the doorstep of Aaron Sorkin and Tommy Schlamme, who were in the early days of their first collaboration, making *Sports Night* for ABC. "Aaron was a huge fan of *Thirtysomething*," Snuffy told us. "He didn't want to do an acoustic guitar show, but he wanted it to be guitar. So, we did *Sports Night* with electric guitar, à la Eric Clapton."

The beauty of Aaron, Snuffy realized, is that, when it comes to music, he's instinctively emotional. He has an unusual way of evaluating compositions for his work on-screen. As Snuffy put it to us, "He either doesn't like it . . . or he cries."

As season 1 of *Sports Night* was drawing to a close, Aaron approached Snuffy and said, "Listen, we're doing this show I've had around for a while—it's a political show—and I'm kind of hearing . . . Americana guitar music." Snuffy replied, "Well, I'm your guy."

Not long after, Snuffy was messengered the pilot script. "It was incredible—Aaron's whole opening sequence was amazing—and I'm thinking we're doing an Americana guitar score for *The West Wing*." A couple of months later, just as the editing process was coming to an end, Aaron called Snuffy back, singing a different tune.

"Listen," he said, "we've been laying in John Williams music, big orchestral music, and it's working really great. What do you think about that?" What Snuffy thought about that is . . . (a) he didn't read music, (b) he'd never written for an orchestra in his life, but (c) he wasn't about to miss out on this project just because of a and b, and so . . . (d) he said, "Sure."

Given his lack of orchestral experience, Snuffy called up his friend James Horner, who had composed spellbinding scores for numerous films, including *Glory* and *Field of Dreams* and *Titanic*. As Snuffy studied the handful of scores that Horner sent over, he noticed a pattern. "What struck me was that there was always—at the core—this simple melody; a melody beautifully orchestrated for a full orchestra. I knew I could do *that*. So, I hired one of the best orchestrators in the business and started writing."

Weeks later, Snuffy was in the thick of scoring *The West Wing*'s first three episodes. Toward the end of the third one, "A Proportional Response," a wide-eyed Charlie Young quietly marvels at the solemn grandeur of President Bartlet's imminent Oval Office address to the nation. For that moment, Snuffy told us, "I wrote this little theme."

Around that time, Tommy Schlamme dropped by the studio to see how the music for the show was coming along. "I played him some of the cues," Snuffy told us. "Then I played him *that* cue. He said, 'Play that again!' I played it again and he said, 'That's the theme, that's our theme!' And then he added, 'We need it this week.'"

With the words "this week" ringing in his ears, Snuffy knew there wasn't enough time to expand that "Charlie in the Oval Office" cue into a full opening theme, orchestrate it, and get network/studio approval before recording it. So he got together with his orchestrator and laid down a version of the main theme with just a synthesizer. (**MELISSA FUN FACT:** None of the first four episodes features the orchestral version of the *West Wing* theme. They used the synthesizer rendition until episode 5. **MARY FUN FACT:** For the truly-madly-deeply nerdy, check out that early synthesizer version, then go bask in the full-on orchestral glory that is the main title sequence in season 1, episode 5.)

According to Tommy, once they'd secured the requisite sign-offs, "we went and got a seventy-piece orchestra." For the scoring session, Snuffy gathered dozens of musicians in a large studio on the Warner Bros. lot. Then . . . Aaron showed up. "I was about to do the first run-through," Snuffy told us, "and I said, 'Aaron, I'm gonna play it for you. See what you think.'"

As Snuffy sat there, "on pins and needles," he couldn't get this out of his head: "God, they're gonna hate it!" But then the orchestra played through the main theme, all the way from that opening flourish to the lofty, airy denouement at the end. "I turned around . . . and Aaron's got a tear in his eye. That was all I needed. The biggest thrill of my life with him."

As richly textured as the orchestrations proved to be, if you listen closely and strip away the instrumentation, the key element truly is its simplicity. At least that's how Snuffy described it to us. "It's like a little gospel piece. It's not as grand a fanfare as it sounds. It's really a very simple melody—just orchestrated beautifully."

When we asked Snuffy what made him call it a "little gospel piece," he didn't tell us. He just ducked off and, moments later, was back with his guitar. Listening to him play the *West Wing* theme, simply picking it out on his acoustic guitar, we found this pared-down version was incredibly moving. It was like a prayer. (If you want to hear it, check out the "Hartsfield's Landing" reunion special. Snuffy plays it on acoustic there, too.)

Despite the constant temptation to go to the well of that ascendent main theme, over the seven seasons of the show Snuffy nearly always resisted it. "I'd try to put it in there, but nine times out of ten I chose not to. A lot of times, if you've got a theme that feels iconic to people, you use it every week. I did the exact opposite. I didn't want to wear it out."

Instead, he reserved the *West Wing* theme for big, sweeping moments and, even then, did so sparingly, only once or twice a season. "I used it when Martin was walking down a long tunnel or a hallway going to a speech or something."

That restraint extended to every part of scoring the show, Snuffy acknowledges; the key was to "stay out of the way of Aaron's words, which I learned how to do."

Given his level of respect for writing, his depth of humility, and his comfort with being just a part of a greater whole, it's no wonder Snuffy Walden found a landing spot in the *West Wing* universe. (And given his talent, it's no wonder he's scored over a hundred projects—including Mary's own show *In Plain Sight*—and has won twelve Emmys . . . and counting.) But even as we talked with him about his distinguished career, Snuffy never lost his sense of perspective. "I wouldn't have any of this," he said to us, "without sobriety."

Ask anyone remotely familiar with him and they'll tell you, Snuffy is a musician, and a soul, whose mantra is "How can I be of service?" That instinct to keep pushing forward, to serve others, keeps him on track and keeps his life fulfilled, musically and otherwise. It is an instinct for helping his fellow travelers, asking them—and, by extension, himself—the age-old question . . . what's next?

★ ★ ★ BIG BLOCK OF CHEESE STORY ★ ★ ★

One Heart with Courage

On June 4, 2016, several members of the *West Wing* cast arrived in Anaheim, California, to attend the closing ceremony of the world's largest conference on addiction, recovery, and justice reform. Convened by All Rise (NADCP at the time), the conference brought together thousands of treatment court professionals from across the globe for four days of education and inspiration.

We were there that day to honor Martin Sheen for his unmatched contribution to the treatment court movement by inducting him into the treatment court hall of fame. This is the highest honor bestowed by All Rise and the treatment court field.

Martin cared about treatment courts before most people had ever *heard* of them. As All Rise CEO Carson Fox told us, "It is easy to forget that, back in the early 1990s, the idea of *treating* rather than punishing people who came before the courts due to a substance use or mental health issue was radical." But not for Martin. He understood that what these individuals truly needed was treatment, support, and hope. "Martin's advocacy in those early years, his continued support for all treatment courts, was instrumental in taking this program from compassionate experiment to the most successful justice intervention in our nation's history."

In 2011, I had the great fortune to appear on Hardball
*with Martin to talk about treatment court. He spoke
with such passion and respect. I remember getting home
to a flood of messages from the community in Buffalo
wanting to get involved and support the program.
That is a* real *impact.*

—THE HONORABLE ROBERT RUSSELL,
FOUNDER OF THE FIRST VETERANS TREATMENT COURT

In addition to honoring Martin, All Rise saw that year's conference as an opportunity to recognize the *West Wing* cast members who had done so much to elevate the issue of treatment courts in the public consciousness. For their work, they would be named Justice for Vets / All Rise ambassadors. Mary, Dulé, Allison, and Richard all came to Anaheim to accept their awards in person and to honor Martin's life's work in championing treatment courts. (Janel and Brad were unable to attend and were deeply sad to miss it.)

As part of Martin's induction, each cast member tried to express in just a few words our profound appreciation for what he had done for us and for so many others.

When Martin hit the stage, he had tears in his eyes. He then delivered a soaring acceptance speech, brimming with humility and gratitude. He thanked treatment court professionals past and present who "work, day in and day out, to restore lives and restore hope." He called them "the embodiment of Robert Kennedy's declaration that one heart with courage is a majority."

Martin closed with a powerful call to action, with words borrowed from a treasured poem by Nobel Prize–winning Indian poet Rabindranath Tagore:

And such courage lifts up our nation and all our people
    to that place
Where the heart is without fear and the head is held
    high, where knowledge is free.
Where the world has not been broken up into fragments
    by narrow domestic walls.
Where words come out from the depth of truth,
And tireless striving stretches its arms toward perfection.
Where the clear stream of reason has not lost its way
    into the dreary desert sands of dead habit.
Where the mind is led forward by thee into ever
    widening thought and action.
Into that heaven of freedom, dear father,
LET US ALL AWAKE!

Postscript: Hey. It's Melissa. The day we inducted Martin held an extra dose of magic for me. My parents were there. As mentioned previously in the book, my dad fought for treatment courts from the early days of the movement. He believes what Martin believes: No one is beyond hope. That my father and mother were able to attend this ceremony to honor a champion of a cause near and dear to their hearts, was—and remains—deeply meaningful to me.

SIXTEEN

KEY EPISODES

"What Kind of Day Has It Been?" and
"In the Shadow of Two Gunmen: Parts I and II"

"Who-got-shot-who-got-shot-who-got-shot?!"

That frantic question, audibly gasped in triplicate, came courtesy of *West Wing* superfan Genevieve Smith Whitford. Otherwise known as "Brad's mom," she perfectly captured the collective anxiety that hung in the air for fans from the harrowing final moments of season 1 to the two-part premiere of season 2.

Following the town hall meeting that ends *The West Wing*'s inaugural season, President Bartlet exits the Rosslyn, Virginia, venue to camera flashes and screeching fans, only to have gunshots ring out around him, his staff, and the Secret Service detail tasked with his security. Season 1's pandemonious closing seconds are a blur of sirens, lights, and screams and serve to tee up season 2's pulse-pounding cold open. C.J., Toby, and the rest of the West Wing staffers—rocked off their feet and staggering about in stunned disbelief—attempt to orient themselves amid the chaos. The question of "who got shot" is, of course, on everyone's mind.

At the time Genevieve Whitford posed that question—six o'clock

Pacific, on season 2's opening night—her son Brad was on the *West Wing* set on the Warner Bros. lot.

Brad had arranged his schedule so he could call his mom when the premiere aired back east. "I told her, 'I think we should watch this together.'" (She apparently didn't take the hint.) "I got on the phone with her when the teaser was playing," Brad remembers. "And she was so upset about Martin, so upset. When it was revealed about me being shot, she said, 'Oh my GOD—I HAVE TO GO!' and just hung up."

Another woman in Brad's life also had strongish feelings about that sudden twist of fate, if for different reasons. Janel Moloney. "I was really hoping you weren't going to be killed," she said to Brad. "I mean, if you die, I'm out of work."

As for Brad himself, ask about "In the Shadow of Two Gunmen," and his mind goes straight to the previous episode. "I remember the end of season 1"—filming the assassination attempt at Rosslyn—"we didn't know who got shot." Then, as Brad remembers it, during the summer hiatus Aaron called him up and broke the bad news: "It's you."

"And he said it like it was a compliment!" Brad told us. "In that moment, all I could think was, *I'm unemployed . . .* But Aaron quickly reassured me that Josh would survive."

Heading into production on that final episode of season 1, Tommy Schlamme had also been in the dark about who got shot. In fact, as he revealed to us, "*Aaron* didn't know." They had, of course, discussed various scenarios, but to that point Aaron, Tommy, and John Wells had not yet decided who would be wounded in the attack. Aaron had asked Tommy to film the sequence in a way that would give them the freedom, in the season 2 premiere, to choose any of the main characters as the victim(s). Naturally, leaving their options open meant returning to the literal scene of the literal crime, which is why, months later, cast and crew wound up right back at the Newseum in Rosslyn, Virginia.

Among the too many stories to count from this trilogy of *West*

Wing episodes was, of course, that explosive, dramatic assassination attempt and the high-end production values it demanded: The colorful slabs of the Berlin Wall visible from the viewpoint of the gunmen firing down into the crowd. The explosive audiovisuals of wailing people and police cars, of shattered bubble-tops and orders shouted in the night: "Close the airports, shut 'em down!" There, armed with a bull-horn and cranes, Tommy Schlamme stood tall, in all his budget-busting glory, amid chaos and sirens and faux-panicked background, directing a helicopter shot. Tommy remembers that night vividly. High up on a scaffold, looking out over this massive assassination sequence, he turned to Aaron. "I can't believe they're letting us do this!"

As for the aftermath—the thrilling teaser of season 2—*The West Wing* shot past midnight and into the next morning. "That moment where Richard finds Josh," Tommy pointed out on *The West Wing Weekly,* "the sky's a little blue because the sun was already coming up." In the face of real-life police ordering production to "wrap out," this big-time network television crew instantly became what Josh Malina would deem "a guerrilla unit."

"People are wrapping," Tommy recalled with a bit of subversive glee. "They're *loading trucks.*" Even some crew were unaware that Tommy and his team were continuing to shoot. "We didn't call action," the director remembers, "I was just rolling." In fact, that alarming moment when Toby falters, spotting Josh, that moment his voice breaks . . .

> **TOBY**
> I need a . . . I need a doctor! I need help!

. . . was shot pretty much under the gun. "We were a student film that didn't have a permit," Tommy says. "We just had to shoot really quick before the police came and threw us out!"

The twin arrivals at the hospital—first, the president, then his deputy chief of staff—kick off what becomes a dual-track narrative over the next ninety minutes. Smooth, clever transitions between the medical crises and a series of "origin story" flashbacks help track how President Bartlet, Leo, and his merry band of brothers and sisters came to be.

There's Josh, working for then senator John Hoynes, on a stroll with ex–Secretary of Labor McGarry. "That Spencer walk," Brad said during one rewatch, "God, I love that."

Soon we land on Sam (and his sleek, chic specs) soullessly protecting oil companies from litigation for WASPier-than-thou corporate law firm Gage Whitney Pace. Then, after grabbing a "fresh" morning hot dog with his old pal Josh, Sam bumps into a woman on the street. This leads us out of flashback and back to the hospital, where Sam just bumped into the nurse in charge. (As Aaron said on the DVD commentary for this episode, "Nice cut, Schlamme!") And speaking of the hospital . . .

Filming on a repurposed set from John Wells's *ER*, the panning cameras landed on a slew of quick vignettes: Zoey beside herself to see her dad alive; Jed on the stretcher, kissing Leo on the cheek; the first lady revealing her husband's MS to Dr. Lee. ("Tell the press, don't tell the press, it's entirely up to you.") Perhaps the most memorable one of all involved Donna, whose naked relief at hearing the president's encouraging prognosis is quickly washed away by her discovery of Josh's dire one. Martin Sheen considers this "one of the most extraordinary performances Janel gave in the history of the series."

As far as Tommy was concerned, the sequence Janel calls "my favorite scene I ever shot" was a heavy lift. Having entered the waiting room on edge, but with little to no intel, Donna ends up at a point of total devastation. On one take Tommy gave Janel this piece of direction: "You are walking through the door knowing that something else bad has happened and you are not being told." He then explained, "If you come in that loaded, by the time the shoe falls"—in other words, once she's told that Josh also got shot—"you're right there with it." And she was.

For Donna's critical exchange with Toby, Tommy walked over to Richard and whispered in his ear. Then, while the cameras were on Janel, and Richard was off camera, he surprised her with a line of dialogue that wasn't in the script. Instead of delivering the dialogue as written ("Donna. Josh was hit."), Richard said, "*Brad . . . he died.*"

"I loved that!" Janel remembers. "It was a wonderful creative surprise and the greatest thing in the world for an actor is to be surprised." That's true, but it only works if the actor is emotionally primed and completely in the moment; if she's able to receive that surprise and authentically react to it. In the hands of a less talented, less prepared actor, that moment wouldn't have happened. In the end, Donna's response played like a dream.

> **TOBY**
> Donna. Josh was hit.
>
> **DONNA**
> Hit with what?

A few scenes after this sober give-and-take with Donna, we discover that Toby is quite adept at casual, confident drunk-flirting. That's what we find him doing in *his* flashback in that smoky bar in Nashua. This moment kicks off the "Bartlet campaign" storyline, the ups and mostly downs of that first presidential run.

More impressive even than Toby's unflagging confidence in the face of a winless election record is the range we get to see from the actor smoking his cigar. As the Toby sitting with his colleagues in the ER waiting room, Richard was somehow twelve types of brooding. Now, at Hank's Tavern, Toby vacillates between vaguely drunk and a funny sort of fatalistic. Except when he goes to Hollywood to recruit C.J. to

the team. Then he's positively giddy . . . because C.J. just fell into
the pool.

As far as physical comedy goes, Allison's talent is hard to top. The
banister, the treadmill, we've said it more than once. But it would be,
shall we say, shortsighted, if we neglected to mention, even fleetingly,
that glorious spill into the pool. While Allison refers to that moment
as "not the sexiest coming-out-of-a-pool scene ever filmed"—the slip-
sliding, panicky file-tossing . . . the shrieks and bubbles and gasps . . .
her imploring Toby to "avert your eyes"—we could watch it all night
long. Take a look at that . . . then turn your eyes to this:

Back in the present, standing at the press room podium, just hours
clear of an assassination attempt she can scarcely recall, a dazed C.J.
stares into camera flashes and a throng of media shouting out questions.
Somehow, with a seeming total lack of effort, Allison Janney manages
to play foggy and shaken and snarky and fun, all at the same time:

> C.J.
> We're confirming now that a suspect
> is in custody, and is being
> questioned by federal law
> enforcement. At this time, we
> cannot—we are not releasing any
> information whatsoever about the
> suspect.

> STEVE
> C.J., can you tell us anything—his
> name, where he's from, ethnicity,
> if you guys suspect a motive?

> C.J.
> Yes, Steve, I can tell you all
> those things, because when I said
> we weren't releasing any
> information whatsoever, I meant

```
except his name, his address, his
ethnicity, and what we think his
motive was.
```

Ha! No wonder Danny gave her the goldfish.

While "In the Shadow of Two Gunmen" is chock-full of scenes worthy of deep dives, there are a few more here that truly stand out. Like this one. We'll call it . . .

MEAN BARTLET

The sequence featuring a cantankerous Governor Bartlet surrounded by unfamiliar staffers was, as Tommy tells it, really fun to shoot. "Our whole thing in the pilot was, 'You're over the hump, you've all been working together . . . in the trenches together—you are *family*.' We spent the whole year doing that . . . and all of a sudden we're in a scene where nobody knows anybody." Bartlet's cranky side is at DEFCON 1 because, as Aaron told Martin, "Leo's the only one in the room whose name you know and who you like!"

```
              GOVERNOR BARTLET
       Which one is Josh?
```

A close eye on this scene reveals an apprehensive staff. "Everybody," Tommy says, "is playing four steps back." Given the show's history, it's an interesting dynamic to watch and a challenge to capture on film. To the cast—to Martin in particular—the director offered insight: "We've fallen in love with this president because he trusts the people around him so much. Here's a man who we now <u>have</u> to believe simply does not trust these people. I mean, really, *genuinely*, 'I don't want these people around!'"

In Aaron's mind, this flashback was pivotal for another reason. "To make it clear to the audience that this—right now—isn't the Bartlet you've watched for a whole year. This is the Bartlet before he *changed into* the Bartlet you watched for a whole year."

The scene ends with a sarcastic outburst from the candidate. It was born, at least partially, from what may seem like a matter of . . . dramatic logistics. As Tommy put it to us, during the writing phase he had gone to Aaron and said that to better set up the episode's last moment, he'd like him to hit a particular line of dialogue one more time, to keep it fresh in the minds of those watching at home. "That's why," Aaron revealed, "I wrote this . . ."

```
                GOVERNOR BARTLET
        I understood the point. We're going
        to South Carolina to set up
        Illinois. When I ask, "What's
        next?" it means I'm ready to move
        on to other things, so—what's next?
```

(**MELISSA:** This flashback! This episode—not only are we getting the origin stories of all the characters, we're getting the origin story of Bartlet's signature phrase! **MARY:** And of our book title!)

After a year of Josh being bathed in the warm embrace of the president, Brad loved witnessing this different side—of both men. "It's so interesting to see Martin play an angry scene. He's such a sweetheart."

Outside a VFW hall in New Hampshire—actually the back lot at Warner Bros. on a street set from *Gilmore Girls*—the two old friends argue about the composition of Leo's handpicked campaign staff. Jed's not president yet, of course, and it shows in his behavior, and Leo's too. In this moment—an exasperated Bartlet asking why his friend is doing this, why he'd pushed him to run—Tommy directed Leo to walk away. "There was something in watching Bartlet pursue him. He has to follow Leo." Damn right, he does. How else would we get to see Spencer whip around and hit us with this classic *West Wing* moment?

> LEO
> Because I'm tired of it, year after
> year after year after year having
> to choose between the lesser of
> "Who cares?" Of trying to get
> myself excited about a candidate
> who can speak in complete
> sentences. Of setting the bar so
> low, I can hardly look at it. They
> say a good man can't get elected
> President. I don't believe that.
> Do you?

That was a seminal moment in what many consider the key "love story" of *The West Wing*—the one between best friends Jed and Leo. But the show's *other* love story had its own origin story in the season 2 premiere . . .

THE JOSH-DONNA "MEET-CUTE"!

Remember the first time these two laid eyes on each other, at Bartlet for America HQ, when Donna kept lying about what she was doing in Josh's office? ("When I said I was assigned to you . . . I may have been overstating it a little.") As originally scripted, despite going on for several pages, the whole bit took place right there. According to Aaron, Tommy suggested that they put the scene on its feet. "I wanted them to have their first walk-and-talk," the director recalls.

Wending past vending machines and in and out of hallways, among bright-eyed low-level staffers, Donna stammers out the story of her sketchy medical student boyfriend and her equally iffy college career.

Tommy had good reasons for turning this sequence from a scene set in an office to a walk-and-talk taking us through campaign HQ, including that it would make the artful doling out of Donna's backstory a bit more visually dynamic. But the most interesting reason, to us anyway, is that it served to tee up its ending. "You so wanted that moment to be still," Tommy points out, "and if it all had been still *before* that, it wouldn't have been nearly as profound." This moment here:

> JOSH
> Donna, this is a campaign for the
> Presidency, and there's nothing I
> take more seriously than that. This
> can't be a place for people to come
> to find their confidence and start
> over.

> DONNA
> Why not?

> JOSH
> I'm sorry?

> DONNA
> Why can't it be those things?

Twenty-six seconds (and ten lines) later, a phone rings. Josh nods. Go ahead. She answers. Without another word, he hands Donna her credentials and Snuffy plays us out.

A WIN, A LOSS . . . AND THE AIRPORT SCENE

Okay, let's cut to the chase: Just as news breaks that Governor Bartlet has secured the Democratic nomination for the presidency, and within seconds of Josh's request for some celebratory Doobie Brothers, Donna breaks news of a different kind: "Josh—your father died." Now at the airport, catching a flight home for his dad's funeral, a dazed Josh looks up to see a trio of identically suited men fanning out around him. This is the moment it dawns on canny viewers that, as his party's nominee, Bartlet—who's just walked into frame—is now eligible for Secret Service protection. It's also when the audience realizes they're finally getting a peek at the folksy, benevolent Bartlet they'd come to know in season 1.

When Brad and Martin first rehearsed this scene, they were directed to take "your father died tonight" out of the equation. Tommy wanted it to simply be "two men talking to each other, who are lonely in the middle of the night and just wanna . . . share a drink." As the scene downshifts, Bartlet admits he's been a "real jackass to you, Josh. To everybody. Toby Ziegler, C.J. Cregg, Sam Seaborn . . ." Always looking to puncture the sentiment, Aaron then came in with the closer.

> GOVERNOR BARTLET
> You gotta be a little impressed
> that I got those names right just
> now.

Watching that moment with Aaron for the season 2 DVD, Martin, who's famously bad at remembering names, wondered if it was some sort of inside joke. "Did you write that for me?" he asked. (He had, Aaron admitted.) Martin couldn't stop laughing. "That's a Martin-ism, less a Bartlet-ism!" But back to the airport . . .

The soon-to-be-POTUS has just asked Josh, "You want me to go with ya?" (On the plane. To attend Josh's father's funeral.) He then starts checking his pockets in search of his wallet. A mix of stunned, moved, and charmed, Josh tells him, "Governor. *California*. You have to go to the ballroom and give a victory speech in prime time and go to California!"

As Bartlet watches Josh head down the Jetway, Leo walks up.

Seconds later, Jed turns to his best friend in the world, looks him square in the eye, and says, "Leo? I'm ready."

But on the day they filmed that scene, the director had an idea. Once they'd gotten the shot of Jed saying, "I'm ready," the camera turned around on John Spencer for Leo's reaction. Tommy pulled Martin aside and privately told him that, while off camera, he'd like him not to say the line as written. Instead, he had Martin look at his friend—at John—and say with purest authenticity, "I couldn't do this without you." To Tommy, the reaction that line elicited from John looked for all the world like he was saying . . . *I'll die for you.* Then the two of them, Jed and Leo, walk off to the sound of a soaring prime-time victory speech . . .

> GOVERNOR BARTLET (V.O.)
> Tonight, what began at the Commons
> in Concord, Massachusetts, as an
> alliance of farmers and workers, of
> cobblers and tinsmiths, of
> statesmen and students, of mothers
> and wives, of men and boys, lives
> two centuries later as America! My
> name is Josiah Bartlet, and I
> accept your nomination for the
> Presidency of the United States!

. . . and a restrained rendition of the *West Wing* theme. This leads directly to . . .

THE LAST WORD(S)

When it comes to the final moment of this episode—a groggy Josh waking up from double-digit hours in surgery—there's a lot we could tell you. We could tell you it's arguably a top three all-time last line of a TV show. We could tell you Aaron admits that "too often" he can get "carried away emotionally," and, as proof, we could tell you that he had initially scripted this scene with Josh surrounded not just by the doctors and Leo and President Bartlet, but by C.J. and Sam and Toby . . . the whole gang. We could tell you that Tommy interceded and advised Aaron, "We can make this an adult thing. It's not the end of *The Wizard of Oz*." But what we really want to tell you is this: Sometimes the simplest approach is the most moving.

When President Bartlet leans down to hear the strained whisper of Josh—his deputy chief of staff and surrogate son—he tells Leo what he heard:

> **PRESIDENT BARTLET**
> He said, "What's next?"

SEVENTEEN

I CAN'T BELIEVE IT'S NOT BUTTERFIELD!

One of the hallmarks of *The West Wing* has always been its insatiable appetite for honoring service. (See also: the concept of this book.) But the appeal of the show isn't just that it honors service. It's that so many of the people who inhabit its world *serve honorably*. While any number of *West Wing* characters could be described as having done so, there may be no purer example of "serving honorably" than the hyper-sincere head of President Bartlet's protection detail, Secret Service agent Ron Butterfield. His mix of quietly heartfelt and tell-it-like-it-is was pretty tough to beat.

Over the years, through conversations with his character's real-life counterparts, Michael O'Neill—the actor who imbued Butterfield with uncommon stillness and understated dignity, the actor Brad Whitford calls "an absolute ringer"—developed an abiding respect for the men and women of the Secret Service, who put their lives on the line every single day.

"What we don't understand about Secret Service agents," says Michael, "is that their entire function is to cover and extract. They don't add a gun to the scene, that's another deadly weapon. They immobilize the president—or whoever their charge is—fold him in half, cover him, and move him out of harm's way, knowing that one of them is likely going to take the bullet. They have to trust the other three to stop the *next* bullet from being fired."

Thanks to movies and mythology, this is one of those things we tend to take for granted. But it's truly remarkable. Their mission is so deeply ingrained in them that they remain true to presidents of either party. They divorce themselves from their personal politics, in the same way that soldiers do. It's an extra layer of patriotism to disagree with everything a person stands for, and *still* say, "I will jump in front of a bullet. I will give my life for yours." It is an understanding that the continuity of government is more important than any one individual. More than just protecting the president, they're protecting the *presidency*.

Not long after landing the role of Agent Butterfield, Michael O'Neill mentioned the exciting career news to his old high school football coach. In a rather fortuitous instance of "I know a guy who knows a guy," that coach put the actor in touch with one of the key, if lesser-known, figures in modern presidential history. As Michael described it to us . . .

"He said, 'Oh, you should talk to my cousin Jerry Parr!' I said, 'Yeah, I *should* talk to your cousin!'" The late Jerry Parr was the Secret Service agent credited with saving Ronald Reagan's life during the March 30, 1981, assassination attempt outside the Hilton Hotel in downtown DC. Michael didn't waste a minute in dialing up Jerry Parr—and, man, is he glad he did.

"Jerry took me through the entire moment-to-moment of the assassination attempt. From the first shot fired—which I think hit press secretary James Brady—to pushing Reagan into the car." (The bullet that struck President Reagan ran down the side of the presidential limousine and slipped just inside the open door. Jerry Parr referred to the bullets fired that day as "cheap"—cheap enough, anyway, to fragment.

"It was," Michael told us, "one of the fragments of a bullet that actually hit the president.")

As Parr shoved Reagan in and threw his own body on top of him, the limo screamed out of the hotel drive, which, at that point, had been thrown into chaos. A vehicle carrying additional agents peeled out after the limo to form a high-speed two-car motorcade. Protocols mandated that the agents secure "Rawhide"—that was Reagan's Secret Service code name—in the safest place possible, the White House. As Michael told us, "They called it the 'Corral,' they were trying to get him back to the Corral."

Inside the speeding limousine, as Parr described it to Michael, his training kicked in, along with a rush of adrenaline. Thinking he'd cut his lip, President Reagan was dabbing it with a paper napkin from the luncheon they'd just attended when Parr observed bubbles in the blood, indicating it was oxygenated, "which meant a lung shot." Parr immediately did what Michael O'Neill referred to as "the critical search," which is when you run your hands up along the back of the head, then down, then to the chest, the sides—to try to locate the entry wound.

Confirming that Reagan had indeed been hit, Parr instantly called the agent in the pursuit car behind him. "Bronco, we have a problem!" Parr then made the snap decision to divert the limousine from the White House to George Washington Memorial Hospital. (Feel free to tell us, faithful *West Wing* viewers, when this all starts to sound eerily familiar.)

Not long after hearing Parr's astonishing account of this consequential piece of American history, Michael shared his peek behind the Secret Service curtain with Aaron Sorkin, who asked, "Uh . . . can *I* talk to him?" With the help of Bob Snow, the show's Secret Service advisor, and the boots-on-the-ground insights of Jerry Parr, close observers of *The West Wing* will tell you it's pretty clear Aaron had his notepad handy. But, on the off chance your memory isn't quite what it used to be—and, really, whose is?—here's an excerpt from what Aaron came up with for the season 2 premiere, "In the Shadow of Two Gunmen: Part I."

```
INT. LIMOUSINE — NIGHT

President Bartlet and Special Agent Ron Butterfield
are in the back of the moving limo.

                         PRESIDENT BARTLET
        Is anybody dead back there?

                         AGENT BUTTERFIELD
        We don't know, we don't think so.

We see Ron's bloody hand, wrapped with some
bandage.

                         PRESIDENT BARTLET
        What happened to your hand?!

                         AGENT BUTTERFIELD
        I got hit.

                         PRESIDENT BARTLET
        Oh God!
        (to the driver) Coop, turn around!
        We gotta go to the hospital!

                         AGENT BUTTERFIELD
        We got to get you to the White
        House.

                         PRESIDENT BARTLET
        We're going to the hospital!
        Let's go!
```

                    AGENT BUTTERFIELD
          I have to put you inside the White
          House, Mr. President. This isn't
          something we discuss.

                    PRESIDENT BARTLET
          This is . . . My daughter is
          throwing up on the floor in the car
          behind us. You're losing blood by
          the liter, not to mention God knows
          how many broken bones you got in
          your hand, but let's make sure that
          I'm tucked in bed before we do
          anything . . .

Blood has started coming out of the President's
mouth.

                    AGENT BUTTERFIELD
          Mr. President?

Ron quickly checks the President for a possible injury. He
feels blood near Bartlet's stomach.

                    AGENT BUTTERFIELD
          G.W.! Blue! Blue! Blue!

The limousine makes a quick 180-degree turn.

   Speaking with Michael O'Neill, it was hard to miss the reverence
he feels for the real Agent Butterfields of the world. You could hear it
in his voice. As he revealed to us, "I still can't say, 'BLUE, BLUE,
BLUE!' without getting, ya know . . . messed up."
   Maybe the reason so many found the earnest compassion of his
Ron Butterfield so convincing, so real, is that for him it wasn't an act.
To call attention to these exceptional men and women, whose every
instinct has them fading into the shadows, Michael O'Neill raised his

voice—often quiet, always direct, and something like paternal—to shine a light on their honorable and unsung heroism.

★ ★ ★

SECRET Service postscript: In the spirit of ending on a lighter note— and dominating your next Wingnut Trivia Night—here, now, is every West Wing Secret Service code name we could come up with. (If the über- geeks in your office find any we missed, have them @ us. We could use the excuse for a reprint.)

> *President Bartlet—"Eagle"*
> *C.J. Cregg—"Flamingo"*
> *Sam Seaborn—"Princeton"*
> *Jed and Abbey's grandson, Gus Westin—"Tonka"*
> *Arnold Vinick—"Big Sur"**

And our personal favorite . . .

> *Zoey Bartlet—"Bookbag"*

---

* Like the sound-editing category in your Oscar pool, "Tonka" and "Big Sur" are the ones that'll put you over the top on *West Wing* Trivia Night. (You're welcome in advance.)

EIGHTEEN

A SERVICE STORY

Janel Moloney

J anel Moloney and Melissa originally became friends on one of their first days together on *The West Wing*, just after the pilot got picked up. Melissa happened to be leaving the set as Janel was coming in to shoot some Donna scenes.

> **MELISSA:** She walked up to me and asked, "Are you Melissa? Someone said you do a program for kids. I want to volunteer." I'll never forget it. She didn't know me, we hadn't even *met*. She just sought me out, ready and determined to jump in and get involved.

Later that week, the two *West Wing* assistants got coffee and talked for hours about Voices in Harmony, the LA-based youth-mentoring theater program Melissa co-founded. Janel began helping out at Voices in Harmony workshops and volunteered to be an official tutor, getting matched with a high school student named Karla Nunfio. They continued working together when Karla moved on to Santa Monica College.

KARLA NUNFIO: I'd tell Janel what issues I was having, what subjects I needed help with, and she'd walk me through it. She was very supportive of me—and very passionate about what she was doing. We would get coffee once a week, sometimes she'd pick me up for school . . . she even got to know my family! Janel became a mentor figure for me.

Over those coffees, Janel and Karla would talk about family or her film class, as well as the differences in their backgrounds and the common ground they shared.

KARLA NUNFIO: Through her belief in me, I began to see beyond my small circle, to set goals and dreams I never would've set for myself otherwise.

Karla spent time studying TV and film production. These days, in addition to her work as a financial advisor for soon-to-be retirees, she freelances as a production coordinator.

KARLA NUNFIO: My time at Voices in Harmony—and with Janel and Melissa—changed my life. I am forever grateful.

Years later, when Melissa was working with All Rise, Karla told her, "Whatever I can do for you guys, I'll do it." Melissa wasn't shy about taking her up on the offer. Since then, Karla has served as a member of the team at All Rise for their annual conference, as production coordinator on a number of PSAs featuring the *West Wing* cast, and as a key volunteer for the Voices of Uganda project. Which brings us full circle . . . back to Janel.

JANEL MOLONEY: When Melissa and her team took a version of Voices in Harmony to war-torn Uganda for the Voices of

Uganda project, a nonprofit called International Medical Corps
played a pivotal role in making it happen. I was inspired to learn
more about—and support—the critical work they do. International Medical Corps provides health services and medical training to communities that desperately need it. They made it possible
for Voices of Uganda to reach and support former child soldiers
and other displaced children who have experienced unfathomable loss and suffered unspeakable tragedies. I wanted to be part
of that effort.

Janel has always been especially drawn to causes that promote the
empowerment of young people. Another nonprofit she supports is
closer to home: Riley's Way Foundation.

JANEL MOLONEY: My friend Lauren Shenkman and the team
she works with at Riley's Way help young people cultivate leadership skills based on empathy and kindness, by cooperating and
connecting across diverse communities. I can't think of anything
we need more—right now and in the future. The kids at Riley's
Way, and people like Lauren, make you feel, even in the middle
of worrying times, that everything is going to be okay.

It's hard to miss a pattern here. While Janel lifts up a number of
charitable endeavors, the ones that stand out for her typically involve
the closest people in her life.

JANEL MOLONEY: When she was in Uganda, Melissa sent photos of herself alongside the children and families that International Medical Corps and their nutrition program helped connect
her with. For me that made an even bigger impact; it really
brought it home. It's one thing to hear about all these amazing,
worthy causes—there's so much need in the world—but it pushes

your inspiration to new heights when a friend is on the ground serving a community, be it in downtown Brooklyn or Northern Uganda.

From Voices in Harmony to tutoring Karla (who is now herself a tutor), from her support of global efforts like Voices of Uganda and International Medical Corps . . . to those in her own backyard, Janel is a prime example of the compounding value of service. What you put in, you get out . . . plus a little bit more. And it all began with her reaching out to Melissa—a person she didn't even know, had never even *met*—once upon a time on the *West Wing* set.

INTERNATIONAL MEDICAL CORPS

The International Medical Corps is a global humanitarian organization dedicated to saving lives and relieving suffering. The mission of the corps, established in 1984 by volunteer doctors and nurses . . . is to improve the quality of life through health interventions and related activities that strengthen underserved communities worldwide. With the flexibility to respond rapidly to emergencies, the International Medical Corps offers medical services and training to people at the highest risk, always working to strengthen local healthcare systems and promote self-reliance.

www.internationalmedicalcorps.org

RILEY'S WAY FOUNDATION

Riley's Way invests in a youth-led kindness movement, providing young people with the programs, support, and inclusive community they need to thrive as change-makers. Riley's Way is committed to supporting these young leaders to build a better world that values kindness, empathy, connection, and the voices of all youth. Riley's Way envisions a future where kind leaders build a better world.

www.rileysway.org

★ ★ ★ BIG BLOCK OF CHEESE STORY ★ ★ ★

Taps

Here, now, a quick peek behind the curtain at How Aaron Sorkin Writes . . . courtesy of Janel Moloney:

I had a meeting in Aaron's office to talk over potential Donna storylines. Right as I'm about to talk, I hear this *tap-tap-tap*. I started to talk again—*tap-tap-tap*. I say, "What is that?" Aaron says, "Oh, that's the bird on my windowsill. That bird has been coming to my windowsill for the past three seasons. It's the same bird tapping on my window. We have done many things to try to get this bird to stop doing this, but this bird continues to do this." The whole meeting the bird kept tapping.

Little did I know, Aaron was just about to leave the show, and I think he was very behind on his writing and was dealing with a lot. Anyway, we have our talk, I go back to the set. Later on that night, I get the newest script [for season 4's "Life on Mars"] and I open it up . . .

INT. JOSH'S OFFICE — DAY

Donna is sitting at Josh's desk, reading, when we hear a noise of something tapping on glass.

                  DONNA

      Stop it.

Tapping.

                  DONNA

      Stop it.

Tapping.

DONNA

Stop it.

Tapping. Donna turns around and speaks to something behind her.

DONNA

You have to stop it.

She turns back around and we hear the tapping noise again. Outside the window where we see a white dove pecking at the glass.

KEY EPISODE

"Noël"

A sk a hard-core *West Wing* fan what leaps to mind when you name-drop season 2's "Noël," and you'll get a diversity of answers. Yelling in the Oval and bagpipes in the hall. The nation's greatest therapist and a badly bandaged hand. A moving speech from Leo and "Carol of the Bells." But before we dive deeper into the Lyman of it all—the suicidal pilot with whom he shared a birthday or how Josh *really* cut his hand—let's take a moment to acknowledge an Ebenezer Scrooge–level character transformation. In the span of twelve months Toby has gone from purest holiday Grinch to official dispenser of Christmas cheer. In the meantime, C.J. and her snooty sidekick (the Dickensian-sounding Bernard Thatch) return a Blue Room painting to its rightful owner while Bartlet schools his young body man in the art of dressing up. Also, we should shout out, Donna-style, "Yo-Yo Ma rules!" just for good (and merry) measure, right? Okay—let's do this.

In the wake of the harrowing assassination attempt in Rosslyn—Bartlet and Josh getting shot, Sam saving C.J.'s life by pulling her to the ground, Charlie learning he had been the intended target—*The West Wing* had spent the first half of its second season dealing with the psychological fallout for various members of the administration. In this episode, the spotlight lands on Josh, who, you'll recall, almost died from that bullet to the chest. What comes next is a beautiful and sensitive look at post-traumatic stress disorder, some tough talk from a soft-spoken wise man (call him Stanley if you want), and a truly legendary Leo McGarry moment. What it all added up to was another Christmas classic.

It's worth noting, first off, that Brad Whitford hated rewatching this episode . . . which is not to say he doesn't think it's good. He does. It took home awards, even one for him, it's a hall-of-fame fan favorite, he gets it. But like many actors, Brad doesn't love to watch himself work. What he did love was to watch Tommy and his crew work. "That whole episode was beautiful . . . all that Christmas music and the decorations, the sets . . ."

But it wasn't just the decor. Brad also remembers the style Tommy brought to the episode. "There was a . . . disequilibrium about it." Yes, the directorial choices for "Noël" kept viewers off-balance, which fell perfectly in step with Josh's agitated state of mind.

Three weeks before the episode begins, upon learning he shared a birthday with an AWOL fighter pilot whose F-16 had inexplicably "gone silent," Josh Lyman was already feeling discombobulated. Now here he was, in a secluded sitting room, across from a man who could help, a man who is "not the paper boy" and swears he's "completely unimpressed with clever answers." A certified specialist from the American Trauma Victims Association, Dr. Stanley Keyworth knew his way around the smug denials of a guy "in nine kinds of pain." (Stanley and his no-nonsense, low-key bedside manner came courtesy of Adam Arkin, who would return in subsequent seasons to help President Bartlet fight off bouts of insomnia. He would also wind up as one of *The West Wing*'s most popular recurring characters, delivering trademark truth-to-power lines like this one to POTUS: "Screw around if you want, but it's your money, it's about to be *my* money . . . and I sleep fine.")

In "Noël," Brad recognized the challenge of playing the PTSD storyline with the actor sitting across from him. "Adam's one of those people you feel so instantly comfortable with. You have to create some blocks." In response to Arkin's hardwired warmth and ease, Brad dialed back Josh's typical snappy charm. "I didn't want the material to sound . . . chipper. I remember not wanting to be as conscious of the rhythm as you are in a fun scene with Donna."

Weeks before, having already filmed the two-part season premiere, "In the Shadow of Two Gunmen," Brad had approached Aaron, who was sitting on one of the numerous golf carts people use to get around the studio lot. After the first two episodes, Brad recalled, Tommy and Aaron had said, "We need to move on to the next story. We're not gonna stay in 'shooting' mode." But now, two months later, the emotional fallout of the assassination attempt was still gnawing at Brad.

"I remember saying to Aaron, 'Look, I'm not begging for an episode here, but it feels a little weird that I got shot four months ago and it's never come up.' Then, in that very sort of Aaron way, he told me, 'I, uh . . . I appreciate that.'" Not long after, the "Noël" script landed in Brad's hands. He was thrilled. Grappling with what was then a rarely explored issue, PTSD, it felt like a chance to push Josh into darker, more complex psychological territory. To Brad, it felt exciting, unnerving.

"It made such sense that Josh, particularly, would not allow himself to process it in an emotionally healthy way, initially." But as happy as Brad was to see it on the page, it was hard to miss the inherent challenge of the storyline itself. "The scariest thing to me was trying to modulate somebody who has so much emotional compression and is covering it." Talking it over, the writer, director, and actor came up with a plan of attack.

"Josh was so gifted at using comedy as deflection," Tommy points out, "that we had to find a way to make it not quite as sharp." So Aaron wrote to it, to keep Josh hiding behind smartass wisecracks . . . but, in this case, had them not quite work. In a sense, he was intentionally playing Brad a little bit out of tune.

For his part, Brad was discovering his own way of coming across as somewhat off-key, borrowing a technique from one of acting's all-time greats. "Throughout the episode, I kept trying to imagine music. I would do these walk-and-talks, trying to hear something else . . . to try and throw myself off. It's something Al Pacino did in *The Godfather* that always resonated with me." Take it from two actors: It's one thing to talk about this technique, but to actually pull it off is seriously impressive.

In seeking the catalyst for Josh's slow-burn meltdown, Aaron's mind went to a storyline—about a suicidal pilot—that he'd considered for a previous episode but had ultimately scrapped. "Suddenly it became clear to me that I could make the pilot story part of Josh's unraveling by presenting a guy who, displaying no signs of mental or emotional problems at all—in fact passing all the kinds of rigorous tests that you would have to pass to become a military fighter pilot—has committed suicide. And happens to have been born the same day as Josh." It was an ideal substitute for what the deputy chief of staff was going through. "I'm an outwardly stable guy and I just put my hand through a window," Aaron pondered on Josh's behalf. "Am I gonna kill myself? What's next for *me*?"

As for Tommy Schlamme, his focus was twofold. One scene between President Bartlet and Charlie, initially scripted as a sit-down in a single room, got put on its feet, winding briskly past a number of Christmas trees. But beyond establishing the White House festivity, there was another reason behind this directorial choice. Contrast. Visually and energetically, the goal was for the therapy sessions to stand out against the other storylines. Tommy wanted to reserve the viewer's urge to settle in and concentrate for the Josh-and-Stanley scenes.

"Very seldom do we do such a singular episode," he points out, "and even in a singular episode there's still some interesting stories going on. What's the president doing . . . C.J.'s story and the Nazi art . . ."

Oh right, C.J.'s story and the Nazi art. This narrative thread gave *West Wing* viewers an amusing and close-up look at the late British actor Paxton Whitehead. Matching C.J. for smarts, height, and laudable posture, the splendid actor's Bernard Thatch was a White House staffer who split his time between the Visitors Office and the Gifts Unit. An actor Aaron remembers first seeing as Sherlock Holmes on Broadway twenty-plus years before, there Paxton stood, arrogant in the Roosevelt Room, calling C.J.'s necklace "a monument to bourgeois taste."

Given the relative weight of Josh and PTSD, that moment of levity was welcome. And it wasn't the only one. Rewatching "Noël" with Aaron for the season 2 DVD, Brad offered his friend a pat on the back: "I just want to say, it's a great comic instinct to have Toby purveying the music in this episode."

On the other hand, that comic run came with a price: an extended walk-and-talk with a nearly Olympic degree of difficulty. Watching Toby and Josh wind their way through the West Wing, Brad couldn't stave off flashbacks of his own: "*That* is a nightmare. A really long walk-and-talk with an absolutely pivotal, subtle moment at the end of it. You're going to screw up most of the walk-and-talks, you're going to blow a lot of takes, and you're terrified that the one that works *technically*"—meaning camera and sound capture it just right, actors hit their marks, get every word letter-perfect—"you're going to just miss that moment in an intangible way at the end."

The pressure was on—for both actors. While Richard was saddled with long runs of dialogue—"Not just any bagpipes, Josh. Those guys are the Duncan McTavish Clarney Highland Bagpipe Regiment" and "Capitol Bluegrass Banjo Brigade, and those guys were featured on local news"—Brad had to land the precarious final beat of the walk-and-talk with the edgy, raw emotion of a nuanced and triggering PTSD moment.

JOSH
I can hear the damn sirens all
over the building!
[long pause] The . . . bagpipes.

It is a skillful, subtle piece of acting. Not long after, Stanley spurs Josh to confront the explosive moment that brought them together in the first place: shouting at the president in an Oval Office meeting (the "scene of the crime," if you will).

JOSH
You need to listen to me! You have
to listen to me! I can't help you
unless you listen to me! You can't
send Christmas cards to everyone,
you can't do it! Forget the SPR,
let's get the IMF loans like we
said we were going to. Listen to
what I have to say about Didion,
and please, *listen* to me!

For Tommy, the moment after that eruption constituted one of his biggest challenges. "Watching Brad get to that point was exciting. The harder job," he reveals, "was Martin."

"Brad was so scary in that scene," Martin said to us, the memory seeming close at hand. "The character had suddenly slipped off the loop. I remember talking to Tommy. 'Why am I so quiet? Why am I not engaging him and telling him everything will be all right, to try to calm down?' Tommy said, 'That's *you*, Martin. That's not Bartlet.'"

Martin's instincts were for Bartlet to pull Josh in, not shut him out. As Tommy would tell us, "He kept saying to me, 'I'm watching him break down. That's somebody I love!'" But, the director explained, until the president got some emotional distance from a guy he considered like a son, Josh wouldn't feel, as Tommy put it, "entitled to let go."

Following an awkward decrescendo, that incendiary scene closes on President Bartlet, shot from behind, at the Resolute desk. It was a tableau Tommy had been waiting to use since the *West Wing* pilot. The idea was to underscore the power of the presidency—to hit home that, as the director put it, "you never do what Josh just did."

Back in therapy with Stanley, a sea change has taken hold. Once cocky and defiant, Josh and his body language have succumbed to humility in the face of the daunting words "post-traumatic stress disorder." Desperate to retain his position at the White House—"That doesn't really sound like something they let you have if you work for the president. Can we have it be something else?"—Josh reveals the tiny cracks in the dam that will soon lead to the flying open of the floodgates.

Meanwhile, the president and Charlie are dressed to the nines for the Congressional Christmas Party and the spellbinding music of Yo-Yo Ma. The regal formality associated with "statesmen" and "times of occasion" is appropriate, of course, but as Brad will tell you, this scene also signals a well-known fact of *West Wing* life: "Aaron loves the tails." So, "Eagle" and Charlie head out, all tux'd up and ready to go.

Okay. Let's take a moment to discuss the character of Rebecca Housman. Mrs. Housman is the Holocaust survivor who recognized a painting outside the Blue Room, which led to an emotional outburst on a White House tour. Tommy read a slew of talented actresses for the role, but none seemed quite right. Then he learned something about his friend director Mimi Leder. (**MELISSA:** Mimi, who directed many *ER* episodes for John Wells, directed "Election Day: Part I" in *The West Wing*'s final season. **MARY:** And me, when I heroically gave my life to save the planet in *Deep Impact*.) Mimi's mother, Etyl, was a Holocaust survivor. But, alas, she wasn't an actor.

Still, in Tommy's view, Etyl's unique perspective—her lived experience—would add an intangible, authentic quality that no amount of talent or training could match. So, he met with Etyl, and after some convincing, she agreed to give it a try. The day they shot that scene was, naturally, an emotional one. Looking back, it's difficult to put into words how lucky we were to have Etyl play this role. The stillness and dignity she exuded, and the depth of what she had survived long ago, felt inexpressibly moving. As a sixteen-year-old, Etyl was sent to Auschwitz. By the time she returned to Brussels, the rest of her family had perished. Her quietly powerful performance in this episode was a real gift, and turned a small role into one that was anything but.

★ ★ ★

ANOTHER non-actor appearing in "Noël" was world-class cellist Yo-Yo Ma, whose virtuosic (and indefatigable) playing of Bach's Cello Suite No. 1 in G Major is the stuff of *West Wing* legend. As they began to film the party sequence, Yo-Yo Ma told Tommy that he'd like to play the piece "live" for every take. Sensing the director's reluctance, he said, "You're worried I won't play it in the same rhythm every time. Don't worry about that."

"And he did!" Tommy says. "We could edit any one of the takes and it would never change the metronome of it!" For Tommy—for everyone—it was genuinely hard to process that mind-blowing level of proficiency. "I'd never worked with someone who so clearly was the best at what he did," he would say years later. "Like Michael Jordan, the question is . . . Who's number *two*?"

Now, as you'll recall, the music Yo-Yo Ma performed (over fifty times) provided the breathtaking score to the montage of Josh's breakdown at the Congressional Christmas Party. Among the most visually stunning sequences *The West Wing* ever produced, it was put together by editor Bill Johnson, whom Tommy credits for his dynamic work on the episode and on this montage specifically. It comprises a brilliant, violent tornado of images, a swirling together of numerous threads: the gunshots, the sirens, the shrieks of the crowd. The world's greatest cellist bowing the strings. The harrowing flash of Josh getting shot, then back at the concert, where he starts to break down.

As the momentum of the music swells, we return to the therapy session, where a heated exchange crescendos in kind. Then—suddenly—everything goes quiet. Except Stanley's shouted question: "*Josh. Josh!* How did you cut your hand?!" As sirens wail and the cello reemerges, we finally see the flashback confession: Josh's hand smashing through the glass of his living room window. It's really quite something. For such a showy moment, what may be most impressive is the way Brad showed restraint.

"It's obviously a raw, emotional part of a raw, emotional episode," Brad told us. "If you push too far on the . . . release of it, it risks kind of . . . cheapening the moment." During filming, Brad was intent on calibrating his performance. For inspiration, he chose a well-respected newsman from a bygone era. "The very most I felt Josh should show emotionally, the most he should release, was . . . what the country got from Walter Cronkite when Kennedy was shot. It would just be hard for me to imagine Josh as remotely realistic or functional if he melted down completely . . . in front of Yo-Yo Ma."

Believe it or not, after everything this chapter's delved into, we've only just arrived at the episode's two most heralded exchanges.

> JOSH
>
> Why would the music have started it?

> STANLEY
>
> Well, I know it's gonna sound like I'm telling you that two plus two equals a bushel of potatoes, but at this moment, in your head, music is the same thing as . . .

```
                      JOSH
        . . . as sirens.

                    STANLEY
        Yeah.

                      JOSH
        So that's gonna be my reaction
        every time I hear music?

                    STANLEY
        No.

                      JOSH
        Why not?

                    STANLEY
        Because . . . we get better.
```

As for the most cherished exchange . . . For many of us—for most of us—it's the one that comes after Stanley sends Josh back out into the world. Exiting the West Wing, Josh crosses through the lobby, only to be stopped by his boss, who's been waiting for him.

```
                      LEO
        This guy's walking down the street
        when he falls in a hole. The walls
        are so steep he can't get out. A
        doctor passes by and the guy shouts
        up, "Hey you! Can you help me out?"
        The doctor writes a prescription,
        throws it down in the hole, and
        moves on. Then a priest comes along
        and the guy shouts up, "Father, I'm
        down in this hole. Can you help me
        out?" The priest writes out a
```

```
prayer, throws it down in the hole
and moves on. Then a friend walks
by. "Hey, Joe, it's me. Can you help
me out?" And the friend jumps in
the hole. Our guy says, "Are you
stupid? Now we're both down here!"
The friend says, "Yeah, but I've
been down here before, and I know
the way out." Long as I got a job,
you got a job, you understand?
```

"When John first did this scene," Tommy says, "it was very hard for him. It became very poignant." The director suggested John pull back on the emotion, to let the score do some of the heavy lifting. "Snuffy's gonna be there," he told him, "*you* actually don't have to. Just . . . talk to your friend." Once John Spencer had a sense of how to attack the scene, well, we don't need Tommy to tell us he was brilliant. But he did.

Before we finish up, let's take a moment to acknowledge that, in an episode where a world-class musician insisted on playing his instrument forty-nine more times than necessary, a bunch of other key figures played their instruments in an uncommon, virtuosic manner: Aaron writing Brad's quips slightly out of rhythm; Brad driving himself to distraction with music in his head; editor Bill Johnson serving up visually symphonic flourishes. So yeah, it wasn't just the cellist.

The episode ends with Donna escorting Josh out the White House gates. Going to get his damaged hand rebandaged, they pass by a choir performing "Carol of the Bells." Soon, thanks to the music (and those faint, intermingling sirens), we'll walk away with the sense that, while Josh may be on the road to recovery, he's got miles to go before he sleeps well. In addition to being a moving and lovely way to send us all off for Christmas break, that final scene, Aaron says, is notable for a couple of reasons.

"First, John Podesta, the last Clinton chief of staff, gave permission for Tommy to shoot inside the gate for the very first time. The other reason, which means more to me, is that it was shot on November eighteenth of the year 2000. At two a.m. that morning my daughter Roxy was born. This is the middle of the night, it's November in Washington, so I have to believe it was awfully cold. But Tommy and Brad and Janel got this choir to sing a song for my newborn daughter and they put it on film and my whole family really treasures it."

Brad Whitford has called this episode of television "the best acting experience I ever had." As an actor, he says, "you always feel like you're swimming upstream. Doing this role, but especially this show, feels like . . . what I imagine surfing feels like."

Everyone needs to feel that way sometimes. To feel, in a seemingly endless stream of "difficult," that some things—sometimes—can be easy. And that we get better. Everyone needs somebody to jump into the hole they're in and show them the way out. And, maybe more than anything, everyone needs a friend to help rebandage your hand, even as sirens—and "Carol of the Bells"—are still ringing in your head.

★ ★ ★

POSTSCRIPT: *The original air date of "Noël" was preempted when Democratic presidential nominee—and outgoing VP—Al Gore conceded the election in an act of noble, old-school patriotism.* (**MELISSA:** Future *West Wing* writer Eli Attie helped compose the historic address, ushering in a peaceful transfer of power. **MARY:** Aw . . . Remember those?)

TWENTY

A SERVICE STORY

Bradley Whitford

F or as long as we've known him, Brad Whitford has been walking the walk, literally and otherwise, when it comes to service. We're not being hyperbolic when we say that Brad is a hero to both of us. He's someone we genuinely look up to. Brad's dedication to fighting for what he believes in—be they causes, candidates, or campaigns— inspires us to keep going with the work we care about most.

Brad advocates for such a multitude of issues that it's practically impossible to try to list them here. (**MELISSA:** Even as we're writing this, he and his wife, Amy, are staying with me in DC because he flew in to receive Brady United's Brady Action Award, which honors champions of gun violence prevention.) Then, of course, there's the campaigning . . .

Brad puts himself out on the political front lines, both nationally and locally, in his home state of Wisconsin. He gives speeches, hosts fundraisers, goes door-to-door, yes, but his efforts extend beyond that, too; he gets down into the details of it. The willing embodiment of boots-on-the-ground leadership, Brad has been an enroller and an organizer at every level, in race after race after race. Meanwhile, when it comes to the actual discourse, he is tirelessly engaged and extraordinarily knowledgeable. Drawing the media spotlight to events, organizations, and individuals, Brad has made an art of lending his voice to lifting up those he believes in, all while encouraging others to do the same. So it's surprising—and also really not—when you reflect on where he came from.

BRADLEY WHITFORD: I was raised a Quaker. One of the main things Quakers believe in is nonviolence. Coming of age in the sixties, with Vietnam, it was particularly volatile. I had older siblings and my brother was a conscientious objector who took a very dangerous principled stand. To avoid serving, you have to answer two questions. "Are you a Quaker?" Yes. "Are you a birthright Quaker?" Which he was. A lot of people at that time were pretending. Then they say, "Are you a pacifist?" If you say "Yes," you qualify as a conscientious objector. My brother got up and said, "I'm a Quaker . . . but I'm not a pacifist, I would've fought against Hitler." I remember my mother wailing in the bathroom because we thought he'd have to go to jail, which was a possibility. He ended up getting alternative service and being on probation.

This is all to say, the political stakes were very active in the house. My mother was probably the most influential person in my life. She was always involved—League of Women Voters, doing stuff for UNICEF, for Earth Day. She was very concerned about the environment. It was just this constant example of getting involved and staying involved. And this goes to what I think *The West Wing* is all about. My very close friend, [the Reverend] George Regas, once said, "Politics is the way you create your moral vision." It's not culture. It's actually *politics* that is the execution of your moral values.

When Brad talks about his background, he sounds like he was *born* to be on *The West Wing*. No wonder he fought so hard to play Josh. As he grew more invested in the show and its themes, Brad's vision of politics—and the moral underpinnings it revealed—deepened.

BRADLEY WHITFORD: I had a two-and-a-half-year-old when we did the pilot, and two more on the way. And the war in Iraq seemed completely insane. Having kids, I felt like their future was being attacked every time the newspaper landed. Now, look, I have real reservations about being, you know, a "blowhard actor," and there are always people telling you to shut up. But to me, there's nothing less democratic than telling people to shut up. And you realize there's this opportunity, politically. There's a way to use it. And the most satisfying way is to use the ridiculous amount of attention you get to give a voice to causes and people you believe in. Anthony Edwards, who was on *ER* then, was a real inspiration to me. When *West Wing* took off, he gave me this wonderful advice: "Just remember, celebrity is currency. You can spend it on yourself . . . or you can spend it on other people."

From the start, Brad knew one cause he really wanted to spend it on . . .

BRADLEY WHITFORD: I have a dear friend, Jon Shestack, who founded Cure Autism Now with his wife, Portia. They have a beautiful son, Dov, who is severely challenged by autism. Early on, when *West Wing* had just started, I went to lobby with them on the Children's Health Act of 2000. That was the first time I realized that being a celebrity could be helpful in shining a light, in getting meetings even. After all the work and organizing put in by Jon and Portia and so many others, autism research wound up receiving much-needed funding. To play a small part in that was hugely gratifying—and eye-opening.

I honestly think that, unless you're nuts, if you get to be part of an experience like *The West Wing*, you know how lucky you are. Then you realize the platform affords you this joyous thing: to be able to be of service, to show up for something you really believe in.

Decisions are made by those who show up.

—PRESIDENT BARTLET, "WHAT KIND OF DAY HAS IT BEEN?"

Over the years, Brad has seen countless people "show up" in seriously impactful ways. But two figures struck him as especially consequential. One of them was Ady Barkan.

Ady Barkan was a lawyer, author, and political activist. In 2016, Ady was diagnosed with ALS, the neurodegenerative disease also known as Lou Gehrig's disease. In 2017, a video of Ady confronting Senator Jeff Flake during a cross-country flight became headline news. In it, he pressed the Arizona Republican to "be a hero" by voting no on a tax bill that many believed would imperil programs—Medicare, Medicaid, Social Security—that people with ALS and other medical conditions depend on. Before the plane landed, the video had gone viral. This incident ultimately led to Ady co-founding the Be a Hero PAC and the Fed Up Campaign, both of which support progressive candidates and the causes they champion. Sadly, Senator Flake (along with dozens of his fellow Republican senators) voted in favor of the cuts.

One of Brad's earliest memories of Ady involved advocacy on behalf of the so-called DREAMers—undocumented immigrants who came to the US as young children, who have lived here and attended school here, and who, in many cases, identify as American.

> **BRADLEY WHITFORD:** There was an event at Senator Feinstein's Los Angeles office . . . for the DREAMers. And there was going to be a counterprotest. I met Ady in a Starbucks near the office. He could still talk, but his voice was failing. Ady said, "Put the guy with ALS in front. If they hit me, it'd be a great picture."

Ady often put himself out front, even as his ALS progressed, because he understood this cold, hard political reality: It is easier to ignore an idea than it is to confront actual human suffering right in front of you. Ady Barkan put himself out front to help others who couldn't. That's not just powerful, effective politics. It's true bravery, up close and personal.

> **BRADLEY WHITFORD:** In his early thirties, this guy got one of the most dire medical diagnoses you can get. He didn't know how much time he had, didn't know how much time he had to be able to *speak*. And he decided to use himself as a political weapon in the fight for healthcare because he recognized how powerful this was. It was more than just something to admire, which of course I do; it was incredibly *effective*. To me, it was extraordinary.

In the 2018 midterms, Democrats won back control of the House of Representatives. Brad saw Ady's messaging and presence on the campaign trail as having a real impact.

> **BRADLEY WHITFORD:** I really do think part of it was the pressure Ady was putting on, strategically, in different races across the

country, where healthcare, which had been a losing issue for Democrats, became a winning issue.

As Brad and Ady continued to work together, they formed a deep, personal connection. In July 2019, Brad and his then fiancée, actress Amy Landecker, got married. No longer able to speak without the assistance of a computer, Ady was there, front and center.

BRADLEY WHITFORD: Amy and I couldn't have imagined how wonderful it would be to have Ady perform the service. His awareness of what love means . . . how short, how precious, time is. It was really beautiful.

Not long after, Brad learned that a film crew had been following Ady across the country as he spoke out for healthcare reform. "I want to see the footage," Brad told them. Once he saw what they'd shot to that point . . .

BRADLEY WHITFORD: I said, "We need to make a documentary about this."

In 2021, with filmmakers Mark and Jay Duplass joining Brad as executive producers on the documentary, *Not Going Quietly* premiered at the South by Southwest film festival. It was awarded the Cinema for Peace Award for the top political film of 2022.

His work with Ady on a number of political endeavors provided Brad with insight that he considers both inspiring and frustrating.

BRADLEY WHITFORD: I think people who've dealt with real tragedy, like Ady, remain engaged even in the face of adversity because they do not have the luxury, the privilege of walking

away. There's no greater privilege than to despair about the political system, to just throw your hands up and say, "I'm out—the
system's corrupt!" I'm lucky. I'm ridiculously privileged. And
honestly, I'd rather use my privilege to stay involved, to get to be
in the trenches with amazing people like Ady Barkan. *That's* a
privilege.

Another organization Brad supports is Fair Fight Action, which
seeks to address voter suppression efforts in Georgia and across America. Why did Fair Fight appeal to him?

BRADLEY WHITFORD: Because I fell in love with Stacey
Abrams! She was originally an incredibly effective minority leader
in the Georgia House, so she had this "How the hell do you do
that?" quality. She reminds me of something Martin said once:
"Oh, we're not necessarily going to *win* this particular race, this
particular initiative. That's not why you do this. You do it because
it's the right thing to do, and with persistence these things pay
off." Stacey and Fair Fight embody that ideal. Overcoming voter
suppression—particularly in communities of color, and when it
comes to the youth vote—requires discipline. In 2018, Fair Fight
drew attention to the mismanagement of elections, the irregu-
larities, the crazy-long lines. They exposed actions—and
inactions—that were, yeah, recent, but also decades-long, en-
trenched, and institutional. The forces looking to make voting
harder are counting on us to stop paying attention, they're counting on us to be quiet. Stacey and Fair Fight work to make sure
that doesn't happen.

Oh, and meanwhile, in 2020, Stacey basically *won* the Senate
for the Democrats. Without those two Georgia Senate seats . . .
The woman *saved* democracy! As cynical and pessimistic as you
can get these days, you see examples like Stacey and Ady, where

single human beings can have a tremendous effect. It's not easy, but it makes a massive difference.

While it's true that one person can make a sizable impact, Brad's boots remain firmly on the ground when it comes to making the world a better, more equitable place.

BRADLEY WHITFORD: It's not like we're going to elect one person and fix this. The fight, as we've learned in recent years, will never end. There's always going to be greed and injustice. But it's like that John Lewis quote: "Democracy is not a state. It is an *act*, and each generation must do its part."

Postscript: During the writing of this book, Ady Barkan died from complications of ALS. His memory, and the legacy he created through his years of fierce advocacy, live on.

BE A HERO

Be a Hero takes on the impossible fights. Big money. Special interests. Powerful politicians. Be a Hero has taken them all on—and won.

www.beaherofund.com

FAIR FIGHT ACTION

Fair Fight Action promotes fair elections around the country, encourages voter participation in elections, and educates voters about elections and their voting rights. Fair Fight Action brings awareness to the public on election reform, advocates for election reform at all levels, and engages in other voter education programs and communications.

www.fairfight.com

TWENTY-ONE

KEY EPISODE

"Two Cathedrals"

The final line in *The West Wing*'s sophomore season is delivered by Leo McGarry, whose eyes are locked on a soaking-wet President Bartlet standing at a podium. As POTUS addresses the White House press corps while a torrential storm rages outside, everyone in the room eagerly awaits the president's reply to a question C.J. had reminded her boss to strategically avoid. "Can you tell us right now if you'll be seeking a second term?"

Wide-eyed, Leo turns to watch his friend Jed answer the reporter's question, and says to himself—and to anyone in earshot—"Watch this."

Nearly a year before that final moment, the first domino had fallen, tipping all the others inexorably toward what would become Bartlet's fateful, wordless answer. That first domino to fall occurred off-screen and looked, oddly enough, like a cigarette.

During a February fundraiser at a Los Angeles hotel, Aaron Sorkin and Kathryn Joosten, who played Mrs. Landingham, had succumbed to their shared habit of ducking outside for a smoke. Standing with Aaron—"by valet parking or something," he vaguely recalls—

Kathryn casually mentioned that the following week she'd be testing for a pilot.

"As soon as she told me that she was going in to test," Aaron would reveal to *The West Wing Weekly* two decades later, "I stopped listening to everything else she was saying . . . and just began thinking, 'How would I write Mrs. Landingham off the show?'"

In that moment, the showrunner knew he'd want to hit Bartlet hard in season 2. "Hard enough," he admitted, "so that this very devout Catholic would question his faith in God, and in fact question his faith in God to God Himself." He also figured, if they were going to dig in like that, they might as well swing for the fences. That meant more than just having Bartlet question his faith. It meant doing so in the middle of what Aaron called "the Yankee Stadium of cathedrals," the National Cathedral in Washington, DC.

While killing Mrs. Landingham in a drunk-driving accident would be (and was) undoubtedly heart-wrenching, that shocking development alone would not justify such a profound leap of faithlessness. That said, in addition to other hits along the way—Josh's near-death experience at Rosslyn, the firestorm surrounding POTUS's multiple sclerosis revelation—what happened at Eighteenth and Potomac (and the fact that Mrs. Landingham had been on her way back to the White House so the president could tell her about his MS) would surely push Jed Bartlet closer to the ledge.

The good news for Kathryn—in addition to her going on to win two Emmy awards for her subsequent work on *Desperate Housewives*—was that Aaron knew the "Two Cathedrals" end game well in advance. So, even before she read the script where her character dies, Aaron was able to assure her that "this doesn't mean you're off the show. You're gonna be back." And she was, and not just in "Two Cathedrals."

The rest of the cast learned about the death of the president's beloved secretary in their own way. But according to Aaron, the revelation was especially tough on one actor. "Everyone prior to the table read had been told Mrs. Landingham was going to die . . . except Dulé . . . who hadn't read the script prior to the table read." To make matters worse, and by quirk of fate, Charlie's devastating reveal—" . . . she's dead"—happened to land at the very top of the page. What resulted is a table read moment to remember.

"Dulé turned the page . . . looked at it . . . and he couldn't believe it." To Aaron, Dulé's hesitation suggested the idea that, if he didn't say it out loud, perhaps it wouldn't really be. "The poor kid. Honestly, we weren't pranking him. It was just one of those 'I thought you told him—' 'I thought *you* told him' kinds of things." Yes, thanks to that miscommunication between Aaron and Tommy, Dulé was left to live through Delores Landingham's death right there in front of the whole gang . . . including Kathryn herself.

"At first," Dulé told us, "I really was wondering if I was reading it correctly. And when I realized I <u>was</u> reading it correctly, I was wondering, *Does everyone understand what I'm reading here?* If Mrs. Landingham has died . . . what does that mean for Kathryn? Is she not going to be a part of the show anymore? At all? It really shocked me."

When it came time to shoot that scene in "18th and Potomac," Dulé held on to the sense of shock he'd initially felt. "At first, I'm trying to have all this emotion. Aaron comes in and goes, 'Charlie grew up in DC, his mother was killed in the line of duty, he has seen violence, he has seen death. You're more used to death than these other people. Just say the information.' It really was a good note. And that's what I ended up doing in the performance."

All things considered—the interwoven flashbacks, the connective tissue between past and present, the transitions that brought them seamlessly together—"Two Cathedrals" is expert writing at its most elegant. But it's also a triumph of direction.

As Aaron put it to us, "I've always felt that, as much credit as Tommy has gotten for the show, he hasn't gotten enough; I eat a little bit of his pizza in that regard." Tommy just intuitively *got* what Aaron put on the page. "He shot it beautifully and got terrific performances," Aaron says. "I wrote. He did everything else."

For the director, his sights for "Two Cathedrals" were set on clarity above all. While a trackable throughline is crucial to telling any good story, this one, which included flashbacks to Bartlet's childhood, required extra-careful execution. As Tommy points out, the episode was "uniquely in the mind of one person. It was a real memory piece. All I cared about was letting the audience know from the very beginning, from the first flashback, that we're inside Jed's head." That meant transitioning clearly from one world to the other. The nervous tapping of a Sit Room cigarette brings Bartlet back from a bygone schoolyard chat with his stern taskmaster of a father . . .

> DR. BARTLET
> Mr. Spence found this cigarette
> butt on the floor in the aisle of
> the chapel.

> YOUNG JED
> People shouldn't put their
> cigarettes out in the chapel, Mr.
> Spence.

> DR. BARTLET
> Well, people shouldn't be smoking
> in the chapel, I think is my point,
> Jed. Do you understand what I'm
> saying?

Perhaps the cleverest transition of all stemmed from a classic *West Wing* go-to: the distinctive slipping on of a sport coat. Due to a lifelong issue with his shoulder, Martin has an unusual way of putting on a jacket. He sort of whips it around and over his head. After decades of doing it, that crazy-looking motion has become second nature. Before you even know what's happening with the jacket, it's on, like magic.

"My left arm was crushed by forceps at birth," Martin explained. "I had no lateral movement with my left arm, so I devised that method when I was a boy." Having witnessed that jacket-whip technique many times, the chance to pay it off as Bartlet backstory was too good for the director to pass up. It was a match-cut Tommy had been waiting years to shoot.

"Wouldn't it be great," he thought, "if I could figure out a way that, as Bartlet's putting on his coat to the funeral, Young Jed's putting on *his* coat?" So, he told the young actor, Jason Widener, to study Martin and learn how to put on his coat the same way. That extra bit of prep paid off—the coat-flip transition is seamless.

Playing a best-friendish big sister to Young Jed was Kirsten Nelson, whose talent Aaron and Tommy had gotten to know while casting *Sports Night*. Kirsten arrived at *The West Wing* audition with a fully formed character; just ask Aaron. "She obviously came into the audition having watched every Mrs. Landingham episode . . . and did the voice without it being like an *SNL* impression. You really saw Mrs. Landingham as a young woman."

A final piece of guest casting came days before production began in DC. At the table read the week before, the role of Jed's father, Dr. Bartlet, had been performed by *West Wing* writer Lawrence O'Donnell. Appearing with Josh and Hrishi on the *West Wing* podcast two decades later, the MSNBC host explained, "At read-throughs . . . we don't have all the guest parts cast. Frequently, writers would read the other parts. That day I had the Bartlet dad part." It was a role that resonated throughout the series, defining corners of the president's emotional and psychological topography, even before viewers had put a face to the name.

Exuding an old-school East Coast frostiness, Lawrence's Dr. Bartlet made quite an impact. At the end of the read, Tommy leaned over to Aaron and whispered, "That's what I want in Bartlet's father!" From there, the team went out to a handful of actors, including Mark Harmon. But, due to a complicated production schedule—this episode had to split its time between DC and the Warner Bros. lot in Burbank—none of the potential Dr. Bartlets could make it work. As luck would have it, this freed up Harmon for his four-episode arc in season 3 as Secret Service agent (and C.J. love interest) Simon Donovan. If he'd taken on "Two Cathedrals," we all would've been denied the joy of watching him teach C.J. how to both shoot a gun and safely shop for the black Vera Wang.

Okay, so . . . Lawrence was packing to fly to DC the next day—he hoped just as a "break glass in case of emergency" option. Around noon Pacific, the phone rang. It was Tommy. "If the next guy turns this down," the director told him, "you're going to have to do it." For Lawrence, the worst-case scenario felt just around the corner. He asked Tommy, "Please call me and tell me that the guy has taken it."

A day later, Lawrence was at the airport and, as he tells it, "the phone's not ringing. I'm in the plane now and the phone's not ringing. They close the door and the phone . . . hasn't . . . rung." Now on his way to Washington, with no word from Tommy, Lawrence was just shy of full-blown panic. Glancing about the cabin, his eyes found, well . . . me. (Melissa. Hi.) He rushed over and explained what he refers to as his "predicament." At that point, Lawrence recalls, he was taking some serious mental inventory: "I have no professional habits as an actor. Is this how I prepare? I don't know. But I'm sitting here with a professional. This feels good, this feels like the thing to do." As the jet settled in at thirty thousand feet, Lawrence and I sat together, running lines for his acting debut.

"We worked on the scenes as we flew across the country," Lawrence said, exhilaration still present in his voice, "which was just invaluable to me." After the plane landed—"kind of late at night in Washington"—Lawrence arrived at the hotel where the cast was staying. It became instantly clear that the news had spread. "There's Martin in the lobby. As I come through the door, he goes—just overjoyed—'My father is here!'" At that moment, Lawrence knew. "It's official: I am doing this."

The next morning, Lawrence found himself standing on the campus of a prep school in Delaware, looking for all the world like he knew what he was doing. But inside, he felt like anything but. "It seemed to me," he remembers, "to be an act of complete desperation on the part of *The West Wing*. Like Hollywood had run out of actors."

Tommy, to this day, remains duly impressed with what Lawrence managed to pull off. "It was not an easy thing to do. He was frightened to death, he really was, genuinely." But that was okay. When it came to this episode . . . "frightened to death" was going around.

"We were kind of nervous the day that we were shooting Martin's big speech at the end," Aaron admitted. (**MARY:** Cursing God inside a church, stubbing out a cigarette on the sanctuary floor . . .) As he arrived at the National Cathedral to rehearse the scene, Aaron couldn't help noticing a rather unusual . . . congregation. In addition to the crew and Martin and some of the rest of the cast, there were several members of the clergy. And some of them seemed a little disturbed by what was about to go down.

One of them in particular, though, was feeling fairly serene—Brad Whitford's friend George Regas. According to Tommy, this man of the cloth, having read the script, offered the following insight: "Unless you question God, you really can't believe in Him." To the director, those words of wisdom were a good sign . . . and exactly what the scene was about.

Aaron's favorite moment with the clergy came as rehearsal was set to begin. "I stepped up to the one closest to me and said, 'You know that he's about to denounce God . . . right?' The man smiled and said, 'Yeah! It's gonna be *great!*'"

> PRESIDENT BARTLET
> You're a son-of-a-bitch, you know
> that? She bought her first new car
> and you hit her with a drunk
> driver. What, is that supposed to

be funny? "You can't conceive, nor
can I, the appalling strangeness of
the mercy of God," says Graham
Greene. I don't know whose ass he
was kissing there 'cause I think
you're just vindictive. What was
Josh Lyman? A warning shot? That
was my son. What did I ever do to
yours but praise His glory and
praise His name? There's a tropical
storm that's gaining speed and
power. They say we haven't had a
storm this bad since you took out
that tender ship of mine in the
north Atlantic last year . . . 68
crew. You know what a tender ship
does? Fixes the other ships.
Doesn't even carry guns. It just
goes around, fixes the other ships
and delivers the mail, that's all
it can do. *Gratias tibi ago,*
domine. Yes, I lied. It was a sin.
I've committed many sins. Have I
displeased you, you feckless thug?
3.8 million new jobs, that wasn't
good? Bailed out Mexico, increased
foreign trade, 30 million new acres
of land for conservation, put
Mendoza on the bench, we're not
fighting a war, I've raised three
children . . . That's not enough to
buy me out of the doghouse?!

The speech goes on from there, entirely in Latin . . . until, that is,
Bartlet lights the cigarette, stubs it out on the floor, and offers up his
go-to-hell bitter end: "You get Hoynes!"

According to Martin, Aaron wasn't sure the Latin bit would work.

WHAT'S NEXT

"So, I asked him, 'Well, why are you using it?' He said, 'Because I want to use God's language.'" (It was also, Aaron confessed on the DVD, a decent way to circumvent the censors.)

Set in this sacred place, the cathedral scene was a real challenge for Martin, a devout Catholic. The Latin only upped the degree of difficulty. "I'd never acted in a foreign language, let alone Latin," Martin confessed. "So, I was presented with a very serious problem. How do I learn this speech, perform it in a public place, and pull it off . . . naturally?"

The answer to that first question was this: "I had about a week and a half to learn the speech, so I went to my local pastor, Monsignor John Sheridan, and we worked on it whenever he was free. He made a few changes." (**MELISSA:** Never let it be said Aaron wouldn't let you alter the lines. All it took was a little divine intervention.)

After getting the Latin down, there was still the issue of finding it within himself to execute the lines naturally in what he considered a holy place. Coupling that with an overt act of defiance like snuffing out a cigarette on the cathedral floor left no room for doubt—delivering this holy jeremiad wasn't going to be easy. Martin just made it look that way. "He was there on take one," Aaron said. "Latin and all."

When we talked to Martin about the confrontation with God, he referred to it as "one of my favorite scenes." But he also revealed something surprising about the sequence. "It gave me such confidence," he said. "Aaron thought it was a big deal. It wasn't. It was delicious. I didn't want to seem like I was showing off, but I was. I enjoyed every bit of it."

This is not to say there was zero struggle going on inside him. Early on, Martin sat down in a pew in front of the church to reflect and catch his breath. "Aaron came up and sat next to me," the actor recalls. "He was weeping and he said . . . 'Thank you.'"

As much as the scene took out of Martin—and as much as he put into it—the results spoke for themselves. There on-screen was a man's fury at God and fate and the unfairness of life . . . alongside a little boy's defiance in the face of a cold and domineering father figure. "That moment of throwing the cigarette," Tommy recalls, "was really powerful. It was . . . the act of a child's rage." It was also, according to the director, the only time he'd ever worked with Martin "when he was going to a dark place." At the end of that trying day, Tommy was happy it had gone so well . . . and happier still that it was over with.

Before we wrap this up, Aaron would like to make one thing perfectly clear: Late into this episode, when a hellacious wind blows open the Oval Office doors to the torrential rain storming the portico, President Bartlet reflexively calls out, "Mrs. Landingham!" Despite her being, well . . . dead . . . the woman walks into the room. According to Aaron (and common sense), "that's not the ghost of Mrs. Landingham. That was Bartlet talking to her in his mind." As for that raging storm clattering the White House windows . . .

To Aaron, "the storm . . . it's a form of baptism . . . of re-baptism." Mrs. Landingham's role there is the same as it was in every storm she ever saw Jed Bartlet weather: To simplify. To calm. To restore in him, as Aaron put it, "a confidence and a love and a purpose." Which brings us back to the beginning, by which we mean . . . the end.

REPORTER (SANDY)
Can you tell us right now if you'll
be seeking a second term?

Aaron went into the last moments of the season 2 finale looking to avoid a *Will he or won't he?*–type cliffhanger. "Asking the question and then going to black seemed . . . just a little cheaper than what we were doing." On the other hand, he realized that having Bartlet answer yes would likely read as anticlimactic. He had to find what he calls "an interesting and poetic way" to otherwise address the question, which is why he'd scattered some body language bread crumbs via Young Mrs. Landingham.

          YOUNG MRS. LANDINGHAM
You stuck your hands in your
pockets, you looked away and
smiled. That means you made up
your mind.

          YOUNG JED
That doesn't mean anything.

          YOUNG MRS. LANDINGHAM
Oh yes it does.

          YOUNG JED
I stuck my hands in my pockets!

          YOUNG MRS. LANDINGHAM
And looked away, and smiled. We're
in.

And there it was. The reporter asks present-day Bartlet if he'll run for reelection. Bartlet sticks his hands in his pockets, looks away, and smiles. A *yes*, plain as day, without a single word.

That deftness and elegance of execution represents *The West Wing* at its best. After an episode full of profound complexity and inner conflict, closing out a season marked by shocking revelation, the camera lands one last time on President Bartlet. Witnessing the stellar work of Aaron, Tommy, and Martin, we're reminded that, like a cathedral or a pressroom full of cameras, the eye of the storm is a powerful place to be. We find ourselves feeling like a wide-eyed Leo McGarry, uttering to everyone in earshot these two precious words:

"Watch this."

★ ★ ★ **BIG BLOCK OF CHEESE STORY** ★ ★ ★

Church Laughter

Odds are, you didn't need to buy this book to guess that Allison Janney is deeply revered by the *West Wing* family. Listening to cast, writers, directors, and even executives sing her praises, we heard variations on the theme of her supreme gifts as an actor. And, obviously, all you have to do is fire up your *West Wing* DVD box set or log on to YouTube or stream it on Max to find ample evidence of Allison's wide-ranging talent. It's right there on-screen in her broken, heartfelt pleas in support of the women of Qumar, or in the stand-alone episode, "The Long Goodbye," where she comes face-to-face with her elderly father's Alzheimer's . . . and, of course, it's up front and center in that fan-favorite sequence from late in season 1 when C.J. lip-syncs "The Jackal."

But while there are countless examples within countless episodes of Allison's being, as Josh Malina put it to us, "effortlessly great on the show," one that stands out for many fans (those of us in the cast included) came in a lighter moment from the show's fourth season, in an episode called "Privateers."

As you may recall, C.J., Will, and Amy Gardner head into the Mural Room to manage a controversy involving the first lady and the Daughters of the American Revolution. In this moment, *West Wing* audiences are introduced to the über–blue blood intonations of actress Helen Slayton-Hughes, who hilariously blurts out, "I'm Marion Cotesworth-Hay!" C.J. is instantly sent into torrents of laughter, followed by breathless, absurd excuse-making . . .

```
                       C.J.
         I'm sorry. I was . . . I was
         thinking of this thing from . . .
         this thing that just happened . . .
         with the deficit! I'm sorry . . .
```

. . . and perhaps the greatest case of fake church giggles ever filmed. As Amy and Will try to cover—offering up an award for Ms. Cotesworth-Hay, "The Francis Scott Key key"—there's C.J. in the background, convulsing with fits of laughter. (Note: No, Amy, it's not "a hazing.")

When we talked to Allison about this hysterical moment from the show, what she remembered most is that "it took a *long* time. More than twenty takes, all told." She also recalls its being nearly as hard as having to *cry* in a scene, if not harder. Especially as filming went on. "I just remember getting to the point where I didn't feel at all like laughing anymore," she said. "I'm a pretty good laugher—it's definitely what you'd call one of my 'special skills'—but it requires a lot of you, a lot of energy. I remember during more than one take thinking, 'There's now nothing funny about this.'"

For the sequence, Allison reached back to a lesson she'd learned on a previous job. "I had to laugh at the beginning of a scene in the play *Inspector Carol*—this was a million years ago—and I realized it was going to have to be, like, an actual *physical* thing I had to do. I'd start moving my stomach over and over, breathing in and out, which was so ridiculous that it would make me *actually* laugh. It's absurd, really, but it gets the job done!"

However "effortless" moments like that one may seem to those of us watching from the sidelines, it's as much a tribute to Allison's tenacity as to her innate talent. As she put it to us, "I just remember not knowing how I could possibly do it again."

But she did do it again. And again and again. And the results are now ingrained in our memories or posted on YouTube or streaming on Max. The best proof of all the hard work that went into AJ making it look so easy—in gut-wrenching moments or ones marked by convulsive church laughter—may have come in something she said to us for the book. Looking back on that hilarious, unforgettable sequence, Allison channeled what we'll call her inner perfectionist: "I've watched that scene since and I honestly think I could have delivered a better take."

TWENTY-TWO

WAYS AND MEANS

The first time Alex Graves ever worked on *The West Wing*, the fledgling director—and self-described "shy guy from Kansas"—designed an elaborate and lengthy opening shot for the iconic episode "In Excelsis Deo." Looking back on that experience, he laughed and said to us, "It looked like air traffic control." From where we stand, the story of that shot, and the manner in which its execution was handled, perfectly captures the ways and means by which the *West Wing* powers that be nurtured—and protected—young artists.

As a film student at USC, Alex had been obsessed with long takes. He admired the famous extended opening shot by Orson Welles in *Touch of Evil* and reveled in the work of French innovators like Jean Renoir and American director Brian De Palma, particularly in *The Untouchables*. When it came to *The West Wing* and designing long takes, Alex wasn't alone. "Tommy was all over it," he reminded us, "he had run with that brilliantly in the pilot."

The first time we sat down with Alex, the passion he feels for his collaborators on *The West Wing* was palpable, particularly as it related to his early years on the show. Decades after the fact, he occasionally teared up as he described a creative culture fostered by people who did more than just support him; they found ways to protect him and what the up-and-comer saw as his vision and his process. Alex still gushes about "an environment Tommy created and Aaron created . . . and John Wells *allowed* against a lot of muscular pounding at his door, I'm sure." The support he felt started on day one.

ALEX GRAVES: I'm on my first day of filming, doing my opening shot of the whole cast around a Christmas tree—it's Allison and Rob, and Richard and Janel, and everybody—the opening shot of the show. I'm on take *thirty* and Tommy appears on set. And I'm so green I have no idea that this is probably not a great thing. I'm like, "Oh hi, Tommy!" Everybody else is probably thinking, "Tommy's come down because we called him. 'Cause this kid's on take thirty . . ." Anyway, I do another take and we don't get it . . . but we're close.

When I'm about to do the *next* take, Tommy sits down next to me at the monitors. Right as I'm about to say, 'Action,' I think, 'Hm. I may be in trouble.' Like, 'Duh, wake up, farm boy!' I yell 'Action' and we almost get it, but . . . we don't. When I say 'Cut,' I notice that everybody on set looks at Tommy.

That's when I realized, Ohhhh, I *am* in trouble. . . . Tommy turns to me, and he leans over. And he says—in a slightly loud voice—"That's a *great* fucking shot." And he walks away. And that's it. I do two more takes, and we nail it. But he left me alone. He left me alone to do my work. Because he could see what I was doing.

The faith Tommy showed in Alex didn't end there. CUT TO: Two years later. The Democratic National Convention has descended upon Los Angeles.

ALEX GRAVES: Clinton's White House was inviting members of the cast to the convention in downtown LA, sometimes even when they're supposed to be filming. I'm on set, shooting, and I'm supposed to have John Spencer at midnight, but he's down at the convention. Suddenly the phone rings. They say, "John Wells is on the line for you." And I'm thinking, O-kayyy . . . John's *never* called me on set. So, they bring me the phone. And he's like—

HOLD ON. You know what? Let's put it in script form.

INT. WEST WING SET — OUTSIDE THE ROOSEVELT ROOM — LATE

A bright-eyed AD hands Alex a PHONE. On the other end is Executive Producer JOHN WELLS.

          ALEX GRAVES (TO HIMSELF)
     He is going to destroy me for going
     so late . . .

          JOHN WELLS (OVER THE PHONE)
     Hey, how ya doin'?

Alex responds, nonchalant . . .

          ALEX GRAVES
     Hi, how are you?

          JOHN WELLS
     I just want to apologize. I am so
     sorry.

          ALEX GRAVES
     For what?

          JOHN WELLS
     Well, for what's going on.

ALEX GRAVES
What do you mean?

JOHN WELLS
Well, you're—we're trying to make
your day and the studio's furious.
And I know that you may not have
the cast you need, and I just
wanted to apologize.

A bit thrown, Alex manages to stammer out a high-voice
version of . . .

ALEX GRAVES
Uh, it's okay, I'm fine, I'll
just . . . I'm gonna shoot . . .

JOHN WELLS
I know you're gonna go over,
so . . . we apologize.

Perplexed, Alex hangs up and, dazed, hands the phone back to
the bright-eyed AD.

ALEX GRAVES: I mean . . . that never happens. I'm like, I don't
know what that was, but wow . . . that seemed really nice.

And it was. But that's not the end. To reset: In this moment, it's
clear to Alex that they're not going to get John Spencer back, and it's a
near certainty that shooting is going to go way over for the night. Then
Alex learned that the studio was "hoping I'd be done by midnight, but
at that point I knew I may not be done by three a.m." So, around this
time . . .

ALEX GRAVES: Tommy walks on set, and it's like, "Tommy's
here—*and he's gonna talk to Alex.*" I've figured out that the

studio's freaking out on John and Tommy . . . like *really* mad.
And Tommy comes over and—

HOLD ON. Let's go back to the script . . .

INT. WEST WING SET — VIDEO VILLAGE/OVAL OFFICE HALLWAY — VERY LATE

All eyes on Tommy as he approaches Alex at the monitors.
Cast and crew are dead silent.

> TOMMY
> Can I talk to you for a minute?

> ALEX GRAVES
> (thinly veiled frantic) I think I
> can be done by midnight. I just
> have to adjust some things and I'll
> probably have to eliminate a couple
> shots. Would that be okay? And I'd
> do this in one shot instead of
> covering it in the three angles I
> was going to—

> TOMMY
> Just . . . come over here.

Tommy takes him over to the corner. Alex thinks to himself:
"He's pulling me aside. To get me away from everybody. What's
he gonna say? Oh God, this must be really serious."

Over in the corner, Tommy glances around, then leans into
Alex, and whispers . . .

> TOMMY
> Just do . . . whatever the
> fuck . . . you want.

And he leaves. FADE OUT.

Okay. That *really* never happens. And it captures one of the things we loved most about our time on *The West Wing*. That sense of holistic commitment—from every corner—to respect the process of whatever work is being done by whichever member of the team, is vitally important. The actors, the director, the lighting department, camera, sound, hair and makeup, background artists, and countless others—*everyone*.

For Tommy to express that level of trust in a young director, who's very early in his career, and who has the studio breathing down his neck . . . is such a gift. For him to decide, "We're just going to protect this kid's vision," is more than rare. Alex called it "magic." The vast majority of the time, it doesn't happen. The vast majority of the time, vision and artistry eventually get chipped away. And if nobody's protective of it, the clock starts ticking in your head. Instead of the work, the *clock* becomes what matters.

That culture of mutually assured protection—of family, and the ways it was established—distinguished the *West Wing* set from all the others the two of us have been on, before or since.

And it wasn't just that we liked one another or laughed a lot or had the good fortune to share great chemistry—it wasn't *just* those things. It was the faith we had in every other person to do their job at a very high level. And, whether it involves art, service, or a day at the office, those things don't happen by accident. They happen by promoting and nurturing unbreakable two-way trust.

It's not magic. It just feels that way.

TWENTY-THREE

KEY EPISODE

"Bartlet for America"

T he morning after Brad Whitford took home the Emmy for his
sensational performance in "Noël," John Spencer was walking
down a street on the Warner Bros. lot. He spotted Brad and Aaron
sitting in the back of a golf cart. As he approached the two freshly
minted award winners—the previous evening Aaron had landed yet
another Best Drama Series Emmy—John got the feeling they'd just
been talking about him. He was right.

Offering a preview of a story he and Tommy had been discussing,
Aaron said, "We're working on a script for you. It's gonna be your
year soon."

As John revealed on the DVD commentary he did with Aaron and
Tommy, "That's the first time I heard of this episode: 'Bartlet for
America.'"

For the lucky few who knew John Spencer, the following observa-
tion won't exactly bowl you over: Multiple times during that DVD
commentary rewatch of "Bartlet for America," he couldn't stop himself
from blurting out his admiration for someone on-screen. At the very
start, just seconds into the episode in fact, the first person to make an

entrance elicited this uncontainable response from John: "I *love* this actor." It was the guy playing FBI Special Agent Mike Casper, aka Clark Gregg (aka Phil Coulson, Agent of S.H.I.E.L.D.).

Minutes later, David St. James appeared on-screen as the shadowy congressman Darren Gibson. He hadn't even spoken yet, he hadn't said a single word. "This guy was *extraordinary*," John raved. "He was wonderful. A silent killer." And don't get him started on Joanna Gleason. ("I can't tell you the joy that was!") For Joanna, the feeling was mutual. "John connected like no other actor with whom I had ever worked. He made you think—made you *feel*—before speaking."

But let's pull back a moment—or rather, pull up, for the thirty-thousand-foot view. Like "Noël," this *West Wing* episode is more focused on a specific character than most, and this time the focus landed on Leo. Thanks to President Bartlet's years-long lie of omission—he had been keeping his multiple sclerosis diagnosis to himself (plus another sixteen people)—Leo is being dragged before a House government oversight committee to testify about what he knew and when he knew it. That's the cover story, anyway. What the opposition party is *actually* planning is to take POTUS's best friend and chief of staff out for a spin and dig into his past struggles with addiction, pills, and Johnnie Walker Blue. To be fair, being in a hotel room passed-out drunk right before your candidate's presidential debate isn't "illegal," but, then, neither is subjecting an honorable man to personal and professional humiliation, so . . . off we go.

In addition to tracking Leo's journey through his congressional testimony, we bear witness to a flirtation with Joanna's Jordon Kendall, the lawyer representing him. "When the camera rolled, and Leo asked what my plans are for Christmas Eve," Joanna remembered to us, "I felt such emotion. It was Leo and Jordon—all business but lonely—connecting." In the meantime, Agent Casper keeps us posted on some church bombings in Tennessee, and we take a trip, via flashback, to the great state of New Hampshire for a series of check-ins with:

1. "Governor" Jed Bartlet—remember him?

2. Jed's old pal Leo, who has a slogan, a grand plan, and a bar napkin he'd like to share.

3. Younger, fresher-faced versions of C.J., Toby, Josh, and Sam, fifty percent of whom team up to chest-pass a basketball through a Bartlet campaign office window.

4. Oh, also—Aaron brings back Delores Landingham and nobody thinks she's a ghost!

So, sure, there's a handful of other storylines driving this episode, but when you give the GPS a closer look, it's clear that all roads lead back to Leo and that damn congressional hearing. For the moment, though, let's return to the beginning. Actually, no—before that.

Even prior to production on "Bartlet for America," the creative team around *The West Wing* knew this story would be different. Deeper . . . more meaningful . . . *personal*. Given John Spencer's openness about his own addiction and recovery, there was already a lot of "there" there. As Tommy told us—he directed this one, too—"Bartlet for America" struck a nerve before the process had even begun.

"Just talking to John about what it was going to be, he burst out crying. I was like, *Fuck! I don't want him to do that yet!*" Tommy looked at John. "I shouldn't have told you about this." But there was no reason to worry. For John, the narrative ground the episode would dig into was extremely rich. Being so moved before filming didn't mean his emotional stores would get "used up." From our time working with John—in scenes in the Sit Room or brushing shoulders through the bullpen—it was evident he was an actor with an impossibly deep emotional reservoir. He wasn't going to run out of tears. "In the end," Tommy recalls, "he did the scene the same way. He just kept finding more and more stuff."

On the day Aaron, John, and Tommy sat together to rewatch "Bartlet for America" for the season 3 DVD, Tommy clocked a line of dialogue from the first two minutes of the episode. He turned to Aaron, noting "the power of a scene you wrote a year ago . . . in 'Noël.' There was never a reference since, 'til this moment, a *year* later. But there was not one viewer who didn't understand that reference."

> JOSH
> I'm gonna help you, 'cause you know why?

> LEO
> 'Cause you walk around with so much guilt about everybody you love dying that you're a compulsive fixer?

> JOSH
> No, Leo, no. It's 'cause a guy is walking down the street and he falls into a hole, see?

The first day of filming "Bartlet for America," John Spencer made his way onto the set of the congressional hearing room, where viewers would spend a sizable chunk of the episode, and was blown away. "I remember seeing this set for the first time, this set was incredible!" To meet production needs, *The West Wing* had taken their show on the road for this one, setting up shop at a different studio. "We were using the set of the series *The Court*," John recalled. (**MELISSA:** *The Court* was a short-lived legal drama starring Sally Field.) "It was a huge feature [of the episode], filled with background artists, and *vast*. You really felt like you were in court!"

Standing there, right hand raised, John discovered something new. "This was," he revealed, "where I first found out [Leo's] middle name was Thomas." Yes, much to the good-natured chagrin of costume designer Lyn Paolo, who had embroidered the monogram *L.B.M.* on the chief of staff's dress shirts, from that line on, *L.T.M.* it was! ("We did have to change Leo's shirts," Lynn told us. "I remember John not wanting to, as he was rather attached to his previous monograms!")

While "LTM" had his hand in the air, Aaron had his head in the past. It's safe to say the writer loved a *West Wing* flashback, and we're right there with him. "Flashbacks . . ." Aaron says, "when we would go back to before they were in the White House . . . became a sanctuary for me. Because the four years I was writing the show [were] the two years before and the two years after September 11 . . . when everything changed. It was nice to be able to take the characters back to before September 11. There was a real freedom there."

When the show would transport us back to the Bartlet team's pre–White House days, you could sense the "before-times" energy on-screen. "I look at these flashbacks," John Spencer once said, "and we look younger. We look a little more . . . innocent."

In that idea, Aaron saw a simple explanation. "You don't have literally the weight of the world on your shoulders," he pointed out. Exactly. At that point, they weren't in the White House yet. The characters exuded what Aaron refers to as a "childlike optimism."

From the days and nights shooting the origin story of Leo pushing Jed to run for president, a couple of stories stand out. In that first flashback—the conversation between Leo and then *Governor* Bartlet—there was one word Martin Sheen apparently didn't know how to pronounce. "Valium." He got there eventually, but for a while during shooting it was kind of touch-and-go. Rewatching the episode, John joked to Aaron and Tommy, "Guess who taught him how to say it!" Then, with a similarly sly smile in *his* voice, Aaron quipped, "Uh, John, there are any number of us who could've taught him how to say it."

Then there was that famous bar napkin. The gold-medal winner for *West Wing* artifacts—with the Paul Revere knife taking home the silver—is the napkin on which Leo wrote those three little words: "Bartlet for America."

```
            LEO
I've been walking around in a kind
of daze for two weeks and everywhere
I go . . . planes, trains,
restaurants, meetings . . . I find
myself scribbling something down.
```

In classic Sorkin form, the reveal of that would-be campaign slogan is unspoken, arriving only visually, when Leo sticks the napkin on an empty easel in the room. It's a beautiful moment. A perfect *West Wing* moment. Getting there, though, wasn't quite perfect. "I remember not being able to stick that up for several takes!" John said. Luckily for everyone involved, literal stick-to-itiveness (and a little more spit) got the job done.

That initial foray into the past provided a glimpse at Jed Bartlet's first steps on the road to 1600 Pennsylvania Avenue. Traveling back to the *present*, "Bartlet for America" dealt head-on with the hard realities of addiction. "In 'In the Shadow of Two Gunmen,' Aaron says, "we saw that Leo was the one who had gotten the posse together. I don't think it's coming as too much of a surprise to us that Leo was the one who got Bartlet to run in the first place. I just think that what makes it particularly poignant in 'Bartlet for America' is the point that Bartlet makes in the very last moment of the show: that this very powerful guy, who is capable of doing so much, literally through force of will and skill and talent, getting all these people together, getting this man elected, couldn't *not* drink the scotch in his hotel room. That glass of scotch was absolutely his undoing. And, to anyone who's familiar with addiction or alcoholism, the sad tragedy is that it doesn't discriminate. It certainly doesn't discriminate for skin color, gender, economic status, IQ. And it has nothing to do with being strong-willed or weak-willed."

John Spencer put it another way. "A person powerful in any other situation . . . can be powerless against something in a cup." Nowhere was that truth more self-evident than in Leo's hotel room with the two donor CEOs and the sixty-year-old scotch they brought in to seal the deal.

That slippery-slope sequence—for Leo, one drink with a group becomes ten drinks by himself—was one John had no issue tapping into. "As an actor," he said, "addiction . . . is not a foreign place for me; it's an easy place to get back to in my mind. I've raided convenience bars. When I ran out of the vodka I turned to the scotch and finally ended with the Bailey's Irish Cream." What struck John was how Leo cannot take his eyes off that glass. "All through the conversation, it's back to the glass." (Watching Leo take that fateful sip of Johnnie Walker Blue, Aaron couldn't help narrating the catastrophic moment: "And a million people leap to their TV screens, 'Oh noooo!!'")

The tale of that downfall, told matter-of-factly by Leo to the lawyer by his side, represented a central love story of the show, Jed and Leo:

```
                    LEO
        The President was at the debate
        site, walking the stage. A podium
        is a holy place for him. He makes
        it his own, like it's an extension
        of his body. You ever see a pitcher
        work the mound, so the dirt does
        exactly what his feet want it to
        do? That's the President. He sees
        it as a genuine opportunity to
        change minds—also as his best way
        of contributing to the team. He
        likes teams. I love him so
        much . . .
```

As lovely and moving as the scene was, Leo's recounting of the moment he fell off the wagon posed a challenge for the director. "We're coming out of something enormously powerful," Tommy said to John. "From an actor's point of view, you're telling that story straight through. When we came back, you hadn't had some metamorphosis, you already knew that truth. Yet we as an audience had a massive metamorphosis." Initially, Tommy couldn't quite figure out how to shoot the Leo-Jordan sequence coming out of the flashback. What he eventually realized is this: "I was trying to make more of it than it was."

Spencer never forgot what made the difference that day. It was a piece of direction similar to the one Tommy had given him for his "guy falls into a hole" speech at the end of "Noël." He reminded John that it was actually a pretty simple scene. "'You're telling a story.' That's the note you gave me."

Meanwhile, there was still the matter of those vindictive House committee members. Enter: Cliff Calley (Mark Feuerstein), aka the first guy not named Josh we ever liked for Donna. As House majority counsel, he confronts shady congressman Darren Gibson, who had the goods on Leo (and was in the hotel room with the Johnnie Walker Blue).

```
                    CLIFF CALLEY
          This is bush league. This is why
          good people hate us. This, right
          here. This thing. This isn't what
          these hearings are about. He
          cannot possibly have been properly
          prepared by counsel for these
          questions, nor should he ever
          have to answer them publicly.
          And if you proceed with this line
          of questioning, I will resign
          this committee and wait in the
          tall grass for you, Congressman,
          because you are killing the party.
```

After the hearing reconvenes (and just *before* Congressman Gibson is set to resume his questioning of Leo), the chairman of the oversight committee, Congressman Joseph Bruno, cuts him off, abruptly shutting the hearing down. Leo gets up, relieved and a bit stunned by the sudden reversal. With Margaret close at hand, he walks out in a daze. His private, personal demons will, it appears, remain private and personal. And, with that, "Bartlet for America" heads off toward its emotional closing moments.

We follow Leo on the long, solitary walk back to his office, where he finds his best friend—not the president, but *Jed*—waiting for him. "I have a present for you," Jed says. It's the napkin Leo gave him all those years ago—"Bartlet for America" scribbled in pen—except now it's framed. Soon, Jed walks out, leaving Leo alone with his gift.

Overcome with emotion, the framed napkin in his hand, Leo sinks into his chair and begins to weep. We get a little emotional. And so does Aaron, during the DVD rewatch, while sitting next to Spencer. "Well," he says, "that's what they give Emmys for, John."

Barely able to get the words out, John manages a sweet, broken reply: "And that's the kind of writing and direction that an actor waits most of his career to have."

In that moment, after listening to John Spencer rave for almost an hour about actors and acting, about Aaron's writing and Tommy's direction; after listening to his boundlessly effusive spirit as it related to every element that went into making this episode of television, we were transported back to our time with John on *The West Wing*. Witnessing him again, armed as always with compliments and a passion for the work, was a little eerie and a lot heartwarming. This, we recognized, is the man we knew. The depth of kindness and humanity in Leo McGarry was mirrored by John every day of his life on the show. That spirit, which so profoundly resonated with us, was reflected in the final words of the episode, delivered by his best friend, Jed:

"Merry Christmas, Leo. That was awfully nice of you."

★ ★ ★ **BIG BLOCK OF CHEESE STORY** ★ ★ ★

The Room Where It Happened

If you were on the tram tour at Warner Bros. Studios in Burbank, you wouldn't hop off at Soundstage 23. We shot there for the run of the show, but honestly . . . it doesn't look like much. Sure, it's fifty feet tall and armed with "elephant doors" for loading in massive set pieces, but from the outside—for a fan on a tram tour—it hardly stands out from the other stages on the lot. You're not going to defy the tour guide by jumping off only to wind up tangling with lot security. But if we told you what's at eye level just inside the front door, you might consider making a break for it, cell phone at the ready, all geeked up to grab a snapshot. It's not C.J.'s briefing podium or the Resolute desk or Toby's pink Spaldeen encased in glass. Mounted on the wall's soundproof padding just inside the front entrance, is a small bronze plaque:

In Loving Memory of Our Friend
JOHN SPENCER
Who worked, won Emmys and
graced us with his passion and talent on this stage.
THE WEST WING
July 14, 1999 to December 16, 2005

That lovely plaque honors a great actor and a better man whose name and heart and soul live on. Still. Right there in Soundstage 23.

TWENTY-FOUR

WILL BAILEY

Origin Story

Okay, let's get back to our origin stories. As with any long-running show, the "original cast" is just that. Original. Over time, fresh faces make their way into the world we've come to know, while others head off into the sunset. Take Sam Seaborn. For such a beloved character to walk out the door was, of course, a big deal. But it was hardly unprecedented.

In TV, as in life, the reason anyone does anything rarely stems from a single factor. It's always a cocktail of issues. Did various financial negotiations go sideways? Yes. Were there disagreements involving billing in the opening credits or the quantity of Sam Seaborn storylines? There were. But it's also true that a key issue behind Rob Lowe's departure was rooted in a conflict that went to the heart of the show.

Central to Aaron's vision for *The West Wing* was, you'll recall, the paramount importance of the ensemble. As the show caught fire and became a bona fide hit, Rob recognized a general (and vocal) reluctance to allow one member of the cast to upset the balance of that ensemble. As he put it to us, "It's coming off of George Clooney blowing up on *ER*. People were like, 'That is never going to happen. We will never, ever, ever, EVER let anyone—ever—be anything more than anybody else. *Ever.*'"

While the natural trajectory of a TV series often bends toward this actor or that one "breaking out," and while that's a perfectly reasonable thing to wish for, the fact is, Aaron had wishes of his own. He wished to stay true to his foundational vision for the series as one built around a constellation more than a star. And so he did.

In the end, Rob and his representatives put out a press release: "As much as it hurts to admit it, it has been increasingly clear, for quite a while, that there was no longer a place for Sam Seaborn on *The West Wing.* However, Warner Bros. has allowed me an opportunity to leave the show as I arrived . . . grateful for it, happy to have been on it, and proud of it. We were a part of television history and I will never forget it." Later, Aaron acknowledged the dual challenge of that new Seaborn-less normal: "It was hard saying goodbye to the character and harder saying goodbye to the actor."

That goodbye was a long one: In the years since Rob left, he and Aaron have worked together multiple times, including on a West End stage production of *A Few Good Men* and on *A West Wing Special to Benefit "When We All Vote."* (More on that later in the book.)

But, as we all know, when relationships end, it is not always on the best of terms. Twenty years after he left, in 2023, Rob's tone about his time on *The West Wing* had shifted significantly. He said that he felt "very undervalued" on the show, and shared that "I did not have a good experience." Personally speaking, it was hard to read these comments, but they were clearly deeply felt. Around the time he left the show, Rob was making more than twice the salary of the core ensemble, and when the cast pushed for equal pay, it seems he took this as an affront. Coupled with what he perceived as the diminishing size of his role, this apparently was the breaking point for him. Maybe it just wasn't a great fit. Rob was—and is—certainly a star. He has gone on to be the face of many shows after *The West Wing.* Perhaps the notion of a true ensemble, where everyone is treated the same, and thinks of themselves as a cast of players, rather than individual stars, wasn't the right environment for him at the time. "I walked away from the most popular girl at school," Rob said of *The West Wing* in 2023, "but I also knew that it was a super-unhealthy relationship, and it was the best thing I ever did."

To us, Rob pointed out decorously that "nobody wants to know that the Beatles fought." And that's true. But what happened happened, and an all-access pass to *The West Wing* wouldn't have been complete without a detour, however slight, down this stretch of Pennsylvania Avenue.

So, yes, as *The West Wing* kicked off its fourth season, a sea change was in the air. In advance of Sam's exit, stage left, Will Bailey showed up, right on cue, in the form of Josh Malina.

The first thing you need to know about Josh Malina is that he is both the meanest person you'll ever work with and the nicest person you'll ever work with. While you may have heard references to Josh's off-screen antics—the merciless teasing, the outrageous long-form pranks, his habit of knocking script pages out of the hands of every passerby—the fact of the matter is he's far, far worse than that. But . . . while Josh often quips that his arrival marked "the beginning of the end of *The West Wing*," we beg to differ. To the contrary, his emergence on the scene represented new blood, a different kind of energy . . . and a bit of that old, familiar Sorkin DNA.

There are plenty of "Mighty Sorkin Players" populating (and re-populating) the various spaces in which Aaron's words have been brought to life, Brad Whitford and Tim Busfield among them. But who has more consistently appeared on stage and screen speaking Aaron Sorkin dialogue than Josh Malina? *A Few Good Men*—the Broadway play (plus the national tour) and the movie. *Malice*. *The American President*. *Sports Night*. Even after season 4, when Aaron exited the "stage" of *The West Wing*, Josh remained—his faithful, glowing ghost light.

The second thing you need to know about Josh Malina is that he procured the job that would change the trajectory of his life and career thanks, in part, to his cousins' choice of high school. Scarsdale High—regardless of how it sounds, we swear it's not a tween show on Netflix—is the secondary school attended by Stuart, Joel, and Rachel Malina . . . at the same time as this other kid named Sorkin.

Years later, Malina's mom suggested that their son reach out to his cousins to help land an audition for Aaron Sorkin's Broadway production of *A Few Good Men*. Thanks to those family connections, Josh got his foot in the door. From there, the rest was up to him.

The good news for Josh was this: When it comes to producing his work, Aaron is more than just a nice guy who does favors for his old classmates. He's someone with a keen eye (and a soft spot) for talent. And Josh Malina is undeniably talented (insert own Brad Whitford joke here), which is how he wound up cast in *A Few Good Men*. How he has *continued* to work with Aaron since is up for debate, but we're guessing this didn't hurt:

"As cast members of *A Few Good Men*," Josh told us, "we got to be part of the Broadway Bowling League. It was fun, we quite enjoyed it. But on one of these bowling nights, Aaron started choking. It was a piece of hamburger, but at first we thought he was just being funny, that he was doing a bit . . . until we realized, Oh, this is a thing that's actually happening. So I ran over and did the Heimlich on Aaron . . . and ended up cracking three of his ribs. That was the downside. The upside was, it kept him alive long enough to put me in *Sports Night* and *West Wing*!"

What can get lost in the whirlwind of Malina's wisecracks and his self-effacing faux apathy ("I'll say anything, I don't care, I'll wear a chicken suit") is that he's practically tailor-made for Aaron's words.

Josh's facility with dialogue and humor can't be taught. He could play sardonic and smart while sleepwalking on his hands in the middle of Times Square. But he can also deliver when it comes to emotions big and small, and does so with a remarkably nuanced sincerity.

But let's rewind a bit.

It's 2001. Josh is on a show on NBC, he's married, with one child and another on the way and—you know what? Here's how Josh put it on *The West Wing Weekly*: "It's Halloween. My pregnant wife is out of town with our four-year-old daughter, trick-or-treating with my in-laws, in Sacramento. I'm alone in my house, having a moment of great satisfaction because I've bought a house, I've done it, with my acting career. That night I get a call saying, 'Don't come in to work tomorrow . . . NBC doesn't love the script, we're gonna rework it,' blah blah blah. Long story short, we never went back to work."

Now, it just so happens that, not long after, Josh spotted a *West Wing* rumor in the entertainment industry trades. Sources had it that Rob Lowe might be leaving the show. "Hm . . ." he thought. "I should probably reach out to Aaron . . ."

So, there Josh sat at his computer, feeling a bit like his character, Jeremy Goodwin, from *Sports Night*. During a hilarious meltdown in the pilot, Jeremy pleads as he interviews for a segment producer gig. "Ms. Whitaker, I would be great at this job! You gotta believe me when I say I've been training my whole life for it!" Indeed, when it came to that *West Wing* vacancy, you could say Malina had been training his whole life for it. And, unlike Jeremy, instead of spontaneously wigging out, Malina kept his cool and fired off what he still remembers as "this shameless, dorky email."

"I noticed this thing in *Variety*," the shameless, dorky email began, "about Rob leaving the show. Just pitching here, but have you thought about hiring somebody who's less well known, less good-looking, and would work for a lot less money?"

Aaron's reply came quick and was pretty much as good as it gets. "Tommy and I were just discussing this!" To this day, Josh isn't sure if Aaron was telling the truth or just susceptible to suggestion, but in classic Malina form, he doesn't really care.

Next thing you know, Aaron told Josh to "meet me at the Four Seasons and we'll discuss." Naturally, Josh was thrilled, but from where he stood, there was little to discuss. As he said to us, "What better role was out there? What opportunity for an actor is better than 'Do you want to be on *The West Wing?*'"

Sitting across from Josh at the Four Seasons in Beverly Hills, Aaron seemed kind of excited about the idea. "He started telling me what the character was like," Josh told us. "He's hitting me with all this information: 'He's a young guy, funny . . .' It felt a little like he was pitching *me* on the character!" Meanwhile, what kept running through Josh's mind was, "Um . . . Aaron? You had me at 'meeting.'"

As Josh described it to us, a bit deeper into the conversation the tenor suddenly changed. "Aaron got really serious and was like, in hushed tones, 'Now . . . just, uh, so you know . . . the character, he, uh . . . he isn't Jewish.'" A moment of bewildered silence later, Josh looked at his friend and said, "So? What do you think, I'm gonna turn it down, like 'I ONLY PLAY JEWISH CHARACTERS!' I literally was like, 'Dude, whatever you say—I'm in, and I don't care. I'm excited to hear about it, I'm excited about all of it, but I don't care about any of the details at all. Whatever it is, I'm going to do it and I'm very, very excited about it!'" (It appears Josh reserves his poker face exclusively for the gaming table.)

From there, Aaron dove into the details of how the initial option period would work. Josh would appear as Will Bailey for six episodes. "Then if we're happy," Aaron told him, "and *you're* happy . . ." Josh knew the end of that sentence. But he didn't wait for it, and he wasn't shy. "Well, *I'm* gonna be happy," he told him. "Just let me know when you guys are."

Obviously, as far as Josh was concerned, the meeting at the Four Seasons was one to remember. In fact, it was so exciting, he couldn't help feeling a bit distracted. As he put it to us, "It's a moment you'd assume I'd want to savor, but I think what I really wanted to do—part of me anyway—was just . . . leave, so I could call my wife and say, 'MELLIE—I JUST GOT SIX EPISODES OF *THE WEST WING*!!'"

★ ★ ★

THE first day Malina ever appeared on the *West Wing* set, the actor whose shoes he was hired to fill hadn't the foggiest idea what to expect. "I felt like everybody on the show knew Josh but me," Rob Lowe told *The West Wing Weekly*, "so I was excited to meet him and see what all the fuss was about." What, then, did the soon-to-be-former deputy comms director think? "He was totally as advertised. So smart, really funny, and just clearly knew how to play the music. It was like he was there *forever*."

That kind of says it all about Josh Malina and his place in the *West Wing* universe. He entered it fully formed and ready to run.

Maybe it's the confidence that comes with years spent developing fluency in the language of Sorkin. Maybe it's the "I don't care" he wears so well. What didn't hurt is something Brad confessed to us in an unguarded moment: "Josh is just . . . hilariously funny."

If you watch the cold open of "In the Shadow of Two Gunmen: Part II" and you haven't watched the first episode, it plays like a horrendous overreaction of the police to a diner putting out his cigarette in an egg.

—JOSH MALINA, *THE WEST WING WEEKLY*

Whatever the reason, from day one Josh walked in with this sense of preordained belonging, like he was already a member of the pack. Which brings us to "Arctic Radar." Episode 10 of *The West Wing*'s fourth season, "Arctic Radar" includes one of the iconic moments—and one of the iconic on-screen images—the series ever saw.

An episode-long battle of egos between two world-class writers, one slumping (Toby) and one on a hot streak (Will), ends in a mutually respectful détente. Compliments are poignantly exchanged, order—and Toby's writing mojo—is seemingly restored, and a note is hand delivered by Will to the grouch who just hired him to help write President Bartlet's second inaugural address.

As Will leaves—for a vacation he will cut short precisely eighteen seconds later—Toby opens the envelope and removes a short handwritten note. The note—"*Sam Seaborn for Congress*" embossed across the top—reads:

> *Toby—*
>
> *He's one of us.*
>
> *—Sam*

"That was huge for me," Josh told us. "It almost made me laugh when I read it 'cause it's Aaron talking to the audience *and* the cast, telling them, 'As King of the Show, you <u>must</u> accept this person. He is what *West Wing* is!'" Malina is convinced that Aaron's generosity in issuing that quasi commandment made a difference in the way he and his character have come to be viewed. And yet . . .

"There are still people who don't accept the premise," Josh says. "People who hate my character and felt like he was an interloper. That's why my Twitter bio is 'Hi, I ruined *The West Wing*.'"

But Aaron knew a transition was coming, and he primed the audience for it—and did so in the most Sorkin-like way. In "Game On," the first Will Bailey episode, there's a key scene that takes place on an Orange County beach. Just after Will confirms that he has more campaign events that day, Sam takes off his tie and offers it up, telling Will that *his* tie "doesn't go." Into that seemingly innocuous handoff, it's hard not to read a passing of the *West Wing* baton. Sam walks away, as Rob Lowe would soon. As the sun eases down and the tide rolls out, one can sense in that exchange the end of an era . . . and the start of something new.

* * *

A SERVICE STORY

JOSH MALINA

Through his commitment to public service, Josh Malina has inspired us, not just for what he's done, but for how he's done it. He lives his personal values publicly and with a brave and enviable audacity. Often sardonic, at times serious, he takes the hits and stands up for what he believes in, Twitter screeds be damned. He's even allowed himself to—hold, please, for a moment of utter mortification—"evolve."

> **JOSH MALINA:** It's a complete one-eighty from earlier in my career to later in my career. I have that innate "Who gives a fuck what some actor thinks about anything of substance?" pulsing through me.

> **MARY:** I also struggled with that. The answer, for me, was that having an opinion on a particular moral question or a matter of policy . . . doesn't have to be as an actor, it has to be as a *citizen*. As a part of a global community, you get to

care about all of those issues. And then, *because* you're an actor, you are blessed with a platform that gets to amplify it more.

JOSH MALINA: That's exactly right. The one-eighty for me was, I'm a citizen. Being part of *The West Wing*, even as a viewer, encourages you to care about civics and about your rights and responsibilities as a citizen, and inspires you to get involved to the extent that you can. So, I've realized there's nothing wrong with putting myself out there as long as I constantly—and I try to—undercut myself and make it clear that I AM NOT AN EXPERT. On *anything*.

MARY: I care about the environment as a mother, as a caring person—I care about those issues as a human.

MELISSA: Exactly. And the thing is, most people aren't area experts. You don't have to be an area expert to care about and fight for the issues that impact your life and the lives of your loved ones and community.

JOSH MALINA: I'm sure I sometimes cross the line into seeming like my opinion matters more than it does. A lot of the time I agree with the people who are like, "Stick to act-ing!" I get it. We have an unfair advantage, being actors. Something I say, as a citizen, is going to get heard or ingested by many more people than the average person on Twitter. I just had to come to terms with the fact that that's a positive, not a negative. That if I share the things I care about, I'll be careful, and I do try to be. I do a lot of speaking engagements for Jewish organizations and I'm always saying, "I'm not an expert on Middle East affairs."

MARY: But I am. Kate Harper is!

JOSH MALINA: Yes! As Will Bailey, I *dated* someone who was!

There was a specific inciting incident behind Josh's one-eighty. In the early 2000s, he was invited by the Jewish Federation of Greater Los Angeles to a rally in support of Israel. The impetus for the rally was not political, and not remotely controversial: "Israel has a right to exist."

JOSH MALINA: This was actually before *West Wing.* I would have been on *Sports Night*, I guess. I told them, "I'm not a celebrity, but if you want me to sit on the celebrity dais, I will." When I arrived, my relative lack of "celebrity" came into even clearer focus. The celebrity sign-in people were like, "Who are you?" I said, "I swear, you guys invited me." I had to spell my name— twice. It was embarrassing. I wasn't offended, I was like, "Why should you know who I am, but . . . somebody called me."

Then he got onto the dais and took a look around . . .

JOSH MALINA: It was Jim Hahn (the mayor of LA) and a great orthodox musician named Peter Himmelman. I was like, "Well, where are the actual celebrities?" (Also, why didn't they know who I was if I'm one of *three* people on the "celebrity dais"?) I spoke to the entertainment liaison for the Jewish Federation afterward and she was like, "Oh yeah, if it has to do with Israel, nobody will come." And I was like, "We're in Hollywood, it's like the Mecca—so to speak—of famous Jewish people. What are you talking about?"

She said, "If it's explicitly about Israel, nobody will come. They'll send money anonymously, they're supportive, but you're not gonna get them out." I remember thinking, That's kind of appalling. Because I'm very critical of Israel, and I'm happy to share that stuff—and I do now—but . . . "Israel has a right to exist." *That's* too controversial to sit on the celebrity dais?!

Once Josh finally landed on *The West Wing*, with its hit-show spotlight, the lure of sharing his thoughts and opinions grew, as he started receiving interview requests.

JOSH MALINA: *The Jewish Journal of Greater Los Angeles* talked to me, so I shared that story. All of a sudden I started getting all this response. Every Jewish website—"BabagaNewz. com" wants an interview! Strangers are writing to me, other Jewish organizations, literally the consul general of Israel in Los Angeles called me: "You should organize a trip to Israel!"

I was clear that I never wanted to put myself forth as any kind of expert, but I could see the positive aspect of using my limited celebrity to draw attention to other things. And as I've gotten more and more educated about issues in that area (though still not an expert), there are critical things I can help bring an eye to. I have opinions about the occupation and what things Israel could do to more fully realize its democratic ideals . . . which, of course, gets me grief from *another* corner of the community.

I mean, I'm a friend of Israel. It just depends what kind of friend you want. Do you want the friend who always tells you that you do everything right? Or the friend that's going to ask you to be *better*?

Josh currently sits on the board of Americans for Peace Now, an organization advocating, through education and persuasion, for a resolution to the conflict between the populations of Israel and Palestine. As flattering as the offer was, Josh initially resisted. He told them, "I support you, I'm interested, I like listening to webinars occasionally . . . but I don't know what my qualifications are to sit on the board." Their reply was, "Whether you like it or not, you have some following, and if you can help bring attention to things . . ."

That Josh is a good man and a better friend will come as no surprise to anyone who knows him. In 1995, when Melissa launched Voices in Harmony, the fledgling organization held a micro-fundraiser at a bar. She remembers it as "super bare-bones—we got a band to play and got the bar to donate all the food, but people had to buy their own drinks. Josh and his family were two of the first three donors in the history of Voices in Harmony. My parents were the others."

JOSH MALINA: There's something in the Talmud that basically says, You don't walk by somebody who's asking for money. My father has lived that to the point where we literally had to stop him once from putting a dollar in a businessman's cup of coffee. "Dad, that guy's not asking for money, he just has a cup!"

AMERICANS FOR PEACE NOW

APN's mission is to educate and persuade the American public and its leadership to support and adopt policies that will lead to comprehensive, durable Israeli-Palestinian and Israeli-Arab peace, based on a two-state solution, guaranteeing both peoples' security, and consistent with US national interests. APN also works to ensure Israel's future and the viability of Israel's democracy and Jewish character through education, activism, and advocacy in the United States, and by mobilizing American support for Shalom Achshav, APN's sister organization in Israel.

www.peacenow.org

HIAS

Welcome the stranger. Protect the refugee. Founded as the Hebrew Immigrant Aid Society in 1881 to assist Jews fleeing pogroms in Russia and Eastern Europe, HIAS has touched the life of nearly every Jewish family in America and now welcomes all who have fled persecution.

www.hias.org

★ ★ ★

TWENTY-FIVE

KEY EPISODE

"Game On"

It's difficult to overstate how momentous season 4 was in the life arc of *The West Wing*. It represents an inflection point as Aaron Sorkin and Tommy Schlamme, the show's creators, left the series they loved so much. You might assume that Aaron and Tommy's run ended with a star-spangled season finale featuring Bartlet and his staff, triumphant on election night. It did not. The story of the president winning reelection is told, of course; it just happened to arrive early in their final season, in episode seven. Aptly titled, "Election Night," the *West Wing* debut of director Lesli Linka Glatter treated viewers to a stellar "victory montage" that included: a blizzard of patriotic confetti, countless waving American flags, a celebratory balloon drop, and what feels, upon reflection, like an eerily prescient cover of Bob Dylan's classic folk song "The Times They Are A-Changin'." They were indeed.

That said, we'd argue that the times *actually* began a-changin' the week before, in "Game On." While this episode didn't exactly signal the end of an era, it did suggest the *beginning* of the end. The first hint at that transition involved the tie we mentioned in the previous chapter (the one Sam let Will borrow earlier in the episode because *his* tie "doesn't go"). Hours later, around one a.m. in a Laguna Beach bar—and just seven seconds before this episode's final credits—Will takes out the tie and tries to give it back:

                         WILL
              Don't forget your necktie.

                         SAM
          Keep it.

Sam said that on his way out the door, without looking back. He didn't even break stride. That sense of *motion*, lasting as it did through the episode's final moments, was a critical element of director Alex Graves's early vision for "Game On." From its opening shot—over Leo's shoulder, tight on a flummoxed, twitchy Toby getting pranked in his office—that first minute, and the forty that followed, could be best described as kinetic.

Before filming began—just as the script had been completed, in fact—Aaron put in a call to Alex. "This is the election episode," he told him. "You'll know at the end of the debate that the winner's going to be Bartlet." From that conversation on, Alex felt compelled to produce "a real razzle-dazzle episode." A day later, Aaron took Alex aside and reiterated what had already been explicitly ordered in the script—"I don't want to FADE IN, you should just CUT in." That instruction, on the page and otherwise, sent the director off in search of what he calls an "edgier . . . fresher" approach.

"I decided to take the camera off the dolly and shoot handheld," Alex says. There were, he explained, a couple reasons for this. "Not only did I think it would inject the beginning of the episode with a fresh energy, I thought it would be fun to see a presidential debate with a handheld camera because [we'd been] conditioned over the years to watching the debates from these locked off, very stoic video positions."

Alex based the visual approach to the final Bartlet-Ritchie debate on those between Vice President Al Gore and Texas governor George W. Bush in the 2000 election. He was intrigued by the idea of shooting behind the debate moderators and their monitors and cameras. Establishing that visceral feeling—"like I was in the room watching two men perform in . . . this theater of the debates"—would, he imagined, "liven things up."

Livening things up fell right in line with Aaron's script. Despite several weighty, consequential events, it's undeniable that "Game On" is pretty darn fun. "We had a ball shooting this," Alex says. "Number one, we were in love with the writing. Number two . . . moving very fast"—due to the handheld camerawork—"really energized the cast. If we weren't laughing," he said, "we were filming. We were having such a good time."

That was the good news. The bad news was, "Page count was long at the table read," Aaron says. It's not terribly surprising, then, that Alex's first cut of the episode came in well over time. "There was," as Aaron diplomatically put it, "a level of concern."

Despite that concern, one of the longest scenes in "Game On" came nowhere near the chopping block. Set on Air Force One, it featured the return of Assistant Secretary of State Albie Duncan. This delightful sequence saw Hal Holbrook's crotchety political operator getting prepped by C.J. for the post-debate "spin room." According to Alex, it clocked in at nine pages. (**MARY:** An average TV scene tends to run one or two pages and can be as short as an eighth of a page.) "Holbrook came on, said hello to everybody . . . and in the hours it took to shoot the scene . . . never once looked at his sides or script."

Of course, that scene staying in meant other things had to come out. A sizable chunk was removed from a Leo story involving a Qumari warship, a shipment of weapons getting redirected to a terrorist group, and Qumar's UN representative, Ali Nassir. The most noteworthy element of that thread was the welcome reprise of Joanna Gleason as Leo's lawyer, Jordon Kendall. Referring to Joanna as "a gold rush of an actress," Alex still marvels at the dynamism firing between those two. "They were like an old, sexy married couple, who . . . no matter how tough the fight got . . . enjoyed every minute of each other." This was, Alex went on to say, just as true of the actors themselves.

They may have made it look easy, but for Joanna Gleason "Game On" was anything but. "It was a challenge because I arrived on set in the early afternoon, and we shot until about four in the morning. But John never flagged—there was much kibitzing, which led to the ease of the on-screen banter!"

Given the crisis with Qumar, the chief of staff has to stick close to home, even as the president and the rest of his team head off to San Diego for the debate. As far as Leo is concerned—he'll say as much, later, to Ali Nassir—not attending the debate is "like missing my brother's wedding." Indeed, in an exchange early on with the soon-departing president, Leo nods him out to the portico for a heartfelt pep talk.

> **LEO**
> There's no such thing as too smart.
> There's nothing you can do that's
> not going to make me proud of you.
> Eat 'em up. Game on.

The idea embedded in that *West Wing* quasi haiku existed in the world of the show . . . and outside of it, too. Even for a position as critical as leader of the free world, certain voters are put off when a candidate comes across as a know-it-all. "That's Bartlet's vulnerability," Aaron points out. "And he's been getting nudged by Toby for a while not to try to run from that. To *be* the smartest guy in the class."

Governor Ritchie, meanwhile, is his perfect foil and polar opposite, the plainspoken "guy you wanna have a beer with" straight out of central casting. This debate episode was, in part, Aaron's reaction to the 2000 campaign and what he saw as Gore "trying not to be himself,

for fear that being himself was . . . unattractive to too many people."
The choice for Bartlet to actually *be* the smartest kid in the class, to
lean in to his intellect and his command of the issues was, for many
viewers—these two included—like a dream sequence come true. "I
could've written the debate with the Republican . . . wiping up the
floor with the Democrat," Aaron says. "The point was that intelligence
isn't a vice." (In a way, this can be seen as an analogy for the show itself:
it's okay to use acronyms and long words, it's okay to talk fast and
underexplain, it's okay to make one big scene out of eight little ones.
Intelligence—in television, as in politics—isn't a vice.)

But enough about the main event (for the time being), let's get to
the undercard: Josh Malina's *West Wing* debut!

The first time viewers ever laid eyes on Will Bailey, he was managing the political campaign of a dead man named Horton Wilde and
barking out orders from the middle of a mattress store in Newport
Beach. Quick refresher: It wasn't that the underdog Democrat vying
to represent California's Forty-Seventh District was "dead in the polls."
He was actually, well . . . dead. *Dead* dead. That's why perfect-looking
Sam Seaborn and his perfect-looking necktie had shown up. To persuade the campaign to, at long last, shut down and spare the White
House (and the party) any further embarrassment. But Will Bailey
wasn't having it.

> **WILL**
> There's a campaign being waged
> here, and I'm not embarrassed by
> it. There are things being talked
> about, things you believe in,
> things the White House believes in,
> and they're only gonna be talked
> about in a blowout, and you know
> it. And you know there's no glory
> in it, and you still come here
> twice and tell me my guy's a joke!

That's quite a moment for a new cast member—playing a weary, rumpled "David" facing off against the well-dressed "Goliath"-size ego and righteous indignation of one of POTUS's best and brightest. Malina, though, didn't flinch. Not in the mattress-store showdown and not in that tense-making press conference scene. Oh yeah—that.

As Josh recounted to us, the fact that the first *West Wing* scene he ever shot was directed by Alex Graves really put him at ease "because I knew him from directing me five times on *Sports Night*." That said, it was a press conference scene, which meant "there were," as Josh put it, "a lot of quick answers and a lot of policy." Press conference scenes can be especially demanding on an actor because, of course, whoever's at the podium—as C.J., Will, and cocky-'til-his-comeuppance Josh Lyman can attest—has virtually every bit of dialogue, interrupted occasionally by a reporter shouting a question . . . at which point you dive into yet another chunk of dense policy.

On his first day, Josh's experience kicked in. "I was in game mode," he says, "and in the right headspace, frankly, because I had trained for this moment. I had done forty-five episodes as Jeremy on *Sports Night*, seven hundred and fifty performances of *A Few Good Men*. I didn't go to acting school, I trained in the Aaron Sorkin Conservatory, and it served me well when I stepped onto the *West Wing* set. I'm sure I had first-day nerves—I am human—but I felt prepared."

Josh's readiness didn't go unnoticed. "He walked in to a team playing ball," Tommy Schlamme says, "and he stepped right in." Piggybacking on those comments, Alex added, "And he did it with incredible grace. He had the crew and cast cracking up half the time when we weren't shooting."

Okay. Back to the main event—that final presidential debate. Everyone (minus Leo) is backstage in San Diego, ready for the bout to begin. When we say "everyone," we're not just talking about C.J., Sam, Toby, and Josh, nervously circling the president prior to his entering the ring. And we're not just talking about Charlie and his episode-long panic about the demise of the president's "lucky tie" or the first lady, who's minutes away from injecting mischief into her husband's pregame ritual. We're talking about Bartlet's opponent, the gentleman to the right of him, both literally and politically.

Governor Ritchie was played with good-ol'-boy bravado by the great James Brolin. That the man was able to come in and hit the ground drawling is as much a tribute to the stellar fortune of an educated guess as to Mr. Brolin's sizable talent. You see, according to Aaron, they needed to cast the role of Governor Ritchie before a scene for that character had even been written. "All I was able to tell you guys about the character," Aaron later reminded Alex and Tommy, "was that his response to [Simon Donovan] being shot was going to be 'Crime, boy— I don't know.' We had to cast it on that basis." That worked out pretty well, and not just because it led to this badass Bartlet moment:

> PRESIDENT BARTLET
> In the future, if you're
> wondering . . . "Crime, boy—I don't
> know" is when I decided to kick
> your ass.

—"Posse Comitatus"

When you think about the seconds right before the president heads out to debate, what do you remember most? The first lady cutting off POTUS's tie with scissors? The mayhem that came next? Or perhaps it's Richard Schiff in the background of the intimate exchange between Jed and Abbey, chomping on a baby carrot. (We'll wait while you cue up the scene and double-check. It's there. As Rob Lowe told Aaron on his podcast, "If you let him, Richard Schiff would enter every scene on a unicycle, juggling a pizza.")

What Tommy loved about this chaotic Abby-snipping-off-POTUS's-necktie sequence was the contrast it featured in Martin, the man at the center of it all. "You have this really great 'low comedy' moment and then . . . he's capable of doing this." By "this," Tommy meant the barrage of knockout punches that Martin then delivers in the debate. His Bartlet doesn't pull a single one:

                    PRESIDENT BARTLET
Well, first of all, let's clear up a
couple of things. "Unfunded
mandate" is two words, not one "big
word." There are times when we're
fifty states and there are times
when we're one country, and have
national needs. And the way I know
this is that Florida didn't fight
Germany in World War II or
establish civil rights. You think
states should do the governing
wall-to-wall. That's a perfectly
valid opinion. But your state of
Florida got $12.6 billion in
federal money last year—from
Nebraskans, and Virginians, and New
Yorkers, and Alaskans with their
Eskimo poetry. 12.6 out of a state
budget of $50 billion. I'm supposed
to be using this time for a
question, so here it is: Can we
have it back, please?

As if that wasn't enough to put the political world on notice that Josiah Bartlet wasn't some soft, elite academic that Governor Ritchie could shove around, there was this:

PRESIDENT BARTLET

```
There it is . . . That's the ten-
word answer my staff's been looking
for for two weeks. There it is.
Ten-word answers can kill you in
political campaigns. They're the
tip of the sword. Here's my
question: What are the next ten
words of your answer? Your taxes
are too high? So are mine. Give me
the next ten words. How are we
gonna do it? Give me ten after
that, I'll drop out of the race
right now. Every once in a
while . . . every once in a while,
there's a day with an absolute
right and an absolute wrong. But
those days almost always include
body counts. Other than that, there
aren't very many unnuanced moments
in leading a country that's way too
big for ten words. I'm the
President of the United States, not
the President of the people who
agree with me. And by the way, if
the Left has a problem with that,
they should vote for somebody else.
```

The president's hammering of Governor Ritchie with those two powerful rhetorical flourishes was an uplifting moment that the campaign, and the show itself, really needed. *The West Wing* would soon face a moment of significant transition, with all the attendant worries and excitements that come with times of seismic change. It would advance toward this pivot point armed with a culture that had long been established—and with the resilience of a cast and crew that knew its

way to greatness. There was, then, good reason for disorienting, debilitating anxiety, as well as an abiding confidence that the level of quality they'd grown accustomed to could be achieved again. This jumble
of emotions was captured—unwittingly and through the eye of a
shaky, distant handheld camera—as two combatants met each
other . . . in the middle of the stage.

                    GOVERNOR RITCHIE
     It's over.

                    PRESIDENT BARTLET
     You'll be back.

TWENTY-SIX

TRANSITION

Ask any elementary school teacher, anyone in the field of psychology or social work, any priest or politician. Hell, ask any *anyone*, and they'll tell you: Transitions are hard. Of course, in politics, they are also an unavoidable and fundamental fact of every administration. And there's something fittingly poetic that *The West Wing* had to deal with losing its "president," Aaron Sorkin, after precisely one full term in office.

Trying to synthesize any given moment of change by speaking to the individuals involved—with conflicting accounts, viewpoints, memories, and agendas—can be a fool's errand. At the same time, certain stories are essential threads to the fabric of a larger narrative. When it comes to *The West Wing*, the story of Aaron and Tommy leaving—and John Wells taking over as showrunner—is one of those threads.

While the following tells the story of a tumultuous period in the life of *The West Wing*, it appears time has healed old wounds. Two decades later, while a melancholy lingers, it pales in comparison to the sense of pride shared by everyone involved. Something else that lingers? An abiding fondness.

During one of our sit-downs with Peter Roth, we brought up this time of transition. The first words out of his mouth were "I love Aaron Sorkin. I have so much affection and deep respect for who he is." John Wells calls Aaron "the greatest writer in the world" and says "Tommy's contribution to the show can never be underestimated." Shooting for the trifecta, Tommy Schlamme says, "I love John Wells," describes Peter Roth as "a wonderful human being," and considers his relationship with Aaron "the greatest creative collaboration I've ever had . . . that I ever will have."

As for Aaron, he often used to say, "I write a TV show. Tommy *makes* one." Still, long after *The West Wing* had come to a close, he reached out to Tommy to share a thought that had come to him after years of producing television. "It never dawned on me," he told his old partner, "that you didn't have a Tommy." To this day Aaron considers his time spent with Tommy—and with John Wells and Peter Roth and the rest of the *West Wing* gang—as among the greatest he'll ever know. "I feel like for four years . . . I had the best job in show business."

All of that said . . . there's a reason that things came to a head, and then to an end, for Warner Bros., NBC, and what Peter Roth calls "the triumvirate" of Aaron, Tommy, and John. And while the reason is a predictable mix of money and time, and time and money, somehow that still left room for surprise.

JOHN WELLS: The one thing I did not expect to happen on the show was for Aaron to leave it.

PETER ROTH: The magic of this show . . . was the alchemy of the three of them. The studio put John with Aaron and Tommy to serve as a check and balance. John is an outstanding and very efficient producer. It was like the three branches of government. In conjunction, not always in agreement with one another, but always proper checks and balances.

As one of the very first *West Wing* fans—a fan before the very first rough cut—Peter felt a bit caught in the middle. (Then again, as chairman and CEO of Warner Bros. Television Studios, that's pretty much the job description.) For a while you can say, Well, we're winning Emmys, we're making something we're proud of, this is TV legacy . . . but, eventually, production budget issues get harder to justify.

PETER ROTH: It was challenging. No question about it. It was a continuum of overage. And that's the way Aaron, I believe, arguably worked at his best, when under pressure.

AARON SORKIN: Those first four years, all those budget overages . . . were due largely to my taking ten days to write a script, instead of eight.

Although . . .

TOMMY SCHLAMME: The first two years had nothing to do with Aaron and late scripts. It had to do with *me*. I was going, "This show has to have this sort of patina to it," so every location we'd go to, every set we would build, had to be The Most Important One in the World . . . with the biggest decisions ever to be made. So the show was expensive to do.

JOHN WELLS: It was coming to a head financially with Warners and, honestly, an awful lot of that was NBC.

TOMMY SCHLAMME: It's a natural thing. It's the battle between creativity and capitalism, it's the world that we live in. These are big-ticket items. The idea that they should just be supportive of *any* way that we want to do it is BS. They *should* have a say in it, they should be able to do that.

PETER ROTH: Coincidental to those increased costs and that increased pressure was that the ratings slightly declined. That then led to pressure from the network on us. Eventually, that led to one of the most traumatic developments of *The West Wing*.

JOHN WELLS: Warners was frustrated with how much it was over budget, so they [said], "We gotta get this back under control. Can we get some other people writing it to help?"

PETER ROTH: There was pressure from the network to change some of the content of the show. And I believe that that—along with the pressure of trying to contain the costs—imposed on Aaron in a way that caused him to say, "I'm not doing this anymore."

AARON SORKIN: I think Warner Bros. and NBC wanted me to leave the show, to be honest. And they're not bad guys for wanting that. [It's] the economics of commercial television. The way that they put it is: "You don't have the guy who designs the car build every car. It's a lot less expensive to bring in people who can just replicate that car."

It felt like I was starting to hear somebody at NBC and Warner Bros. kind of start to do the dishes and put the empty beer bottles away. And I thought this was the time to go.

JOHN WELLS: Aaron was also just exhausted from trying to write or rewrite every single episode. He was getting pretty burned out.

TOMMY SCHLAMME: At the end of the third year, I had already gone to Aaron to say, "Listen, I'm thinking about slowly pulling out." That was one of the reasons, even in the second year, that I wanted Alex [Graves] and Chris [Misiano] to be executive producers. I wanted them to be able to do the Christmas shows and the season premieres because those were really the bigger shows.

In a momentous *West Wing* season 2, Tommy directed four pivotal episodes: The premiere—"In the Shadow of Two Gunmen: Parts I and II"—"Noël," and "Two Cathedrals." As the show's producing director, that meant more than just being behind the camera.

TOMMY SCHLAMME: It was not just . . . "I can't do all these shows." My job was becoming . . . putting out fires.

AARON SORKIN: Tommy and I for several months—ever since Christmas—had been talking about . . . "Should this be our last season? What do you think?" Neither of us was going to leave the other one there alone. We were going to go at the same time.

TOMMY SCHLAMME: Both John and I knew that it was coming down from the network that Aaron needed to allow other people to write scripts. I never thought for a second that Aaron would accept that, nor did I think it was a good idea. But they thought it might solve one of the problems. If six scripts a year—out of the twenty-two—were written by someone else, then whenever Aaron was behind, that script was ready, and that script could go and he'd have more time to catch up.

There was just this one detail . . .

TOMMY SCHLAMME: Everybody knew Aaron was not going to do that. For two years, Warner Bros. had been saying, and John had been saying, "You gotta let people [help]." And now John was getting more pressure: Can this be sustained this way?

The answer was, well . . . no. At least not in a way that everyone could live with.

JOHN WELLS: Everybody always thought they'd be the one [to] convince Aaron. There was a line of 'em. I said, "I think you're misreading the man, guys. I've known him a long time . . ."

TOMMY SCHLAMME: It became, finally, John saying, "The studio now has said that you have to let them do it. There's no alternative."

JOHN WELLS: We had a meeting at Peter Roth's office, where Peter said to Aaron and Tommy and me, "Look, you know, [NBC] is upset. I need you to deal with the budget and get the scripts done."

Aaron said, "Yeah, I'm not going to do any of that." Peter said, "Well, then this isn't going to work." Aaron stood up and left, and Tommy went out to speak with him in the hall. Then Peter stood up and said, "So, that's done," and went back to his desk. I was like, "What's done?" And he's like, "He just quit."

I went out in the hallway and Aaron was out there, talking to Tommy. I said, "Peter thinks you just quit." And he's like, "What?" I said, "You just quit. I was there. He said, 'You gotta do it' and you said you wouldn't and walked out."

And that was, sadly, that. According to Tommy, Aaron's decision was not impulsive, he'd thought it through, but it did come quick. And it came with a request.

TOMMY SCHLAMME: He said, "I can't do the show that way. Will you leave with me?" I went, "Aaron, maybe you haven't heard me, but that's not gonna be that hard a decision. Of course I will."

Then John went to talk to Tommy, thinking he might stay on.

JOHN WELLS: Tommy's like, "I'm not coming back."

PETER ROTH: It was a very difficult meeting . . . beyond just how deeply sad I was.

JOHN WELLS: Once Peter called [NBC] and said, "Yeah, he quit," they wouldn't take any other meetings to talk about it. But I was sort of like, "Excuse me, guys. What do you think happens next?" They went, "We keep on making the show."

TOMMY SCHLAMME: It was heartbreaking to Aaron. I mean, there's nothing in him that wanted to leave, but there was nothing in him that would say, "I'm going to let other writers write the show." That's just not the way he works.

We asked Peter if he ever thought, "Should we even keep doing it?"

PETER ROTH: I did have those moments a number of times. When you lose the creator of a show, there's a bit of heart and soul that's lost. But John Wells is a fabulous producer and is to be applauded for what he did.

TOMMY SCHLAMME: Aaron and I both went home that night to write a press release—separately. Then we came in in the morning. We talked to John about it. At that point, there was no "What's going to happen next year?" It wasn't like, "Let's talk about it," or "Is John gonna take over the show?" It was just clear. Aaron knew what he was doing. It wasn't like, "Oh, fuck, why did I do that!"

JOHN WELLS: I told [NBC], and then Peter, that we'd take a shot at [continuing the show]. I'd put a staff together . . . I'd work in the room. I told him I thought the transition was going to be rough . . . just the writing itself. Aaron does something very specifically and we can get close to sort of mimicking some of it because there's enough of it, enough rhythm, that we understand it, but it's going to be different.

Then came perhaps the hardest part—breaking the news to the cast and crew.

TOMMY SCHLAMME: We told them on April 30 that we were leaving the show.

AARON SORKIN: We were in the middle of shooting the last episode of the season.

TOMMY SCHLAMME: We were already racing to get this episode finished, to get it on the air in two weeks. I think it was like three days before the end of the season because part of what we both had decided was we needed to do this *before* hiatus. We needed to . . . tell the people that we so loved and so admired and so respected that we were gonna leave the show.

AARON SORKIN: We went right over to Stage 23 . . . to tell the cast. Because a press release was going out.

JOHN WELLS: We were sitting down with the whole cast to say we intended to go forward and hoped we'd have everybody's support to try to continue.

TOMMY SCHLAMME: It was very emotional. I remember trying to have body language that said, "This is okay. Everything's gonna be okay." Like to a kid with a skinned knee. Not like "God, I don't know what's gonna happen . . ." which is what I felt. I felt confident about *me* leaving and the show being okay. I am a true believer in "graveyards are filled with indispensable men." But . . . it was the language of Aaron. There were very few who could get into that without it sounding a little like mimicry. It was so organic with him.

This was, of course, a shocking moment for everyone on the show.

BRADLEY WHITFORD: I remember, very clearly, sitting in the Roosevelt Room when Tommy and Aaron called us in. I burst into tears.

DULÉ HILL: I remember Tommy getting up with Aaron right beside him. Tommy said he and Aaron were leaving the show. They'd been on this journey together and they would be leaving it together. I remember being shocked. I was like, "What do you mean you all are leaving? Do you know what you just said?"

ALLISON JANNEY: I was hoping they were joking. And then it started to sink in and all my abandonment issues kicked in. I didn't know how we would go on without them! It was a really sad day.

MARTIN SHEEN: I was shocked. I wanted the writing staff and producing team to continue because I knew it was the best blend going and it could go as long as we stuck together. I felt the ground really start to shake. I felt that we were very vulnerable. I thought it was a death knell. I didn't know if we'd last another year.

JOSH MALINA: One by one, people tearily got up and questioned whether or not the show should continue. I remember my saying, "I haven't been here that long; I vote strongly for continue."

JOHN WELLS: I had that conversation with Aaron and Tommy, and they were both, "No, keep making the show!" The show wasn't done.

BRADLEY WHITFORD: I remember thinking this is what it would be like if I was a Branch Davidian and David Koresh left. It was really disorienting. Knowing they were going to be gone . . . it was scary. You didn't know if it would go on.

Of course, it did go on. But first, John Wells had to rally the troops.

JOHN WELLS: One of the things I said to Martin—and John Spencer, he and I had known each other for a long time, which was helpful—I said, "We fulfill a place in the American culture right now, in which we can talk about things nobody else is talking about in an entertainment space. We can continue talking about things that need to be talked about, about public service, seeing people in public service as heroes, who are giving up a lot of their lives to try and make all of our lives better." I didn't know if it'd be a year or a couple of years, but [I figured] as long as we can do it, we should keep trying to because who knows when the next opportunity will be to have that conversation on television.

Despite John's reassuring words of wisdom and brave face, these were uneasy times for him as the new showrunner.

ALEX GRAVES: John sat me down privately and he said, "Aaron and Tommy are leaving, I have to take over. And I'm going to get crucified because I've got a hit show in *ER* so I'm a huge target, and the greatest writer in the world just left the show. And we have to carry on because there are various movements afoot to quash the voice of democracy and Aaron created a show that's the voice for democracy."

As if these straits weren't dire enough, there was also the dead-serious family drama the president and first lady were facing, thanks to some Qumari terrorists choosing to ruin Zoey's graduation night.

JOHN WELLS: I called Aaron. "All right, you quit. Bartlet is not in the White House, and his daughter is kidnapped. What happens next?" He goes, "I have no idea. I'm kind of glad I got out of it because I don't have a solution." I said, "What do you mean you 'don't have a solution'?"

Aaron may not have had a solution, but he gave John's team plenty of places to go.

AARON SORKIN: In pool there's something called a "leave." A really good pool player doesn't just want to get the three ball in the corner pocket, they want to set up the next four shots after that. They want to give themselves a good "leave." I wanted to give the season 5 writers a good leave. I didn't want to have them have to start off with a blank piece of paper. "What do we *do*?" I thought it'd be easier if they had to finish something.

JOHN WELLS: It was not my favorite time, but . . . we had a good time in the writers room when we started to try and pull it together. We sat down and started writing. I didn't really have an ambition to take over and continue the legacy of this fantastic show that Aaron and Tommy had created. I was just hopeful that we would do okay.

ALEX GRAVES: John was as positive, decisive, and encouraging as he could possibly be. Part of the reason was we *had* to, and part of [it] was . . . he wanted the show to keep going to keep taking care of everybody on the show, the family on the show—*and* the family of the audience. It's a great show to have on the air. Just typing "FADE IN . . ." after Aaron left had to be a terrifying proposition. And John did it. He just plowed forward . . . cracking a joke or laughing, through the whole thing, never letting any stress show.

DULÉ HILL: I was thankful John Wells would still be there. He is a dynamic talent and I trusted that, in his more than capable hands, the show would have a life, that we would have our own Camelot.

Josh Singer's arrival in *The West Wing* writers room coincided with John's new role as showrunner.

JOSH SINGER: I didn't understand at the time, but . . . John wrote those first two scripts of the first season after Aaron. He put his name on those because he knew that we were going to get hit because they weren't going to be Sorkin scripts. He basically said, "I will take the body blows. I am going to protect my team."

Writer Debora Cahn, one of the crossovers from the Sorkin years to the Wells era, still can't quite process her good fortune in having had such a diversity of showrunner experience.

DEBORA CAHN: I felt like I worked for Dionysus . . . and I then went to work for Apollo. I got opposite ends of this incredible spectrum and would not have wanted to miss out on either one. Aaron taught magic and resilience. Because to work for him, you had to have a lot of resilience. And John taught structure—how do you tell a story, how do you build out a season, how do you really run a show?

As John and his team pushed through the growing pains of *The West Wing*, season 5, that leadership in the room was reflected on-screen. The "leave" they were left with—Zoey being taken, President Bartlet's controversial choice to invoke the Twenty-Fifth Amendment and step aside—ultimately pays off in a dramatic tableau:

Amid flashing lights and cop cars, Marine One sets down on a field outside Calverton, Virginia. Jed and Abbey Bartlet hurry across an expanse of farmland to a dazed and battered Zoey and take her in their arms. Charlie is trailing right behind.

This represented a major turning point for *The West Wing* and its brand-new commander in chief, John Wells. But John wasn't alone. He was armed with a team of smart and willing collaborators . . . and with the enduring groundwork of the show's creator.

> **ABBEY**
> There're gonna be more days like
> this. It starts now. It's going to
> be harder this time.
>
> **PRESIDENT BARTLET**
> Yeah, I know. We can still have
> tonight, though, right?
>
> **ABBEY**
> You got lots of nights. Smart
> people who love you are going to
> have your back.

The transition had begun.

★ ★ ★

PART III

THE TRANSITION

THE JOHN WELLS ADMINISTRATION

PEACEFUL TRANSFER
OF POWER

Years before winning the Best Original Screenplay Oscar for *Spot-light*, Josh Singer was a first-year member of John Wells's writers room. Just a kid with a laptop and a dream . . . and a room in a house on the island of Kauai. Confused? We'll let the writer spell it out: "Every year, John would take all the writers on retreat to Hawaii. We'd sit together and beat out the season." (**MARY:** Going on a Hawaiian retreat to plot out season 5 of *The West Wing*? I can think of worse ways—and worse places—to spend a week.)

"It's all totally new to me," Josh told us. "It's my first job, we're in Hawaii—it should be really exciting, right?" (**MELISSA:** Right! *Yes.* What's with the "should"?!) "But what it is, actually, is stressful beyond belief. 'Cause I've never been in a writers room, everyone else there has an amazing résumé, a million credits. I'm scared to death. I hardly speak the first three days. I walk up to John at one point—during a break—and go, 'I know I haven't said much, I hope that's okay . . .' John just smiles, pats me on the back, and says, 'That's all right, it's probably better if you don't say anything for about six months.' He was joking, obviously, but it was also so generous." As Josh put it on *The*

West Wing Weekly, "It kind of [took] the pressure off. He was making a point that you're here to learn. That's the wonderful thing John did, and I'm sure still does, for staff writers. You're getting paid to *learn*." Never was that more apparent than in the run-up to season 5.

Albert Einstein allegedly said, "The measure of intelligence is the ability to change." Starting in the fifth season of *The West Wing*, that old adage was put to the test. Following the departure of Aaron and Tommy, John Wells took over the room as head writer and showrunner. His approach to leading the staff represented a clear divergence from the unique writing process Aaron had employed over the first four seasons.

As hard-core *West Wing* fans will tell you, the season 5 premiere dealt with the Twenty-Fifth Amendment. John Goodman's curt, intimidating, vexingly likable House Speaker Glen Allen Walken becomes president after Bartlet steps down in the wake of his daughter's kidnapping.

With the specter of that first post–Aaron/Tommy *West Wing* episode hanging over him, John Wells approached Josh, issuing the young staff writer his first official assignment: Write up a memo on various situational protocols, including, "What would you call Glen Allen Walken? Would you call him 'Mr. President'? Would you call him 'Mr. Acting President'?" Josh dove in with the unbridled, directionless enthusiasm you'd expect from a rookie with something to prove and no clue what the hell he was doing.

"I wrote a twenty-five-page memo with seventeen pitches for 'ways this would be a really cool thing to do with the Twenty-Fifth Amendment in your episode.' None of it made it into the script." But the fact that the memo was unusable was kind of beside the point. The object lesson of these exercises was twofold: To train young writers and to instill in them a sense of shared mission, of *team*. "Most people say they go to law school and learn a different way of thinking. I went to John Wells's screenwriting school and learned a different way of thinking."

Having worked under both John and Aaron, Debora Cahn can speak to how different each leader's style was from the other's. "On some shows," she told us, "when you are writing your episode, you're not in the writers room for those weeks. John did not believe in that."

Lauren Schmidt Hissrich was another young writer who served under both showrunners. (Years after her time in the *West Wing* writers room, Lauren went on to create and run the successful Netflix series *The Witcher*.) "John makes those meetings mandatory," she told us. "Doesn't matter if you're shooting, if you're writing . . . you are expected to be in that room and responsible to the other writers. It crafts this feeling of real independence and real responsibility, while also [making it clear] that you're not alone, that you can go seek help. It's not just on you."

John Wells's affection for his years leading the *West Wing* writing staff is palpable. "We'd start the writers room with an hour-and-a-half conversation about politics," he told us. "Everybody just talking. It's name-dropping now, but Eli Attie is really good friends with [Secretary of State] Tony Blinken. They were best men at each other's wedding. Lawrence would have a whole ton of stuff he wanted to rail about that he heard from somebody on the select committee in the Senate." (If you're having any trouble figuring out who "Lawrence" is in this scenario, tune in to MSNBC, ten p.m. Eastern, and look for the guy railing about what he heard from somebody on the select committee in the Senate.) "Eli would have a bunch of stuff from National Security or the State Department. We'd have other advisors or people come in over the phone like [President Reagan's chief of staff] Ken Duberstein. And then we'd talk issues. Who could be president if it was a woman? Could a woman get elected? You talked about that . . . about Social Security policy . . ." Listening to John reminisce about the room, we felt a little jealous. Smart people around a table, back-channeling trusted experts, the passionate exchange of ideas, getting paid to listen to Lawrence O'Donnell go off about politics? Count us in.

The previous way of working had clearly differed. Supplementing Aaron's own storylines, his staff would research and pitch and write up memos for other potential narratives. From there, Aaron would weave it all into the script. This is how it came to pass that Brad Whitford's mom, Genevieve, asked a perfectly reasonable question: "How can Aaron write every episode? What if he gets hit by a bus?!"

In the latter stages of the series, having spent time in the writers room himself, Brad asked how John Wells was able to stomach a process so different from his own. Without skipping a beat, John told him, "No matter how you would prefer to work, you have to give way to talent. And Aaron is a mind-boggling talent." That was, as Brad pointed out, "an audacious adjustment" on John's part, as well as "an astute piece of producing."

John Wells was, and is, an exceptional producer. That he was able to pick up the mantle after Aaron and Tommy moved on, and navigate the artistic, logistic, and personal rocky shoals left in their absence, was a tribute to his leadership. But it also spoke to his talent. His talent as a writer and as a person of uncommon vision allowed John and his staff to continue producing top-flight episodes while embracing a process that was, for this show anyway, entirely new.

_____TWENTY-EIGHT_____

KATE HARPER:
ORIGIN STORY

Disclaimer: Hey. It's Melissa with a quick reminder. In the spirit of The West Wing *and its desire to reflect our best hopes for capital-D Democracy, Mary and I are doing a church-and-state thing for our origin stories. Aside from connecting the dots on her timeline—and offering a follow-up fact check—Mary has taken a hands-off approach to everything that follows except for this: "I'd rather eat glass than write about myself."*

★ ★ ★

THE deputy national security advisor serves as a member of the executive office of the president and, as the National Security Agency's second-in-command, holds a prominent seat on the National Security Council. The nature of the critical work this deputy performs fluctuates with each administration's governing philosophy. But two things can be said of every individual—Republican or Democrat, dead or alive, real or fictional—that has ever held this office:

1. The role constitutes an indispensable cog in the machinery that is "national security."

2. The role hardly ever has anything to do with their bangs. . . .

As we learned from her boss (National Security Advisor Nancy McNally), Kate Harper was "top of her class at Annapolis." Also, with the possible exception of Admiral Fitzwallace, Commander Harper was about as "alpha" as the Bartlet administration ever got. And, yes, the badass backstory—a four-year run in Naval Intelligence, her shadowy ties to the CIA, that time she piled a stumbling-drunk secretary of labor into a sedan on the back streets of Havana—brought a hint of espionage to the West Wing of *The West Wing*. But beyond the uncommon intrigue of her heavily redacted résumé, it was Kate's tight-lipped, sly charm—boosted by moments of disarming insecurity—that stood out during her tenure in the second term of the Bartlet administration.

Mary McCormack's circuitous route to series regular on *The West Wing* began in "the Congo, of all places." The Congo, in this instance, was actually the island of Oahu . . . more specifically, the set of *ER*, where she was preparing to play Debbie, a tomboy-meets-Batgirl Red Cross worker. Her very first take on the hit hospital show was shot by veteran director Chris Chulack, who helmed dozens of *ER* episodes over the years.

"As soon as Chris yelled 'Cut!'" Mary recalls, "he walked over to give me a note on my performance. I knew exactly what he was going to say. So I got ahead of it: 'I know, I know, I get this note all the time, I talk too fast, I promise I'll slow down!'" Mary can't remember what Chulack's note actually was, but, turns out, it had nothing to do with how fast she was talking. What she does remember is what he said next.

"God, no, don't slow down! On this show we *want* you to go fast. Whatever you do, don't slow down!" In that moment—on *ER*, in Hawaii, for crying out loud—the New Jersey native felt like she'd come home.

Just about a year later, she would be invited to join *The West Wing*, a show for which talking fast wasn't just tolerated; it was a job requirement. That, as it happens, would not be Mary's first time on a political show, having played a young Republican lobbyist on the George Clooney / Steven Soderbergh project *K Street* for HBO. In this entirely improvised show, the actors were asked to name their characters. Mary went with "Maggie Morris," blending her maternal grandmother's name, Margaret, with the surname of her soon-to-be husband. (For Mary, this would not be the last time a "Margaret Morris" showed up on set.)

Unfortunately, after just one season, Clooney and Soderbergh decided to pull up stakes on their experimental exploration of the DC lobbyist subculture. (Find the DVD box set of this little-known show. Mary's on it with John Slattery, Roger Guenveur Smith, Mary Matalin, James Carville . . . It's a fun watch.) But—good news—not long after that, Mary got a call from John Wells.

During Mary's brief run on *ER*, John had floated the idea of her joining *The West Wing*, but *K Street* got in the way. Now the decks were cleared. From that very first fast-talking take in her very first scene on *ER*, Mary already knew and loved the culture of a John Wells production. It was, in her view, a perfect match. As she put it to me, "It all felt—seriously—too good to be true."

As the two parties looked to hammer out the final details of her deal, and as if there wasn't enough to celebrate, Mary was gearing up for a celebration of an altogether different sort. The musical *Cabaret*—in which she'd made her Broadway debut five years before as the boozy, floozy nightclub singer Sally Bowles—was coming to a close. Following the final performance, a big bash was being thrown in its honor. Anyone who got to see Sam Mendes's legendary revival could probably envision what that late night was like. (The Kit Kat Klub took its partying pretty seriously.)

So, imagine Mary's surprise when she realized two days later that she was pregnant, and had been at Studio 54 the night of *Cabaret*'s closing party. "I didn't have any idea at the time, and I'd definitely had a drink or two." (SPOILER #1: The baby was fine. SPOILER #2: The baby is in college now. Still fine.)

So, yes, Mary and her husband had just received amazingly great, life-changing news. It's just that the amazingly great, life-changing news came with a bit of a hitch.

"The *West Wing* contract negotiation was almost finished, and now I suddenly had this very relevant, very impactful piece of information that, quite honestly, may have derailed the whole thing. Of course, you don't have a legal obligation to tell a producer you're pregnant, but, at the same time, I *knew* John and liked him tremendously. It just felt wrong not to say anything . . . which is how it came to be that I told John Wells that I was pregnant before I told my mom."

Mary had no idea how John was going to react, but, in the end "there was no hesitation, no high-voice hemming and hawing, no awkward pause or silence. There was just an immediate, sincere, enthusiastic 'Congratulations!' He was so genuinely excited for me and Michael, just . . . as a person. And—knowing him as I do now—as a dad."

Before Mary could express her own apprehension about . . . well, *all* of it, before she could finish saying she understood if this would be a deal-breaker—"before I could even get it out"—John cut her off, saying, "Don't worry about it. This show," he assured her, "is a real family. We've got <u>tons</u> of babies!"

"He had to have been at least a little concerned," Mary points out now. "But he kept it free of any negative *anything*. It was a real gift, one we'll never forget."

Talk to John about this gesture and his focus stays, to nobody's surprise, on the community and the elements within it that need to be cultivated. "If we don't allow talented people to live their lives outside of their work, they're not going to be available to us to be on the show and be good. We do that in all kinds of areas. People get sick, and we keep them on payroll and tell them to get better. You've got to create that world."

Sitting on her bed a week before officially becoming a cast member, Mary cracked open the first *West Wing* script ever to feature the character of Commander Kate Harper. The episode, "Talking Points," would be a first for another reason too. It was the directorial debut of Richard Schiff. Having previously worked with Richard on a number of other projects, including Steven Bochco's *Murder One* and the big-budget action movie *Deep Impact*, Mary was familiar with his talent and her respect for him was sky-high. The fact that an actor she knew and admired would be directing her first episode was a positive. That said, it didn't exactly slow the pulse.

Before Mary and her first-day jitters set foot on the *West Wing* stages, there was the not-so-little matter of her initial costume fitting. What she remembers most from that day was being "just pregnant enough that my boobs were huge." Taking it all in stride, costume designer Lyn Paolo told her not to worry, explaining, "I just finished doing this for Mary-Louise Parker—it's no problem!"

From that day forward and throughout her pregnancy, Mary went in for weekly fittings. And between Lyn's various tricks of the trade and a series of strategically placed raincoats, cardboard boxes, and a leather folio or two, the actress's constantly evolving figure remained as close to a cover-up as *The West Wing* had seen since Leo got pulled before Congress. Now, back to her first episode . . .

Mary came to the stages on day one staring up at a pretty high bar. Just imagine. Joining an established group of actors and friends on a runaway hit (and a well-oiled machine) was a daunting task even in the most typical circumstances. Doing so with one of the core cast directing television for the first time and, oh yeah, who was also an actor she really looked up to? That pushed the bar even higher. Plus, as Mary points out, "Richard is not that big into small talk. He's a professional and he's serious and on that day he was bound to be a little too preoccupied *directing the episode* to trot out the welcome wagon." So, bear all of that in mind, then realize that the scenes Mary was set to shoot on day one included . . .

1. Getting instantly thrown into the ring with this trio of heavyweights: Anna Deavere Smith (NSA Director Nancy McNally), Lily Tomlin (President Bartlet's secretary, Debbie Fiderer), and the *Apocalypse Now* guy currently manning JFK's Resolute desk in the Oval. And, in running that fairly harrowing gauntlet, her Kate Harper had to . . .

2. Go toe-to-toe with Fiderer about "code-word clearance" and the wisdom of how she maintains her outer-office workspace. After which she had to . . .

3. Go toe-to-toe with President Bartlet about the virtue she saw in France's opposition to extraditing a pair of "bloodless murderers" to the US. Meanwhile . . .

4. Her performance had to strike a delicate balance of speaking truth to power, respecting the chain of command, and being at least a little bit charming. Oh, and she also had to . . .

5. Convincingly show off her character's ability to speak fluent Arabic! This has to rank pretty high on the all-time list of most daunting first days. What a kindness John and his writers room showed Mary, saving Kate Harper's fluency in Mandarin for a later episode—you know, once the new girl got her feet wet. (**MARY:** Thanks to the season 6 episode "Impact Winter," all these years later I can still say, "I understand, but the president would really like to get off the plane. Do you have a hydraulic lift?" in Mandarin. **MELISSA:** Mary may be the only actor in the history of *The West Wing* to walk and talk in three different languages!)

Point being, it was a lot for a first day on the job—and that's not even taking into account all the sniffing! (What's that? The, uh . . . the sniffing?) Oh. Yeah. Um . . . Mary?

"I have this thing that happens when I'm nervous—my left ear clogs, and I have to sort of sniff to make it 'pop,' to even out the ear pressure. I tried to do it subtly, all while half explaining, half apologizing to Anna Deavere Smith or whomever."

Huh. Wow. But, wait—couldn't all that sniffing come across a little like you have . . .

"A drug problem? Yes. Yes it could. So, I'm nervous and emotional and it's my first day on *The West Wing* and I'm going around to the other actors, telling everyone about my ear pressure, how all that sniffing isn't what it looks like—'I don't have a drug problem!'—which, of course, just makes you sound like *you have a drug problem*. That first scene with Anna Deavere Smith, she was so welcoming, and then meeting Lily Tomlin—who's sweet and a genius and legitimately a *legend*—and the whole time I was basically Scarface."

But then there was Martin—"generous, chatty Martin," as Mary puts it. "What a lifesaver he was. He gave me such a warm welcome." Walking onto set, he greeted his fellow child of Ireland with a great big smile and more than a touch of a thick Irish brogue.

"Mary Catherine McCormack, all the saints and all the . . . somethin' else," Mary (mostly) remembers him saying. "I don't know how he put it exactly, some funny Irish turn of phrase. What I do know is that he *loved* that I was Irish. It's possible I may have crossed myself." Given the degree of difficulty on that first day of filming, that was probably a wise move.

Okay. Let's talk about the bangs. Originally, Kate Harper had bangs, but down the line, the *West Wing* powers that be saw that hairstyle as too "youthful" and "not sufficiently Washington, DC." We bring up Kate's hair now because of one thing: message boards.

Most *West Wing* cast members knew enough—even in these early Netscape days of the internet—to turn a blind eye to message boards. Message boards were the birthplace of snark. (Anyone else remember TelevisionWithoutPity.com?) They were not where any actor would go looking for validation and support. Except Josh Malina.

"Josh would pore over these boards, seemingly all day," remembers Mary. "Gleefully. If he found something—anything—negative, it was like winning the lottery for him. He would torment us endlessly." Malina was indeed relentless. And for Mary the gods of the message boards gave Josh the gift of this nickname: "SheBangs." It was like Mary's Secret Service code name for that first Kate Harper season.

Josh clearly has a lot to answer for, but if there's one thing you can't do, it's put Mary down. She's an unstoppable force. And there are few greater pleasures than watching her nail a four-page dramatic walk-and-talk about the inexorable onset of hostility in the Balkans and then on "Cut!" seeing her do a victory moonwalk through the set, along with her iconic "*West Wing* Clap" (da-duh-DUH! da-duh-DAH!), which would take over the room like a wave at a soccer match. I'll never forget Mary whooping and clapping a particularly thorny scene in the Oval when she and Allison finally got it . . . "C'mon, *West Wing*! C'mon, *West Wing*!"

It's true that *The West Wing* was a family before Mary came. But I genuinely can't imagine that family now without her. Look closely at Kate Harper and it won't take you long to see—beneath the serious, professional, military shell—a twinkle in her eyes. That's Mary. She brought to *The West Wing* what she brings everywhere: edgy wit, boundless warmth, and lifelong friendship. And occasional bangs.

★ ★ ★

A SERVICE STORY

MARY MCCORMACK

(Quick reminder: This is still Melissa. Mary remains off to the side for this one.)

Mary McCormack is the proud daughter of a corporal in the

United States Marines and the proud granddaughter of a Purple Heart recipient. Her passion in support of veterans and their families runs bone-deep. Driven by their example, she's been inspired to play a small part in advocating for those who have put their lives on the line for our country and those who continue to do so at this very moment. When it comes to veterans issues, Mary puts her money where her mouth is. I should know. She is a Justice for Vets / All Rise ambassador and is constant in her support for the work we do there. That support began early.

MARY: When you started at Justice for Vets (a division of All Rise), I jumped at the chance to play even a tiny role in such a great mission. Over the years, I've known a lot of people who struggle with substance use and with mental health disorders. Adding on to that the trauma experienced while serving, it's no wonder some have difficulty transitioning once they're back home. All Rise makes sure our military men and women get the treatment they have *earned*. Over the years, I've been extremely lucky to meet so many veterans whose lives and relationships have been saved—truly saved—by veterans treatment courts.

I'm proud to say my sister, Bridget, was a major proponent of treatment courts as a justice on the state supreme court of Michigan, and later as that court's chief justice. She saw their value up close and in action and was instrumental in their success across Michigan. Bridget also sits on the board of All Rise. Meanwhile, my daughter Rose has joined her aunt at a number of veterans treatment court graduations, singing the national anthem.

All Rise isn't the only veterans cause Mary holds close to her heart.

MARY: Every May for the last seven years, I've been fortunate to take part in the National Memorial Day Concert for PBS. This event honors the military service and sacrifice of all our men and women in uniform, their families, and those who have made the ultimate sacrifice for our country. I always bring my daughters to Washington for this event because I think it's important for them to understand that Memorial Day isn't about cookouts and a day off from school. It's about something inexpressibly profound. This past May, my eleven-year-old, Lillian, came along with me and was so moved that she's decided that next year she'll be joining our ranks as a concert volunteer. Over the years, I've said this a lot about the Memorial Day concert and it's true: "This is a chance for us as a nation to say thank you, to honor the fallen, to let Gold Star Families know that their loved ones did not die in vain, and that we will not forget them."

Another cause Mary holds close was summed up publicly by a member of her own family . . .

MARY: My cousin Carl Nassib played defensive end for seven NFL seasons and three NFL teams: the Browns, the Raiders, and the Buccaneers. In addition to rushing the passer and stopping the run, Carl made his mark on professional football when he posted a video on Instagram in 2021 that included this succinct and moving message: "I just want to take a quick moment to say that I'm gay. I've been meaning to do this for a while now, but I finally feel comfortable enough to get it off my chest."

With that short message, Carl changed the world a little bit. He certainly changed the culture of the NFL. Carl's very public coming-out video spoke to millions of people, including me and my family. In just over a minute, on a video shot in his own backyard, he captured a powerful idea: that no one should feel not seen or less than because of who they are or whom they love. I'm so proud of him. He's a real hero of mine.

Carl finished by saying, "I'm going to start by donating $100,000 to the Trevor Project. They're an incredible organization. They're the number one suicide prevention service for LGBTQ youth in America and they're truly doing incredible things."

There are few causes that speak to me more than this. Helping people be seen, helping erase a stigma that has caused people untold pain and real harm, that has endangered generations of people . . . few things are as important.

I'm proud and inspired by my cousin Carl, and I'm heartened by the positive reaction his coming out evoked.

Mary is also a passionate advocate for commonsense gun legislation.

MARY: In 2019, my three daughters, Margaret, Rose, and Lillian, were standing just outside a nail salon near our home in Los Angeles, waiting for our babysitter, Monica, to settle up inside. Suddenly, a man waving a gun burst out of the storefront and pushed past the girls, running into the busy parking lot. Moments later, LAPD officers stormed out after him, guns drawn, screaming commands that mixed with the screams of fear from the people outside. It all happened so fast. Monica was still inside. Amid the chaos of the moment—guns pointed everywhere, all the screaming—a woman working in the mattress store next door pulled my girls inside, shoved them onto the floor, and hid them safely under a bed. Every time I drive past the mattress store, I think about that woman—her name is Tanya—who risked everything that day, who ran toward the gunman to pull my girls to safety.

All this time later, every morning, when I send my daughters out the door, I think, "What if something happens? What if this is the last time we'll ever talk?" I can't imagine I'm the only parent who has that terrifying thought as they send their children off to school. Or to the movies. Or to the mall. I'm guessing that's pretty common these days. Common . . . but not normal. Many of us have been lucky so far. But when faced with the reality (every day 120 people in the US are killed with guns and more than 200 are shot and wounded), it's hard not to think, How long until it's our school? How long until it's our movie theater, our mall? Our *turn*?

It's unacceptable. Our daughters and sons shouldn't be huddled under a bed unless they're playing hide-and-seek.

As a mother of three, and just as a citizen, too, I am a loud, proud supporter of the work done by organizations like Moms Demand Action. I honestly can't believe that keeping our kids safe is a thing for which actual advocacy is required, but here we are. I mean, the commonsense gun measures they support—an assault weapons ban, enacting safe-storage laws, strengthening background checks, banning high-capacity semiautomatic weapons—are literally as popular as *Italian food*! (Maybe that's because the gun homicide rate in the US is twenty-six times higher than that of other developed countries.) It's a shame that, despite those reforms polling so well, we have to take to the streets, hold rallies, and beg our representatives to do the right thing—to keep our kids safe. But I'm so grateful that Moms Demand Action organizes those of us who do.

If you combine the populations of Great Britain, France, Germany, Japan, Switzerland, Sweden, Denmark, and Australia, you'll get a population roughly the size of the United States. We had 32,000 gun deaths last year. They had 112. Do you think it's because Americans are more homicidal by nature? Or do you think it's because those guys have gun control laws?

—TOBY TO CONGRESSMAN HENRY SHALLICK, "BARTLET'S THIRD STATE OF THE UNION"

JUSTICE FOR VETS

Justice for Vets is a division of All Rise that transforms the way the justice system identifies, assesses, and treats our veterans. Justice for Vets provides training and technical assistance to bring together local, state, and federal resources to directly serve justice-involved veterans including specific training and resources for veterans treatment courts. Justice for Vets keeps veterans out of jail and prison and connects them to the benefits and healthcare they have earned.

www.allrise.org/jfv

THE TREVOR PROJECT

Our long-term vision is to build a world where we are no longer needed—where every LGBTQ+ young person is loved and accepted for who they are, and therefore not at higher risk for suicide or mental health crisis. Until then, we'll continue to meet the need sustainably and refine our efforts intentionally so that we can provide support to every LGBTQ+ young person who needs it.

www.thetrevorproject.org

MOMS DEMAND ACTION

Moms Demand Action is a grassroots movement of Americans fighting for public safety measures that can protect people from gun violence.

www.momsdemandaction.org

★ ★ ★

KEY EPISODE

"The Supremes"

Toward the end of Cameron Crowe's 1989 coming-of-age classic, *Say Anything*, there's an exchange between the film's quirky young couple as a 747 flies them off to Europe and an uncertain future.

> DIANE COURT
> Nobody really thinks it will work, do they?
>
> LLOYD DOBLER
> No. You just described every great success story.

As we pored over interviews with the key players behind "The Supremes," we couldn't get that moment out of our heads. We'd heard numerous variations on that theme, regarding *The West Wing*'s fifth season generally and its seventeenth episode in particular. As many wondered how the series would overcome the losses of Aaron and Tommy, John Wells and his staff set off to tell a story about a pair of

Supreme Court vacancies and the odd couple (one liberal, one conservative) with whom the president hoped to fill them.

According to writer Debora Cahn, back then there was "an accepted assumption that you couldn't write anything about the Supreme Court." More than one network had tried, only to have those efforts (ABC's *The Court* and *First Monday* on CBS) die on the vine. "It just never worked," Deb told us. "It's hard to dramatize . . . hard to understand what the issues are at that level. It's hard," she explained, "to find ways to make it *alive*."

John Wells never bought into the conventional wisdom that you can't dramatize the SCOTUS. As Deb put it to us, "John was like, 'You *can't*? Well, we will!'" (John, it should be noted, is the person who devoted multiple episodes of the then most popular show in the world, *ER*, to the political crises in the Congo and Darfur. This was a brave creative choice, and quite unheard of, and those episodes are to this day some of the finest hours of network drama we've ever seen. Fortune, as they say, favors the bold.)

"The Supremes" was shot during a period of somewhat bumpy transition. But executive producer Alex Graves says, "We just kept making the show for ourselves, and tripped and sailed and had failures and successes [and] found our way."

Eight weeks earlier, John Wells had come into the writers room with what Deb considered a truly preposterous assignment. "Debora," he told one of the greenest members of his staff, "you're doing the Supreme Court episode."

"That was one of those times where I then went and threw up," Deb says now, laughing. "It was ridiculous, I just didn't know that kind of stuff!" For the record, Debora Cahn, who created Netflix's 2023 political show *The Diplomat*, is never not one of the smartest people in the room—any room. And her gift for self-deprecation is off the charts. "It was a really great team of people coming up with the philosophical backbone of the thing, and then I was adding flowers and cookies and cats and shoes, and . . . doors opening and closing . . . and drunk people." (Drunk people like Josh Lyman, who found himself, even before downing his share of "a twenty-one-year-old Glenlivet," head-to-toe intoxicated by one Evelyn Baker Lang.)

> JOSH
> I love her. I love her mind. I love
> her *shoes*.

A brief refresher: Josh divines a plan to fill not one Supreme Court vacancy, but two. Instead of nominating a centrist (who would fly through the Senate confirmation process), he suggests they convince the elderly incumbent chief justice ("liberal lion" Roy Ashland) to step down, opening up a second seat on the court. Then, Josh explains, President Bartlet could nominate *two* jurists, one from each side of the ideological divide. This would constitute a history-making, legacy-securing gambit.

"That was John's first year running the show," Deb points out. "And it was one of those classic moments in the writers room. He knew he wanted to do a big Supreme Court episode, and he had this really great idea: *What if liberals and conservatives each got one?*"

The politics of this maneuver were as complicated as the weighty issues facing any candidate on a SCOTUS short list. You see, the writers wanted the nomination of the liberal justice to be as messy as possible. Finding an issue that was disqualifying on its face for a prospective jurist was key to the conflict required to drive that story. So, they reached out to political consultant Ken Duberstein, who identified "the biggest obstacle you can put in the middle of a confirmation fight," one that would really "kill a nomination." Deb was not disappointed. It was an issue on her radar.

"We wanted to make the problem abortion," she told us. "That [the character] had gone through it, and that that would become the central issue of the fight for the nomination." This upheld the room's initial idea that the "dream choice" for the progressive justice should be a woman. This, in turn, led to the writers grappling with their own version of a dream choice. For the role of Evelyn Baker Lang, Debora recalls, "We knew we wanted a star."

Enter Glenn Close. From her very first costume fitting, "she wanted to know about every case her character referenced," Deb told us, "every legal principle forming her argument." As Lyn Paolo sized Glenn for Evelyn Baker Lang's outfits (and, we suppose, those lovable shoes), the actress pulled out a list of questions for Deb, Alex, and Josh Singer, the staff writer armed with a Harvard law degree. Looking at the three of them, Glenn said, "I want to go to law school in the next six hours."

"Part of attracting an actor of that caliber," Deb points out, "is making sure the role is meaty enough. I wrote monologue after monologue for this character. Long, very talky scenes . . . a lot of lines. Poor Glenn had to just talk and talk." Like in the Roosevelt Room scene, where Toby and Josh are going through the motions of prepping Lang for a judiciary hearing they all assume she'll be far too progressive to land. (**MELISSA:** This is the speech that drives the bewildered staffers out of the room and Josh in the direction of a burgeoning shoe fetish.)

> **EVELYN BAKER LANG**
> If you're Webster, the question is
> "Where do you stand on Roe v Wade"
> and the answer is judicial rulings
> shouldn't be based on personal
> ideology, mine or anyone else's. If
> you're Davies, the question is "How
> would you approach a D and X case,"
> because he's the drum banger on
> partial birth, and the answer is I
> don't comment on hypotheticals. If
> you're Malkin, you're from

```
        Virginia, so you ask about my
        decision in Drori. I take you point
        by point from the doctor to the
        father to Casey to undue burden to
        equal protection, back to Roe, at
        which point you can't remember the
        question and I drink my water for a
        minute while you regroup.
```

In a follow-up scene, minutes later, she drops the real bombshell:

```
                EVELYN BAKER LANG
        Let's see. In high school I snuck a
        copy of Lady Chatterley's Lover out
        of the public library and never
        returned it. In college I got a
        marijuana plant from my roommate as
        a birthday present. And in year two
        of law school, I had an abortion.
        [BEAT] Can I get some water while
        you regroup?
```

At the rehearsal of the first *West Wing* scene Glenn Close ever shot, director Jessica Yu was taken aback. "Everyone introduced themselves, and [Glenn] sat down and said, 'I want you all to know that I'm very nervous.'" The humility of that moment really moved Jessica. "She wasn't trying to disarm everyone else," she says. "[A *West Wing* episode] is a different thing—the pace of shooting, these speeches that you have to learn . . . the pace of the scenes themselves . . . She was *nervous*."

Speaking of the director, we'd be remiss if we didn't acknowledge how lucky we were to have Jessica Yu helm three episodes of *The West Wing*. An Emmy and Oscar winner (for Best Documentary Short Subject), she directed "The Supremes" while five and a half months pregnant and in a previous season had directed a *West Wing* episode while *six* months pregnant! (**MARY:** Badass.)

Hey. Melissa here. Not long before this episode went into production, my nephew James was born. I decided that my character *also* had a newborn nephew that looked suspiciously (and exactly) like my real-life nephew. So I put his "coming home from the hospital, looking adorable in a little blue snowsuit" picture on Carol's desk. There was a shot that I saw was going to start on a phone and then pull back. So I stuck his little picture next to the phone and I said to Jessica, "I have a new nephew. Any chance you can get that in the shot?" And it's totally in the shot! I told my nephew, "I made you a star, kid. You're one day old and you're on national television!" Okay, back to the search for the next Supreme Court justice(s) . . .

Finding a worthy adversary for Evelyn Baker Lang—one who could rival not just her intellect but her complexity and appeal as well—was a tall order . . . and key to unlocking the magic of "The Supremes." Debora and the other writers saw a template in real-life Supreme Court "Odd Couple" Ruth Bader Ginsburg and her conservative counterpart, Antonin Scalia. It was "the two of them giggling together," Deb told *The West Wing Weekly*, "going to the opera together . . . enjoying each other's company . . . enjoying arguing with each other . . ."

For Judge Christopher Mulready, whose judicial philosophy was anathema to every soul in the Bartlet administration, *The West Wing* tapped the stellar film actor William Fichtner. (**MELISSA FUN FACT:** William went on to play Allison Janney's husband on *Mom*.)

From the start, Debora knew what she was looking for in a Judge Mulready. "You wanted someone who walked in the door and had a little . . . touch of evil immediately," she says, "but could then totally undercut it, which [Bill] just did a great job with." That said, the first few takes between Fichtner and Richard Schiff weren't quite where they needed to be. "These two guys were so excited to work with each other," Deb says, "that they were both being a little deferential." Then Jessica pulled Bill aside and employed some advanced directorial tactics. "You are so much smarter than Toby Ziegler," she told him. Understanding how to communicate exactly that, Fichtner began checking his watch and feigning disinterest. The scene, according to Deb, "popped to life."

The sparks between Mulready and Lang, on the other hand, were fanned early in the writing process. Deb asked Josh Singer to come up with a legal argument that showed off the "intellectual muscularity" of the jurists. "What's something they could argue about, where they both know that they're yanking each other's chains, but nobody else listening to it knows?" Josh outlined various legal scenarios that would thread that rather particular needle. Deb settled on this one:

>   MULREADY
>   Mr. Ziegler was trying to convince
>   me the Defense of Marriage Act is
>   unconstitutional.
>
>   EVELYN
>   (chuckling) DOMA? *He* was trying to
>   convince *you*?
>
>   TOBY
>   What.
>
>   EVELYN
>   He doesn't need convincing.
>
>   TOBY
>   Well, I wasn't doing a particularly
>   good—
>
>   EVELYN
>   He's yanking your chain. He would
>   never uphold DOMA. He might not love
>   the idea of gay marriage, but he
>   hates congressional overreaching,

```
and Congress doesn't have the power
to legislate marriage. The issue
isn't privacy.
```

```
                 MULREADY
Or equal protection.
```

```
                 EVELYN
It's enumerated powers. He'll have
an easier time knocking down DOMA
than I will.
```

As for the rest of the *West Wing* gang, that snappy Debora Cahn dialogue served its purpose, and then some. What could have been the not-so-merry-go-round of stuffy jurisprudence became instead a lively carousel of what Deb calls "engaging elements for people who did not have an interest in the judicial system." Case(s) in point . . .

C.J.'S SPECIAL SOMEONE

C.J.'s effervescent storyline involves an off-screen suitor and a texting session. (**MELISSA:** Well, to be a stickler, it was an IM session. IM is short for "instant messaging," which was the prehistoric version of texting.) C.J.'s giddy glances at a laptop screen schooled viewers in filling a moment without a single line of dialogue. Typing on her computer, and positively abuzz with flirty delight, C.J. seems practically drunk on fresh infatuation . . . then gets *actually* drunk on that Glenlivet.

Which is what makes it all the more remarkable that, on the day of her biggest scene—a two-page rant at Toby and Josh—Allison was battling a 103-degree fever and a stomach flu. It was the last of three scenes shot that day.

"We were running over," Deb recalls, "and then there was a lighting problem. And all this time that we're running three hours late,

Allison's puking in her trailer." Eventually, with the first two mammoth Roosevelt Room scenes finally in the can, the AD calls for Allison. "She comes out of the trailer, marches into her office . . . the camera rolls, and she blazes through these two pages of text!"

It was, Deb continued, "flawless." When Jessica Yu called "Cut!" the crew just stood there, stunned. Jessica shot a second take—just because you have to—and then, still looking green fifteen minutes later, Allison sped off the lot.

DONNA AND COOKIES AND CATS, OH MY!

According to Debora, the inspiration for this "runner," which would prove pivotal in the Supreme Court storyline, began with Allison's mother. "There's this place in her hometown," Deb says, "that has these unbelievable cookies." (**MELISSA FUN FACT**: Ashley's Pastry Shop—it's in Dayton, Ohio. You should probably go there. Now.) "Once a year Allison's mom would send this massive box of them. There's this huge announcement on the set—'THE COOKIES ARE HERE!!'—and everyone comes running." This care package of amazing treats gave Deb the idea for Donna's mom having sent really *horrible* treats. For the record, Deb would like everyone to know: "Allison's mom's cookies were not dry." Also, they didn't come in a cookie tin with a picture of two cats on the lid.

Ah, yes. The cats. Shadrach and Meshach. The ones that forced Donna's folks to admit that, after thirty-nine years of marriage, they'd "outgrown compromise . . . so they got both." This is what plants the Great Justice Compromise in Josh's brain. Just like Donna's parents and the cats, when it came to those SCOTUS vacancies, the Bartlet administration "got both."

THE REASON FOR THE SEASONING

As a way of lightening the potentially impenetrable subject matter of this SCOTUS storyline, Deb peppered the episode with dashes of farcical spice. But that wasn't the only grounds for all the spirited fun. Having Lily Tomlin spritz a boisterous Josh outside the Oval, hearing a half-in-the-bag C.J. croon "American Pie" with Mitchell Ryan's Senator Pierce, or hearing a prospective chief justice exclaim, "Josh Lyman is gesticulating wildly!"—it was all therapeutic for Debora, who was dealing with troubles close to home.

"It was," Deb says, "a . . . bizarre situation where we started working on this story at the beginning of December, which was just as my mother was starting to get very, very ill, and passed away eight weeks later. I think it was this incredible escape. It's why I chose, as much as possible, to write the episode as a comedy. I needed comedy to get me through the judicial system, which I didn't understand, and I also needed comedy to get me through that period of time where it was . . . trips to the hospital and doctors and consultants and second opinions and a situation that was just getting worse and worse and darker and darker. A lot of this was written in her apartment . . . in her hospital room. The fourth act, which turned into a drunken French farce . . . was really inspired by the fact that I just needed to laugh."

Reflecting on the episode a year after its initial broadcast, director Jessica Yu went back to the beginning. "When I read the script," she said, "[it] felt so Aaron-esque to me. There were things about the pacing and the music of the language—and the humor too—that made me think of those really wonderful scripts that you just had such pleasure *reading*, let alone seeing and directing."

High praise like that is music to Deb's ears. After all, as she's said before (another dive into self-deprecation), "All I ever hoped to be was a successful Aaron Sorkin mimic."

Reflecting on this close examination of "The Supremes," it struck us that the episode represents not just the resilience of *The West Wing*, but also the strength and messiness of democracy itself. Asked for his impression of Justice Mulready, Toby captured that well:

```
              TOBY
    I hate him. I hate him—but he's
    brilliant. And the two of them
    together are fighting like cats and
    dogs . . . but it works.
```

That idea—that arguing honestly and 'til we're blue in the face can lead to the best outcomes—goes to the heart of the show. That's why, to us, this constitutes a watershed episode: While the shifting sands from the Sorkin years to the Wells era experienced ups and downs, "The Supremes" submitted clear evidence that one of the key DNA strands of *The West Wing* could and would continue; that potentially dry policy points could be spun into entertaining and compelling narratives; that the "sugar" of that wonderfully captivating storytelling could help the medicine go down, even when that medicine constituted supremely impenetrable subjects like the highest court in the land.

Above all, it confirmed that regardless of whose hand is on the tiller—especially if it's connected to John Wells—*The West Wing*'s sense of hope, inspiration, and aspiration would remain on a forward course . . . and full steam ahead.

THIRTY

FIRST, FAMILY

F riends," it's been said, meme'd, and stitched on samplers and throw pillows, "are the family we choose." Given that we spend half our days at work, it's no surprise that we inevitably find those friends there, and that sometimes those friends become our family. They're present for weddings and divorces, the births of your children and the deaths of your pets. They get you through the bad times and celebrate the good. Aaron himself may have put it best.

"I like bands more than solo acts," he says. "I like team sports more than individual sports. In success you have somebody to high-five along the way, and failure is a little bit easier when there's somebody in the foxhole with you." Sound familiar?

We're a group. We're a team. From the President and Leo on through, we're a team. We win together, we lose together. We celebrate and we mourn together. And defeats are softened and victories sweetened because we did them together.

—TOBY ZIEGLER, "WAR CRIMES"

"Ever since *The West Wing*," Aaron once mentioned to Malina, "I've been looking to duplicate that experience." To us he said, "I wanted everyone involved with the show to feel pride of authorship . . . as much as I do, or Tommy does, or anyone else. I just loved the spirit on that set so much." It's difficult to articulate the impact made by that spirit, by such a strong sense of "family," not just on our personal lives, but on what we brought to work and what we put on-screen. But you know what? We're gonna give it a try.

LIFE . . . AND THE OTHER THING

On September 3, 2004, Michael and I welcomed our first child into the world. Margaret McCormack Morris. Throughout the pregnancy, John Wells and everyone over at *The West Wing* couldn't have been more supportive, emotionally and in all the other ways. Production was mindful of my shooting schedule, making sure I always had plenty of time to get to my doctor's appointments. And every time I came back with a sonogram picture in my hand, it got passed around the cast and crew. They were so excited, like family. They also shot around my increasingly visible belly. And days before I had the baby, Martin gave me a blessed rosary—he gave me one for the births of Rose and Lillian, too. I held them through each delivery.

After Margaret was born, my maternity leave was set to run through three episodes of production. One morning, when Margaret was just six days old, my phone rang. It was director Chris Misiano.

In addition to being an executive producer on *The West Wing* at the time, Chris was—is—also a dear friend. He was calling to check in on the baby, to offer his congratulations, and to see how I was doing. I told him, "I'm feeling good." After a pause, he said, "*How* good?" Silence. Then . . . "Okay. Don't hate me, but . . . is there any world where you'd be able to come in and work?" (Turns out, the show had hired an actor for a role and, for various reasons, it just didn't work out. Suddenly they found themselves having to recast the role and reshoot scenes. This meant seriously revamping the production schedule—and fast—so . . .)

"You'd just be sitting at a desk," Chris quickly assured me. "We'd make it really easy for you . . . and only if you feel completely comfortable with it."

As crazy as it seemed in the moment, the truth was, I couldn't wait to bring Margaret to work and introduce her to all these people I considered, in a very real way, her family. So, seven days after Margaret McCormack Morris graced us with her presence in the world, her presence was required on set. Seven days into her life, I became a working mother.

Sure, there were times where we had to "Cut!" and "Go again" because I would look down and realize it was apparently time to nurse the baby. And, yes, Lyn Paolo had to procure *eight* of the same shirt for those scenes. But here was the headline: I could have my baby there with me all day. I knew then, and I know now, that that was the best gift a working mother could get. I got to do work I love while holding my baby between takes—having my *best friends* hold my baby between takes, and pass her around the *West Wing* set. It was magical; it was heaven. I felt like I won the lottery.

Margaret is eighteen years old today. (And by "today" I mean . . . *today*. Like . . . as I'm typing this sentence.) By the time this book is published, she'll have completed her freshman year of college. But I'll never forget my very first "Bring Your Daughter to Work" day . . . and all the ones that followed. There is also this . . .

While we were writing *What's Next*, my father, William McCormack, passed away. He was a profoundly decent and subversively hilarious man, and it was—is—a crushing loss. The support I received from Brad and Melissa, Allison and Janel, and the whole gang has been crucial. They just scoop you up. Not long after my dad died, Melissa and I had our first interview with Martin for the book. At the end of our conversation, we got to talking about my dad, the loss of him, how much I missed him, and then Martin said this: "You know, Mary, there's an old Irish saying, I don't know if you've ever heard it: 'We never get over our fathers. And we're not required to do so.'"

It moved me then and it moves me now. And I'm so grateful. For all of it. Melissa?

MOTHERS AND DAUGHTERS AND TELEPHONE CALLS

My mother always said, "You'll never regret showing up for your friends." She was right about that. (She's right about most things.) Looking back on the work we've happily revisited for this book, Mary and I couldn't help but notice the correlation between the deepening sense of a *West Wing* "family" and the service projects we undertake together. It's not that surprising. The more we show up for one another, the stronger the feeling of family becomes. But it's not just that. It's also about putting in the time. And Lord knows on *The West Wing* we put in the time.

> **ALLISON JANNEY:** I haven't spent as much time with my own family as I did with my *West Wing* family. The number of hours we spent together is extraordinary. We were a good family. Like all families, we weren't without our issues, our little . . . brushfire controversies. But it all always worked itself out. Seven years is a long time. A lot of things happen.

> **MELISSA:** Allison's right. Over those seven years, I met an amazing group of civic-minded, hilarious, and talented people; I got paid to act (which I would've done for free and which supported my nonprofit work); and with this *West Wing* family by my side,

I went through the best of times . . . and the worst of times. Like the night my mother almost died.

Alone in a hotel room not far from the hospital, looking to grab a few hours of sleep and shaking from adrenaline, I called Allison, I guess for empathy—she's got plenty to spare—and then called Janel for something else entirely: "Get it together, Missy! Do what you need to do for your mother. You need to be on top of every little detail, she needs you to be her advocate. Every day people die in hospitals. Don't let your mother be one of them!" I realized in that moment I needed both of those calls . . . and that nights like that are how families are born.

Of course, having friends who are family isn't just about talking you off the ledge. It's about fun stuff too, like weddings and cookies and happy little accidents.

Before *The West Wing* came into my life, I attended the wedding of a friend, Harrison Hobart. At the reception, I was chatting with a lovely, elegant woman, who was "best friends" with Harrison's parents. The families had known each other forever, the kids played together as children, the whole bit.

Upon learning I was an actress, Macy—that was the elegant woman's name—positively lit up. Her daughter was an actress too and was, in fact, currently performing in a play in New York. That's why she couldn't attend the wedding. Macy said she hoped her daughter and I would meet along the winding road of show business, insisting, "You two will *adore* each other!" CUT TO . . .

The Warner Bros. lot . . . years later. Allison invites me to her trailer. Her mom's visiting and she brought cookies from Ohio. (Remember the cookies Deb Cahn referenced in the last chapter, about "The Supremes"? This is the origin story of *those* cookies!) I'm walking toward Allison's trailer when I see this woman who looks vaguely familiar. "OH-MY-GOD-IT'S-THE-ELEGANT-

WOMAN-FROM-HARRISON-HOBART'S-WEDDING!"
Yep. It was Macy Janney. I met her years before I ever met Allison. And she was right. (*She's* right about most things too.) We
did adore each other. Still do.

Coincidences and Allison seem to go around. Like the fact that she
and Martin and Rob Lowe *all* grew up in Dayton, Ohio. But that's not
the end of it. How about this bit of kismet: Years into the show, Allison
and Rob were talking about their old hometown . . .

ROB LOWE: Where'd you go to high school?

ALLISON JANNEY: Miami Valley High School.

ROB LOWE: That was the fancy school. I was only there once. I
was in their gymnasium, they were putting on a production of *A
Funny Thing Happened on the Way to the Forum.*

ALLISON JANNEY: I was <u>in</u> that play. It was my acting debut!

These days, even as we've gone our separate ways, the cast still
manages to connect and catch up in our various corners of the country.
In some cases, it's at one of Allison's famous West Coast "Wig Parties"
(it's exactly what it sounds like and, before you ask, YES, there are
pictures), other times it's dinners and game nights on the East Coast
with "Carol" in the nation's capital.

MARY: Melissa has had so many of us crash with her (and her
housemates, Eric and Ben) in DC that we started calling their
house "*West Wing* Airbnb."

BRADLEY WHITFORD: Amy and I stayed there last year and
upgraded it to "The *West Wing* Embassy."

MELISSA: For my fiftieth, I went to my parents' house in Philly. My friend Shannon and my mom planned a bunch of surprises for me, culminating in a good old-fashioned birthday party. The night before the party, I came home to find Allison hiding under a table with my nephews. She jumped out and nearly gave me a heart attack! The next day brought another unexpected visitor— Janel. We had a *West Wing* sleepover at my mom and dad's!

JANEL MOLONEY: Melissa and I have always been family. I just codified it by making her godmother to our son Julian.

MELISSA: Janel and Allison aren't the only *West Wing*–ers who've been to my folks' place. One year, when he was in Pennsylvania, playing Nat King Cole in *Lights Out*, Dulé showed up there on Halloween.

DULÉ HILL: I had to try your mom's famous "Witch's Stew"!

It wasn't just the cast with whom we developed this sense of family. It was the crew as well. Now a producer, Julie DeJoie worked as Tommy Schlamme's assistant back on *The West Wing*. Jeff Halvorsen, the man she married, was a set dresser in the Art Department.

JULIE DeJOIE: I spent fourteen to sixteen hours a day on this show. This was our lives. I met Jeff on *The West Wing* . . . So, my future husband was there, my best friends . . . I mean, without the show, we wouldn't have our kids! We have *West Wing* babies!

DYLAN MASSIN (UNIT PRODUCTION MANAGER): One night not that long ago we started counting and we got somewhere between seventy-five and one hundred babies born on the show! I got married on that show. I bought a condo. I had a daughter. I sold my condo and bought a house. I had another daughter. In that seven-year period there was all this family, all this life.

LAUREN LOHMAN (ASSISTANT TO AARON SORKIN): My introduction to Hollywood began the last week of casting *The West Wing* and I've been with Aaron ever since. I wish I hadn't been so young because I didn't realize how special this was and how lucky we all were.

KRIS MURPHY (REPORTER KATIE WITT): Aaron created a family. As a cast, we survived triumphs and tragedies just like any other family.

LLEWELLYN WELLS (LINE PRODUCER): We had an exceptional family feeling on *The West Wing*. The cast, the directors, producers, the crew . . . the background actors that appeared in the bullpen scenes, they became part of the family, which is not normal in television.

RAMÓN DE OCAMPO (OTTO): Unknown to a lot of people—including myself at the time—Martin is intensely proud of his Mexican heritage, and, upon hearing my name, he whipped out his driver's license to show me. "My name is Ramón," he said, "and my first son is Ramón, too. Ramón, Carlos, and Emilio. I wish I could have kept my name, but when I started in this business all those years ago it was looked down upon to have a name so . . . ethnic. I kept it in my real life, though." I whipped out my own license because my middle name is Martin. So, we were both Ramón/Martin. It was a great bonding moment that doesn't really happen on sets very much with the new guy and the guy on top. He made me feel welcome, like I belonged.

JILL CROSBY: On my first day as department head of Hair for *The West Wing*, Allison Janney sat down in my chair. Sometimes in life you meet a person and feel like you've known them forever. A lot of people felt that way about Allison. She was always present, engaged, and just . . . one of us. Allison, to me, is a dear friend. *Beyond* "dear friend"—she's family.

Adam Ben Frank was one of *The West Wing*'s much-beloved assistant directors. A turning point in his personal life came later in the show's run.

ADAM BEN FRANK: Being in the closet, you do what you think is normal because you want to fit in. I wanted to be normal. *The West Wing* gave me the nudge to come out. I thought, These people are going to be my friends for the rest of my life, they're my family. I can't leave and not be known fully. One Friday night before the show wrapped, a bunch of us went to Firefly for drinks, and I told everybody. It was like setting off a glitter bomb. I came into the show this big lump of clay and left a beautiful boss!

I didn't want to be friends with you
and have you not know.

—JOSH TO C.J., "THE CRACKPOTS AND THESE WOMEN"

Holli Strickland was a *West Wing* production assistant. (She, too, is much beloved.)

HOLLI STRICKLAND: "Five-dollar Fridays" is a little on-set lottery. They do this on a lot of shows. On Fridays, you'd put in a five-dollar bill with your name on it, then, at the end of the night, one five-dollar bill is drawn. Whoever's name was on it won the

whole pot. Everyone participated—lighting, grips, sound, producers, directors, actors—so it ended up being a hefty little pot.
Of course, the odds aren't great, and I didn't win. Everyone knew
I had been saving up to go backpacking in Europe for two weeks
during hiatus and because I was so young they always took me
under their wing. I didn't know it at the time, but someone
started a second bucket. Just for me. My two-week trip ended up
being just over two *months* because the cast and crew were so
generous. Martin was so happy for me, but he was like a worried
grandpa. He found out that Spain was one of my stops and insisted that I meet his sister, Carmen. I ended up staying with her
family for a few weeks, and then she made me check in with her
by pay phone every few days from whatever country I was in. She
told me Martin had been calling almost every day, asking if she'd
heard from me, just to make sure I was okay.

AMERICAN DAD

In addition to bringing Aaron and Tommy's show to Warner Bros.—
and then to Wednesday nights at nine—John Wells was the guardian
of all things *West Wing*. Managing conflicts between his fellow creatives and those holding the purse strings, he put himself in the middle
of it all and handled it with impossible calm. When Aaron and Tommy
left, he kept his head about him and the series afloat, leading it, and all
of us, to safe harbor.

In the run-up to the show's final season, John got creative to make
the budget work, so he could keep as many cast and crew as possible
(yep, even Malina) gainfully employed.

JOSH MALINA: I remember John calling me to his office [and]
saying . . . "I think I've figured out a way to keep you on the show.

You'll do eleven episodes next season. You'll do about half the season. How does that sound?" And I was like, "It sounds eleven is better than being fired."

MARY: He called everyone in. Everyone had that meeting.

JOSH MALINA: Part of the discussion was the show had become tremendously expensive.

MARY: If we wanted to have another season, then—

JOSH MALINA: "Here's what I can do." Which I just thought was a very straight-up and lovely thing to do. In this business, most of the time . . . you find out when nobody calls to tell you to show up three months later. The other thing he did, which is completely unheard-of, was, he said, "And for the last two episodes, I'm going to give you a raise. So that when you're looking for another job, your quote will be higher than what it is now."

MARTIN SHEEN: John was the only producer I ever worked with who told me the truth, the whole truth, and nothing but the truth all the time. If he didn't have the money, he didn't have the money. I believed him.

MARY: When I went in to meet with John, I could tell he was trying really hard to puzzle things together. And honestly, as much as I wished I could do all twenty-two, I was thrilled to get to do even one episode. So I told him, "However many I can get . . . sign me up." Then he said . . . "You should come back to *ER* for a few episodes." Because I had a new baby, he wanted to make sure I had enough work. I mean, John Wells . . . There are no words. Except these four from earlier in the book: "He's a real dad."

POLITICS OR . . . THE BAR

RENÉE ROSENFELD (SCRIPT SUPERVISOR): Compared to other shows I'd worked on, the *West Wing* set was completely different. I so enjoyed getting to have conversations about current events and politics. It is the last and only job I had where no one left the set.

JULIE DeJOIE: During a lighting setup, people didn't leave, they just . . . gathered. Sitting in the Roosevelt Room, somebody would tell a story. I'd wonder, "Is this just Tommy's game to keep everybody awake, telling these stories?" Then Aaron would come down and join in. It was very social.

MELISSA: On *The West Wing*, no one went to their trailer. We mostly just hung out and talked. In a sense, we're still sitting around the campfire. Life gets "kids-busy," friendships get harder to maintain . . . but you fan the flames and send up the bat signal. Whoever tilts it toward the sky, the rest of the family shows up.

Our friend first AD and director Andrew Bernstein put it well:

ANDREW BERNSTEIN: The family feeling that that show had—cast *and* crew—made you want to be a participant in what other people were interested in. I just wanted to hang out, be in that family, any way I could. Yes, I'm political, and I was interested in that stuff . . . but the more I could hang out with Mary, Melissa, Richard, Brad, and Martin, the more I wanted to. If it took you in a political direction, great. If it took you, ya know . . . to the bar, great.

If friends are the family you choose, service represents—to borrow a line from "Posse Comitatus"—the things we choose to care about.

To us, that's what this chapter, this book, and this *family* are all about: taking you toward service . . . and, sometimes, to the bar. As a wise man (named Sorkin) once said, "It's all right to be alone in a big city if you can find family at work."

The Wingnuts and
The West Wing Weekly

Just as any discussion of the *West Wing* family would be incomplete without a shout-out to the Wingnuts, any discussion of the Wingnuts would be incomplete without a shout-out to *The West Wing Weekly*. In our research for this book, the podcast has been a source of endless value. It's also done more than any post–*West Wing* anything to stoke the fire of the fans, galvanizing and expanding an international community of *West Wing* watchers. (We see you, UK fandom.) For those readers less "podcast adjacent," a primer:

The West Wing Weekly is a rewatch-and-recap commentary podcast that explores, episode by episode, the seven-year run of the series. It is the brain-child of superfan Hrishikesh Hirway, whose co-host is *West Wing* cast member Josh Malina. For those who have not yet experienced this fun, sharp, bantery program, an early exchange in the podcast's first episode sums it up with a decidedly familiar breeziness:

HRISHI
It's like having a little book club
for watching *The West Wing*.

                    JOSH
        Yes, a book club where only two of
        its members can actually speak.

                    HRISHI
        Right.

                    JOSH
        Which for me, is the best kind of
        book club.

                    HRISHI
        Also, one that doesn't require
        reading books and only watching TV.

In addition to analysis, insights, and anecdotes, many podcast episodes feature guests from the *West Wing* cast and crew
or from the real world of politics, media, or academia. For instance, one week Richard Schiff might be on to talk about his
memories of shooting "In Excelsis Deo." The next might have
Joe Biden's then future chief of staff Ron Klain—podcast code
name: "Papa Smurf"—discussing what it's like to put together a
Supreme Court vacancy "short list." So yeah—it's a great podcast, with a fiercely loyal listenership and a fun, familiar *West
Wing*–style sign-off. ("Okay. Okay. What's next?")

We've talked about Malina plenty in this book, but let's take
a moment to focus on his co-host. When it comes to *The West
Wing*, Hrishi is a true believer. Seriously, he's like a missionary,
walking-and-talking the earth, seeking out converts. Through
the years, he's lured countless unsuspecting friends into the
West Wing universe by plying them with his top two irresistible episodes. "I make people watch 'Shibboleth' from season 2
and 'Take This Sabbath Day' from season 1." Yep, he goes right
for the jugular. They're hooked.

Asked for a favorite *West Wing* moment, Hrishi went back to "Shibboleth" and the classic he-gave-him-the-knife speech. "The feeling of family that gets expressed . . . when Bartlet—*President Bartlet*—says, 'Charlie, my father gave this to me and his father gave it to him, and now I'm giving it to you . . .' That's workplace drama at its best. That the guy who is the lowest in the pecking order in the executive office is being treated like a son by his boss . . . is just so beautiful."

What we love most about *The West Wing Weekly* is that it really seems to rally people, providing a clubhouse that they've been looking for since the show went off the air. It's been a real gift to so many fans, and to a lot of causes, which brings us to . . .

MELISSA: Of all the appearances I've done on behalf of All Rise, *The West Wing Weekly* has been the one piece of media that's helped elevate our cause more than any other. I get approached all the time—on the streets of DC, at the train station, in restaurants—and often they're staffers on Capitol Hill, and even a few elected officials. "We're huge *West Wing* fans," they tell me, "but we really love the work you're doing now with treatment courts! We heard you talk about it on *The West Wing Weekly!*" The support we have received from the Wingnuts and *The West Wing Weekly* has been, and continues to be, extraordinary . . .

One year on my birthday, a *West Wing* fan reached out on social media to the All Rise Twitter account, asking what I wanted as a gift. My colleague who runs the account, deputy communications director Brooke Glisson—our Sam Seaborn, if you will—asked me. What I really wanted was for more veterans to be able to attend our veteran mentor training "boot camp." These men and women are crucial to the success of treatment courts. "So," I told Brooke, "if someone's willing to donate some scholarship money for that . . ."

Somebody was.

That podcast listener donated in honor of Melissa's birthday, then tweeted about it. Soon, *West Wing* fans—and *West Wing Weekly* listeners—got wind of it and they started contributing too. "We raised over fifteen thousand dollars and were able to send a whole group of veterans to our mentor boot camp training for three days. The ripples of that are huge! That was a gift that Josh, Hrishi, and their community gave to me and to my community, and we couldn't be more grateful. Best present I ever got."

While the podcast has helped spur a sense of community among fans of the show, the Wingnut culture it tapped into has, of course, been there all along. It exists in big cities and small towns, in this country and overseas. They express themselves in *West Wing*–themed tattoos and college courses based on the show (*The West Wing*: Power and Principle in the American Political System, University of California, Berkeley; *The West Wing* as History, American University). Wingnuts name their pets after *West Wing* characters, and some of them do that with their kids. I mean, we haven't exactly run the numbers on this, but we can safely estimate that there's roughly half a dozen families out there with a pair of dogs named C.J. and Toby; a few sets of parents with little Josh Lymans running around. (For that latter group, the briefest of warnings: Do not let him anywhere near the message boards. It won't go well. It never does.) Meanwhile, thanks to streaming services like Max, and podcasts like *The West Wing Weekly*, a whole new crop of would-be Wingnuts, including Mary's three daughters, are discovering the show.

We'll end with this: Josh, Hrishi, and every single Wingnut...
we just want to say thank you. Thank you for watching the show
(and rewatching the show and re-rewatching the show), for
reading the book (feel free to reread the book), for supporting
our causes, for passing the baton to a new generation, and for
expanding our *West Wing* family. Okay. Okay. What's next?

THIRTY-ONE

"WALK-AND-TALK THE VOTE"

W hen it comes to *The West Wing*'s mix of family, service, and politics (fictional and otherwise), one August day in 2012 stands out as especially memorable. In that case, the trusty *West Wing* bat signal drew former colleagues from in front of and behind the camera. It all began with a pair of state supreme court vacancies and a "*West Wing*–in–law" (Mary's sister, Bridget McCormack), an associate dean at the University of Michigan's law school, who was vying for one of the open seats. (It's Melissa. As a fan of both Bridget and Mary—I see myself as the missing McCormack sister—I'll take the lead in this proceeding.)

Weeks before that fateful Saturday in August, Mary and her husband, Michael, had been brainstorming creative ways to help her big sister. Given that Bridget was running in a state election and that her name would appear in the oft-overlooked "nonpartisan section of the ballot," even the faintest spotlight could provide a game-changing bump. So maybe Brad or Richard could record a video endorsement on their iPhone. Or Allison. And . . . could they possibly get Martin to lend his voice to the cause? So they reached out.

In what should have come as no surprise, but did, everyone said yes. Which is great, of course, except that all of a sudden, the McCormack team realized they were going to need a director. Former *West Wing* director of photography and all-world good guy Michael Mayers signed on. And, oh yeah, what on earth were we going to *say*? Mary called up her old *In Plain Sight* colleague John Cockrell, who scripted a snappy public service announcement / campaign short called "Walk-and-Talk the Vote." (**MARY:** John has been one of my best friends since we were seventeen and both in the a cappella group the Pipes, in college. Even then he was the smartest, quickest writer I knew. He and I have worked together wherever possible ever since. The fact that he was never on the staff of *The West Wing* is one of those small wrinkles in the fabric of space-time. John is a true Wingnut [and SportsNut? if that's a thing?]. I've never met anyone who loves the show as much. He was a natural choice to write "Walk-and-Talk the Vote"—which at the time was the most significant "new" *West Wing* incarnation yet. In fact, the first new *West Wing* scenes since the end of the show. The look on John's face as the cast assembled that day is about as great a memory as you can have. Imagine a six-year-old stumbling onto a walk-and-talk between Santa Claus and the Easter Bunny and you can begin to picture it.)

From there, Mary remembers, "we got crewed up. All of a sudden, what we'd initially pictured as a fast-and-loose, half-assed iPhone video had morphed into a full-fledged day of filming—with a crew and call sheets . . . craft service . . . That level of generosity from my *West Wing* family, and also just the *comprehensiveness* of it . . . I was so touched. I still am."

The ten-hour shoot took place in a Burbank postproduction facility dressed up as a makeshift West Wing. What made this event extra special is that it boasted a nearly all-volunteer cast and crew. Every actor, writer, and producer, all the hair and makeup people, lighting and sound, set designers and dressers, electricians and prop masters—

even crafty and the catering services—worked for free. All for a good cause, a great candidate, and the very best reasons.

While Allison, Mary, Janel, and I got finishing touches on our makeup and hair, we sat in an office going over our lines. Brad and Richard grazed over at craft services. Just a stone's throw away, Malina was rehearsing the first scene, throwing a tennis ball, Toby-style, against the wall of his office. ("For the record," John Cockrell said to us, "a decade later I still hate myself for not specifically scripting the ball as a 'PINK SPALDEEN.' It haunts me to this day.")

With all the creativity that went into every aspect of "Walk-and-Talk the Vote," it was the production designer, Denny Dugally, who had to get above-and-beyond inventive. She and her team raided storage units at work and home and brought set dressings and props—an American flag here, an eagle statuette there—and, in the Mickey Rooney / Judy Garland spirit of yesteryear, embraced their inner "We're gonna put on a show!" Drab postproduction offices, editing suites, and conference rooms transformed into a remarkable semblance of *The West Wing*.

Meanwhile, as other cast members trickled in, Mayers strategized his opening shot, Mary's husband, Michael Morris, showed up with their three daughters in tow (one of them, Lillian, brand-new!), and Mary and Malina got ready to roll. Oh, and the candidate we were there to endorse thanked everybody in sight as production geared up for the day. The next several hours resembled a rowdy summer camp reunion as we caught up with one another and reacquainted ourselves with the characters we'd last played five years before. Walking-and-talking, passing the baton, battling busted coffeemakers and bantering with friends, we had the time of our lives . . . again. (And in a subtle homage to Tommy Schlamme, the day went long.)

It was a total dream. We instantly fell back into old habits: the fast and easy on-set conversations, the constant teasing and fits of laughter, Brad and Allison goofing off while going over lines . . . and all of us rolling our eyes at Malina and what one can only loosely refer to as his "jokes."

I don't know why, but nothing makes me feel quite so good as the sight of colleagues enjoying each other outside work.

—PRESIDENT BARTLET TO JOSH AND LEO,
"THE CRACKPOTS AND THESE WOMEN"

It culminated in shooting a scene around a conference table, talking about issues we care about, issues that state supreme courts take up every day: civil rights, the environment, workplace protections, voter protections. As if that weren't enough, we were graced with the presence of legends Lily Tomlin and Martin Sheen, who both prioritized this get-together because they believed in the candidate, the cause, and the family of friends who asked for their help. Then, as Martin closed out the video with a trademark flip of his blazer and his trademark line, "What's next?" we were finished. Almost.

At the end of the day, the final setup and shot came down to . . . the candidate. Poor Bridget—the one on-camera presence who wasn't an actor had to film her piece of the ad in front of the remaining cast and crew. "I'm Bridget Mary McCormack, and I approved this message." And yet . . . after a few takes, the future state supreme court justice nailed her line, blushed at the applause, and that was that. CUT TO . . .

Several weeks (and many hours of editing footage) later, the four-minute video went viral on social media, generating millions of views across multiple platforms. (It lives on, as everything does, thanks to YouTube.) Just days after that, we eagerly tuned in to MSNBC's late-night cable news show, *The Last Word*, hosted by former *West Wing* writer-producer Lawrence O'Donnell. Thanks to Lawrence, viewers got to see not just a clip of the video, which is what we had hoped for, but the entire thing! He also interviewed Bridget for a segment, during which she made the case for her candidacy while underscoring the importance of nonpartisan elections like the ones for state supreme court.

"Walk-and-Talk the Vote," it's worth noting, was as much a public service announcement as a campaign ad. And the subject of that PSA remains a legitimate issue—not a major one, but not a minor one, either. Many state and local election ballots include sections that even savvy voters remain unaware of. As Martin's President Bartlet points out in the video, "If people fail to realize a straight-ticket-vote doesn't count in the nonpartisan races, if they just casually vote the party line, their interests will continue to go unrepresented!"

On November 6, 2012, Barack Obama and Joseph Biden won reelection over their GOP challengers, Mitt Romney and Paul Ryan. Meanwhile, in the great state of Michigan, Bridget took one of the three open supreme court seats while earning more votes than any other candidate, the incumbent included. In 2018, Bridget was selected by her peers to serve as chief justice and remained in that role until she retired from the court in 2022, having won reelection in 2020. Her legacy is best characterized as one of bipartisanship, of fundamental change, of increased citizen accessibility to the court, and of giving voice to disenfranchised people in search of more equitable outcomes. Bridget is also a champion of treatment courts and a member of the board at All Rise. *The West Wing*'s Evelyn Baker Lang would be proud.

Looking back more than a decade later, it would appear the whole chaotic, fun-filled enterprise undertaken on that summer day went off without a hitch. And it did. Except . . .

Between coordinating production, acquiring network and studio approval, and the race to get all these people together in one place on one day, one thing got lost in the shuffle. And it was sort of a big deal . . . which Mary realized less than an hour after we wrapped. Her urgent text to one of the producers went a little something like this:

"Ohmyfuckinggod! *We forgot to ask Aaron!!!*"

(Oops.) Yes, the one permission we had neglected to lock down was the one that mattered most. So Mary wrote him a panicked mea culpa. (**MARY:** Just popping in to say that I was literally *sick* with worry. Okay. Back to Melissa.) Here's how Aaron replied:

> Mary,
>
> You're so sweet to write. Bridget sounds awesome and I wish I lived in Michigan so I could vote for her. I'm very flattered that you and she would want to use *The West Wing* to help her campaign and I'm proud that the gang can always be counted on to pitch in. Let me know if there's anything I can do to help.
>
> Aaron

Two more emails and four months later . . .

> Dear Mr. Sorkin,
>
> I want to thank you for your incredible generosity in allowing us to use your characters and your intellectual property for the campaign video we made. Over a million people saw the *West Wing* video, and the earned media around it was unbelievable. In a name recognition race like the state supreme court race, this truly might well explain the outcome. I am so grateful for your kindness in permitting us to run with it with your

blessing. And I promise to make the Michigan Supreme Court a fairer institution while I serve on it, and to improve the way justice is done in our state. Thank you.

Warmly,
Bridget McCormack

Justice McCormack,

I was so happy that Mary and the cast were able to help in the election of such a worthy jurist. I don't envy you your job but I wish you the wisdom of Solomon and I look forward to breaking the law in Michigan so that I can meet you someday.

Best,
Aaron

(LEFT)
Martin calls numbers on the Bingo Bus
on one of the annual trips to Vegas.
Courtesy of Annette Sousa

(RIGHT)
A poster for Martin's famous Bingo Bus trips, created by *West Wing* background actor
and stand-in John Wan. John was known for making lots of creative invitations, cari-
catures, and posters during his time on the show.
Courtesy of Peter James Smith, poster by John Wan

Cast and crew gather in front of Martin's Bingo Bus, having just arrived in Las Vegas.
Courtesy of Maxine Penty

After production assistant Holli Strickland's *West Wing* bicycle was stolen—it had been a crew gift—makeup artist Greg LaCava bought her a new pink bike, which led to various cast and crew posing with "the pinky bike" all over the Warner Bros. lot, including here, on top of President Bartlet's desk in the Oval Office.
Courtesy of Allison Janney

Deputy National Security Advisor and Chief of Staff tied up in red tape. And pink tape. And black tape. *Courtesy of Allison Janney*

Toby Ziegler

The crime for which Mr. Ziegler has been charged is of the utmost serious
In nature. He was charged with leaking top-secret, confidential, government
Secrets to the press. This action could have jeopardized the intelligence
Community of the United States. His trial is pending.

Now, therefore, be it known that I, Josiah Bartlet, President of the United
States of America, in consideration of the premises, do hereby grant unto
Toby Ziegler a full and unconditional pardon.

In testimony whereof I have hereunto signed my name and caused the seal
Of the Department of Justice to be affixed.

In this District of Columbia, on this twentieth day of January in the day of
Our Lord.

Josiah Bartlet   Aaron Sorkin
President of the United States   Pardon Attorney

Bartlet's pardon letter for Toby from the series finale, "Tomorrow." Notice the
name of the pardon attorney.
Courtesy of Matthew Truex, Warner Bros. Corporate Archives

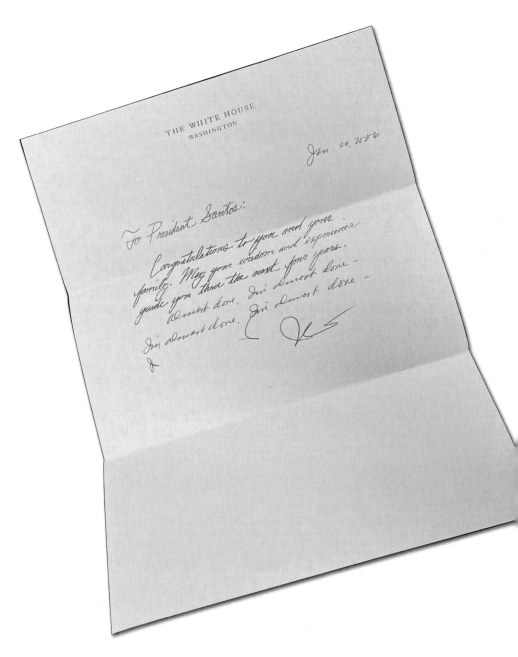

The actual prop used in the series finale scene when President Bartlet writes his transition note to President Santos. Props prepared the first part of the letter. The second, in Martin Sheen's hand, was written during the filming of the scene, and it says, "Almost done, I'm almost done, I'm almost done . . ."

Courtesy of Blanche Sindelar, Warner Bros. Corporate Archives

West Wing cast in front of Marine One. Yes. That's a genuine typo. Even the greatest art department in TV has a bad day once in a while.
(L-TO-R: John Spencer, Martin Sheen, Mary McCormack, Richard Schiff, and Josh Malina)
Courtesy of Mary McCormack

(Penn Jillette, Lawrence O'Donnell) After seeing magicians Penn & Teller do a flag-burning trick in Las Vegas, Lawrence knew he wanted to write it into a *West Wing* episode. The trick became a plot point in season 6's "In the Room" when it was performed by Penn & Teller at Zoey Bartlet's birthday party.
Courtesy of Lawrence O'Donnell

Allison Janney and executive producer John Wells on the very last night of the very last episode of *The West Wing*. *Courtesy of Allison Janney*

Mary and soon-to-be president Barack Obama at a 2008 campaign rally at the University of New Mexico in Albuquerque. He had been bingeing *The West Wing* in the car on the way to the rally. Forty-eight hours later he was elected the 44th President of the United States. *Photographs by Michael Morris*

Allison and Melissa at the Human Rights Campaign gala in Washington, DC, October 2015. *Courtesy of Brendan Kownacki*

Allison and her niece Petra, whose nonprofit, Amelia Air, flies in and rescues pets from overcrowded kill shelters then flies them to more populated areas to place in forever homes. Also pictured: Dutch, Sippy, and Henry. *Courtesy of Allison Janney*

March 8, 2016: Here we are outside the Steven J. Ross Theater as then Chairman of Warner Bros. Television Group, Peter Roth, and Warner Bros. hosted the rollout of a Justice for Vets PSA starring the cast of *The West Wing*. (L-TO-R: Peter Roth, Melissa Fitzgerald, Mary McCormack, Allison Janney, Brad Whitford, Richard Schiff, and Dulé Hill) *Courtesy of Brendan Kownacki*

Holding Justice for Vets challenge coins and celebrating Martin Sheen's induction into the All Rise Treatment Court Hall of Fame, June 4, 2016. (L-TO-R: Travis Howard, Melissa Fitzgerald, Dr. Alice Chen, Surgeon General Dr. Vivek Murthy, Hon. Bridget McCormack, Richard Schiff, Martin Sheen, Allison Janney, Mary McCormack, and Dulé Hill) *AP Images for All Rise*

October 17, 2016: Mary, Dulé, Allison, Richard, Melissa, Josh, and Brad celebrate the unveiling of Allison's star on the Hollywood Walk of Fame.

Photograph by Everett Collection Inc / Alamy Stock Photo

The wedding ceremony for Brad Whitford and Amy Landecker, officiated by their dear friend and renowned activist, the late Ady Barkan.
Courtesy of Brad Whitford

Photo booth strip of
Melissa, Mary, and Allison
at the celebration of
Brad and Amy's 2019 wedding.
Courtesy of Mary McCormack

Aaron Sorkin answers a question on the *West Wing Weekly* podcast finale. Hrishikesh Hirway, Josh Malina (standing); Tommy Schlamme, Martin Sheen, Brad Whitford (front row); and Timothy Davis-Reed and Peter James Smith (back row) look on. More than thirty members of the cast and crew were together onstage for this mini-reunion at the Ace Hotel in Downtown Los Angeles, in front of an audience of more than a thousand fans. *Photograph by David G. Marks, davidGmarks.com*

Campaigning together in 2016. (L-TO-R: Richard Schiff, Josh Malina, Brad Whitford, and Dulé Hill) *Photograph by Michael Morris*

Behind the scenes (and face shields) while filming "A *West Wing* Special to Benefit When We All Vote" during the COVID pandemic, October 2020. (L-TO-R: Emily Procter, Melissa Fitzgerald, Allison Janney, Janel Moloney, Dulé Hill, and Richard Schiff) *Courtesy of Melissa Fitzgerald*

Martin and Melissa at The Kennedy Center in October 2023 before their final performance of A. R. Gurney's *Love Letters* in celebration of Recovery Month/All Rise. *Photograph by Karla Nunfio*

Martin rallies the troops on the National Day of Solidarity during the WGA and SAG-AFTRA strikes, outside the Disney studio lot on August 22, 2023.
Photograph by Jack E. Herman

The practical joke war between Josh Malina and Brad Whitford never really ends. Not even on the picket line, during the National Day of Solidarity.
Photograph by Michael Morris

Aaron Sorkin, surrounded by *West Wing* cast and crew, picketing for the WGA and SAG-AFTRA on the National Day of Solidarity, August 22, 2023.

(L-TO-R: BACK ROW: Melissa Fitzgerald, Ron Ostrow, Ramón de Ocampo, Evan Arnold, Richard Schiff, Aaron Sorkin, Brad Whitford, Allison Janney, Mary McCormack, Peter James Smith, Kim Webster

FRONT ROW: Janel Moloney, Chris Ufland, Josh Malina, William Duffy, Dulé Hill)

Photograph by Michael Morris

Brad and Mary backstage at *Boeing Boeing* at the Longacre Theatre on Broadway, 2008. Mary was nominated for a Tony for her performance, and the play won for best revival.
Courtesy of Mary McCormack

Melissa, assistant director (and "beautiful boss") Adam Ben Frank, and Allison Janney at one of Allison's famous Wig Parties, this one for her birthday in 2004.
Photograph by Kristin McArdle

The very last Gail's goldfish bowl prop from the very last episode of *The West Wing*.
Courtesy of the Warner Bros. Corporate Archives

KEY EPISODE

"The Debate"

One of the most memorable episodes in the history of *The West Wing* came in the show's final season. "The Debate," the show's first and only live episode, was the brainchild of showrunner John Wells and writer Lawrence O'Donnell, who had written two of the most pivotal episodes of season 6, including "In God We Trust." Directed by what had to have been a frantic and exhausted Alex Graves, "The Debate" was produced twice—once for an East Coast audience, then again for folks on the West Coast. For now, here is an oral history of the two-and-only "live" episodes *The West Wing* ever aired, in (mostly) Lawrence's own words.

LAWRENCE O'DONNELL: It was the riskiest thing the show ever did, and I was the only one who didn't understand how disorienting it was because I had done a lot of live television. It's not live drama, but the idea of "it's live" was something I understood technologically. I knew some of the people in the special live crew who had to be hired for this, who never worked on any other episode. But I also knew that I *couldn't* know how much pressure was on the actors. It's different from a play, you're not gonna get the same rehearsal time. A play you're gonna have an audience of fifteen hundred, not fifteen million. The nerves that come with a "live event" affected the characters too.

> **SENATOR VINICK**
> You have no idea what this feels
> like. "Terrified" doesn't begin to
> describe it.

LAWRENCE O'DONNELL: It began with John Wells saying, "I want to do a live episode." No idea what it was gonna be about, but they had done a live episode on *ER*. (**MELISSA FUN FACT:** And our own Tommy Schlamme directed that one.) I came up with the suggestion that ours should be a debate, mostly by process of elimination. What else could it be? If we do a debate, you'll get to use all those conventions of live television. You'll be able to re-create something—you have a shot list. You know what it's supposed to look like. And the audience will have a visual familiarity.

One of the things about presidential debates is that they tend to be boring. I had to come up with how to loosen this up and get out of that stupid "thirty seconds to reply" and canned thirty-second stuff.

So, I decide I'm gonna have one of them propose throwing away the rules. When you throw away the rules, it becomes a more lively thing, right? And that's gonna be good for Alex as the director because scrapping the rules means fewer rules for the cameras and everything becomes less static. It's something I'd always hoped a candidate would do. It would be a really smart move because it puts pressure on the other guy to agree to that and, if he doesn't, risks making him look weak. Like "I need this format to protect me."

The subject of the episode was set. Now it was time to write the thing. While writing, Lawrence was in frequent contact with Jim Lehrer. (Lehrer, who died in 2020, was a Hall of Fame journalist, perhaps best known for his work on *PBS NewsHour*, who moderated twelve presidential debates across forty-plus years in a long and storied career.)

> **LAWRENCE O'DONNELL:** I told Jim, "I want one of the candidates, after the rules get recited, to say exactly what the audience is thinking, which is, "Those rules are stupid. Let's just get rid of the rules."
>
> SENATOR VINICK
> We could go on with this ritual and
> let the rules control how much
> you're going to learn about the
> next President of the United
> States. Or we could have a debate
> Lincoln would have been proud of.
> We could junk the rules.
>
> **LAWRENCE O'DONNELL:** I finished my pitch . . . and there's this silence on the other end of the phone. This is when I expect Jim to bail out. He says, "I've been waiting decades for a candidate to do that."

Lehrer had anchored more televised debates than anyone in history. I actually asked him to do it for "The Debate" and he really, really wanted to, but he told me, "I can't do it. PBS has a rule, saying we cannot participate in fictional depictions like this. And I wrote the rule." So, Jim Lehrer was out. I asked Tom Brokaw, same thing. Tim Russert, same thing . . ."

FORREST SAWYER: Lawrence called and said, "We'd really like somebody who's done this sort of thing before. Would you do it?" I said, "Sure . . . but how much do I have to pay you?"

LAWRENCE O'DONNELL: Forrest Sawyer was perfect because he had all that gravitas of the anchorman because he was one. And because he was not working at NBC News anymore, he was able to do it.

Prepping for this ambitious undertaking meant more than actors having to learn larger-than-usual chunks of dialogue. The ramifications extended to production overall.

LAWRENCE O'DONNELL: We wrote Jimmy Smits a little lighter in the other episode we were working on so we could schedule extra rehearsal for them in "The Debate."

Lawrence and Alex Graves would then ferry Jimmy and Alan "off campus" to a separate rehearsal room outside Warner Bros.

LAWRENCE O'DONNELL: We would rehearse this like a play for hours, for two weeks. That was just heavenly. We've got our actors, the director Alex Graves is here, "the playwright" is here . . . I wanted this to go on for a month! Because suddenly we're in the theater world!

JIMMY SMITS: We had the luxury of rehearsing all that time. Well . . . "all that time"—we had an extra week.

ALAN ALDA: It was a real adventure for the two of us because there really was not much time to rehearse. And they were shooting Jimmy in another episode!

One difference maker is that all the actors involved had extensive experience in front of live audiences. That included the candidates on-stage and their handlers, as well, one of whom—Janeane Garofalo—had logged over a decade doing stand-up comedy.

LAWRENCE O'DONNELL: You had Ron Silver and Alan Alda, who'd been on an awful lot of Broadway stages. Jimmy had a lot of stage experience. They just kept saying, "We're doing a play, we're doing a play!" Alan just loved it.

ALAN ALDA: Can we go do this? Can we take this out as a play and go do it?!

Of course, Alan's enthusiasm didn't mean there weren't frustrations along the way.

ALAN ALDA: It's an hour of material you're supposed to at least be familiar with, and Lawrence kept changing it as he got more ideas! And if you have five versions of something in your head, you don't know which one to pick when it's time to speak. So we relied on teleprompters.

Despite the teleprompters, just like theater, the live episode came with a sense of "anything can happen."

ALAN ALDA: The second show had a completely different audience. They thought they were at a Democratic rally. They kept applauding every time Jimmy Smits said something. I started a line and they were still making noise, so I said, "No, wait a minute, I got something good to say here." That shut them up.

JIMMY SMITS: If I had to name a top five of what I've done . . . that live debate episode is up there. It was what I imagined it would be like in the 1950s when they were doing *Playhouse 90*.

LAWRENCE O'DONNELL: The backstage stuff that begins the debate, that's all live. In another show that all would have been filmed ahead of time and just attached to the live piece. But our claim [was that] this is live television, start to finish. So when you see Ron [and] Janeane . . . working with their candidates, that is happening live. They are walking them to that stage live . . . but it's like you're in a *West Wing* episode . . . then when we come out onto the stage, it's going to pop into, you know . . . TV.

ALAN ALDA: Problem was, I needed glasses to see at a distance and glasses hadn't been established for [Vinick]. So, for the first time in my life, I had to put in contact lenses.

Hmm . . . What could possibly go wrong?

ALAN ALDA: On the first show, five minutes before air, I'm still trying to get my contact lens in and I couldn't. And with my fingers in my eye, there's no sense of concentrating on the show. I just had to get the contact lens in, otherwise I wouldn't say any of the right words!

The next fifty or so minutes saw two veteran performers engaged in rhetorical battle over tax reform, immigration, Medicare, Head Start, global warming, and other hot-button issues—all while trying to keep their talking points straight and their eyes on one of the many hidden teleprompters.

LAWRENCE O'DONNELL: The only things comparable to the kind of directing Alex was doing in these two performances . . .

are *Saturday Night Live* and sports. Because you don't get to go
back and edit—it's really happening. It was unlike any directing
Alex had ever done . . . it was incredibly high-pressure [and] a
fascinating challenge to see him rise to.

It's hard to choose the best moment of the "The Debate," but if
forced—and, for the record, our editor, Jill, *is* (affectionately) forcing
us—we'd go with this one:

> SENATOR VINICK
> I'm sorry. I shouldn't have used
> that word. I know Democrats think
> liberal is a bad word. So bad you
> had to change it, didn't you? What
> do you call yourselves now,
> "Progressives?" Is that it?
>
> CONGRESSMAN SANTOS
> It's true, Republicans have tried
> to turn liberal into a bad word.
> Well, Liberals ended slavery in
> this country.
>
> SENATOR VINICK
> A Republican President ended
> slavery.
>
> CONGRESSMAN SANTOS
> . . . What did liberals do that was
> so offensive to the Republican
> party, Senator? I'll tell you what
> they did. Liberals got women the
> right to vote. Liberals got
> African-Americans the right to
> vote. Liberals created Social
> Security and lifted millions of

```
elderly people out of poverty.
Liberals ended segregation.
Liberals passed the Civil Rights
Act, the Voting Rights Act.
Liberals created Medicare. Liberals
passed the Clean Air Act, the Clean
Water Act. What did Conservatives
do? They opposed every one of those
programs. Every one. So, when you
try to hurl that word "liberal" at
my feet, as if it were something
dirty, something to run away from,
something that I should be ashamed
of, it won't work, Senator, because
I will pick up that label and I
will wear it as a badge of honor.
```

Boy. That kind of unapologetic fortitude sounds like something progressives—and not just progressives—would respond to. To borrow those words from the late Jim Lehrer, "We've been waiting decades for a candidate to do that." Also, Alan was right—it would've made a great play.

While it's true that "The Debate" constituted a big idea, ambitious in scope and with a high degree of difficulty, for the principals involved, it represented something more quietly meaningful.

LAWRENCE O'DONNELL: It was a deeply personal experience for all of us, and we kind of didn't want it to end.

By throwing out time-honored rules in favor of something new—a true exchange of ideas—and by pointing out the pointlessness of thirty-second answers, by showing what could happen next, this episode offered up something to aspire to. It played to the intrinsic human need for something to believe in and modeled for our future selves a better version of our present.

A SERVICE STORY

ALAN ALDA

Between his work on Marlo Thomas's 1970s-era children's album, *Free to Be . . . You and Me*, his title role in *The Seduction of Joe Tynan*, the exploration of sociopolitical dynamics with Ellen Burstyn in *Same Time, Next Year* and, above all, his multiple-award-winning role as Hawkeye Pierce on the legendary TV show *M*A*S*H*, Alan Alda is one of the all-timers when it comes to the confluence of entertainment and activism. The last four decades, though, have seen his civic engagement steer clear of politics. Now he drives toward a different intersection. The one connecting two of his passions: science and communication.

ALAN ALDA: I was doing the science television show *Scientific American Frontiers*. It worked because I was able to make real personal contact with the scientists, which helped them get out of "lecture mode." I did it the way I would have if I was in an improvisation with them. Really paying attention, really responding in a genuine way. One time when I was at USC, I said, "Can we get twenty engineering students for three hours?" I asked each of them to talk to the other nineteen about their work for two minutes. After everybody did, we improvised for three hours . . . and then they spoke again. Everybody was amazed, including me, that they were much clearer, and related better to the audience.

From then on, every time I was at a university I'd say, "Can't we start a communication program, so we could turn out scientists who are not just fine scientists, but good communicators?" Well, nobody said yes, except Stony Brook in Long Island, which was close to where I lived. The Alda Center was established there about twelve years ago. Ever since, we've been training scientists here and all over the world.

My podcast, *Clear + Vivid*, is about communicating in every aspect of life. Whatever money that makes goes to the Alda Center. So, it's all tied together like almost everything I do.

We felt beyond lucky to have Alan as a fellow *West Wing*–er, and we feel the same way about his participation in our book. So here's a brief montage of Alan Alda stories from on and off the set of *The West Wing* . . .

THE ICE CREAM SCENE AND THOSE FUCKING BOOTS FROM *M*A*S*H*

Before Lawrence O'Donnell began writing the script for the season 6 episode "In God We Trust," John Wells came to him with a request. "Is there any way you can get Alan Alda and Martin Sheen in a scene together?" This is how it came to be that Lawrence and the writers came up with a storyline involving debt ceiling negotiations between Senator Arnold Vinick and President Bartlet. When it came time to direct the much-anticipated sequence, director Chris Misiano was nothing short of starstruck. "This was the first episode I got to do with Alan," he says. "For someone who grew up watching *M*A*S*H*—watching Hawkeye—to actually get to work with this man . . ."

Early into shooting the Bartlet-Vinick standoff, it wasn't all peaches and ice cream. Actually . . . it was. That was the problem. Alan and Martin were getting along so famously that in the first few takes the dynamic between them was reading far too chummy.

As Misiano recalls, "Lawrence is standing behind me at the monitor going, 'Uh . . . they really gotta get *mean*. They don't really like each other . . . these two guys are having a great old time . . .'" And that was in the *first* half of the negotiation scene, in the Oval. They hadn't even gotten to the ice cream yet.

Oh right. The ice cream. This scene stemmed from a story Lawrence recalls hearing about a time during the Cuban Missile Crisis when Bobby Kennedy and JFK were sitting in the kitchen, eating ice cream out of these big tubs. "On *The West Wing* you're always trying to find a place to put [characters] other than the Oval." So, Lawrence set the second half of the Bartlet-Vinick summit in the kitchen, over pistachio and coffee ice cream. (Alan, it should be noted, *hates* coffee ice cream.) The ice cream scene was shot the day after the Academy Awards had kept Alan up late, celebrating his nominated turn in *The Aviator*. "The Oscars kept him up 'til one in the morning," Misiano says. "We kept him up 'til *three*.")

Chris had another memorable moment with Alan, in the waning days of *The West Wing*.

CHRISTOPHER MISIANO: During a break while we were shooting the series finale, Alan and I were walking on the lot. He looked at me and said, "So, you ready for it to be over?" I was like, "Yeah, you know, sure, it's been a nice run . . ." He put his arm around my shoulder, smiled and said, "It's going to be harder than you think." It was pretty clear he was talking about how he felt after *M*A*S*H* ended.

As we were finishing up our interview with Alan, the conversation turned to the topic of memorabilia. Other than a Vinick campaign button, he doesn't have much from *The West Wing*. Then we asked, "But you probably have *tons* of stuff from *M*A*S*H*, right?" We're so glad we did.

ALAN ALDA: I kept my boots and my dog tags. The dog tags had the names of real soldiers who had died in World War Two. The boots were the same ones I wore every day on *M*A*S*H*. I tried to sell them for charity once, for twenty-five thousand dollars. Nobody bought. I still have those fucking boots.

Alan is also the proud owner of the world's shortest *West Wing* origin story:

ALAN ALDA: John Wells called up and asked if I wanted to run for president. I told him that sounded like a great idea and it seemed like fun.

And it was. For all of us. Now—who's got twenty-five grand for Hawkeye's fucking boots?

Postscript: On July 28, 2023, we and the rest of the civilized world were thrilled to read that Alan sold those fucking boots. "The boots and dog tags I wore every day that we filmed M*A*S*H *just sold at auction for $125,000—all going to the Alda Center for Communicating Science at Stony Brook U. I'm very grateful. The Center is thrilled. And so am I."*

———

THE ALAN ALDA CENTER
FOR COMMUNICATING SCIENCE

The Alda Center opened in 2009 as a result of collaboration between Alan, Stony Brook, and Stony Brook's School of Communication and Journalism, with Brookhaven National Laboratory and Cold Spring Harbor Laboratory. Oh, and look for the *Clear + Vivid* podcast wherever you get your podcasts!

www.aldacenter.org

★ ★ ★

★ ★ ★ BIG BLOCK OF CHEESE STORY ★ ★ ★

Vinick's Hometown and
a Key to the City

LAUREN SCHMIDT HISSRICH (WRITERS ASSISTANT, WRITER): In the beginning of season 6, this small California town began to lobby for Arnold Vinick to be from Santa Paula. I'm not sure how they got my name, but out of the blue they began writing me. So, I wrote back and before I knew it, we'd started a correspondence. Turns out, in a subsequent episode we had to establish where Vinick was from. So, I said to the other writers, "Can we say Santa Paula?" And we did. I ended up getting the key to the city! I went and spoke at their town hall and I still have the certificates. I'm an honorary—and very proud—citizen of Santa Paula!

And from this we learn the power of good old-fashioned lobbying.

THIRTY-THREE

GONE

There were a lot of good days on *The West Wing*... Looking back, armed with a perspective that only time can offer, you could say that, when it came to *The West Wing*, there was only one truly bad day.

December 16, 2005

BRADLEY WHITFORD: I got a call from my assistant—I was at my kid's school—John had had a heart attack and was at this hospital in West LA. I jumped in the car. I got there and went up. The door was closed and the nurse said, "He's in there. Some friends of yours are in with him, but . . . he's gone." I went in, and Stockard was standing there with John's friend, the director Lee Rose.

LEE ROSE: I walk in the room and John's assistant Kim is there . . . his friend Stephen is there . . . and Johnny is dead. I called Stockard and said, "You need to come to the hospital."

STEPHEN PFEIFFER: Stockard immediately stopped filming and came over.

STOCKARD CHANNING: I went to the hospital . . . but I got there too late.

BRADLEY WHITFORD: He was gone. And I'm suddenly in a room with everybody. There was some concern about reporters finding out. We wanted to protect him. So we were with him for many hours. There were a lot of tears; tears alternated with dark humor.

ALLISON JANNEY: I was in a restaurant, I'd just finished lunch with a friend. I couldn't believe my ears. "Gone." I was stunned. There is no "ready" for a moment like that. I got in my car and headed over. I stayed there in John's hospital room with Brad and Stockard and Lee for quite a while. It was such a sad, strange time . . .

STOCKARD CHANNING: I had to call Martin's manager—I didn't have Martin's number with me.

MARTIN SHEEN: Oh God, I lost a brother. I absolutely adored him.

JANEL MOLONEY: I'd just walked out of my parents' house, I was in the car, still in the driveway, when Brad called. "I have bad news. John Spencer died."

MELISSA: I was in Santa Monica, in the living room of my apartment, when Janel called. "Hi, Missy. Are you sitting down?" When I told her I wasn't, she said, "Can you be?" So I walked over to the sofa. "Okay. I'm sitting down." She told me flat out. "John Spencer died." I was stunned. (And glad I was sitting.) All I could think—all I could say—was . . . "No. No."

RICHARD SCHIFF: I was doing a play in New Jersey. Brad called to tell me John was gone.

DULÉ HILL: I was at my house in Woodland Hills. I pick up the phone, "Hey, Brad, what's happening?" He said, "I'm sorry to tell you this, but . . . Johnny's gone." It took me a minute to grasp what he was talking about. It just didn't make sense. Finally, somewhere in that pause, I realized that he was talking about John Spencer. I said, "Oh, my God . . ."

MARY: We were back east for the holidays in New York. I was holding Margaret—and decorating the tree with Michael and my mom—when Brad called. I was happy to hear from him for about five seconds, and then he just . . . said it. I was genuinely shocked, thunderstruck. You hear something like that and you feel knocked off your mooring, just truly and totally disoriented. The last thing I remember is handing Margaret off to Michael.

LYN PAOLO: I was at the mall shopping for John when I found out that he died. A suit for Leo for the next episode. Can you believe it?

JOSH SINGER: The show was on hiatus for two weeks. I was at LAX, waiting for a flight to Philly, when I got the call. I was stunned.

JIMMY SMITS: I was on the 405, headed south, just over the Sepulveda Pass, coming home from work. I was on the phone talking to John Wells about decisions they were making in the writers room. Suddenly, he had to get off the phone. A few minutes later he called me back to let me know that "Spence" was gone. This had just happened, he didn't have any details. I pulled over. I was just numb.

BRADLEY WHITFORD: Somebody came into his room and we stepped out as they did what needed to be done. We rode down on the elevator with him on a gurney. Suddenly, we're standing out on the street. John's wheeled into a hearse and taken away. You're just . . . We were in shock.

MELISSA: A bunch of us—Brad and Stockard and Martin, Lee and Tommy and Aaron, Jimmy Smits, Lyn Paolo, Allison, Janel, Eli Attie, and others—got together at John's home. We sat around in a circle—on couches, on the floor, in chairs—sharing our memories of him. It was such a long time ago, so much life has happened since, but I still remember it vividly.

STEPHEN PFEIFFER: *West Wing* was a family with such a strong bond. And that family came to rally.

LYN PAOLO: I remember being in a circle and Martin saying we should all hold hands. He was leading the prayer. He gave such a beautiful speech about John being in a better place. I was devastated—we all were—but I remember thinking, "God, I wish I had his faith."

ELI ATTIE: It was like a member of the Beatles just died. It just had a feeling of . . . somehow the whole thing has been broken in some way.

MELISSA: The get-together that night was incredibly raw. It was also . . . complicated. We felt deeply sad, of course, but in addition to tears and heartbreak there were beautiful stories about John, off set and on, about what made him "John."

ALLISON JANNEY: It just meant so much to be in John's home, in his space, being around his . . . you know . . . his things. One thing I still remember is being sent home with a painting I was told "John would've wanted you to have." It was by an artist we both loved.

MELISSA: Since the funeral fell around the holidays, I was home with my family in Pennsylvania. Josh Singer, whose parents lived nearby, came over with his dad.

JOSH SINGER: My father, who was always a believer in showing up to these things, offered to drive with me and Melissa to the funeral in New Jersey. I remember it being cold and bleak, and that there was a Catholic Mass, which gave me insight into the world from which John had come.

ELI ATTIE: I had never been to an Irish Catholic wake before. There's this tradition of the big corkboard of pictures of the whole life and there was something amazing about it. John had a fifty-something character actor's face as a four-year-old! And you're watching him grow into his face over the course of this board. This guy you only knew in this one intense, wonderful phase of his life, and you're seeing him step into his greatness in photographs . . .

LEE ROSE: At the funeral home, Mary-Louise Parker and I go into the bathroom. Mary-Louise looks up and goes . . .

MARY-LOUISE PARKER: "Okay, you know what, God, I need a word with you! Your *assistant* needs an assistant—because you took the wrong guy!"

LEE ROSE: I nearly peed my pants. It was the first time I had laughed since John died. Later that night, Mary-Louise, I think Richard Schiff was there, Bradley, myself—we went to dinner in the Village. Strangers kept walking by, saying, "I'm so sorry."

KRISTIN CHENOWETH: Two weeks before Christmas, I caught John smoking in the alley. I said, "Gimme that cigarette!" He goes, "Kristin, every day without a cigarette is hell. I just want this one." I said, "Okay, but no more after this!"

He said, "I'll tell you what. If I die, I have one request. I want you to sing 'For Good' at my funeral." I laughed. "Well, that won't be for a while." And then he passed away.

PETER ROTH: He passed away so suddenly. We were all so shocked. I remember Aaron asking me if they could use the Stephen Ross Theater at Warner Bros. to have a memorial service, which I was thrilled and honored to be able to do.

RON OSTROW: The theater was packed. That tells you something about how people felt.

LEE ROSE: Everyone got up and spoke. Stockard spoke, Marty, Aaron, Tommy, Brad. And Jimmy Smits because they'd been on *L.A. Law* together too. Mary McDonnell spoke too, and some people Spencer had done theater with. It was beautiful.

KRISTIN CHENOWETH: I didn't think I could do it. Then I felt him, I felt John say . . . "You're gonna do this because I *asked* you to, just the other day!" So . . . I did. And it was horrible. I sounded like a frog. But the important thing is . . . he loved that song, loved the message: "Because I knew you, I have been changed . . . for good."

ALLISON JANNEY: What I remember most from the Warner Bros. memorial is that Kristin sang "For Good" so, so beautifully.

PETER ROTH: I was really weeping. Because it wasn't simply Kristin's relationship with John, it was everyone's relationship with John.

America has lost a giant tonight.
And I've lost a friend.

—MATT SANTOS,
"ELECTION DAY: PART II"

Bradley Whitford's Eulogy

First of all, John would be pissed off that his memorial today is actually a forced call on what will be a full day of shooting. I met John Spencer when a teamster picked me up to go to the read-thru of the first big movie I ever got, *Presumed Innocent*, in New York in 1989. I had a small part, but John's was substantial. He was practically curled up in the back seat of the van and he was terrified. You could see it. When I asked him if he was okay, he said he wasn't sure. This part was the biggest break of his career. And it would be the first time in his professional life that he had ever tried to act sober.

Walking up Broadway with him after the table read, he was giddy. It had gone well. He could do it without the booze. And as he pointed out a Blarney Stone he used to black out in, he told me that acting was going to save him.

And he was right. John held on to acting for dear life. He reveled in it, built his life in service of it, treated each opportunity to do it as a privilege to be prepared for and executed with the care of a Japanese tea ceremony. Lines had to be down cold, the props just so. Like any good actor he was trying to get to the place where he could relax, just be the guy, and maybe let a little crazy out. Let's face it, working on a one-hour television show for this long involves a crushing level of intimacy.

The good news is that we all have a job. The bad news is that the overexposure to each other required to make a television show means that we will inevitably end up walking around together in nothing but our emotional underwear. We are with each other from the puffy dawn to the gaunt night. We fail in front of each other. We get mad at each other. We laugh with each other. We keep each other going. We all know, and I'm not just talking about the actors here, we all know that we will be revealed to each other. It is a place with all of the nourishment and all of the horror of a family.

Add the medieval caste system that is show business, the wacky financial stakes, the emotional carnage of being overvalued and undervalued (often on the same day) . . . and you have, well, you have stage 23 here at Warner Bros. Studios. (By the way, there is no question that we could be making a far more interesting show than the one we are all so proud of being a part of. But the camera is pointed the wrong way.) So when we say we have lost a brother, we mean it literally.

I wish John could have known the horrible loss we feel at his passing. I wish he could have heard the voices of countless strangers who tell me how they feel like they have lost a friend. They feel like they knew him, and it is a testament to his acting and his decency that they actually did. He brought it all to Leo. He was vulnerable, he was a bull, he was funny, he could scare the hell out of you, he was on fire, he was held back, he was revealing, he was hidden. He had seen it all, and it hadn't been pretty. But there was still something funny about it.

John was great to imitate. His body was evidence of the punishing mileage he had racked up and of the strength, optimism and the raw defiance necessary to get the thing going.

Everyone knows that John didn't have a face. He had a mug. It was an unlikely combination of a comedy mask and an old catcher's mitt: hugely theatrical yet somehow honest, familiar, and broken-in at the same time. His default expression was a smile. When he laughed his mouth flew open so wide that he was blinded by his ample eyelids and eyebags, like a boxer in need of a cut-man.

And his legs were impossible. It didn't make sense that they worked at all. They were bowed like a couple of Irish harps that were strung way too tight. But he got them going with a roly-poly hot coal walk-with-a-wince that only made sense once he hit his signature cruising speed. In those crappy flip-flops that Betty was always slipping on him. When John told me he was going to have surgery on his legs next summer, I remember thinking, thank god. Finally. What ocean of denial did you have to be swimming in to think those unsnapped vaulting poles were ever a viable means of transportation? But of course he was going to wait till hiatus. He needed them to get him to work.

I love you, John. Thank you, my friend. I will never forget you.

Richard Schiff's Eulogy

To John from Richard.

I am a great actor! You can laugh if you want . . . for seven years John Spencer has been trying to convince me—to get me to say out loud, "I am a great actor." And so, to honor John, I have said it. For those of you who know me, you know how ridiculously impossible that is for me to say. Never mind that I still think I suck. That's not the point.

John Spencer came at you with love like Joe Frazier came at Muhammad Ali with fists. Think about it. John Spencer would come at you, short and powerful, forehead first with fiery eyes and loading the left hook with compliments and adoration and admiration, respect and absolute and pure love. And throw them at you with ferocity and determination and grit and he would not let up, no matter how you ducked, bobbed, weaved and side-stepped. And, sure enough, he'd catch you with that hook and buckle your knees.

He had the spirit of the boxer, you see. He was a fighter. He fought his demons that way and day in and day out he was triumphant over them. Batting them down as they popped up like so many Jack-in-the-boxes, trying to divert his focus, his drive, his will to be the best human being he could be. And his great weapon was acting. He loved acting like no one I've ever met. He loved the make-up, the robe, the slippers, the trailers, the prizes, the gossip. He ate it, and dreamt it, drank it, devoured it like steak. And to do it right he kept those demons nearby, allowing them life to live through his acting and so always walked that dangerous, courageous line—the line only great actors and artists must tread on. And John Spencer was a great actor.

I was doing a scene in the Oval Office on *The West Wing*. A tough scene. John was doing the Warren Leight play at the Taper and had to leave the set by five PM every day to make his show. So he was shot out first. All day long I was doing this very hard scene and all day it was going well, alive in the moments. When I was being shot, I expected it to go just as well. But John had left for the play and when I looked over to his chair where he had been sitting all day, the scene suddenly stopped. Someone had replaced John in his chair and the scene stopped. You see? And I realized that all day in my glances over to John I had received this great gift. One look from Leo and I had been filled with substance, with purpose, with clarity. And now with John gone, I was empty. And the scene stopped. The play was over. And I had to start again by myself and I hated it. I told him that the next day. I thanked him for his great gift to us; his generosity, his presence. John was always there for us—off camera, giving, constantly and totally and forever giving.

I am not present at the memorial because I am doing a one-man show in New Jersey, of all places. When I told everyone of this choice to do this play I was greeted with such remarks as: "Are you out of your mind?" "Why on Earth are you doing THAT!?" But John responded with, "Oh that's great!" "It's going to be so great for you," "What's the play?" "You're going to kill them!" and so on and on. And so each and every day as I wait, terrified, in the wings to embark on this wild expedition on stage, I talk to John. And I thank him for his faith in me. And I think: "If John were back here, as fearful and shaking as I am, he would smack down those demons and put the proverbial mouthguard between his clenching teeth and tear out on that stage and conquer all." And so I thank him every night. I thank him for all that he has given us and will keep giving us.

At his funeral in New Jersey, I watched his friends and family and the other Catholics present reach over and touch his casket to say goodbye. And so I did as well. I felt a rush, an electric surge coming through my hand from his casket. I was reaching out and touching him to say goodbye. I had missed the chance in Los Angeles. Some believe that the soul stays around for a couple of days before it embarks on the next journey, wherever that is. Well, John had stuck around, I think. To say goodbye back to us. And wouldn't it be just like him; one last act of generosity to let us say goodbye. To stick around for a little, just a bit more, conversation and companionship. To chat about the things in this world one more time.

What's the greatest thing you can say about someone? That without them you would not be who you are. John Spencer has changed my life for knowing him. And I will always love him for it.

And so with severely buckled knees, lying flat on my back on the canvas, in fact. I say this for you John: "I am a great actor." And one day, maybe one day, if I keep talking to you, keep listening to you, I'll be, just maybe, as great as you.

★ ★ ★

IN talking to the cast and crew about John, we came away with, frankly, what we'd envisioned and hoped for: memories and anecdotes about the wonderful actor—the wonderful man—behind the wonderful Leo McGarry. What we didn't bank on—though, in retrospect, we should have—was the spectrum of affectionate John Spencer imitations. These attempts at his sly, winky, gravelly-voiced intonations are, of course, not exactly translatable on the page. You'll just have to trust us. They are undeniably charming, oddly moving, and hilariously terrible. (There are so many bad ones, it's hard to choose. We'll go with Malina. Honestly—all of a sudden Spencer's a *pirate*?!)

Here, now, is just a smattering of cast and crew impressions—and, you know, *impressions*—of the late, great John Spencer. Gone too soon, but never forgotten.

Melissa Fitzgerald (Carol Fitzpatrick)

The West Wing aired at nine o'clock every Wednesday night. On Thursdays John would make the rounds to tell everybody about something they had done in the episode, then talk about it, dissect it. He would just find that teeny-tiny moment. And, look, I didn't have a whole lot of moments on that show. But if I had one, even if I didn't have a line, he'd note it and talk to me about it. I saw him doing that with everybody, no matter how big or small their part was. I was so touched by that. I'd tell him, "John, my *mom* wouldn't have even noticed that moment!" He saw the littlest things. And the biggest things. I loved Thursdays.

Dulé Hill (Charlie Young)

We were in DC, filming, and we were given a motorcade. The park police were there. We're in this white van and they're doing their whole thing like when the motorcade comes through, how they clear a path for the president. And we're all like, "This is cool, can you *believe* this?!" That would always be Johnny. He would look at me—I can see it now—with a huge smile on his face: "You wouldn't get this if you were on a cop show!"

Emily Procter (Ainsley Hayes)

Walking down the hall for her first-ever West Wing *scene, Emily Procter overheard John Spencer shout to Tommy Schlamme—this is how she put it to us, accent included—"Hey, Tahmmy, if the new girl doesn't work out, we don't have to keep her, right?!"*

> EMILY PROCTER: And Tommy's like, "Yeah—of course, John." I'm *walking* onto the set. I was like . . . in the room. And then we rehearsed the scene. (Afterwards, he said I could stay.)

From that mischievous moment of Spencer razzing the new kid, John and Emily enjoyed what she calls "this really special relationship."

> EMILY PROCTER: One time, early on, he called me on the phone. "Uh, Emily, it's Jahn. Jahn Spensuh." You know I'm not doing his accent right. [She *really* wasn't. And it was hilarious, God bless her.] And I was like, "Yes, John, how can I help you?"
> "I'm wondering if you want to come over. Come have breakfast with me."
> We had bagels and orange juice. It was lovely. And then he was like, "Let's run our scene for next week!"

But Emily didn't have her script. That didn't stop John, though. He handed her a copy he'd printed. There was—she could tell—a method to his madness.

> EMILY PROCTER: John had this pool that took up a huge part of his backyard and he had all of these roses—John loved roses— that were still in pots. He put a couple of pots by the water and a

coiled-up hose and he made an obstacle course with all this garden equipment! We had to weave in and out and do the scene and go close to the water. And *time* it.

Emily quickly realized this wasn't just a fun, creative acting exercise, this was John taking a new kid under his wing, getting her ready to fly. (And walk-and-talk.)

EMILY PROCTER: He said, "I want you to know, it's gonna go very fast." My scenes before that had been just standing in his office and he knew I was going to have to do movement. I don't know that he got anything out of it. I think it was *all* for me, it was all a gift.

Mike Hissrich (Producer)
I had worked with John Wells on a series that was set in New York. *Trinity*. John played this soft-spoken Irish father. When he was cast as Leo, I expected a similar sort of soft-spoken character. What I always remember is that scene in "A Proportional Response" where Leo dresses Bartlet down with that speech. The Charlemagne speech.

My friend, if you want to start using American
military strength as the Arm of the Lord,
you can do that. We're the only superpower left.
You can conquer the world, like Charlemagne.
But you better be prepared to kill everyone.
And you better start with me. 'Cause I will raise
up an army against you, and I will beat you!

—LEO TO PRESIDENT BARTLET,
"A PROPORTIONAL RESPONSE"

That was something I hadn't seen from John before. I got chills when we shot it. That scene in Leo's office was a clash of two titans . . . waiting to see which one blinked. It was Shakespearean. I remember thinking, "Wow, John has *that* in his toolbox, too."

Anna Deavere Smith (National Security Advisor Nancy McNally)
John was very serious about his work. But he also had a sensitivity, a fragility. He was no-nonsense, but there was a kind of vulnerability in his work that I think is wonderful. It's really useful for an actor, especially a male actor, to have.

Michael O'Neill (Secret Service Agent Ron Butterfield)
I had done a play and a couple films with John in New York. So, I got to know him through work. My first day on the *West Wing* set, he took me by the hand, and vouched for me. He introduced me to everybody . . . basically saying, "He's one of us." I'll forever be in his debt for that.

Dave Chameides (Steadicam Operator)
John always had those Tea Tree toothpicks on him, always had a box. The minute he came in the door, he would come up to me because he knew I liked them. He would open it like a cigarette box, he would flip it, and just one would come to the top and I'd take it and he would smile at me. He must have gone through a box a day.

Allison Janney (C.J. Cregg)
I loved his work ethic and his professionalism. When he arrived on the set he wanted to work. He didn't like the pranks, didn't like to screw around, just . . . "Let's do our job." He just loved acting, and he loved actors, he loved all of us. Especially Stockard. Stockard and John became very good friends. I loved their friendship, loved them hanging out in his trailer.

Mindy Kanaskie (Co-Producer)

John and Stockard had an old theater friendship. They were East Coasters who knew each other's secrets and history. There was a different kind of deeper love with them.

Lawrence O'Donnell (Writer, Executive Producer, Dr. Bartlet)

John did a play in LA called *Glimmer, Glimmer and Shine*. I think there's maybe two other people in the cast, but it feels like a one-man show because John's on that stage . . . holding the stage in a way I've never seen before in theater. I sat there watching this, overjoyed and surprised . . . and a little bit embarrassed to discover that on *The West Wing* we were using one percent of John Spencer. It made me retroactively understand those read-throughs. I felt that there was this Rolls-Royce engine humming along in that room. He was a Rolls-Royce of an actor. When you see him do that walk-and-talk, like the one at the beginning of the pilot—if you saw that after seeing him do *Glimmer, Glimmer and Shine*, you'd go, "Well, yeah, no kidding."

Allison Smith (Leo's Daughter, Mallory)

John Spencer was the consummate actor, but even more . . . a consummate friend. There wasn't a day that went by that he didn't hug me on set. I can see him now: Leo in a suit, striding right over, arms wide. I never had a dad of my own. I borrowed Mallory's.

In 2001, I took over John's dressing room at The Mark Taper Forum after *Glimmer, Glimmer and Shine* to do *QED*, a play by Peter Parnell. On opening night, John left me a note:

> *To my Mallory,*
>
> *Theatre and roses,*
>
> *Dad*

Stockard Channing (Abigail Bartlet)

Sets are all about the downtime and who you're talking to. John just became one of these people who you're sitting there with, and someone says, "You're wanted on set" and you go, *"We're still talking!"* That friendship, it just clicked from day one. It deepened into one of the most profound relationships in my life. He was just so in love with acting, had such energy and ebullience and he was brilliant and precise . . . and I miss him to this day.

Christopher Misiano (Director, Executive Producer)

When Spencer died, I inherited some *West Wing* scripts he had in his house. They were marked up with all these slashes and little notations—the script was scored, almost like a piece of music, to give a sense of rhythm to the lines. When Aaron left and Debora Cahn's first episode came out, John came running up, grabbed me, and whispered in my ear, "She's got the *rhythm*!!" That's how important it was to him.

Whenever John wanted one more take, he'd would say, "Hey, 'Christmas'"—that was his nickname for me—"can I have one more for my mother?" I've taken that with me. Ever since, I'll tell an actor, "Hey. Do one for your mother." And usually they're the best takes. In those moments, I always think of Johnny.

Rob Lowe (Sam Seaborn)

John Spencer could do more with three words than most actors can do with three *scenes*. Week in and week out, I would watch him say, "Thank you, Mr. President," and make it mean five thousand different things. It could mean "I love you" or "I'm angry with you." "I don't agree with you" or "I'll run through a wall for you."

Eli Attie (Writer, Producer)

In season 3 of the show, "Bartlet for America" aired. There was a screening during crew lunch. I was sitting a row or two behind John and . . . when the episode ended—when Bartlet made that incredible, magnanimous gesture to Leo—John was just sitting there watching, with tears streaming down his face. Aaron appeared in the aisle and was also tearing up. He just went over to John and hugged him. It was two people who understood that problem, sharing an unspoken conversation about it through that episode of television. It was such an incredible moment because you saw the love that was part of that show, that people expressed toward each other, often through the work. It's just one of those moments I'll never forget.

John Amos (Admiral Percy Fitzwallace)
To work with John Spencer was a joy. He was always in the moment, which of course made it easy for me to be equally in the moment. I miss John. I've worked with so many actors who felt that they were more important than the role that they were portraying. He was the antithesis of that. He could not lie. There was no lie in the man.

Holli Strickland (Base Camp PA)
One of my favorite *West Wing* memories is taking a picture—black-and-white—of John. We were shooting a formal scene that day so he's in a tux—a white shirt and cuff links—and he's kissing his dog Zoey on the mouth! I was later told by his family that it was the last picture ever taken of John.

Richard Schiff (Toby Ziegler)
John loved every single aspect of acting. And not just the acting. He loved all of it—the costumes . . . the trailers . . . the makeup. He'd show up early in the morning in the makeup trailer for a little pampering. He had a whole ritual. He'd just lie back in his chair, and he'd have on those two little eye pads. I wanted to be in and out in two minutes. Meanwhile, John was over there on the other side in his fluffy slippers in a robe with his eye pads and his quadruple caramel whatever

on the table . . . and he'd be gossiping with the makeup people for two or three hours. He just loved the whole thing.

Julie DeJoie (Tommy Schlamme's Assistant)
My favorite thing about John Spencer was that whatever he did, he did it one hundred percent. When he was acting, he gave everything, every time, to the role and to his fellow actors. When he drank coffee, it was the biggest cup of coffee they made. When he smoked, that cigarette never stood a chance. When he wore cologne, he wore the hell out of that cologne. When you had a conversation with him, you felt like there was no one else in the world. And when you made him laugh that enormous laugh, there was no better feeling.

Kim Webster (Ginger)
John Spencer was a Jersey boy. He was no bullshit. He was just the salt of the earth.

Ramón De Ocampo (Otto)
We were doing a long walk-and-talk, and during a little break I was by my trailer, stretching my calf out on the step. John comes up and says, "Lemme show you something." He walks me into his trailer and goes, "You know what it is?" Digging into his closet, he said, "It's the shoes." And he takes out his slippers. His soft, memory-foam, beat-up, comfortable-as-hell slippers. "You can have these, they're a gift. Wear them on the set. In fact, if you're not walking so much, they'll probably let you wear it during the scene." I remember thinking that that was what this show was—these incredible artists who I looked up to, these giants of the field, giving you slippers to support your feet.

Lyn Paolo (Costume Designer)
John Spencer used to say coming to his wardrobe fittings was his "hourly shrink session of the week." He would come in and tell me

everything that'd happened that week, just bleed it all out. Then he would go, "I feel better now," and toddle off to the set, leaving the scent of Eau Sauvage behind. I'm not kidding—in the Warner Bros. aisles you can still get a faint whiff of it when you walk past his double-breasted suits. Seriously, they're still there, and there's still this faint aroma of John Spencer, and it makes me so happy every time.

Alex Graves (Director, Executive Producer)
In my weepy eulogy of John at one of the celebrations, I said, "I loved John's face." I used to come up with shots that I could do to work the topography of his face.

Josh Malina (Will Bailey)
It was my first table read—in the Roosevelt Room. Everyone's sitting around the big table . . . the actors, the department heads, the writers, the producers, a lot of people. I remember walking in and feeling really psyched to be there . . . but it was a daunting room. I remember John Spencer walking up to me and introducing himself: "Hey, how ya doin'? John Spencer! I just loved ya on *Sports Night*!" I don't even know if he really watched *Sports Night*, but that's not the point. John was that guy who would go out of his way to be warm, to make you feel good, to make you feel like you *belonged*. I'm sure I'm guilty of not always honoring his memory this way, but I try to do it when I'm a regular on something and not the new guy.

Jimmy Smits (Matt Santos)
John and I did a play together . . . twenty years before . . . at the New York Shakespeare Festival. Then we worked together for all those years on *L.A. Law*. So, when I came to *The West Wing* . . . I felt like Spence vetted me for everybody. "He's okay." There was a touchstone there. We kind of kept finding each other.

Matthew Del Negro (Bram Howard)

I remember, he had a little scene . . . like a pass through an office. And they were setting up the lighting, and he was looking around, and he's looking at the desk, and he goes over and opens this drawer, and he pulls out this pen, and he goes over to [director] Chris Misiano, and he's, like, "I really think I'd have this in my pocket. Jed gave me this." He was like a little kid—and this was season 7! He was so into the details, and so excited to be there . . .

Bradley Whitford (Josh Lyman)

He was wrestling a vicious monster of addiction that he was well aware was always "in the next room," he would say, "doing push-ups." There are people who lug the big sack of humanity and self-loathing and failure around with them because it's part of them. And they have the guts . . . to hack through the jungle with a dull machete, despite this . . . They are some of the most beautiful actors on the planet. John was one of those guys.

Andrew Bernstein (First AD, Director)

When I directed one of my first scenes with John, he was alone in Leo's office, watching a videotape. No dialogue, he puts the tape in and watches this thing on the TV. We started rolling and a practical light in the room started flashing, the bulb started going. So, the [director of photography] starts hitting me, "You gotta say cut, the light's not working." Right as John was getting out of his chair, I said, "Cut, cut, cut," and he storms out to the monitors and starts in on me about how he was gonna get up and fix the light bulb, how "that was something *real*." I was like, "I'm sorry, they told me to say cut!" He's like, "Don't ever do that, I *live* for those moments!" To me that was the greatest directing lesson of all time—and one of those things that stays with you forever. John never saw problems, only opportunities. That's what

I miss about him. He allowed magical moments to happen, where light bulbs would flicker and you were allowed to fix it.

Joanna Gleason (Jordon Kendall)
I sat with John for the first time in the congressional hearing scenes in "Bartlet for America." It was a huge scene with much coverage, and we started talking and talking. For six hours between takes! We had many theater folk in common, but the conversation wandered for miles in every direction. Just before one take, he shared with me that his friend Jessica Lange could kill a cow and butcher it!

William Duffy (Larry)
Whenever he would pay me a compliment, it would mean so much. Every once in a while, we'd finish a scene, he'd look at me and go, "Nice." (**MELISSA:** For the record, Duffy's Spencer impression was quite possibly the best we heard. But don't sleep on Brad. His is no joke.)

Mary McCormack (Kate Harper)
Acting with John Spencer felt like the scariest privilege. Every time I did it, I got better by degrees. It was like hitting with a tennis pro, I felt him lift my game. My memories of working with John pop with a mix of color and gravity. Rehearsing in fake Camp David or the fictional streets of Havana. Playing CIA dress-up with Leo, trying to lug him into a car. One second he's playing drunk off his ass, the next—a split second after "cut"—he's the sweetest gentleman actor you'd ever hope to know. And when you're treated like a pro by the *ultimate* pro it instills a confidence in you that feels indelible. I'm a better, more confident actor today because I sat in the Sit Room across from that man.

Peter Roth (Chairman/CEO of Warner Bros. Television, 1999–2021)
I remember that every time I saw John, it was the biggest hug, the warmest response, the most lovely of human beings.

John Wells (Executive Producer, Showrunner)
John Spencer was the heart and soul of the series. The anchor. Both as Leo and as an actor. There wouldn't have been a *West Wing* without John. The day he agreed to play Leo was the day I knew the show was going to be a success.

Aaron Sorkin (Creator, Showrunner)
John came from a hardscrabble background, working-class New Jersey. He ran away from home when he was fifteen years old. He mostly played tough guys, even if they were good guys . . . there was gravel in their voice and a map of the world on their face. He was always the happiest guy on set, he was always bucking everybody up.

He had a habit of making his job look easy, which it definitely wasn't, but then came "Bartlet for America." In that episode he would need to reveal that on the day of Bartlet's final debate with his (un-named) opponent, Leo had relapsed in his recovery from alcoholism and was passed-out drunk in his hotel room. These are the kinds of memories—nightmares—that live forever in the bones of an alcoholic or addict. The shame is overwhelming.

On the day we were shooting the scene in the hotel suite I could see John was hurting. His performance was fantastic but to me it looked like torture. Tommy likes to shoot a lot of takes and you can't argue with the results. I'd been giving John his privacy all morning (he didn't need any notes) but I went to him after the fourth or fifth take and said, "I'm going to ask Tommy to move it along." John said, "No. It's my chance for something good to come out of it." He knew I knew what "it" was and I wanted to give him a speech about how everything good came out of it—you're here—but he was working.

You ever stop thinking of this as Leo's office?

—JOSH TO C.J., "TOMORROW"

Martin Sheen (President Josiah Bartlet)
At the mention of John, I laugh. I laugh just thinking of him. Because I did my own makeup, I was always a little ahead. I had a lot of time to waste. I'd go over to the hair-and-makeup trailer just to get ten minutes of gossip with him while he had his hair done. He'd be lying there with his head back, he would have cucumbers on his eyes, and he would be bitching about something and I'd start laughing and laughing. I began to realize he was doing it on purpose, to give me a laugh. I'd say, "Johnny, how you doin'?" I called him Johnny, by the way, no one called him Johnny, I did that just to see if I could get away with it and he never corrected me. "Johnny, how you doin' today?" (**MELISSA:** It was at this glorious point that Martin would, for the first of many times, launch into the most committed of the John Spencer imitations we heard during the research for this book.) "Ah, Marty, ya know I am tellin' ya this . . ." "Ya know, I said this" or "Aw geez, I cursed her out, I gotta make amends." If they had taken the word "amends" out of John's vocabulary, he wouldn't know what to say.

We were the oldest ones in the cast, both old New York stage players. A couple of old drunks who were now sober, thank God. And we knew we were onto something very special, all the players were so brilliant, so committed. And yet we knew that if we ever came to the set not knowing our lines, or undisciplined or bitching about something, being late . . . We knew that as long as *we* kept that discipline, nobody would slack off. So we felt this very real sense of responsibility. It really was like we were the parents.

We had these little signals, looking at each other—a moment, between takes—"Can you believe this? Can you believe what we're doing?" It was gratitude . . . an awareness that it's probably never going to happen again like this in our careers. I adored him. He was such fun. What a wonderful actor and human being. God love him.

★ ★ ★

IT'S Sunday, September 22, 2002. We are in the Shrine Auditorium in Los Angeles for the 54th Primetime Emmy Awards. John Spencer's beaming face is framed up with his fellow nominees: Victor Garber, Freddy Rodriguez, Dulé Hill, Richard Schiff, and Bradley Whitford.

The words "and the Emmy goes to . . . John Spencer!" bring a roar from the crowd, a crowd that is suddenly—instantly—on its feet. Amid thunderous applause, and a "bomb-swell" of Snuffy Walden's soaring *West Wing* theme, John pushes himself up out of his seat. On the other end of a back-slap from Dulé, John hugs Martin for a long moment, kisses Allison, then Stockard, and embraces Brad and Richard before dashing up the stairs to the stage—fast, like the moment might somehow slip away. Receiving his Emmy, he takes to the microphone, flashes that incandescent smile of his, and starts to speak:

"I've never wanted to do anything but act. It saved my life. It's the reason I get up in the morning . . ."

THIRTY-FOUR

KEY EPISODES

"Election Day: Parts I and II" and "Requiem"

The sudden passing of John Spencer turned the world of *The West Wing* upside down. It was an emotional and spiritual blow to all of us who loved him, of course. But there was work to be done. As John would have pointed out quicker than anyone, "the show must go on." And so it did.

Soon after John died, Brad Whitford was approached by *West Wing* showrunner John Wells. "He very delicately told me, 'John's family doesn't think he would be averse to us sort of . . . dealing with his death in the show.'" This is how it came to be that, within a matter of weeks, Brad went from serving as a pallbearer at a real-life funeral to *acting* as a pallbearer at a fictional funeral.

John's death affected a number of episodes that were already, to varying degrees, in progress. Season arcs had long been planned out, episode outlines had been put together, scripts written . . . The sudden absence of a character as central as Leo McGarry—the running mate to Democratic presidential nominee Matt Santos—was hardly a plot point to be glossed over or written around. A substantial overhaul would need to be undertaken. The thing is . . . everyone—writers included—was on hiatus for the holidays.

As Josh Singer told us, "John Wells almost immediately reached out to all the writers and said, 'Hey . . . given what's happened . . . we should talk about which episodes need to change, and also how we want to think about the rest of the season.'"

Over the remainder of the hiatus, Josh and the rest of the writers followed the showrunner's lead. After they all took what John Wells called "a minute to process," the showrunner would start sending out emails and the reshaping of *West Wing* season 7 would begin.

Josh Singer's script for "Welcome to Wherever You Are" was set to start shooting as soon as the holiday break ended. "Spencer wasn't supposed to be in my episode," Josh remembers, "but he *was* supposed to be in the next one" (Lauren Schmidt Hissrich's "Election Day: Part I," directed by Mimi Leder). "So there was immediately work to do." As the writers refashioned episodes within the parameters of this unthinkable new normal, some tent-pole plot points came into focus:

In the waning seconds of "Election Day: Part I," Annabeth Schott would discover an off-screen Leo unconscious on the floor of his hotel room.

In "Election Day: Part II," while the rest of the country was learning who their next president would be, Leo's colleagues from the Bartlet administration (and the Santos campaign) would, in a series of emotional vignettes, learn about his perilous collapse, followed not long after by his death.

A third episode, "Requiem," would open with Leo's funeral and unfold through the rest of that day. As his loved ones grappled with his death and memorialized his life, gatherings would range from ruminative to commemoratory . . . and, at times, amusing.

Set against the political ramifications of Leo's passing (the ground-game calculus as it pertained to West Coast voters, the hasty search for a new VP), the personal drama was appropriately reflective, in mood and otherwise. The on-screen action paralleled what so many of us had recently experienced. Acting out the storylines felt truly surreal, given that we'd lived them just weeks before.

For Eli Attie, who co-wrote both "Election Day: Part II" and "Requiem," processing the emotion of John's death presented a challenge unique in his career. "To have to go from that shock to a lot of furious typing," he told us, "it's one of those times in your life when you really *cry* as you're writing something, and I definitely did, working on some of those scenes." Then again, he knew he wasn't alone. "We all had to go through this exercise. You don't get to face it on your own time, you don't get to have your own ways of processing a loss, you're *given* a way to process it: Write about it, and mourn the character that way."

Donna. I'm going to tell you something shocking.
Except we don't have time to be shocked. So I need
you to just hear it and go back to work.

—TOBY TO DONNA, "18TH AND POTOMAC"

For some, the memory of shooting "Requiem" remains tenuous at best. "I don't remember filming it," Dulé Hill told us. "I only remember walking with the casket. If you asked me about another scene from that episode, it's just gone. But I vividly remember the casket . . . and walking down the aisle." What struck him in those moments, he told us, was "just the weight of it."

This came up with Stockard Channing too. She talked about a

scene where the first lady and the president are mourning side by side. "Martin and I were sitting together," she said, "the two of us were a mess. It was just a heavy feeling."

What affected Brad Whitford most was that inconceivable familiarity. "Even though I felt like it was a good thing to do . . . it was just like, "What the *fuck*?! I was pushing his real casket—just a few weeks ago—now I'm wearing *makeup* and doing it."

Filming Leo's death and funeral was disquieting for many of the *West Wing* cast and crew, and extremely difficult emotionally. Jimmy Smits, though, saw a silver lining. "It was cathartic in a way," he told us. "We were able to put that love on celluloid, independent of the actual memorial service. Things that are there now. Forever."

When we spoke to Kristin Chenoweth about this bewildering moment in time, one question rose above all: How much too-close-to-home was it to be the member of the cast who had to break the news on camera and say those words out loud? ("He died, Josh.")

As easy as it may seem for an actor to tap into the emotion on the page, those scenes were, for obvious reasons, terribly challenging to play. "I had to be the one to find Leo," Kristin says. "I didn't want to do it, I didn't know *how*." Then she got a little help from her friend.

"John always had a Jolly Rancher in his pocket," she told us. "And I was always like, 'Get the green apple, I want the green apple!'" Now, one thing you need to know about TV is that, when it gets cold, the wardrobe department provides these parkas called "warming coats." Naturally, Tinker Bell–sized Kristin was outfitted with a rather petite one. "They'd give me a child's coat and make a big joke," she said to us with a laugh. "'We got your warming coat at Gap Kids!'"

"The day that we came back after John passed," Kristin told us, "they couldn't track down my little Gap Kids parka!" So they handed her this big coat and, what do you know, "I reached into my pocket and . . . Jolly Ranchers. I was like, 'Okay, John, I hear you. I'm listening.'"

Go back and watch that moment—"He died, Josh." The heartbreak on Kristin's tearstained face, the punched-in-the-gut shock on Josh's as he absently gathers her into his arms . . . in that one second, those two captured what so many of us had felt on the other end of the phone just weeks before.

Shooting "Election Day: Part II" (written by John Wells and Eli Attie, beautifully directed by Chris Misiano) felt, in some ways, like a journey into uncharted territory. The raw, close-to-the-bone quality of the storylines was unique to the series. This time the energy was different. This time it was quiet, slow, loaded . . . and full of words unspoken.

> *In a hotel corridor, in the midst of Election Day chaos, Donna tells Josh that Leo was found unconscious in his room. "He wasn't breathing."*

> *C.J. hangs up her phone, stunned. She asks Margaret, "Is the president in his office?"*

> *In the middle of a low-key rant about the lame duck mundanities of his office, President Bartlet looks up to find his chief of staff in a daze, her eyes filling with tears. "C.J., what is it?"*

Given what the cast and crew had recently gone through, it's not surprising that this was a charged episode. It was also a tricky one to execute. "It was a tall order to do this well and respectfully," Malina said on *The West Wing Weekly*, "and for it to land emotionally . . . without it feeling that it was either overly sentimental or . . . manipulated. When you know what happened in real life, it makes it that much more difficult to dramatize in a way that's done tastefully. I think Eli and John and Christopher and the cast did very well."

I know he's your friend. He's my friend too.
But we can't be sentimental about this. . . .

—LOUISE THORNTON TO CONGRESSMAN SANTOS,
"ELECTION DAY: PART II"

"Election Day: Part II" weaves back and forth between the spreading news of Leo's death and some compelling war room pandemonium—vote counts, exit polls, red states, blue states, ever-changing electoral math . . . and the dueling whiteboards of competing presidential campaigns. (**MELISSA:** It's like an hour-long behind-the-scenes dramatization of Steve Kornacki at the Big Board.) Little did viewers know that, in the *West Wing* writers room, the election results had been similarly touch and go.

"I think it's now somewhat widely known that we had planned on Vinick winning the election," Josh Singer told us. (**MARY:** Um . . . spoiler? For some of you?) The point, he said, was "to cement the idea of the continuity of democracy . . . of the peaceful transfer of power . . . of the idea that there's no 'right' party, that both parties have things to contribute."

John Wells has summed up Santos versus Vinick this way: "We went back and forth on whether the Republican should actually win the election. We thought that that could be a very interesting thing to do and then watch that transition and see what happened to our characters as they left government."

After John Spencer died, though, the showrunner and his staff began internal discussions as to whether they should reconsider. According to Josh Singer, "A number of us worried that the loss of Leo and the loss of the election would be too much for the show to bear." After some debate, John and the writers room called it—for Congressman Santos.

"The way John Wells guided and managed that discussion," Josh said, "was as democratic as I've ever seen on a writing staff. It left everybody in the room feeling pretty good about things." That said, there was at least one person involved who wound up a little disappointed.

"I was really rooting for my character to win!" Alan Alda told us effusively. "I was so caught up in winning that, when I was watching the episode—remember, by then we'd shot everything—and the vote came in, I thought I still had a chance!"

As episode 16 turned to episode 17, the shock and raw of "Election Day: Part II" gave way to a subdued, meditative mood in episode 18. "Requiem" writers John Wells, Debora Cahn, and Eli Attie built a narrative around Leo's funeral that felt appropriately ruminative, but also gave us periodic pops of fun with the collegial swapping of Mc-Garry war stories.

> **PRESIDENT BARTLET**
> You remember that trip to Seattle during the first campaign, when he couldn't find his umbrella, so you grabbed a garbage can to hold over him?
>
> **MARGARET**
> And it still had garbage in it.
>
> **PRESIDENT BARTLET**
> Leo ended up with a three-course meal on his head!
>
> **MARGARET**
> Dry as a bone, though.

On *The West Wing Weekly*, Josh Malina described his sense of filming the memorial as "sort of impressionistic," noting the unusual "mournfulness of shooting the funeral of a buddy." While he'd played funeral sequences before, laying Leo to rest was, of course, starkly different. "There often was kind of a black humor to shooting these scenes, talking about the death of a character played by a friend who's, of course, alive. This was a very odd, sad, meaningful exercise. It felt absolutely like a tribute to John . . . a coming together."

That "coming together" represented another moving element of the episode—all the wonderful cameos. With his camera roaming the congregation, director Steve Shill and his team captured the raw emotion on the familiar faces of actors from seven years of *The West Wing*. While numerous current staffers, deputies, and assistants were spotted grieving in the church pews, Shill also landed on several former cast members whose characters had long since left *The West Wing*. This mass influx signaled a desire to honor a fallen friend by participating in what felt like—what *was*, in a very real way—a holy occasion.

"I thought it was sweet and right that they included as many people from the cast as could make it," Malina said. "My guess is there was a much wider net cast for anybody that it would make sense to have at the funeral. Depending on availability, anybody that could come was there, and I thought Steve Shill did a good job of sharing with us who's there, giving everybody a little bit of a moment."

Not everyone could make it back. According to Rob Lowe, "The only reason Sam Seaborn wasn't at Leo McGarry's funeral . . . is because I was in Europe shooting a movie and we couldn't get my schedule to permit it. It was one of the great heartbreaks."

While it was indeed disappointing that Sam wasn't there, his old sparring partner, Ainsley Hayes, was—tearfully paying her respects to the man who originally hired her and, later, angling for a job as White House counsel in the Santos administration. Others present included Leo's daughter, Mallory; Zoey, Liz, and Ellie Bartlet and the grandchildren; a pair of VPs ("Bingo" Bob Russell and John Hoynes); Danny Concannon; National Security Advisor Nancy McNally, and, seated in the back, ex–communications director Toby Ziegler and his ex-wife, Congresswoman Andy Wyatt. There's an Amy Gardner sighting too (and not just at Leo's memorial). While the homecomings of these characters brought brief flashes of "where are they now?"–type fun to the proceedings, more than anything they imbued the episode with precisely the gravity, scope, and history the moment called for.

Some found the undertaking difficult to process, even disorienting, but the episode offered a chance for healing as well. During downtime between takes or while the crew positioned cameras and lights, stories began to fly. "You'd take a break," Malina says, "and the conversation was about John. So, we had our own sort of counterpart to the scenes with President Bartlet and the groups of people remembering [Leo] . . . telling funny stories . . . and laughing in remembrance of the special person that was John. That happened a lot on set while we were shooting his funeral."

> JOSH
> Leo used to tell these tall tales
> to test how gullible you were. Like
> how he played Davis Cup tennis
> before he blew out his knee.

> WILL
> How he hustled chess games in
> Washington Square Park.

> DONNA
> How he was a train conductor.

> JOSH
> Minor League baseball player . . .

> PRESIDENT BARTLET
> If you were buying it, the stories
> kept gettin' bigger and better.

                         C.J.
          My favorite was how he almost made
          the Olympic Luge team in 1962.

                       ANNABETH
          He didn't make the Luge team in
          1962?

                         WILL
          There weren't any Olympics in '62.

Filming "Requiem" hit Stockard Channing especially hard. But, like her friend John, Stockard's a veteran, a consummate pro. "They *had* to tell the story," she said to us, "because he had to die as Leo." While her inner "actor's actor" understood the necessity of it, producing Leo's final chapter represented one of the strangest moments in her life.

"We were on the lot," Stockard said to us. "It was a Friday night, late, end of the day. Martin and I actually had to sit on a chair while a grip carrying a flag over his shoulders had to pretend to be the coffin. It was the most bizarre combination of reality and fiction. For Martin, I'm sure, as well. But . . . you have to do it. That's what we do."

Following the funeral, as he despairs in the limo with the first lady, President Bartlet appears withdrawn, steeped in grief. Leo was his best friend. More than a chief of staff, he was a partner . . . a *brother.* The last thing he wants to do is put on a happy face and play host at a post-service get-together. Yet just a little while later, after steeling himself outside the door to the reception, in he strides, all smiles and handshakes and slaps on the back.

                   PRESIDENT BARTLET
          Why all the long faces? Leo would
          be furious to think we were all
          standing around feeling sorry for

```
ourselves! We need some music. Do
we have any music?

                CAROL
I have a CD player in my office.

            PRESIDENT BARTLET
That's the spirit . . .
```

And now he's off, cheerleader in chief, kissing a teary-eyed Debbie Fiderer on the cheek, greeting C.J. with a smile and a "How ya holdin' up?" Finally, he taps Leo's beloved assistant Margaret on the shoulder. "Hey, kid," he tells her. "Leo loved you. You knew that, right? I don't know how he could've done it without you." That whole sequence is, as Malina rightly put it, "so presidential. He just snaps to it and . . . really buoys everybody."

It's funny how time works. More than a decade later, the act of committing to film the last moments of Leo McGarry feels not at all bizarre or disorienting to us. More than ever, it feels right, like a loving way to honor the life, heart, and soul of John Spencer.

At the end of these three key episodes, just four *West Wing* offerings would remain. The spirt of Leo, like the spirit of the man who played him, would continue to make its presence felt all the way through to the end of the series. But these storylines—the ones with Leo at center stage—felt like a swan song of sorts. The palpable sense of a bittersweet goodbye, that ache of reluctant farewell, was captured in the very last line of "Election Day: Part II."

Leo's former deputy and protégé, in the quiet aftermath of a historic electoral win, wanders slowly around the Santos / McGarry war room, the very picture of pensive. With memos and campaign posters strewn about and a champagne bottle on the floor, we see the whiteboard, its map completely filled up now, almost equal parts red and blue. Josh Lyman's gaze (and the camera) lands on a photo of Leo

McGarry—of John Spencer. A twinkle in his eyes, Leo stands beside his running mate, hands held high in victory.

In that moment, speaking for the campaign as Josh, just as he seemed to be speaking for the *West Wing* cast and crew, Brad Whitford delivers those final, heartfelt words. They come out sad and hushed . . . in a whisper—like a prayer: "Thanks, boss."

THIRTY-FIVE

MEANEST MAN
IN THE WORLD

Ask any watcher of *The West Wing* and they'll tell you, the show saw its share of practical jokes. Olives in Will's pocket. Amy Gardner's office doors falling down. C.J. and Charlie's back-and-forth in "Hartsfield's Landing." (Her *desk* collapses!) And speaking of C.J.— and speaking of Will—how can we forget the turkeys in her office and the bicycles in his?!

While these moments were plenty entertaining, they pale in comparison to the relentless off-camera pranks pulled by the meanest man in the world, Josh Malina. As director Chris Misiano told us, "There were days that I wanted to fucking strangle him!" True enough and same here, but every now and then, even Josh's archnemesis, Brad Whitford, describes him as "a joy on the set." We'll second (and third) that. Don't tell him we said this, but Josh is hilarious, smart, always prepared, and genuinely kind. His cruel talent for pranking, though, must be seen to be believed. To kick things off, here are a few practical joke allegations, courtesy of our chat with Brad, and a rebuttal or two, courtesy of our chat with Josh.

BRADLEY WHITFORD: The thing is, Malina has no sense of proportional response. If I used a hand buzzer on him, he would, you know, pick up my daughter from school and not tell me.

We heard he'd put open bags of flour on top of the door so they would fall on Alex Graves's head when he walked into his office.

JOSH MALINA: Gotta say, that does sound like me.

BRADLEY WHITFORD: He once got a crane and hoisted Alex's golf cart onto the roof of the soundstage.

Wow. The degree of commitment, the amount of planning, the involvement of teamsters, *permits* . . .

BRADLEY WHITFORD: He used to fill cars with dirt.

(**MELISSA:** What does this even *mean?*)

JOSH MALINA: I definitely hid an onion in Janney's trailer, so that it would slowly rot.

MARY: A classic.

JOSH MALINA: Brad always read books on set. Every time he walked away from his chair, I ripped out the last few pages of what-ever he was reading. Also, we were once on an airplane together, and when he fell asleep, I took his Kindle and bought *Mein Kampf.*

BRADLEY WHITFORD: He'd put toothpaste on your trailer door. Or Vaseline.

JOSH MALINA: I stole Alex Graves's iPod, erased all eight thou-sand songs, essentially rendering the device useless, and reset the controls to Mandarin. Turns out it is *very* hard to set it back to

English once it's set to Mandarin. In retaliation, Alex literally hit me in the balls.

BRADLEY WHITFORD: I had a very sweet assistant who would leave supportive little Post-its in my trailer. Just cheerful messages like, "Have a great day!" "Breathe . . ." "I have the time and space to do everything that I need to do." Stuff like that. I come into my trailer one day and Malina's left a *hundred* Post-its: "You're losing your hair." "There is no happiness." "The reward is death." "You've peaked."

Malina remembered it slightly differently . . .

JOSH MALINA: They were motivational! "You are *not* a horrible person." "They *won't* find out what you've done." "No, seriously, people *like* you."

This prank war didn't end there. It didn't end at all.

MARY: On our *West Wing* cast text chain, on Twitter . . . they're still constantly duking it out.

MELISSA: Their ongoing Twitter war is like exercise for them. Like a boxer on the speed bag. Those daily little jabs are just to stay in shape, to keep strong for the one-two punch jumbotron moments to come.

While Josh has an extra-special relationship with Brad when it comes to pranks, from time to time we've all found ourselves on the wrong end of Malina.

MARY: Thanks to Josh, I still can't set foot on any set without white-knuckling my sides, like a death grip.

FYI, "sides" are miniature script copies of each day's scenes. They're distributed to cast and crew at the beginning of every day.

MARY: You'd be in the middle of rehearsal and he'd come by and slap 'em out of your hand. Over and over. You're like, "Okay, it's happened three times now," and you think, "Surely not again." Because now it's annoying—now *everyone's* annoyed. That's when he doubles down. He'll just do it 'til you're laughing *again*. Past tears—he gets you through the tears and then back to laughter. He's like a performance artist. It just never, ever ends.

MELISSA: Yeah, it's maddening, the slapping. And hilarious. What else, Brad?

BRADLEY WHITFORD: It's three thirty in the morning on a Friday. We're about to wrap, you could see the director realize he's finally gonna get to go home, get some sleep, see his family. What he doesn't know is that Malina has gotten his keys from the teamsters . . . and, throughout the day, started filling up his trunk with props—Teddy Roosevelt's Nobel Prize, two orange traffic cones, a bunch of computers. We finally wrap, we're driving out . . . and Burbank PD's there because Josh has called security and the director is stunned, looking inside his trunk filled with all these computers and props and stuff!

MARY: Josh is horrible.

MELISSA: Meanest man in the world.

Apparently, Malina's penchant for practical jokes on his fellow *West Wing* cast members goes all the way back to his fellow cast members in the stage production of *A Few Good Men*.

BRADLEY WHITFORD: Josh almost got fired for this thing he did to the soldier who had to stand still in the tower.

RON OSTROW (REPORTER JOHN): That was me. I'm putting on my costume one day and it's like I'm being stabbed with these needles. I rip off my shirt and I'm like, "Aiigghh!!" Josh had put itching powder in my costume. Except it isn't really powder and it doesn't make you itch. It's little pieces of fiberglass and it hurts!

That wouldn't be the last time Ron found himself the target of Malina's pranks.

RON OSTROW: I was doing my taxes, telling Josh about a particular deduction or whatever, something which was perfectly legal. Then one day I get a phone call from the IRS. They had gotten my tax return and were auditing me. The problem was . . . I had not actually filed my taxes yet. It was Josh's father on the phone.

Engaging your *parents* in the plot? Malina is the Zodiac Killer of pranking.

Which brings us to Camp David. Allow me to set the scene. (It's Mary, by the way.) I was about six months pregnant. It's DC hot, we're rushing though the work, trying to get through all the exterior scenes because at any moment . . . the cicadas are coming. They nest in the earth for *seventeen years* and then crawl out all at once, and swarm. It's biblical. I'm bug-averse and can't even deal with gnats, and these cicadas are enormous and whitish with bulging red eyes and just . . . horrific. They're hell-bugs. On the first day at Camp David, we just spot a few, here and there. They're gross, but you can cope. By the end of day two, we saw whole trees moving. I would leave my trailer holding an umbrella just to get to set—*and you could feel them banging into it.*

They were flying through the air, every surface looked like it was alive, it was a waking nightmare. I finally got safely inside. Standing there on set, all of a sudden I feel this creeping thing in my ear. There was one inside my ear! I dropped everything and screamed. It's literally my biggest fear. It was Malina, with a twig. Torturing a pregnant woman. I think I actually cried.

> **JOSH MALINA:** My memory is that you did cry.

> **MARY:** Because I thought for sure one had crawled into my ear and was going to eat my brain with its red eyes. I remember crying, like, "I'm pregnaaaaaaant!"

> **JOSH MALINA:** I should have factored that in. Is it too late? It's never too late to say you're sorry.

> **MARY:** Sometimes it's too late . . .

> **JOSH MALINA:** I don't know if I've told you this before, but Alex [Graves] is one of the all-time great prank-inappropriate retaliators. On *Sports Night* I rearranged the furniture in his [office]. Then I'm walking to the set and all of a sudden somebody is *emptying a fire extinguisher* on me.

> **MARY:** Yeah, too far.

> **JOSH MALINA:** I was like—dude, there's "pranks." You can put your furniture back. I have to go *change* now, I'm at work!

Dylan Massin, our unit production manager and, later, a co-producer on *The West Wing*, provided further evidence of Alex's willingness to go "the full Malina."

> **DYLAN MASSIN:** Although a sweetheart of a man, something happens to Alex when he gets pranked. You would do something

like soak his chair in water so that when he sat in it, he would get all wet. The chairs are all black, so you couldn't see it. A perfectly good prank. And then he would slash all four of your tires.

Things really heated up between Josh and Brad toward the end of the show.

BRADLEY WHITFORD: It was Valentine's Day. It's a big scene, during the election. Santos and Vinick. There's a lot of people there. I get on set and I see Jimmy across the room. He comes over, throws his arms around me and, like, in my ear . . .

JIMMY SMITS: "Those are the most beautiful flowers I've ever gotten and that note meant the world to me. I love you too, man. Seriously, the flowers are more beautiful than the ones I gave *my girlfriend*."

BRADLEY WHITFORD: I'm over Jimmy's shoulder and I'm like, "What?" Turns out, months before, Josh had snuck into my trailer and stolen some of my personal stationery, I guess thinking, "This'll come in handy someday . . ." So Josh sends Jimmy this gorgeous bouquet of really expensive flowers and a note—that he wrote on the stationery he stole from my trailer all those months before—about how deeply meaningful it had been working with him, and how much he meant to me personally, and how beautiful he was. Which is probably why Jimmy kept saying—

JIMMY SMITS: "Those flowers are more beautiful than the ones I gave *my girlfriend*."

MARY: Late in the run of the show, *Ellen* was doing a *West Wing* retrospective. They had a bunch of us on, brought out a cake, the whole thing. Jimmy said he had five thousand bucks for anyone who shoved cake into Malina's face on camera.

JIMMY SMITS: Josh got wind of it and started running.

MARY: I eventually got him. Jimmy donated five grand to the Juvenile Diabetes Research Foundation!

MELISSA: Malina gets a face full of cake and the JDRF gets five thousand bucks? Win-win!

BRADLEY WHITFORD: Obviously, I had to get Josh back. I happened to find out who was editing the "In Memoriam" reel at the SAG Awards . . .

MELISSA: Hold on. What?!

BRADLEY WHITFORD: It would've been incredible. Josh would be declared <u>dead</u> at an awards show. But the editor chickened out. And thank God he did because it would've been horribly insulting to the memory of anyone who *actually* died that year.

That's when Brad did what he calls "the greatest thing that I've ever done, or ever will do."

BRADLEY WHITFORD: I got to write another *West Wing* episode, and I realized that I had the opportunity to create a situation where Malina would have to say, multiple times, "I'm a terrible actor" on national television. The whole episode was constructed to make this happen.

C.J. has found out that the president's son-in-law, who's running for office, is having an affair. Will Bailey is now the press secretary and she's chief of staff. So C.J. tells Will about the affair. He says, "Oh, my God, why did you tell me that?!" She says, "Because you're the press secretary. You have to deal with the press." His line is, "Exactly. I can't act! I'm a terrible actor. I don't like to pretend!" I still have it on my phone. I bring it out all the time, just to make me laugh.

In 2023, Brad convinced someone to play that audio clip over the sound system before the curtain rose on Josh's performance in the Broadway play *Leopoldstadt*. A couple of weeks later, Brad trolled Malina again—this time with video—at a New York Mets game. As Josh sat in the stands, that *West Wing* clip—"I can't act! I'm a terrible actor. I don't like to pretend!"—played up on the jumbotron at Citi Field. What began as small, if inspired, skirmishes had escalated into perhaps the largest-scale, most grandiose war between two actors the world has ever seen.

This is not to say the war is over. Or that Josh Malina is finished. God help us all.

Don't get us wrong. The meanest man in the world is also a pretty nice guy. But, Josh, listen. No matter what they tell you, keep in mind the words of a man with a gift for the long game and an endless supply of Post-its: "You are *not* a horrible person." "They *won't* find out what you've done." "No, seriously, people *like* you."

THIRTY-SIX

MARTIN SHEEN, NUMBER ONE OF NUMBER ONES

Over the years, a sizable portion of the commentariat, and a decent chunk of pop culture consumers, have pointed to the gentleman at the center of *The West Wing*'s West Wing as the ultimate liberal fantasy of a US president. Erudite but tough, progressive but "traditional," he's armed with the heart of a poet, a generational talent for soaring oratory, and the willingness to kick a little ass if you shoot his personal physician out of the sky. A national father figure who loves his Fighting Irish, though not as much as he loves his wife, he's a master of chess who looks sharp in a tux and comes with a great head of hair. Jed Bartlet—Bible-quoting sports fan and heir apparent to JFK—is, they'll tell you with an almost patronizing shake of the head, simply too good to be true.

Perhaps he is. Except for the smoking, an apparently lifelong obliviousness to the Butterball hotline, and the odd questionable joke, the man doesn't have a lot of bad habits. But if you're legitimately looking for "too good to be true," Jed Bartlet may have met his match in the fellow who filled out his suits. Martin Sheen is the real one who's too good to be true.

We know what you're thinking. That's gotta be hyperbole run amok, right? Well, reserve judgment until you've heard from those of us who know him well. To us, he has been, and continues to be, an inspiration, both on the set and off—through his leadership, his fierce commitment to social justice, his presence. Many of us on *The West Wing* could walk-and-talk. Martin walks the walk and talks the talk. Ask anyone. Ask *everyone*.

Mary McCormack (Kate Harper)

You want to know who Martin is? He's the guy who doesn't care how powerful you may or may not be. That's who Martin is.

When I brought Margaret to set—she was only a week old; it was literally day one for me as a working mother—Martin came into my trailer in full-on grandpa mode. "No, no, no, the music in here is all wrong—you need classical music!" he said. "And the lighting . . ." He quickly ducked out to his trailer. A few minutes later he came back holding a gorgeous wood-carved antique lamp. That lamp stayed in my trailer through the end of the show, and when we wrapped for good, Martin gave me the other one. "Janet insisted I bring this in for you. Margaret has to have the set." Eighteen years later, those antique lamps have had pride of place in all three of my girls' bedrooms.

Martin was born to be "number one on the call sheet." He took that responsibility seriously. The influence of his example went beyond simply cultivating a sense of mutual respect on set. In fact, it went beyond the set entirely, and beyond the years we spent working on *The West Wing*. It's different being a number one. For better or worse, you're a real tone setter. ("As number one goes, so goes the show . . .") I think Martin probably affected more sets than he'll ever know. Those of us lucky enough to have become "number one on the call sheet" elsewhere took what we learned from watching him and carried it with us for the rest of our careers. On *In Plain Sight*, the show I did after *The West Wing*, it was important to me to establish a culture of professionalism

and to exhibit and encourage respect and support for every department. It was important to be kind. I may not have been as successful
as Martin in that capacity—there's no way I did it as well—but it mattered to me to try. That's just one of countless Martin Sheen ripple
effects that began on the Warner Bros. lot long before I ever even got
there. But don't take my word for it. Just ask Dulé.

Dulé Hill (Charlie Young)

I took how Martin was on *West Wing*, and I brought the same energy
with me to *Psych*: "We're all going to love each other, we're going to
respect each other, we're going to have a good time. We're making television." That's the domino effect of how things can happen. I'm sure
Martin probably didn't even realize that the way he was on *The West
Wing* had a huge impact on a production that was happening for the
next eight years in Vancouver. On *Psych* it was always love—and anyone who wasn't respecting each other, James [Roday Rodriguez] and I
would both step in. "We're not doing that here. We're here having
fun. We're here bringing the best of ourselves." That's a clear line from
Martin.

Melissa Fitzgerald (Carol Fitzpatrick)

Martin is like a second father to me. I think about him every single
day. I ask myself, "What would Martin do in this situation?" He and
my parents are my "lookups." They set the bar for integrity, decency,
and service. My life is immeasurably better for knowing him.

The first time I traveled to Northern Uganda, it was to volunteer
with International Medical Corps. I was back in Los Angeles for just a
couple of days when my phone rang. It was Martin. He wanted to
make sure I had gotten home safely; he'd been worried about me.
When I mentioned I had to get off the phone soon to go edit video
footage I'd taken on my trip, he said, "Would it be helpful if I narrated
it for you?" I said, "To have Martin Sheen narrate my film? Yes. Yes,

Martin, it would be very helpful." We edited it, Martin narrated it, and International Medical Corps was thrilled to use it to showcase the work they were doing.

These days, working in DC, I still try to follow his example. In the office, at events, I go up and introduce myself—to everyone. Until you work with Martin, you don't really know what good "set etiquette" is. The message that simple act sends—at work or anywhere—makes everyone feel comfortable. It not only brings out the best in people, it's also just . . . kind. That's Martin.

Martin and his wife, Janet, came to Washington in January 2020 and stayed with me! We hung out in our pajamas, we cooked, watched football, laughed and talked for hours. In other words, a perfect weekend. They were in town so he could "get arrested with Jane Fonda." They were protesting climate change with the organization Fire Drill Fridays. (Look it up!) Janet and I sat in the car eating trail mix while we waited for Martin to get arrested so we could pick him up after he got bailed out.

(**MARY**: Melissa was driving the getaway car!)

Allison Janney (C.J. Cregg)

I adore Martin Sheen. I could tell you he's a stunning actor to work with, incredibly generous, wildly talented, and one of the best scene partners I've ever had—those things are as true as anything I know. But more important to me is this: Martin's goodness is so authentic, so deep. He's a protector and a father figure . . . but also kind of a goofball. So, there's this brotherly element to it, too, that he brings to the table. Stir it all up—his charm and skill, the depth of his thinking, the sincerity of his friendship and of his devotion to living decently and with others in the front of his mind—and what you get is Martin Sheen. Yes, at times he couldn't remember our names and he used to call me "the Big Lady," but honestly . . . to me he's just a prince. And that trade-off? That's a *steal*.

Frankie Bruno (On-Set Costumer)
Martin was such a gracious Number One. He is so genuine, so lovely, and just . . . authentic. God bless him—he couldn't remember anyone's name, but he really knows who you are.

Josh Einsohn (Warner Bros. Casting)
I needed to deliver something to Martin's trailer and was told his daughter, Renée (who recurred on the show as "Nancy"), was in there and to just pop it inside. I stepped in and my jaw hit the floor—Martin was right there having his lunch! He was still mostly in costume, so it was like walking in on Martin Sheen *and* President Bartlet. I put the envelope down, apologized, and started to duck out when he said, "No, no . . . here, come have a seat and eat. I have so much more here than I need." It was like lightning striking as I realized that all the activism I'd seen and heard about came from a deeply genuine place. I mean, his first thought at seeing a random crew member was to invite them to eat some of the food off his plate. He barely knew who I was and was inviting me to break bread with him!

Kim Webster (Ginger)
Martin was like my West Coast dad. I was going through some health issues and I'd become friends with Renée and she told him. They just swept in and took care of me. Everything I needed, from nursing care to equipment, even vitamins they thought might help. There wasn't anything they weren't willing to do. He's just a real-life angel to me.

Bradley Whitford (Josh Lyman)
I always thought the key to the chemistry in the show was our unabashed affection for Martin and belief in him. Given all that stuff he's been through in his life and landing in a place of moral action . . . he's truly beloved.

Martin and I were making an entrance, we're about to enter C.J.'s office, but it's one of those things where there's a couple minutes in the scene before you enter. Were we standing offstage, nervously preparing to act brilliantly? No. We're close to each other, whispering—'cause Allison's acting right next to us—about a *West Wing* softball game. I whisper, "Oh, you play softball?" He goes, "Oh yeah, on *Apocalypse* we played every Sunday." And there's a pause . . . and I'm like, "Really? . . . *Dennis Hopper* played softball?" And Martin starts to laugh, and he goes, "Yeah, Dennis played second base." I said, "How? How could he *function?*" And Martin said, "No, he'd lie on his back and say, 'I'm second base, I'm second base!'" I burst out laughing. We had to cut!

The bottom line is, there was just a lot of joy. I think joy is always the secret sauce. The palpable joy brought by certain performers. That's the Beatles on *Ed Sullivan* or Dennis Hopper playing second. That's Martin Sheen.

Llewellyn Wells (Line Producer)

When the show got to be a bigger hit, and we went to DC to shoot exteriors, we couldn't pull him away from the crowds. I'd be like, "Martin, you have to come film!" Sometimes I'd have to wade in and pull him out and say, "Thank you all very much!" Then, still shaking hands on his way back to set, he'd say, "Gosh, sorry I don't have more time!" He was just so grateful to his fans and wanted to connect with them in a real way. If you hire Martin, that's what you get and you're lucky to have it.

Marlee Matlin (Joey Lucas)

It was the White House Correspondents' Dinner and I was *very* pregnant. When I arrived in line to meet President Clinton, I was told my name was not on the list and that I could not enter. Martin, who was standing right in back of me, said, "What do you mean she's not on the list? She's part of our show; she is in the cast!" They still refused to let me in. At that point, Martin said, "Well if she can't go in, I won't go in. Period." I pleaded with him not to miss it because of me. But he stood fast and refused. Eventually, a Secret Service agent let us both in.

Annette Sousa (Background Artist)

He would bring in ice cream carts. At midnight! He would do anything and everything for us. We were having such a good time on set, we felt like family. And he knew who regular background were, he kept track of it, who each person was. He would walk up and ask how my trip to Ireland was.

Josh Malina (Will Bailey)

If the top dog is cool, down-to-earth, and professional, then everyone else kind of has to behave well too. I've been very lucky on the series I've done—Mary on *In Plain Sight* and Kerry Washington on *Scandal* were both great leaders, as was Martin on *The West Wing*. He was always prepared, kind to everyone in the cast and crew, and happy to be there. That made the set of *The West Wing* a wonderful place to be.

Renée Rosenfeld (Script Supervisor)

I remember walking onto the stage on a Friday morning with Martin. I said, "So what are you doing this weekend, Martin?" And he looks at me and says, "Renée. They're at it again—'Star Wars' [the controversial missile defense system]. So I'm going out to Brandenburg, we're going to protest. And if I don't get arrested, there's a barbecue on Sunday."

A couple years later, I was taking four days off to go to Germany with my father's oldest and youngest sisters for the commemoration of the deportation of the Jews from the town my family was from. Before I left the set that night, Martin walked over to me at the monitor and reached in his pocket. He says, "I want you to take this. If you need some strength, hold on to this." And he gave me his rosary. To this day, it's one of the kindest things anyone's ever done for me.

(**MELISSA:** A word about those rosaries. Whether it's Mary and the births of her daughters or Renée and the Germany trip, you knew you were really in the *West Wing* family when you got a rosary from Martin.)

Tommy Schlamme (Producing Director, Executive Producer)
I came to rehearsal and the chairman of the Joint Chiefs, Fitzwallace, played by John Amos, is coming into the Oval Office. They had rehearsed it before I got there. When John came in, Martin hugged him. The president is *hugging* the chairman of the Joint Chiefs. Fitzwallace had all his medallions on and he was in military garb . . . Martin said, "I hadn't seen John in a long time and, you know, Bartlet probably hadn't seen Percy in a long time." And I said, "Yeah . . . I just don't think you guys hug. I know *you* hug, and I know you hadn't seen John in a long time . . ." It was just Martin wanting to tell his friend "I love you," that "I'm happy to see you. Now—are we going to war with Cambodia?" That irrepressible warmth is the reason, I believe, that Martin tested through the roof.

Aaron had this perception that the reason the president shouldn't be a major character in the show is that everybody's character would get altered so dramatically by his presence. If you read the pilot, the president is sort of patriarchal, his ten-speed bicycle, New England, Waspy . . . a person you don't approach easily. So, this show about the "satellites" would get altered by this person being there. Well, the opposite would happen. Martin would be in the center of a scene and everybody was their *best* self, not their most restricted self. And what started to evolve is that people felt empowered and loved by him. It completely changed the complexion of the show and allowed Bartlet to be *a* character, not the central character that altered everybody. That was the benefit. The drawback was that he would occasionally hug Fitzwallace.

John Amos (Admiral Percy Fitzwallace)

I had always been an enormous fan of Martin Sheen, for as long as I could remember. He's a superb actor, and what I found working on *The West Wing* is that he's the most giving actor. He helped me in every way imaginable.

Lesli Linka Glatter (Director)

I remember on that first episode I directed, I was like, "Oh my God!" He literally shook hands with all of the background—every single person. It was like he *was* the president.

Greg LaCava (Makeup)

We were out on location, they were doing driving shots of Bartlet in the presidential motorcade. During a setup, they passed a McDonald's and decided to pull into the parking lot. Martin—being Martin—went inside to say hello to everybody, which means, of course, that he's got to get everyone's name. And then—again of course—he asks, "You need any help in the drive-through?" All of a sudden, he's working the window, taking orders—he even has on the headset! You should've seen them when they pulled up for their burgers and fries. That's the thing with Martin, no matter the job, on *The West Wing* or at the drive-through, it's an occupational hazard—he just loves to meet new people.

Anna Deavere Smith (National Security Advisor Nancy McNally)

Martin is an extraordinary individual, not only because his heart and mind and politics are in the right place, but he's also a kind of actor who almost doesn't exist anymore. He's an actor from the ground up, a model of the craft, an entertainer in the old sense of the word.

Janel Moloney (Donna Moss)

Martin truly cares about everybody, but I always got the sense that he cared about the "little guy" more than anyone. He has this spiritual path where he takes care of the birds that need to be taken care of . . . because the big, strong birds can fly wherever they want. And protecting the little guy, that's built-in. Martin does that on a daily basis.

Dave Chameides (Steadicam Operator)
I remember [First AD] Doug Ornstein coming to set and there being a little huddle. He said, "Listen, we gotta move Friday's work to Monday because Martin is going to be protesting a nuclear something and is probably going to get arrested. So Friday is out, but we think he'll be out of jail by Monday. So we'll move it to Monday." They're not saying, "We're totally screwed! How can he do this to us?!" It was just, "Martin's going to be out, Martin has the thing." I stood there, thinking, How great is it that this is just *normal*?

Lyn Paolo (Costume Designer)
Martin was outside, chatting, when a Warner Bros. tour came by. This woman was on the back of the open-air car and he said, "Are you cold?" She goes, "I'm freezing!" So he goes, "Oh here, borrow my coat." His *on-camera overcoat*. And off the tour went! I get a panicked call from Frankie [Bruno] on set: "We can't find Martin's coat!" Now, the double to the coat had been shipped to DC because we were going to shoot exteriors, so I didn't have the double. So the whole costume department is out running around Warner Bros. trying to find this cart with this woman, and everyone on set is waiting. And I'm tearing around in *my* golf cart—it was like Wacky Racers—to get Martin's coat back. We finally found her and we got the coat! That's Martin in a nutshell—the shirt off his back! Literally.

Stockard Channing (Abigail Bartlet)
I'll always remember Martin coming to set and the sound guys playing "Hail to the Chief" on a boom box.

Yervant Hagopian (Utility Sound Technician)

We went to shoot at an army base. Maybe a thousand soldiers had signed up to be extras. Martin was scheduled to work in the morning and be done before lunch. Once he saw the number of soldiers who volunteered their time, he had his grandson Taylor (who worked as his assistant) come to the base with boxes of headshots. Martin signed autographs, took photos, and talked with every soldier who stood in line. He didn't leave 'til well after dark.

Richard Schiff (Toby Zeigler)

So many of our scenes were right on that emotional edge, something very profound would be happening . . . and then Martin would crack me up and I couldn't stop laughing. It's his sense of commitment. You see his eyes, like he's trying not to betray that he knows that he fucked up, he's trying to save it. It's not like they go cross-eyed. It's as if they *wanted* to go cross-eyed, and he's holding them still . . . with all of his energy.

Carla Ward (Background Artist)

On Good Friday they filmed the inauguration scene with a couple hundred background actors. One of them passed out from the heat. Martin jumps up, runs up the stands. He was the first person to reach her and shouted for something to shade her. He was handed an umbrella and he held it over her the whole time while people attended to her.

I don't know how many godchildren Martin has, but I feel blessed that one of them is my son, Matthew. I could think of no better role model for Matthew than Martin. He puts his money, his time—and occasionally his freedom—where his mouth is.

Mike Hissrich (Producer)

Martin just loves to act. Period. He loved doing those great scenes with Spencer, just two people in a room on their feet, acting. No matter how much work I had to do, I'd try to get over to set when those scenes came up. That was always the best time to go over to just sit and watch.

Adam Ben Frank (Second AD, First AD)

Because Martin always had to say hello to everybody, we'd call him in early, especially on days where there's a lot of background actors. We would say, "All right, bring him in for the greeting process." We built that right into the schedule.

Debora Cahn (Writer)

It was my first solo episode and the first time I was on set as the writer. There's a scene with Martin and John Spencer in the Oval Office. Martin pulls me aside: "Can I talk to you for a minute?" And he says, "You've written a line here, and it says 'It's really incredible.' I would love to have the president give it a little bit more emphasis. So, if it's okay with you, I'd like to change it to 'It *is* really incredible.' Is that okay with you?"

And I was, you know, standing there, shaking—it's Martin Sheen—like, "Yes, Martin Sheen, it is okay. Thank you. Thanks for checking it." I mean, it was so crazy. I was this little tiny pipsqueak, what do I know, I've never done this before. He's Martin Sheen.

David Katz (Background Artist, Toby Stand-In)

When I was a little kid, my parents owned a liquor store on the campus of Marquette University. It's a Jesuit school. Martin gets invited to open up the library there. When he comes back, he has this box. He'd opened the library, so they gave him a box of Marquette ties, T-shirts, hoodies. And he brought the box back for me. He carried it with him *on the flight*. That's the thing about Martin. He knew about us. He listened. He remembered my parents!

Mindy Kanaskie (Co-Producer)

I lived in an apartment in Burbank. At the time, my kids had a two-wheeler and a tricycle. When we went down to ride bikes that weekend, they were gone, stolen. I mentioned it at work. The next day two bikes from Toys"R"Us were delivered to my apartment. Martin had heard about it and sent them. I went down to his trailer and knocked on the door. "Martin," I said, "you got my boys bikes! Thank you!" And he goes, "Well, of course! Kids need bikes." He wouldn't let me make a big deal about it. Just . . . "Kids need bikes."

Kevin Falls (Writer, Co–Executive Producer)

The Democratic Convention in 2000 was taking place in the Staples Center. A producer asked if I wanted to hop in a transpo van and head to Staples with Martin Sheen and a few others. Of course, security was tight and we were dropped off a mile away, so we walked. The closer we got to Staples, the more people recognized Martin. Delegates, construction workers, people walking by—they're all yelling Bartlet's name and Martin is waving to everyone like he's president. By the time we get into Staples Center, it's a crush of delegates trying to shake Martin's hand. A few of us turned into Secret Service agents in an effort to escort him to his seat. It was a little scary, but a lot of fun. President Clinton was speaking that night, but I'll bet some delegates remember Bartlet's entrance more.

Timothy Busfield (Danny Concannon)

I'm walking out of my trailer and I see Marty headed across the lot. He flags down a tour bus and calls out, "Can you give me a ride?!" I remember hearing everybody screaming. He gets on and, like an actual tour guide, says, "Hi, everybody!" and starts answering questions. You could still hear his voice as they headed back toward the main gate.

Holli Strickland (Base Camp PA)

I was having crazy pain in my mouth and I couldn't get a dentist appointment for weeks. Martin, being Martin, saw that I was in pain. Suddenly, I have a voicemail from the dentist's office saying, "Can you come in tomorrow morning?" Martin had called for me.

Alex Graves (Director, Executive Producer)

My favorite sound forever from *West Wing* was walking onto Stage 23 and hearing Martin laugh on the other side of the soundstage. And the reason he's laughing is 'cause Brad's there and he's the funniest man alive. It happened all the time. I'd walk onto the stage . . . and Martin would be just howling. It's still my favorite sound.

John Wells (Executive Producer, Showrunner)

My favorite moment of Martin's from the final seasons is the simple shot of Bartlet in the window of Air Force One as he leaves Washington after his final day as president. Everything that played across Martin's face—extraordinary.

John Spencer (Leo McGarry)

From a 2002 interview with CNN's David Daniel.

Martin has become one of my closest friends in my life. I just adore the man. And as an actor . . . I'm given the role of a man who is devoted to this man who he thinks is great, who he thinks is capable of leadership and greatness and kindness, who's a unique individual. Well, that's exactly the way John feels about Martin. I would love to be as good a human being as Martin Sheen is. I'm not sure I've ever met another person like him in my entire life. And then to have the honor to act with him and to act in a parallel environment: two friends, two friends.

Aaron Sorkin (Creator, Showrunner, Executive Producer)

There are a million things that I want to share about Martin, but I'll lead with this: Martin worked incredibly hard and obviously did a beautiful job. And look, this guy was in *Apocalypse Now*, this is Martin Sheen, and respect is owed. We had to fight Martin at the end of the first season—"we" being Tommy and myself—when it came time for Emmy submissions. For Emmy consideration, the studio or the network can submit the *show*, but the actors have to submit themselves, and Martin was insisting on submitting himself in the Supporting Actor category. He felt this is a show that doesn't have a star, it's an ensemble, and "it will be an insult to the other actors, particularly John Spencer, if I submit myself in the Best Actor category." The only way Tommy and I got him to change his mind is we convinced him that by submitting himself in a Supporting Actor category, he'd likely be taking a slot away from one of the other actors. That's the only thing that got him to do it.

★ ★ ★

THE domino effect of Martin Sheen's leadership on *The West Wing* family is, of course, impossible to quantify. In thinking about the book, Mary and I were deliberate about this: We wanted it to be clear to Martin how he has affected all of us, and how the role model he was (and is) continues to affect infinitely more people than he realizes. Which is kind of perfect because, well, that's what service does.

For so many of us from *The West Wing*, Martin Sheen's impact was profound. We learned from his example that justice is an intentional act, a decision to behave a certain way, to stand up and speak out. And to remember that community, equality, and respect are holy things . . . and that family is too. We learned from him that families eat together.

Amen to that.

THIRTY-SEVEN

SIN CITY AND
THE BINGO BUS

Ask your typical *West Wing* über-fan—your hard-core "Wingnut"—about the cast's best-known extracurricular adventures and they'll likely point you to Google for tales of virtual fundraisers or boots-on-the-ground campaigning in, say, Wisconsin or Ohio. Perhaps they'll steer you to YouTube for a Sorkin-flavored parody, where multiple cast members walk-and-talk for a good cause or a supremely talented state justice.

But there's another off-site *West Wing* exploit that few have ever heard of, and fewer still have seen. The Martin Sheen Vegas trips. (Um . . . "The Martin Sheen *what now?*") You read that right. Many count these trips among their best and brightest *West Wing* memories, and, until now, hardly anyone outside of the show knows a single thing about them.

We'll open with the abridged version: On several occasions during the run of *The West Wing*, Martin Sheen gifted the cast and crew an all-expenses-paid trip to Las Vegas. This generosity extended to every branch of the show's family tree, from core cast to background artists and crew. Giving thanks and paying respect to the work of every individual on the team is part of Martin's DNA. And if that was what these trips were about—if he had, say, splurged to send a bunch of co-workers off on a fun-filled weekend to a resort casino, on his dime—that would've been lovely. Amazing, even. But it wasn't just some distant dazzling *THANK YOU* in flashing neon lights. Martin rode along on the bus with everybody. Oh right, sorry, we should've mentioned—there was a bus. Or, well, actually . . . buses.

The number of people who went on the Vegas trips grew over the years, eventually clocking in at around a hundred cast and crew, so one bus wasn't gonna cut it. And, every time, speeding through Death Valley with everyone else, there he was—the life of the party. Telling stories and cracking jokes, Martin was the ringleader, buzzing down the aisle and making sure everyone was feeling included and having fun. As *The West Wing*'s dialogue coach, Hilary Griffiths, pointed out to us, "A lot of people might think, I spend enough time with these nuts, I don't want to be spending a weekend with them! Martin," Hilary says, "was quite the opposite."

According to Kim "Ginger, get the popcorn!" Webster, the trips often took place around Thanksgiving "for the Thanksgiving orphans who couldn't get home to their families." John Spencer attended a number of times, as did Kathryn Joosten. Having Leo and Mrs. Landingham along for the ride made the trip extra special for many crew members, and not just because they got to know those series regulars a little better and in a totally different context. The two seasoned veterans never failed to bring a splash of color to the adventure. The memory of John pulling up at the Warner Bros. lot in a shiny black limousine still brings a smile to the face of background artist Carla Ward. "He'd take a limo to the bus and take the bus to Las Vegas!" she told us. Kathryn Joosten, meanwhile, left her own mark, not figuratively, but literally—on the inside of one of the buses. (More on that down the road.)

If you're wondering if this kind of event is par for the course when it comes to Hollywood productions, we assure you it is not. To get a keener sense of just how rare it is, we sat down with Maxine Penty, a background artist who also served as Allison Janney's stand-in for several seasons. Maxine came onto the show later in its run, but early on had heard rumblings of this unorthodox tradition. "Someone said, 'Oh, Martin takes us all to Vegas every year!' I'm like, 'What now?' 'Oh yeah, he treats us. We play bingo!' I couldn't believe it. But lo and behold, here I am on the bus going to Vegas and, sure enough, playing bingo! It was unfathomable to me." On many productions, background talent are quite literally told not to speak to the lead actors. Martin, though, doesn't think of hierarchies like that. Everybody's equal—that's just how he's wired. Meanwhile, back on the Bingo Bus . . .

"We would gamble all the way there," Devika Parikh ("Bonnie") told us. Yes, as they rumbled through the Mojave toward Sin City, she and the rest of the gang would engage in those raucous games of bingo. Not just for cash—for *Martin's* cash. Martin would bring a case of money with him, so people would have enough to gamble with when they arrived at the casino. Plus, every one of them was handed an envelope with a hundred dollars inside. "There were cash prizes," Kim remembers, "regular prizes, all kinds of stuff. I won over a thousand dollars in bingo!"

The ride wasn't just about games and prizes, though. And it wasn't just about Martin's presence on the bus. It was about his *presence* on the bus. "He'd come along and nudge everyone," Maxine told us. "'Have ya won, kid, have ya won something?'" If you hadn't, that was simply not gonna fly. By God, you were not getting off that bus unless you'd won some of his cold, hard cash! So, thanks to Martin, everyone felt like a winner on the Vegas trip, even before they got to Vegas. Then they got to Vegas . . . and it was more of the same.

"We would pull into the Riviera parking lot," remembers Peter James Smith (the Ed half of "Ed and Larry"), "and everyone would pile off the buses. Then we'd head into the hotel, where Martin had arranged rooms for all of us." What Peter recalls most vividly is "all these people in the casino wanting to take pictures with us. It was pretty exciting."

Years later, Devika remains overwhelmed by Martin's generosity. "The fact that he even thought to do this for us and then put us up in Vegas? And treat us to see *O*—that was my first time ever seeing Cirque du Soleil!" Oh yeah—we almost forgot. He also took everyone to see Cirque du Soleil. (**MARY:** It's ridiculous at this point, right?)

And, again, just doing that would be more than enough, way beyond "more than enough." Except, wait 'til you hear from our friend background actor / stand-in David Katz. His plus-one on that Vegas trip was his wife, Cece. What sticks out in his memory is standing in line at the Bellagio to see that Cirque du Soleil show. "Martin had an extra ticket and there's this older lady trying to buy one off somebody. Martin just gives her the ticket. Like, 'Here's a ticket, there ya go.' And she got to sit next to Martin!"

But wait, there's even more! That's thanks to the presence of yet another background artist, Annette Sousa. Like so many others on *The West Wing*, Annette had prior Aaron and Tommy experience from her time on *Sports Night*. Annette remembers fans clamoring for snapshots with Martin and other members of the cast and still marvels at "President Bartlet" making his way through the Bellagio. "You should have seen him trying to get through the crowd!"

The casino whirlwind of it all—the clacking of chips and the ding-dinging of bells, the camera flashes and high-roller VIPs—was surreal. Then all of a sudden you look up and Margaret Hooper, Leo's faithful assistant, is spot-lit onstage with a mic in her hand. Talk about surreal. But it's true. Shortly before landing on *The West Wing*, NiCole Robinson started doing stand-up and she performed more than once during our trips to Vegas.

It sort of blows your mind, right? As Devika pointed out to us, "He made sure everybody won money on the way there so we had spending money—for something he was *already* paying for . . ." Devika couldn't contain an incredulous laugh. "I mean . . . who *is* this man?!"

But it's not just a matter of marveling at Martin's remarkable generosity. As Peter James Smith points out, it was "family-making."

Looking back on her experience, Devika appreciated the real, tangible effect those annual jaunts to Vegas had, professionally and otherwise. "I think it made us come together more as a family, as a functioning cast. We forged lifelong friendships."

Know who else felt that way? Dulé. As a series regular, spending time away from set with the crew and background artists meant a lot to him. "I loved the Vegas trip! The Bingo Bus? I'd do anything to go on the Bingo Bus with the *West Wing* family one more time."

For Annette, one image remains especially indelible. "We were at the Riviera, it was Martin and me at the slot machines. He had his hair hanging over his face and his glasses weren't on. He had this look like he was back in the 1950s or something. He looked like James Dean."

Of course, as with most endeavors in life, trips like this didn't happen by accident. They required serious prep and exhaustive logistical planning. "The idea initially came from [Martin's son] Ramón," Martin told us. "He had said, 'You've got to celebrate these folks. Take 'em on a trip.'" Ramón helped organize the three-day, two-night stays, but he didn't do it alone. Right there with him, booking rooms, renting buses, was a cast member you've likely never heard of. Lenore Foster. Lenore was a beloved *West Wing* background actor and a nurturing presence on set. Many saw her as the Mama Bear of that group.

Over the years, thanks to her involvement and cooperation with the Sheen family on the Vegas trips, Lenore and Martin grew close. After her time on *The West Wing*, Lenore made her way into service, working as a TSA officer at LAX.

"One day I was going through security and Lenore was checking the bags," Martin says. "She looked up and yelled at me, 'Mr. President!' I said, 'Oh, my God!' She risked her career, climbing over the security station to give me a hug!"

After Lenore passed away, early on a Saturday in December 2019, Melissa called Martin. "I knew how close they'd been from having worked together on those trips." When Melissa broke the news, Martin said, "Oh, God bless her. What an angel. What a sweet woman." And she was.

According to William Duffy (the Larry half of "Ed and Larry"), "after the show on Saturday night, Martin would sign off to the rest of us with, 'See you at Mass tomorrow!' The next morning I'd come down to the lobby and walk over to find Martin. I'd say, 'Ready for Mass?' He'd say, 'Yup. Off we go . . .' Then a few of us would head out for the half-mile walk—chatting about *The West Wing* or family, our childhoods—with fans excitedly greeting Martin all the way from the Riviera to Guardian Angel Cathedral."

That must've been a sight to see. A procession of hungover *West Wing* acolytes . . . and Martin, the former altar boy, leading the way into a church in Sin City.

"In we walk," Annette told us, "and people were like, 'O-kay . . .' They were so shocked to see President Bartlet at Mass on a random Sunday in Las Vegas. It's such a precious memory for so many of us."

(It is with crushing disappointment that we confess our failure to procure even one measly photo from those Sunday morning Masses. But then again, what happens in Vegas—even in church—stays in Vegas.)

As for leaving Las Vegas . . .

Anyone who's driven there will tell you, leaving Las Vegas is no fun at all. Four-plus hours on the I-15? Well, maybe it's no fun for you, but we're guessing you never took that ride with Martin Sheen. You see, the trip back home was almost as raucous as the bus ride up.

"The first year," Martin remembers, "everyone would win money on the bus and then lose it. The whole idea was for them to have extra Christmas money . . . and they were losing it all in Vegas." (**MARY:** You see where this is going?) "So, I said, 'Okay, fine. We'll do bingo when we're coming *home* too and we'll have the bigger jackpots then.'"

We'd take a moment to marvel at this, but we don't have time because we have to tell you about Martin's TOTALLY NORMAL OBSESSION with tracking down a Thanksgiving card. We'll let Annette field this one . . .

"Coming back from Vegas, we stopped in Barstow—because Martin wanted to get a Thanksgiving card." (**MELISSA:** Honestly, taking everything into account, that may be the single craziest sentence in the book. Is "Thanksgiving card" even a thing?) "He made the bus driver stop at the mall." Followed by a growing crush of fans, seeking autographs and photos with President Bartlet, Martin cheerfully crossed the lot and headed inside, a bona fide POTUS Pied Piper.

We interrupt this anecdote to let you know that Martin going into the mall to find a Thanksgiving card (three days after Thanksgiving) is not the only crazy part of this story. It's not the story at all, actually, so much as prologue to this: Remember that reference to Kathryn Joosten "leaving her mark"? It's time we got to the bottom of that.

As Martin's going in to get the card . . . Kathryn Joosten is on one of the buses making people laugh. (The bus driver, for the moment and for reasons unknown, is nowhere to be found.) All of a sudden she spots something and—HOLD ON. You know what? We're going "script mode" again.

INT. BINGO BUS — A BARSTOW PARKING LOT — DAY

Various *West Wing*-ers slump in their seats, hiding behind sunglasses and worse for wear. ANNETTE SOUSA sits several rows back, not far from JOHN SPENCER. Toward the front of the bus, KATHRYN JOOSTEN is waxing sarcastic to a captive audience. Then . . . .

Kathryn's eyes land on something:

A FLY on the windshield. Grabbing her NEWSPAPER, she rolls it
up and approaches the front of the bus. And . . . WHACK. Got
him! After a moment, the WINDSHIELD of the bus *cracks*,
spidering all the way down one side. Oh. My. God. All the air
is sucked out of the bus.

                    JOHN SPENCER
        Oh *shit*!

                    ANNETTE
        She broke the windshield. She <u>broke</u>
        the windshield!

Kathryn turns tail, hustles down the aisle toward Annette and
John, and ducks into a seat behind them.

                    KATHRYN
        (a paranoid whisper) Annette—don't
        say anything!

                    ANNETTE
        (whipping around, appalled) What?!

At that very moment, the BUS DRIVER climbs back onto the bus,
sits in his seat, taking in the wreckage of his once pristine
view. His expression falls. He looks around. WTF?

It's those oddball moments—barking out numbers on the Bingo
Bus, a random stop-off for a random greeting card, a windshield taken
out by the potent swat of a real-life Landingham—that turn a "trip"
into an *adventure*.

Turning a trip into an adventure—that's the gift of Martin Sheen,
quite literally the gift that keeps on giving. Like we said, he could've
just written a check and treated everyone to a well-earned weekend
getaway. Even that is way more than most of us ever do. The deeper
gift he gave was his time and his friendship.

In earlier chapters we dug into "the culture of *The West Wing*," but when it comes to "the *spirit* of *The West Wing*," it's impossible to miss whose shining example lit the way. The signs are all around us. To Sin City and back again.

★ ★ ★ **BIG BLOCK OF CHEESE STORY** ★ ★ ★

On Background

Hey there, it's Mary. One of the key jobs of the AD department involves managing and directing the actors often referred to colloquially as "extras" or "background." When I came on to *The West Wing*, I was struck by how excellent the show's background was. Because they aren't always. And unrealistic background acting can really take you out of the scene you're watching. Which brings us to Andrew Bernstein. In all my years in film and television, I've never worked with a better first AD than Andrew, who would go on to direct three *West Wing* episodes and, ultimately, become an esteemed and sought-after director in his own right. I remember saying to Andrew back then how the background actors moved with such purpose. He explained, "Well, we actually give them places to go. The form they're getting signed by C.J. is an actual form." (Props to Property Master Blanche Sindelar for that!) Andrew would tell them, "That desk over there is where you pick up this form, get it signed by C.J., then return it to the office down that way . . ." They weren't just crosses, they were crosses *somewhere*, to do *something*. Not only did that make for better television, it meant treating these actors like the professionals they were. Everyone does better work when everyone's being respected.

Maxine Penty had just landed on the show when an AD directed her to do a cross in the middle of a complicated walk-and-talk. "I said, 'Okay,' and then one of the other background actors went, 'Ohhhh, you're doing the suicide cross?'" Maxine didn't know what that meant. But it didn't sound good. "On the walk-and-talks," she says, "the 'suicide cross' meant you had to time it perfectly and slide in between the Steadicam guy walking backwards and Martin and Allison or whoever . . . it's about a six-foot gap . . . and somehow you had to wipe the lens." (**MARY:** A wipe is when an actor crosses very close to the camera so that their body obscures the lens for an instant. These wipes can be very helpful in editing.) "The suicide cross was absolutely terrifying—you're pressed up against the wall in the corridor, your heart is pounding, then you go and, my God, you gotta make it, you can't mess that up. It's a major reset, it's just terrifying."

Actor John Wan remembers the way Aaron and Tommy handled background and stand-ins like him on both *Sports Night* and *The West Wing*. "They treated people with so much respect, no matter what their position was. It was like, 'You're on the show, you're a professional, you're here for a reason. And we *trust* you.'"

Hi, it's Melissa. As Carol, I spent a good amount of time working with Andrew, who became a dear friend in the process. And on camera I spent a good amount of time outside C.J.'s office and inside the press room—two places where Andrew and the other ADs deployed a lot of background artists. Many of these actors worked on the show for the full run of the series . . . and it showed. They were exceptional people who were exceptional at their jobs. Talented, creative, key members of the cast, *The West Wing* background was, for my money, the best on television.

THIRTY-EIGHT

REUNITED . . .
(AND IT FEELS SO GOOD)

A West Wing *Special to Benefit*
"When We All Vote"

I t should've been like herding cats. Or spinning plates. It should've been like herding cats while spinning plates. All of these lives—once stitched together by early-morning calls to set, overtime shoots pushed deep into "Fraturday nights," and periodic trailer hopping on the Warner Bros. lot—had become so far-flung, so scattered, that successfully finding our way back to literal common ground seemed like the stuff of miracles. Except it wasn't. Sure, schedules and geography were complicating factors, but the will was there. The main culprit was the same for us as it was for everyone else in the world: COVID-19.

Everybody should have to stay
inside for three months so that
they truly appreciate the outdoors.

—JOSH TO C.J., TOBY, AND DONNA, "THE MIDTERMS"

Negotiating its testing and travel protocols was undeniably a challenge. And it didn't just come together like magic. It required focus and effort and *intention*. It took a slew of phone calls, text chains, and a shared sense of mission, but ultimately, thanks to spreadsheet technology, the good kind of group-think, and a little bit of faith—something vaguely akin to "celestial navigation"—we'd made it.

Weeks shy of what many of us considered the most important election of our lifetime, we had all reunited to film a staged adaptation of "Hartsfield's Landing," a fan-favorite episode from the show's third season. In support of encouraging voter participation in the fast-approaching 2020 election, on September 18 we descended upon the Orpheum Theatre in downtown LA. Once again, and at long last, the cast and crew of *The West Wing* were breathing the same air. (In the middle of a pandemic.)

And it all started, appropriately enough, with Aaron Sorkin and Tommy Schlamme.

AARON SORKIN: My lawyer was on the board of the Actors Fund, which is a charity that helps out mostly older actors, but anyone who works in the theater . . . during tough times. [The Actors Fund now goes by "the Entertainment Community Fund."] Because Broadway, off Broadway—all theaters—had shut down because of COVID, the Actors Fund was kind of overtaxed. So, I was asked if I might do some kind of benefit . . . a Zoom table read of an episode. That's all it was supposed to be, a Zoom for the Actors Fund.

Then George Floyd was murdered. Along with Breonna Taylor. It was the summer of 2020 . . . I thought that we should do something bigger. I was put in touch with When We All Vote, which is chaired by Michelle Obama, Lin-Manuel Miranda, and a few other people. I contacted Tommy, Brad,

Richard, Allison—the usual gang—and said, "Listen, do you want to do a Zoom table read for When We All Vote instead? It'll be a nice get-out-the-vote thing, just to make sure every *West Wing* fan goes to the polls.

(**MARY:** Just real quick—the Actors Fund wasn't forgotten. The *West Wing* cast did a fundraiser for them too.)

Enter Tommy Schlamme, a man who, as Aaron joked-while-meaning-it to us, "will not settle for a Zoom table read."

TOMMY SCHLAMME: I never could imagine going back to do the show again. I felt like, "I don't want my child to be *eight* again. I loved him being eight, but . . . he's *this* now, that's who he is." It was so precious and so beautiful, there's nothing but "it could break," you know? But then . . . to do it for a higher purpose, to have the excuse to be together again?

AARON SORKIN: Tommy has what turned out to be a really good idea. He says . . .

TOMMY SCHLAMME: Let's find a theater and restage an episode of the show as a *play*, and then I'll shoot it as a play, sort of in the style of a contemporary *Playhouse 90*.

AARON SORKIN: That got me really excited. In my head, I'm going through the Rolodex of episodes we should do. "Hartsfield's Landing," which ends up being a valentine to voting . . . I thought, This should be good. But, as with almost all of the episodes from the first four years, I haven't watched it since the night it aired. The reason for that is I'm terrified the show won't live up to my memory of it. But I've got the DVD box set . . . and I watched "Hartsfield's Landing" and it was great! I don't think

I've ever had that positive a response on the rare occasions that I've watched something I've written later on. Usually, it's like my high school yearbook picture—"I don't quiiiiiiiiite mind. I'm sure it was okay *then* . . ." But "Hartsfield's Landing" was beautifully shot, beautifully lit, the performances were fantastic, so I knew this was gonna be a winner.

BRADLEY WHITFORD: So this "Zoom table read" had now evolved into a filmed staged reading. Then I got a call from Tommy. It felt like I was in a time machine. Suddenly, we're back at the end of season 1, trying to figure out the best way to shoot the assassination at Rosslyn. At the end of the call, he goes . . .

TOMMY SCHLAMME: By the way, everybody's gonna have scripts, but Martin really wants to be off book.

BRADLEY WHITFORD: That was his way of letting me know I'd better get off book because this was gonna be a complete redo of the thing.

For the "complete redo," Aaron enlisted the help of former political operative (and former *West Wing* writer) Eli Attie . . .

AARON SORKIN: Where there were any act breaks—where there would ordinarily be commercials—I wanted to write interstitial material for various people to make "get-out-the-vote" pleas. Sometimes it was . . . actors from the show. Sometimes it was Bill Clinton.

ELI ATTIE: We had a ball. It was so delightful, emailing with Aaron all day again.

TOMMY SCHLAMME: I just couldn't wait to see everybody. I remember walking around. "Cathy Bond's there! And there's Lyn

Paolo!" It was like *The Wizard of Oz*: "And *you* were there, and *you* were there!" So, there was that joy . . . but I was in terror. Because I thought this could really fail. And [at first] Aaron wasn't reeeeeally supportive of the way I was doing it. He was still, "They should have scripts, they should just be in chairs onstage."

AARON SORKIN: It was gonna be actors, stools, music stands . . . You step forward when it's your scene.

MELISSA: That's what I thought it was!

TOMMY SCHLAMME: That's what *everybody* thought it was, which is why I was in terror!

AARON SORKIN: It was supposed to be two days of shooting at the Orpheum, but because Tommy's directing, it was *four* days of shooting at the Orpheum.

BRADLEY WHITFORD: There was something joyous about the whole thing. Then, in the doing of it, through Tommy and Aaron's ambition, you could feel it turning into something that was going to kind of overtake your life. The day before Janel and I are doing all our stuff—on one day—Tommy comes to me and goes . . .

TOMMY SCHLAMME: Aaron's gonna write a thing for you. You're going to do the intro. Aaron'll get it to you. Don't worry, it's gonna be really tight, really short.

BRADLEY WHITFORD: In the car at a stoplight, this long text comes in with the script on it. I'm like, "Fuuuuuuck!!" I call Tommy because I have to do it the next day. Suddenly I'm at a stoplight screaming like Josh, "*There is no way I'm doing this without a teleprompter!*"

While Brad was memorizing his lines via text and screaming at intersections—unlike Donna, it appears he *does* stop for red lights—other cast members began to trickle in. (And again, at that point it was the depths of COVID—pre-vaccine—so we were under hyper-strict protocols. Preproduction rehearsals on Zoom, six feet apart and shielded up when in person, daily testing . . . it was serious.)

DULÉ HILL: Walking in, it was like time stopped and went all the way back to Stage 23 at Warner Bros. It was such a heart-warming feeling to see everyone's beautiful faces again.

MELISSA: My job is based in DC, but because of COVID, I'd been working from home. I was able to take some time off work and fly out to do the special. I stayed with Allison.

ALLISON JANNEY: When Melissa got to my house, I told her I had a Zoom rehearsal with Tommy and Dulé for a scene I had with Dulé.

MELISSA: I said to Allison, "Oh! *I'm* in a scene with you and Dulé, which scene is it?" Allison flipped through her script and then . . .

ALLISON JANNEY: I looked at her: "You enter during this scene. Let's surprise them!"

MELISSA: I hadn't told Dulé when I was arriving, so he and Tommy didn't know.

ALLISON JANNEY: We were in my kitchen. Melissa was off to the side.

MELISSA: Tommy was about to read my line when I popped in on my cue. It's a pretty rare thing to see Tommy Schlamme speechless!

Arrivals for the HBO Max special, while unprecedented—all the swabs and tests and face shields—were otherwise sweetly familiar. The joyful faces and voices of cast and crew were streaming in, catching up . . . and falling into old habits.

RICHARD SCHIFF: I was struck by how easily we all fell right back into rhythm with each other.

BRADLEY WHITFORD: It was nostalgic and exciting and kind of awkward . . . a little like sleeping with your ex. And we wanted to throw our arms around each other, but with COVID, we couldn't. It was . . . an elbow-bump with Janel, then go to your separate trailers.

Once we got onstage, it was more of the same—everyone six feet apart and super vigilant about keeping everybody safe, especially Martin. That last part was a challenge.

BRADLEY WHITFORD: We had to keep reminding him about the six feet. He really wanted to hug us.

MARY: Of course he did. It probably took everything he had not to!

As onstage rehearsals began, cast gathered for the opening scene, which included *West Wing* reporters played by Chuck Noland and Tim Davis-Reed. It was the same old Martin.

CHUCK NOLAND: It was me and Tim meeting Bartlet at the airport, asking him questions. Allison and Martin were all the way across the stage. Martin comes over and goes, "Hi, I know you guys, you're Chuck and Tim, right?" Martin was never great at remembering names, so we were surprised and touched that after all these years, he remembered. Then he goes, "Of course I remembered . . . after the Big Lady reminded me."

Then there was the new guy . . .

AARON SORKIN: We needed someone to read John Spencer's part, and I wanted to get someone who I knew John would respect. And that was Sterling K. Brown.

STERLING BROWN: That I was even asked was a tremendous offer. Honestly, that was my show . . . and [there were] acting crushes that I've had for years.

When it came time to do the actual work, as Tommy predicted . . . Martin came to play.

BRADLEY WHITFORD: You can tell when people don't know their lines and have to kind of . . . rev up. Martin had a lot to do in that episode and he's not even looking at the sides. He was really ready.

AARON SORKIN: Sterling was scared. I had to reassure him. "No, no, no, hold the script in your hand. Everything's gonna be fine." He shows up and sees Martin and Richard rehearsing their first chess scene, and Martin is completely off book.

STERLING BROWN: Martin Sheen is eighty years old . . . he has the most lines in the episode by far and he's talking about chess moves and people in India . . . tricky stuff. I was like, "Oh, so *this* is what's happening." Everybody else saw and started rehearsing their scenes by their trailers outside.

AARON SORKIN: Sterling went, "This is the *opposite* of what you promised me!" And all of his scenes are with Martin.

MELISSA: Sterling kept saying, "I was told that I could hold the script!!" He was joking. He had such a good spirit about it.

STERLING BROWN: I didn't have much to do in the episode, but I was like, "Can I just sit in the audience and watch?" I was like a kid in a candy store.

With cast and crew seeming to pick up right where we all left off, it really was, as Brad said, like a time machine. There was Richard wandering around, bouncing a ball (**MELISSA:** The Spaldeen!), and Dulé offering up his signature click-clacking soundtrack.

DULÉ HILL: I always say, "I tap-dance everywhere." But I *really* love tap-dancing in special moments in special places. To be able to tap on that stage during that script was a way of giving thanks and honoring the journey of *The West Wing* and the relationships we've built.

MELISSA: A bunch of us were standing at the front of the stage between takes when Dulé started to tap. The joy he had in sharing this with us—the joy we had in watching him—brought me back to the countless times we saw him dance on set through the years.

Despite the esprit de corps flying around the theater, not everybody grasped the director's approach to the piece. At least at first they didn't.

MELISSA: Tommy had a vision for that episode that I could not picture for the longest time. Then, standing over at video village, waiting to make an entrance, I saw the camera sweep across the theater and I was like, oh my God . . . I see it now! It was so brilliant and beautiful and everything made sense . . . I'll never forget that moment.

But it wasn't all easy-breezy.

Some of us had a heavier lift than others. Some of us had to spit out phrases like: "an invasion of Penghu Islands" and "Keyhole shows ten AH-1W helicopters" and "on the tarmac at Chingchuankang" and "Xinhua's reporting the live fire exercises." And when we say "some of us," we really mean . . . just one.

ANNA DEAVERE SMITH: Because we were in lockdown, I spent the entire time . . . in my hotel and then in my trailer . . . either repeating the words over and over, listening to the pronunciation of a word or watching video of Condoleezza Rice and Madeleine Albright.

MARY: I really feel her pain. All the ten-dollar words—so stressful. But it's an occupational hazard of the National Security Advisor game.

TOMMY SCHLAMME: I'd seen other [Zoom] productions . . . and they were great, everybody was "together" again . . . But this was a show that had created a sort of visual palette.

Yes, Tommy had a clear idea for the special's key visual elements. This meant yet another "reunion"—the return of the show's original production designer, Jon Hutman.

JON HUTMAN: Tommy called me. At that point they had already scouted the Orpheum and didn't really love what the bare stage looked like. So we built the brick background and the wood floor with a faint checkerboard pattern. It was my first time designing for theater since just after college.

Tommy and Jon talked about different "zones" of the stage, how the episode would flow from one scene to another and which elements could effectively suggest the Oval, the offices, double doors, arches. But even as they wanted to clearly define those spaces, the design team very consciously wanted viewers to feel they were in this empty theater.

JON HUTMAN: The Mural Room had four chairs and a chandelier . . . with the theater's fly-rail ropes clearly visible in the background. That was intentional. Tommy's vision was for this to be "the show seen through the filter of a theater."

Every element, the theory went, would feel organic to the old show, while bringing something fresh to the table. That extended to the performances as much as anything.

JANEL MOLONEY: The difference was interesting . . . the "will they, won't they" of it . . . because I'm so much older and Brad's so much older . . .

JOSH MALINA: "Will they, won't they?" It's more like "Will they, *could* he?"

JANEL MOLONEY: To play Donna again felt so easy, like putting on this really comfortable costume, like, "Oh, I remember this."

ROB LOWE: [When *The West Wing* initially aired] I was more exuberant, puppylike and bright-eyed. Playing Sam in those scenes with that quizzical, searching, enthusiastic positive energy was something now I had to *play*, whereas [in 2002] it was just built in.

MARTIN SHEEN: I knew the chess scenes with Toby were going to be powerful. Because it was an election year, they were more important, and so tense. What Richard was playing . . . gave me goose pimples when he yelled at me. I'll never forget that.

```
                       TOBY
        You're a good father, you don't have
        to act like it. You're the President,
        you don't have to act like it. You're
        a good man, you don't have to act
        like it. You're not a regular guy,
        you're not just folks, you're not
        plain-spoken . . . Do not, do not,
        do not act like it!
```

MARTIN SHEEN: It was a far better scene now because both of us had matured. He was *urgent.* That was the most memorable part of that show for me, his performance.

From Emily Procter's soothing Southern drawl reading the stage directions . . . to the gorgeous, acoustic *West Wing* theme emanating from the fingertips of an on-screen Snuffy Walden . . . through dueling chess matches between Bartlet and his senior staff . . . and all the way to the cool and surprising transition to the 2002 "Hartsfield's Landing," the special felt rooted in the original version of the show, but abstract and theatrical in a wholly new way. It felt at once timeless and timely.

In the end, what was a massive collaboration—and, as Malina put it, "an ode to theater"—came down to one man's vision.

AARON SORKIN: There's no one in the world who loves Tommy Schlamme more than I do, there really isn't. Tommy, with "Hartsfield's Landing," just hit it out of the park. He staged it beautifully, lit it beautifully, shot it beautifully. I don't care that it took four days. The whole time . . . it was like nothing had changed.

A West Wing Special to Benefit "When We All Vote" raised the visibility of—and, according to Aaron, over a million dollars for—an organization whose sole mission is simple: to increase voter participation in each and every election. For those of us who had the privilege of being there, it was that and so much more.

We got to gather together. We got to return to the scene of the time of our lives and revel in the spirit of reunion and democracy. When it was all over, we didn't want to go.

"After we finished filming," Allison remembers, "something dawned on me. I turned to Melissa and said, 'You're working from home, right?' She said she was. So I said, 'Well, if you're going to work from home, why not work from *my* home?'"

I stayed with Allison for six weeks. You want to know why I finally flew home?

I had to get back to *vote*!

★ ★ ★ **BIG BLOCK OF CHEESE STORY** ★ ★ ★

Labor of Love

By the late summer of 2023, the Writers Guild of America had been on strike for 113 days, the SAG-AFTRA actors for 40 days. August 22 was declared the National Day of Solidarity, which is how it came to pass that Aaron Sorkin, the cast, crew, and fans of *The West Wing* took to the streets outside the Disney studio lot, joining thousands of our union brothers and sisters to raise picket signs, march in protest, and make our voices heard.

Josh Malina's sign made good on a promise he'd issued the night before. It read, "I CAN'T ACT. I'M A TERRIBLE ACTOR. PAY ME." And his wasn't the only *West Wing*–fashioned sign. Another pointed out that "DONNA WOULD'VE FIXED THIS BY NOW!"

As chanting picketers continued their boisterous laps around the towering studio gates, a number of us made our way onto a makeshift stage to address the crowd. Brad spoke briefly, as did Richard, but the keynote speech was delivered by Martin.

"Clearly this union has found something worth fighting for," he said, "and it is costly. If this were not so, we would be left to question its value. And so now we are called to support the union, support the leadership, and to stand together for the long haul, and to stick to it like a stamp! The studios are always seeing what is and asking 'Why?' Let us continue to dream things that never were and say, 'Why not?'"

Listening to him speak, and looking around as he exhorted the crowd, it was impossible to miss the innate ability Martin still has to inspire, energize, and uplift; the gift he has not just for words, but for using them to bring people together in service of a common purpose. It's the same life he breathed into President Bartlet.

And so it was that on a hot mid-August morning in 2023, at the corner of Keystone and Riverside in Burbank, California, hope and solidarity got a shot in the arm, and labor got the love it deserves. An already union-strong movement—and an already strong family of friends—enjoyed a kind of renewal that day. Renewal, despite the fact that our commitment to one another, to work and service, and to what we believe in, never really fades. It sticks, as a wise man has been heard to say, like a stamp.

THIRTY-NINE

STAY ALIVE

The West Wing, Hamilton . . . and Washington

The ripple effects of *The West Wing* are wide-ranging in the realms of politics and media, the local kinds and otherwise. During the run of the series, and in the decades that followed, countless political leaders, staffers, journalists, and activists have pointed to the show as having played a role in driving them toward their chosen careers. A similar impact has been felt in the world of entertainment. A steady stream of next-generation actors, writers, directors, and designers have reportedly drawn inspiration from the show. This enduring influence can be found in one of the iconic works of art in our lifetime, the musical *Hamilton*.

The trio of figures most responsible for that Pulitzer Prize–winning piece of theater are its Tony Award–winning writer and star Lin-Manuel Miranda; its Tony Award–winning director, Thomas Kail; and the Tony Award–hoarding show's Tony Award–winning orchestrator and musical director, Alex Lacamoire. To say that they're all big *West Wing* fans is something of an understatement. Lin-Manuel says that he feels like *The West Wing* has been "injected into my veins," having watched the entire series several times, and having seen some of his favorite episodes many more times than that.

For the creator and star of *Hamilton*, the appeal of *The West Wing* went beyond the writing, performances, and aspirational themes that first struck a chord with him back when he discovered the show in reruns on Bravo. It originates with the show's fictional universe, which was one he could relate to . . . and one with which he's deeply familiar.

LIN-MANUEL MIRANDA: My dad's been in politics for as long as I've been around. [He] worked in community organizing for a really long time. When I went to college, he went from "nonprofit" to "for profit," so he could help me pay for college.

Luis Miranda Jr. has spent decades working in and advocating for, among others, New Yorkers and the city's labor force. According to his son, Luis is "basically a democratic political lobbyist." Put another way . . .

TOMMY KAIL: His dad is Bruno Gianelli.

LIN-MANUEL MIRANDA: My dad is Bruno Gianelli.

Played superbly by the late, great Ron Silver, *The West Wing*'s Bruno Gianelli was a campaign manager and political consultant whose party allegiance was, unlike Luis Miranda, decidedly fluid, but whose core belief in America was similarly rock-solid.

LIN-MANUEL MIRANDA: What I liked about *West Wing* was I kind of understood the way politics worked because I'd seen it firsthand, with my dad's work—being the kid dragged to a meeting on a weekend . . . doing my homework in a corner while they're deciding who's going to run in a district. So, between my upbringing and *West Wing*, I was interested in how politics works, without actually being interested in *working* in politics.

In addition to being set in a world he knew intimately, *The West Wing* possessed a theatrical quality, was created by a playwright with a musical sense of fast-paced wordsmithing, and featured a cast of veteran stage actors choreographed into flowing walk-and-talks. Plus, the show revolves around a group of flawed patriots, including a world-class leader and a right-hand man or two (or three or four) looking to achieve great things and do a little good, with the country's best interests in mind. Sounds pretty appealing . . . and pretty familiar. For every C.J., Josh, and Toby, there's a Laurens, a Lafayette, and a Schuyler sister or two. (And Peggy.) Playing Alexander Hamilton's Leo to George Washington's Jed Bartlet, Lin-Manuel Miranda relished the many parallels. Even if, according to the writer, most of them were unintentional.

LIN-MANUEL MIRANDA: A good amount of the *West Wing* references in *Hamilton* are subconscious; like "mind at work," which seems so deliberate.

Because before I look for anything,
I look for a mind at work.

—SAM SEABORN TO AINSLEY HAYES,
"THE U.S. POET LAUREATE"

I'm lookin' for a mind at work,
I'm lookin' for a mind at work. . . .

—ANGELICA SCHUYLER,
"THE SCHUYLER SISTERS," *HAMILTON*

Whether the writer consciously tracked the connections between one of his favorite TV shows and the Broadway hit he and his team brought to revolutionary life, there's no denying their predominance. "The references," he concedes, "keep showing up." Like that tender moment from "The Women of Qumar," when Toby stands at the back of the press room and, in a gesture of empathy and affection for C.J., places his hands over his heart.

TOMMY KAIL: In "One Last Time" there's a moment where Hamilton does the Richard Schiff heart moment. That's not pre-scribed in all the companies. That was for Lin and Chris [Jack-son]. That's a steal from *The West Wing*.

On the other hand . . .

LIN-MANUEL MIRANDA: One that was totally subconscious . . . is in "That Would Be Enough." That song has no historical pre-cedent, there's no textbook I got that from. It was just a very real moment of "I love you, no matter what."

So long as you come home at the end of the day,
that would be enough.

—ELIZA TO ALEXANDER,
"THAT WOULD BE ENOUGH," *HAMILTON*

LIN-MANUEL MIRANDA: Then I later see Bartlet saying it to Ellie and I was like, "Aw, shit! I took that too!"

> The only thing you ever had to do to make me
> happy was come home at the end of the day.
>
> —PRESIDENT BARTLET TO HIS DAUGHTER ELEANOR, "ELLIE"

Don't feel too bad, Lin-Manuel, even Aaron stole that one. (From himself.)

> The only thing you have to do to make me and
> Mom happy is come home at the end of the day.
>
> —CASEY McCALL TO HIS SON CHARLIE,
> "WHAT KIND OF DAY HAS IT BEEN?," *SPORTS NIGHT*

LIN-MANUEL MIRANDA: It's a testament to how many times I've seen all these [*West Wing*] episodes. The only real deliberate one is something called "The Redcoat Transition." It's not on the album, but it's the transition between "You'll Be Back" and "Right Hand Man." The drum fill is the "Previously . . . on" drum fill. Every time I was backstage during it . . . I'd whisper to Chris Jackson: "Previously . . . on *The West Wing*."

Chris Jackson originated the role of George Washington in *Hamilton*. According to Lin-Manuel, Chris, too, is a "huge *West Wing* fan." Then there's Tommy Kail. The *Hamilton* director has gone so far as to deem *The West Wing* "an influencer," both artistically and in terms of his partnership with his own personal Jed.

TOMMY KAIL: The relationship between Leo and the president... is an incredibly formative one for me, especially in my dynamic with Lin. [Jed and Leo] are two people that had such a deep affection and love for each other. It just *was*. You don't have to say it all the time, you show it in a gesture . . . you give somebody a napkin.

You do indeed. In fact, in reference to both the TV series and the musical they had created together, at one point Tommy gave Lin-Manuel a version of the "Bartlet for America" napkin. As a sardonic nod toward how long *Hamilton* had taken to gestate, the scrawl on the napkin read, "MORE THAN ONE SONG A YEAR."

When Lin-Manuel looked at the napkin, he knew precisely what his *West Wing*–themed reply had to be.

LIN-MANUEL MIRANDA: Right on cue, I said . . . "That was awfully nice of you."

Months later, on *Hamilton's* opening night, Lin-Manuel returned the favor, framing the napkin and presenting it to Tommy, as Jed did for Leo. This wasn't just a *Hamilton* thing. Throughout other collaborations, the two friends and colleagues saw the nature of their dynamic as distinctly "Jed and Leo."

LIN-MANUEL MIRANDA: It was a very handy metaphor during the making of both *In the Heights* and *Hamilton*. I'm Jed in this scenario, out in front and articulating a vision for a show, and Tommy Kail's wrangling a creative team to make that vision come to life in every conceivable detail. There's a huge distance between writing the thing and *making* the thing, just as there is a huge distance between our ideals and beliefs . . . and making them law.

The crossover connections between *The West Wing* and *Hamilton* aren't exclusive to the collaborative or thematic common ground of the two shows. They include some of the actors themselves. Like that time a pair of Wesleyan alums found themselves face-to-face at four in the morning in the university library. Picture Lin-Manuel, sitting there, frantic, writing like he's running out of time . . .

LIN-MANUEL MIRANDA: [I'm working on] my commencement speech, and Bradley Whitford's on campus. He's like, "Hey, let's get coffee!" It was probably as *West Wing*–y as real life got—here comes Bradley Whitford to take me out for coffee while I'm trying to write a speech! So, he became an instant friend. He just loved [*Hamilton*] and was an early town crier for it. Then Richard Schiff came and became a *literal* crier. We both burst into tears, in each other's arms, when he came to see the show. It [was] amazing, person by person in the company coming to see it. We freak out when we see those guys.

One of our favorite stories about the creative forces behind *Hamilton* involves one of our favorite stories from *The West Wing*.

BRAD WHITFORD: The line Leo says to Josh at the end of the a-guy-falls-into-a-hole speech—"Long as I got a job, you got a job"—Lin says that to Tommy Kail every time they talk to each other.

This spirit—of looking out for each other, of "I am my brother's keeper"—represents additional connective tissue between *Hamilton* and *The West Wing*. Lin-Manuel and the *Hamilton* creatives have done much to promote good in the world, to look out for as many "others" as they can. This, he suggests, stems from a kind of patriotic empathy that runs through the musical, and whose spirit he observed in *The West Wing* as well.

> **LIN-MANUEL MIRANDA:** I've been heartened to see that the many actors who have participated in *Hamilton* have also been inspired to service. So much so, in fact, that we created a separate online platform called Ham4Progress devoted to causes and issues important to the actors who tell this story every night.

Listening to Lin-Manuel speak about *Hamilton* and its philosophical bedrock, you can't help but hear the echo of what Aaron, Tommy, and John instituted as core *West Wing* values: a vision of America, at its best, as an exercise in argument—periodically respectful, often combative, and always passionate—in service of better outcomes.

> **LIN-MANUEL MIRANDA:** We have a show that, in telling *Hamilton*'s story, brushes through the messy and contradictory origins of our country. If there's any particular viewpoint, it's that our country is flawed because humans are flawed, and the disagreements present at our founding are the disagreements we're *still* grappling with. What *West Wing* and *Hamilton* share is a vision of people with honestly earned, often clashing beliefs of what this country is and could be.

We would be remiss if we didn't mention the granddaddy of all *Hamilton* / *West Wing* crossovers. It came at the curtain call for Lin-Manuel's last Broadway performance in the title role. For Lin's final bow, as a surprise tribute to the star and creator of the show, *Hamilton*'s music director (and fellow Wingnut), Alex Lacamoire, and his orchestra struck up the *West Wing* theme. Yet another Wingnut, Chris Jackson, was in on it too and playfully nudged Lin-Manuel out for one last center-stage moment, to the tune of Snuffy's music. It was a perfect, emotional goose-bumps moment. That was the final beat for the original cast of the latest greatest story ever told. The *first* one took place, appropriately enough, in the actual White House.

As part of an Obama administration event, "An Evening of Poetry, Music & the Spoken Word," Lin-Manuel performed the first cut from what, at the time, was set to be a hip-hop concept album about the life and times of "the ten-dollar founding father." On that May night in 2009, early into the first term of another aspirational, inspirational American president, Lin-Manuel had this to say about George Washington's right-hand man: "Alexander Hamilton . . . on the strength of his writing . . . embodied the word's ability to make a difference."

That notion—that words can make a difference—lives at the heart of each of these shows. Whether they originate from the mind of Aaron Sorkin or John Wells, Lin-Manuel Miranda or Alexander Hamilton or one of the countless unsung heroes "in the room where it happened," words have the potential to inspire, cajole, convince, and transform. And, every so often, when they find themselves in just the right hands, they can offer a road map to who we were and who we are . . . and who we hope to be. Which takes us from *Hamilton* . . . to Washington.

★ ★ ★

AS mentioned at the top of this chapter, countless Washington, DC, residents, from activists to political leaders and their staffers to members of the media, reportedly landed in the nation's capital thanks, at least to some degree, to *The West Wing*. Here they are, Wingnuts all.

State Senator Mallory McMorrow (Michigan Senate)

On April 19, 2022, a state senator from Michigan's Thirteenth District took to the floor of the Michigan statehouse to respond to some false allegations made against her in a fundraising email.

No child alive today is responsible for slavery.
No one in this <u>room</u> is responsible for slavery.
But each and every one of us bears
responsibility for writing the next chapter of
· history. Each and every one of us decides what
happens next.

—MALLORY McMORROW, APRIL 19, 2022

Within hours, video of the speech went viral for its soaring rhetoric, for the cool confidence, the fiery passion—the commonsense appeal to the better angels of our nature. You should really check out the whole less than five minutes on YouTube. It's positively Bartletesque.

SENATOR McMORROW: I went to college at Notre Dame and Martin Sheen was our commencement speaker the year before Barack Obama came.

My mom taught me at a very young age that
Christianity and faith was about being part of a
community; about recognizing our privilege
and blessings and doing what we can to be of
service to others.

—MALLORY McMORROW, APRIL 19, 2022

While State Senator McMorrow admits "you can never watch it too many times," the moment *The West Wing* really left its mark on her came in season 2.

> **SENATOR McMORROW:** Once we got to the "Let Bartlet be Bartlet" episode, the show embodied "This is what government can and should be at its best." We always joke that our job is actually *Parks and Recreation*, but we <u>want</u> it to be *The West Wing*. How hard everybody works—our staff running around at all hours of the night, trying to put all the pieces together—that's what came through in the show. These are fictional characters, but they're grappling with the same issues we do in real life. It's refreshing that I can go to bed at night knowing I tried. It's not always going to work, but you're going to try together. We accept that our day-to-day is *Parks and Recreation* . . . but we aspire to be *The West Wing*.

Eden Tesfaye (Senior Official at the Centers for Medicare and Medicaid Services)

As an official in the Department of Health and Human Services, Eden Tesfaye knows what it means to dedicate a life to her fellow Americans.

> **EDEN TESFAYE:** *The West Wing* has inspired so many generations of political operatives—Republicans and Democrats. It's the show we all watch after a campaign loss, a bad vote on the Hill. The show is a beacon of inspiration to all of us in this line of work.

> **PRESIDENT BARTLET**
> We made it to the New World, Josh.
> You know what I get to do now? I
> get to proclaim a national day of
> Thanksgiving. This is a great job.

EDEN TESFAYE: I love the episode "Shibboleth." I watch it around Thanksgiving each year. It continues to inspire me to keep fighting for those who can't fight for themselves: people like my mother, father, and other immigrants who come to this country with a dream for a better life for their themselves and their families.

Brendan Boyle (PA District 2)

Founder and co-chair of the "Blue Collar Caucus," Brendan Boyle was the first member of his family to graduate from college, having earned a degree from a certain university that the show held in high regard.

CONGRESSMAN BOYLE: I watched *The West Wing* from day one. I graduated—like Bartlet—from Notre Dame. I was a government major and wanted to do exactly what I'm doing now. Eventually I landed in the House of Representatives. More than twenty years after the show debuted, it's still with me. There are days now when you'll be part of passing some legislation—like right before we passed the [2021] infrastructure bill, just before midnight . . . after *years* of trying. The applause on the House floor when we hit 218 votes. I'm thinking, "This is really a *West Wing* moment."

Then there's the congressman's former chief of staff, John McCarthy. Long before rising to his current position as "Deputy Assistant to the President and Senior Advisor to the Counselor to the President," John was an eighth grader who "watched the show religiously" and, in college, "organized on-campus screenings." As he put it to us, "*The West Wing* made me want to work in Washington and ultimately the White House." No wonder he and Brendan hit it off.

JOHN McCARTHY: Brendan and I both love politics and think there's a nobility in public service, so the show really resonated with us. We would reference it constantly. Still do. Whenever

there are things happening in public life today, we will often send
each other texts with clips from the show.

The show's idealism appealed to Brendan, not just as a self-
proclaimed "political junkie," but also as a young man trying to figure
out his version of what's next. These days, that idealism has met
head-on with the hardscrabble reality of a life and career in politics.

CONGRESSMAN BOYLE: Watch episodes from twenty years ago
and see. The gun issue is exactly the same now. It's funny how
reluctant some are to label *The West Wing* "reality" compared to
other political shows. When *House of Cards* was big . . . I enjoyed
it, it's so outlandish and crazy . . . but for a lot of people that's their
perception of Congress. I tell them, "No, it's nothing like that at
all. *The West Wing* will have a happier ending more often than
day-to-day, but it's a far more realistic portrayal of what it's like to
work in politics." They're really surprised by that. People can be so
cynical that they won't allow themselves to believe that good
things can happen. But they can. *The West Wing* wasn't lying.

Kurt Bardella (Political Operative, Press Secretary, Commentator)
Prior to becoming a familiar face on cable news as a journalist and political commentator for MSNBC, Kurt Bardella served as deputy communications director for Republican representative Darrell Issa and as
a spokesman for the far-right media platform Breitbart News. In 2017,
disillusioned after decades spent serving Republican administrations
and causes, Kurt left the GOP. Through the years, though, one thing
hasn't changed. He's always been a hard-core Wingnut.

KURT BARDELLA: I discovered *The West Wing* by accident. I
was a junior in high school and with my mom in a thrift store in
San Diego. There was this VHS set of "For Your Consideration"

screeners. Rob Lowe was on the cover of one. Schiff . . . Brad Whitford . . . Allison. And it was a show about politics. I said, "I'm interested in politics—why not?!" *The West Wing* made that world a little more accessible and, even though it was fictional, gave me some foundational understanding of how this world might work, what I might do in it.

Despite working for most of his career as an avowed Republican, Kurt never really disagreed with the politics of the show.

KURT BARDELLA: Everybody around me was a Republican, so I wasn't getting the other half of the story—outside of *The West Wing*. And at the time there was all kinds of stuff about the show being "preachy," about the "liberal bias in Hollywood." But as a Republican, I never felt that way. There was always someone taking the other side. At times from *within* the administration . . . C.J. would present the contrarian view in an artful, intelligent way.

We gave both sides in almost every argument. Most of the time, our heroes won, sometimes they didn't, but when they didn't, we kind of understood why that was okay, and that's just the way the government is supposed to work. I think that's what spoke to people who were actually doing this every day . . . that are actually trying to accomplish movement for the better.

—PRODUCER MIKE HISSRICH, INTERVIEW FOR *WHAT'S NEXT*

KURT BARDELLA: Republicans weren't painted as necessarily evil. They were coming from different perspectives but had good hearts. So many people who served during the Bush years are huge fans of the show—I came up as a Republican working with them. *The West Wing*, at least when I talked about it in my circle, was never frowned upon. We *all* watched.

In some ways, you look at *The West Wing* like a time capsule from a different moment. The people coming up right now probably can't imagine a time in which *The West Wing* even happened because our entire democracy is built on the premise that the losing side will accept that they're the losing side. I don't know if there is anything left that's bipartisan because once you've crossed a threshold where just believing in democratic norms isn't a bipartisan thing anymore, everything else goes up in flames. *The West Wing* now . . . it's aspirational. This is what we need to be. This is what we're trying to get back to.

State Senator Sarah McBride (Delaware State Senate)

In 2020, Sarah McBride made history as the nation's first openly transgender state senator, winning her bid to represent Delaware's First State Senate District. On Tuesday, November 5, 2024, she will look to make her mark once more, this time as US Congress's first openly transgender member. Long before achieving these milestones, Sarah counted herself as a member of the Obama-Biden White House, the national spokesperson for the Human Rights Campaign . . . and a <u>massive</u> fan of *The West Wing*.

SARAH McBRIDE: I can still remember when my parents mentioned to me this show about the president's staff. I was probably ten years old and already enraptured with politics. As a young trans kid buried deep in the closet, politics seemed like the place where I could help make the world become kinder and more just.

I'd count down the hours on Wednesday nights until a new episode of *The West Wing* would air. It was a glimpse into an environment filled with people I saw myself in: passionate, curious, inspired by the possibilities in our politics, and committed to seeing them become a reality. From the death penalty and gay rights to gun safety and healthcare, each episode gave me a language to more fully understand my own youthful values and opinions. But as I've grown up, it was the deeper personal and moral questions that the show grappled with that stay in my mind. As I wrestled with the decision to move from advocacy to elective office, taking on races that were unprecedented for people like me, and uncertain what to do, I would hear the immortal words of Mrs. Landingham in my mind: "You know, if you don't want to run again, I respect that. But if you don't run because you think it's gonna be too hard or you think you're gonna lose, well, God, Jed, I don't even want to know you."

What a valuable lesson for all of us: We don't owe it to someone else to pursue a new opportunity, but we do owe it to ourselves not to let our fear of hard work or of losing stand in the way of putting ourselves out there.

Reggie Love (Former Special Assistant / Personal Aide to President Obama)

As President Obama's "body man"—his Charlie Young, if you will—Reggie Love had an up-close and personal look at the nation's forty-fourth commander in chief. Now a senior advisor at Apollo Global Management, back in 2008 Reggie's pursuit of politics and public service led him to the doorstep of a fellow *West Wing* fan.

REGGIE LOVE: Because the president had loved the show, when he was a candidate I bought the seven seasons on DVD and would carry that box of DVDs with me. I carried it the whole campaign, because every night he would watch an episode or two. And there would be [times] where you're like, "Man, you're kinda draggin'. We got a big day today. Did you stay up watching five episodes of *The West Wing* last night?"

Then when my brother got to DC, he watched *The West Wing* with me. I've probably had five sets of friends who've watched my DVD box set of *The West Wing*. I still have it.

MARY: In 2008 I was in Albuquerque, shooting *In Plain Sight*. Three days before the election, Michael and I went to a rally at the University of New Mexico to see then senator Obama deliver one of his last campaign speeches. He brings the house down and bounds off the stage and comes over to greet our section. It's a quick grip-and-grin—he's got to hightail it out to someplace else. I'm standing there, cheering, all caught up in the moment, and— I swear—Obama looks at me and goes, "Oh my God, you're Kate Harper!" I was like, "No, no, no—*you're* the next president of the United States in, like, forty-eight hours!" He said, "You're the *national security advisor!*" Later, Reggie told us . . .

REGGIE LOVE: We were literally in the car on the way to the rally, watching the Peace in the Middle East episodes!

That's what Barack Obama, soon-to-be forty-fourth president of the United States, was doing as he drove to one of his last campaign stops—bingeing the Camp David episodes in the back of the car!

Bill O'Brien (Senior Advisor for Program Innovation at the National Endowment for the Arts)
Two decades before Bill O'Brien's career path led him to the National Endowment for the Arts and the nation's capital, he was the producing director and managing director of the Los Angeles theater company

Deaf West. In 1999, Deaf West's board president alerted him to a *West Wing* audition for "Kenny," the sign language interpreter for a Deaf pollster, Joey Lucas, played by Marlee Matlin.

> **BILL O'BRIEN:** The thing that struck me right away is that they were treating Joey Lucas as an exceptionally gifted, visionary pollster who had something to contribute. Her Deafness was never called out. They just allowed her to exist as a super-high-functioning person—the smartest person in the room most of the time—without commenting on it.

Now the senior advisor for program innovation at the NEA, over time Bill's appreciation for *The West Wing* has grown, even as he sees it as "an idealized way of thinking about politics."

> **BILL O'BRIEN:** It's easy to brush aside politics. But to see people in government fight the good fight . . . that's what *West Wing* was so good at. Josh Lyman . . . and everybody who gathered at Leo's table . . . were constantly barraged with challenging situations that are hard to unpack. They would [approach] a problem with "I don't know, but I'm going to try and I'm going to be anchored in what I believe is best."

María Teresa Kumar (President/CEO of Voto Latino and the Voto Latino Foundation)

President and CEO of the country's largest effective Latino voter registration and Latino youth advocacy organizations, María Teresa Kumar advised President Obama's Task Force on 21st Century Policing and currently serves on the National Task Force on Election Crises, the Brookings Institution's Working Group on Universal Voting, and the board of Emily's List. Also, she was in on *West Wing* from day one.

MARÍA TERESA KUMAR: *The West Wing* stood out from its first episode for its intelligence, humor, and clever storytelling. But the reason the show has left an enduring mark on so many people is its relentless heart—its unflinching thesis that there are good intentions and genuine humanity everywhere you look in the political process. While that might not always feel like the world we live in, it gave us a reason to believe in our better angels. That very much drives my work. I try to help our political process find its better angels, to help empower people to believe that their voice counts in our democracy.

Asked for a favorite *West Wing* moment, María came up with a couple . . .

MARÍA TERESA KUMAR: Among so many great moments in the show—including the final season showing Matt Santos (played by the excellent Jimmy Smits) becoming America's first Latino president—there are two lines that always stick with me. In "Hartsfield's Landing," C.J. and Josh are discussing a small town's peculiar voting practice. The eminently quotable press secretary says that "freedom is the glory of God, that democracy is its birthright, and that our vote matters." May that always be true.

The second moment is from "H. Con-172" and stands out because of what it says about leadership, and about what we should demand of our leaders.

I may not have had sinister intent at the outset but there were plenty of opportunities for me to make it right. No one in government takes responsibility for anything anymore. We foster, we obfuscate, we rationalize. "Everybody does it." That's what we say. So, we come to occupy a moral safe house where everyone's to blame so no one's guilty. I'm to blame. I was wrong.

—PRESIDENT BARTLET TO HIS STAFF, "H. CON-172"

MARÍA TERESA KUMAR: Imagine a world where leaders on both sides of the aisle had that type of moral courage. That's the standard to which we should hold elected officials—or anyone charged with authority. *The West Wing* was full of the power of persuasion. We need more of that—a culture in which we can disagree without being disagreeable, a country where good ideas have a chance to break down partisan divides.

Patrick Murphy (Iraq War Veteran, 32nd Army Under Secretary, Former US Congressman)

As the first Iraq War veteran ever to serve in Congress, Patrick Murphy is a trailblazer. Having served in the Obama administration as the nation's 32nd Under Secretary of the Army, he is now a "vet-repreneur" and Wharton Business School lecturer.

PATRICK MURPHY: *West Wing* flat out inspired me to go into political public service. After coming home from Iraq, I ran for Congress and got a chance to work with the phenomenal cast on the repeal of the discriminatory "Don't Ask, Don't Tell" policy, and later did so in the Pentagon when leading the army.

As a devout Catholic and former federal prosecutor, for me "Take This Sabbath Day" had a special meaning on the tough issue of the death penalty. The president wanted one of the three religious leaders he spoke with to give him the answer—should he allow the death penalty to be executed as ordered by the courts? What always struck me about this episode is the heavy burden of leadership. Acting on behalf of everyone, setting aside his own personal religious beliefs, weighs on the president's conscience, as do the consequences of his action or inaction. Watching it—and rewatching it—just humanized President Bartlet and the life-and-death decisions he faced. It went above and beyond the pomp and circumstance of his position. That's what drew me in as a viewer, and still does—the man behind the office.

There's certain decisions I have to make while I'm in this room. Do I send troops into harm's way? Which fatal disease gets the most research money? . . . It's helpful in those situations not to think of yourself as the man but as the office.

—PRESIDENT BARTLET TO FATHER THOMAS CAVANAUGH, "TAKE THIS SABBATH DAY"

(**MELISSA FUN FACT:** In our interview with Martin, we got to talking about "Take This Sabbath Day" and his longtime friend Karl Malden, who played the priest, Father Thomas Cavanaugh. "At the end of that episode," Martin told us, "you know how the priest puts that purple stole around his neck for Bartlet's confession? Karl told me, 'This is the stole I wore in *On the Waterfront*.' And the Bible he used was from *On the Waterfront*, too. He kept them for all those years.")

Jonathan Lovitz (US Department of Commerce)

Having once upon a time spent his life as an actor, it makes a kind of cosmic sense that Biden-Harris administration appointee Jonathan Lovitz is a devoted fan of all things *West Wing*.

> **JONATHAN LOVITZ:** One of the most beautiful moments of *The West Wing* was when Donna calls her teacher from the Oval and says, "I'm in the Oval Office with the president of the United States and it's because of you." To the *West Wing* cast, crew, and writers: I'm in DC working for the president of the United States . . . and it's because of you. Thank you.
>
> The one thing I brought from home for my office on my first day as a presidential appointee was my favorite coffee mug, which says, "Lead Like Jed. Advise Like Leo. Think Like Josh. Speak Like C.J. Argue Like Toby. Write Like Sam."

US Senator Tammy Duckworth (US Senator for Illinois, Iraq War Veteran)

In addition to serving in the US Senate, Tammy Duckworth is an Iraq War veteran, a Purple Heart recipient, and a former assistant secretary of the US Department of Veterans Affairs, who was among the first handful of Army women to fly combat missions during Operation Iraqi Freedom. Back when Tammy was in grad school, she and her friends "would all sit around and watch *The West Wing* as a regular thing. We loved it." One of this Democrat's all-time *West Wing* moments involves the show's most visible Republican.

SENATOR DUCKWORTH: When Ainsley Hayes is introduced there's a discussion on the Equal Rights Amendment. She talks about how there's no way she would ever vote for it because women already have equal rights, why would you need to reaffirm something? When I first watched the show, as a graduate student thinking about politics, this storyline taught me that people who maybe I don't agree with are just looking at the problem from a different perspective. I've carried this attitude through my life, especially into my work in Congress. I always assume the other person loves this country as much as I do, but they're just looking at the problem in a different way. I try to remember that when I deal with my colleagues on the other side of the aisle—they're going to have a different solution from me, but it doesn't mean that they're not coming from a good place—which has led me to be able to do a lot of bipartisan things.

Senator Duckworth's level of devotion to the show is unquestionable. But in case you're wondering . . .

SENATOR DUCKWORTH: I took DVDs of *The West Wing* to Iraq with me. There were two TV series I took to watch at the end of my mission there—*M*A*S*H* and *The West Wing*. It helped me unwind at the end of a hard mission day or to remind me who I was beyond a Blackhawk pilot flying combat missions. I had volunteered to go to Iraq, even though I absolutely opposed the war. *The West Wing* was helpful because, despite my opposition to the war, the show reminded me it was all about loving a nation more than yourself. I was able to be proud of my service as a soldier.

Contemplating her number one moment from the series, the senator went with a season 2 classic . . .

SENATOR DUCKWORTH: In "Noël," Leo tells the story to Josh about someone falling into a hole. The only person who can help him get out is a friend who jumps in and says, "I've been down here before, and I know the way out." When I talk to veterans with post-traumatic stress—I do a lot of peer visitation work— that's the approach I try to take: This isn't about me trying to do a good deed and tell you how it is. I'm just here to listen to you, sitting in this pit of despair, because I've been in a pit myself. Let me try to find the way out with you.

Eric Fanning (22nd Secretary of the Army)

Prior to serving as secretary of the Army in the Obama administration (the first openly gay head of any military department), Eric served as acting secretary of the Air Force and chief of staff to the secretary of defense. Eric is the only person to have served in senior positions in the Departments of the Army, Navy and Air Force. While he was, of course, a big fan of president number forty-four, Obama wasn't the only POTUS he admired.

ERIC FANNING: I loved most that the Bartlet administration fought hard for their beliefs, but allowed for numerous attempts at bipartisan compromise—some successful, some not so much. But it was always more fun when they succeeded, like in two of my favorite episodes. First, when the president allows the govern-ment shutdown, and spontaneously travels to the Hill, ending in a defeat for Speaker Haffley. Second, when Josh and Toby come up with the compromise to nominate a conservative and a liberal to the Supreme Court. (My all-time favorite.)

It's a rare day that Eric doesn't find himself noting some matter of public policy, leadership, or politics and contextualizing it with a reso-nant *West Wing* storyline.

ERIC FANNING: The example I always point to is Toby secretly working on a compromise on Social Security. When Josh finally discovers what's happening, he tells Toby, "We do what's possible. We exploit what's not. That's how we win elections." Nothing better sums up DC.

It isn't just Eric's professional life that's been impacted by the show . . .

ERIC FANNING: My husband, Ben, was so inspired by *The West Wing* that when he decided to transfer from Northwestern University he chose to go to George Washington University, here in DC, which is where we met. So I guess I have *The West Wing* to thank for my marriage!

Stacey Abrams (CEO of Sage Works Productions and Former Georgia House Minority Leader)

Over the last eight years, the American political landscape has seen several transformative leaders, including Stacey Abrams. Credited with an upsurge in voting rights legislation and electing Democrats across the country, including a pair of US senators from her home state of Georgia, Stacey continues to advocate for equity in, and the expansion of, voting in America, alongside nonprofit and advocacy organizations such as Fair Fight Action and Fair Count. Given her jam-packed dance card, it's hard to believe she has time to watch TV, let alone rewatch it. But she does. In fact, she's made time in her busy schedule for *The West Wing* since its inception.

STACEY ABRAMS: When *The West Wing* launched in the fall of 1999, I'd previously cut my teeth in politics by working on the Clinton campaign in 1992 as a college sophomore, and I'd interned for two different departments in the executive branch in college and grad school. I remember eagerly awaiting the premiere (as lauded by *TV Guide* and *Entertainment Weekly*). Once I watched my first episode, I never wavered. I can quote C.J.'s narration to her dad about the senator too stubborn to ask for help but getting it from President Bartlet anyway, the quiet pathos of Leo counseling Josh about climbing up from pain, or the prescient floor speech at the convention that gave rise to Matt Santos.

The West Wing is a constant reminder of how politics can be both noble and guttural—and necessarily both. Not only did I faithfully watch all seven seasons, I also own the entire DVD box set. I continue to revisit entire seasons or watch favorite episodes in times of discontent or for inspiring reminders of what we can imagine if we are willing to try.

Two of those favorite episodes are, as Stacey put it to us, "exemplars of why I fight for democracy."

STACEY ABRAMS: The first is Donna's frantic hunt for someone to cast a vote to cancel out the mistake on her absentee ballot and finding Jack Reese (and romance). His willingness to trust a fellow citizen who did not share his politics is a tremendous statement about the vitality of a shared democracy. The second is when Admiral Fitzwallace reminds an assembled group of the role the military played in desegregation. While not a commentary on voting, he spoke to a collection of congressional leaders who refused to accept the power of their actions. Our votes decide who speaks for us and what they say on our behalf.

When it comes to social engagement, advocacy, and organizing, few figures in American politics today rival Stacey for influence and

visibility. Considering the people who brought her up, that's no surprise. Also no surprise? Her deep-rooted connection to *The West Wing*'s
spirit of civic responsibility.

> **STACEY ABRAMS:** I was raised by parents who believed in service
> as a fundamental component of our lives. *The West Wing*'s call to
> service is imbued in every episode, particularly those that show-
> case the limits of action. In those moments, like Toby's funeral
> service for a forgotten vet or Charlie's mentorship of a young man
> whose guide (Simon Donovan) is lost to violence, we are reminded
> by *The West Wing* that service does not preclude pain and loss but
> is a critical antidote to apathy. The big moments of an election are
> exciting, but true service is lived in the times in between.

Secretary Pete Buttigieg (US Secretary of Transportation, Former Mayor of South Bend, Indiana)

The nineteenth secretary of transportation in US history, back in 2019
the presidential candidate we'd first gotten to know as "Mayor Pete,"
told the *Harvard Crimson* that in his college days he used to host "*West
Wing* watch parties." In 2023, he had this to say to us . . .

> **SECRETARY BUTTIGIEG:** A lot of us were brought up to be skep-
> tical of the integrity or intellect of politicians. So this portrayal of
> a group . . . the president, most of the characters . . . who are just
> smart people doing their best with incredibly hard situations, was
> really meaningful as I was figuring out whether public service
> might be something that I would want to commit my life to.

In recent years, *The West Wing* has occasionally hit a little too close
to home for the secretary. Like that time he was watching "The State
Dinner" at the end of a long day at the Department of Transportation.

SECRETARY BUTTIGIEG: We were dealing with . . . either the rail labor or another supply chain–related labor issue and there was a storm warning bearing down on Guam, and a ship that is actually part of the DOT's fleet was at risk. I was like, "This is the plot of this show!" There's a Teamster strike going on, and there's a hurricane, and the navy ship is caught up, and the president's calling the ship. I was like, "Oh, man, this is supposed to be taking me *somewhere else*!"

Then again, the "art imitates life" of *The West Wing* isn't always so stressful.

SECRETARY BUTTIGIEG: There are these little gems you find retroactively, like the Big Block of Cheese Day. This group is presenting on wildlife crossings and *we're* also building those now! Not in the preposterous way suggested on the show (by Nick Offerman!), but to keep elk and deer and moose from having to cross interstates, and cars from crashing into them. Or another example: I love the episode ["20 Hours in America: Part I"] that turns on the confusion about time zones in Indiana, because I lived that. It still comes up from time to time, even though we cured the worst of our time zone confusion from the mid 2000s.

> JOSH
> Wait. Wait. No. No. You're not . . .
> We changed time zones? We changed
> time—we changed time zones?!

SECRETARY BUTTIGIEG: That episode throws people who are in the DC bubble into the realities of people out where I grew up . . . where people maybe don't want to hear that you "work at the White House," and may or may not be for you, and are just trying to get through their lives.

In TV or cinema, we indulge a little bit in the fiction that you just win people over with honeyed words or that perfect expression. You can go too far in that direction and forget that people are where they are because of their interests, and their incentives, and their culture, and their upbringing, and their geography, and their surroundings, and you're not necessarily going to win them over because you said something better than the last guy said it. *But*: There really is something to be said for *persuasion*, for how you say something. You can reach somebody who might not have otherwise been reached if you can just get something across more clearly. I think that's really important to remember in public life.

The portrayal of people who are very, very capable, and yet are struggling every day because the things they're trying to do are so very hard . . . is inspiring, and was certainly inspiring for me in trying to figure out what to do with my life at about that age when *The West Wing* landed. I hope we can recover a little bit of reverence for our democratic institutions that, while tattered even then, was just *stronger*. There was a kind of awe about the weight of the work that people in those roles have to do, and the trust placed in these institutions and the very human people who run them.

In the end, for this young politician who traded his *West Wing* dorm room watch parties on Wednesday nights at nine for the day-to-day grind of the office of the mayor of South Bend, *The West Wing* became something of a beacon.

SECRETARY BUTTIGIEG: Back when I was mayor, we would have an abundance of *Parks and Recreation* moments, a healthy quota of *Veep* moments, far too many moments that were like something out of *The Wire*. But once in a while, beautifully, there would be a moment which made you think of *The West Wing*.

★ ★ ★

THE night Aaron Sorkin first attended *Hamilton* on Broadway, Lin-Manuel tweeted out, "Sorkin. Was. Here." When a Twitter follower asked him if Aaron knew how much Lin-Manuel loved *The West Wing*, the *Hamilton* star tweeted back, "I mean, he saw the show, so he does now."

This handful of conversations with high-profile Wingnuts—theater icons and public servants alike—underscores the lasting nature of two works of political pop culture. And confirms that entertainment can encourage us toward paths that push beyond the stage or screen and into the rooms where it happens. They serve as a reminder that, if you wait for it—and if you're very, very lucky—art can be eternal and non-stop; that its impact can endure and inspire fresh, new, ever-evolving pursuits, artistic and otherwise; that what comes next can leave you satisfied. In this way, both of these shows—the ideas they represent and the vision they share—manage to pull off something of a magic trick. They manage to stay alive.

———— ★ ★ ★ ————

A SERVICE STORY

MARLEE MATLIN

If we took a poll of the top Joey Lucas moments from *The West Wing*, we're guessing the results would wind up in a dead heat. There was that time the administration's favorite pollster offered a counterargument to making English the official language of the United States:

                    JOEY [KENNY]
        Aside from it being bigoted and
        unconstitutional, it's ludicrous to
        think that laws need to be created
        to help protect the language of
        Shakespeare!

Then there was the scene in Josh's office when (through her trusty sign-language interpreter Kenny) our pal Joey confronted the deputy chief of staff with a hypothetical polling sample that hit a bit too close to home:

                    JOEY [KENNY]
        If you polled a hundred Donnas and
        asked them if they think we should
        go out, you'd get a high positive
        response. But the poll wouldn't
        tell you it's because she likes
        you, and she knows it's beginning
        to show and she needs to cover
        herself with misdirection.

Our pick, though, came in "Mandatory Minimums" from season 1, where we were treated to this four-line exchange between Joey (sans Kenny this time) and Josh re: his "Joey Lucas suit."

                    JOSH
        I wore this suit, special today.
        This isn't my regular Tuesday suit.

                    JOEY
        You have a regular Tuesday suit?

                    JOSH
        No.

                              JOEY
           For me?

                              JOSH
           Yeah . . . So . . . Okay, I gotta
           go.

When it comes to investing in Josh's various romantic entangle-
ments, it's easy to get caught up in the Donna vs. Amy Gardner
sweepstakes. But Josh Lyman–Joey Lucas would've given either of
those pairings a serious run for their money.

Just as she did as Joey Lucas on *The West Wing*, Marlee Matlin
sets the bar high when it comes to service. "Service," Marlee said,
"has always been a part of my life, ever since I visited schools as a
child, performing and bringing a positive light to the accomplishments of Deaf and Hard of Hearing kids. I strongly support the
issue of equal rights for those who face barriers because of how
they are perceived as persons who are Deaf, Hard of Hearing or
otherwise disabled." That high bar extends to her work in support
of my organization, All Rise, as well. Her speech and recovery
story remains a highlight of our 2020 conference and gave hope to
so many.

Reflecting on *The West Wing*, Marlee acknowledges the show's
deep impact on her community. "In the creation of Joey Lucas,
Aaron Sorkin essentially said that a Deaf person can be *anything*—
even a White House pollster—reinforcing the tenets of the Americans with Disabilities Act, that no one with a disability or who is
Deaf or Hard of Hearing should be treated any differently and has
a right to the same freedoms as everyone else. I'm so grateful that,
as a Deaf person, I was able to play a role in the highest echelons
of government service."

Indeed, Aaron's putting the words "Joey" and "Lucas" on the page, and Marlee bringing them to life, resulted in real-world changes, including along Pennsylvania Avenue. "My presence on the show helped lead to a real-life Deaf woman working in the White House as the official receptionist, Leah Katz-Hernandez. She told me that my role inspired her to eventually work in the White House."

One last Marlee story: When I was volunteering in Uganda, I visited a center for the Deaf and met with some of the people there. I mentioned Marlee and that she had won the biggest award any actress could receive. (The Oscar for her performance in *Children of a Lesser God*.) One of the women asked, "The award for Best *Deaf* Actress?" I said "No. For Best *Actress*." She started to cry. Marlee's life and career accomplishments are hard to overstate. Her impact on so many, inside and outside the Deaf community, is truly global.

THE NATIONAL ASSOCIATION OF THE DEAF

The National Association of the Deaf (NAD) is the nation's premier civil rights organization of, by, and for Deaf and Hard of Hearing individuals in the United States of America.

www.nad.org

★ ★ ★

FORTY

KEY EPISODE

"Tomorrow"

The very last sequence filmed on the very last episode of *The West Wing* perfectly captured what the finale was about. In the show's all-time slowest walk-and-talk, President Bartlet ambles his way through the West Wing, offering thanks to the family of people who made his White House run. Unhurried and with a laser focus on each successive staffer, he offers handshakes and gratitude. It is a heartfelt, one-by-one valedictory speech.

Of course, by the time "Tomorrow" had finally arrived in 2006, Aaron Sorkin's tenure at the show he created in 1999 had long since ended. But, as much as anyone, he would have appreciated a nod—thematic, tonal, and subconscious as it may have been—to the finale of a formative television series from his youth. Yes, as John Wells, Chris Misiano, and the company of *The West Wing* brought seven years of story to a reflective, meaningful close, you could hear a whisper of *M*A*S*H*'s iconic last chapter, "Goodbye, Farewell and Amen."

His chopper hovering up, up, and away from the 4077th, Hawkeye Pierce looks down at his best friend B.J.'s farewell note—a bunch of rocks spelling out "GOODBYE." Jed Bartlet—now a civilian flying on what, minutes before, was still Air Force One—unwraps a present from the family of *his* best friend. As he pulls out the framed "Bartlet for America" napkin he once gave Leo for Christmas, it's hard to miss the sense of full circle, the permanent legacy of things not seen.

On the last day of production, the *West Wing* set felt a lot like a family reunion. With cameos aplenty—everyone getting a moment to shine—the energy around the place was a bittersweet mix of opening night and the last day of school. Even the ex–alpaca farmers of the Bartlet administration were feeling ambivalent. "The last show," Lily Tomlin told us, "I couldn't stop crying. We were handing the Oval Office over to Jimmy Smits. I just couldn't believe the show was coming to an end, or that the presidency was coming to an end." Lily wasn't alone. That raw emotion was everywhere you looked, and it was so from start to finish.

"We scheduled the episode so that Martin saying goodbye would be the final scene," director Chris Misiano told us. "It just felt like that needed to go last. Everybody was able to be in the same room and on our set. The atmosphere in that lobby was incredible. I mean, *everybody* was there." (That "everybody" included old friends Aaron Sorkin, Tommy Schlamme, Julie DeJoie, and Lauren Lohman.)

Eli Attie remembers crowds gathering around the monitors. "[At] video village there would be more and more people as the night went on and we got closer to that last shot," he says. "It was really something."

Brad Whitford once described Chris Misiano as "the Shaker director." Chris agrees. "My basic instinct generally is . . . simple. It's clean lines, not a lot of adornment." As overflowing with emotion as this series finale was destined to be—both within the story and for the actors bringing the West Wing to bustling life one last time—this Shaker director with the gift to be simple was the perfect match.

An early example of that comes as President-elect Santos and his soon-to-be first lady, Helen, are at Blair House, prepping for Inauguration Day. She's tying his tie (as opposed to cutting it off).

> HELEN SANTOS
> "Come on, it'll be an adventure . . ."
> That's what you told me when you
> wanted to run for city council, and I
> didn't want you to. "Come on. It'll be
> an adventure."

It's a sweet and simple scene, requiring nothing more than a couple of close-ups and the chemistry Jimmy Smits and Teri Polo had shared across two seasons. There was this moment, too, from later in the episode backstage at the inauguration.

> HELEN SANTOS
> Man, I hope Janet Spragens has her
> TV on.
>
> PRESIDENT-ELECT SANTOS
> Who?
>
> HELEN SANTOS
> Senior year. She beat me out for the
> last varsity spot on the swim team.

For Chris Misiano, the easygoing intimacy John Wells put on the page informed what the director wanted to see on-screen. "I'm not gonna make a lot of cuts in this. This is just these two people. We're just gonna push in slowly and do it in one shot. That's all it needs."

If President and Mrs. Santos are the promising sunrise slipping into view, President Bartlet and the first lady are the sunset, still radiant, even as they dip slowly toward the horizon. In an episode the

director calls "a love letter" from John Wells, these presidential marriages complement each other all the way through the various passings
of batons and too many goodbyes to count. Among these moving,
intimate moments, a quietly powerful one has Dr. Bartlet and her husband gazing out a White House window on their final early morning.

ABBEY
You did a lot of good, Jed. A *lot*
of good.

As we began our dive into "Tomorrow," it struck us that, while
moments like that one (and the episode overall) have been described as
contemplative, meditative, reflective—you know . . . all the big
"tives"—there's quite a lot going on. Josh and Donna are waking up in
bed together, Mallory's stopping by C.J.'s office to deliver her family's
going-away present for POTUS (and to cringe for a sec upon hearing
that Sam's engaged). Oh, and speaking of Sam, he's not just engaged—
he's back! Returning to the place he considers "home, sweet home," the
prodigal Sam is set to fill that *West Wing*–iest of roles: Josh Lyman's
Josh Lyman (aka Josh's deputy chief of staff).

Actual Josh Lyman, meanwhile, is taking his last, best shot at convincing C.J. to join the Santos administration. Honestly, though, what
are the odds? This time tomorrow, everyone's favorite Pulitzer Prize–
winning hopeful romantic, Danny Concannon, will be waiting "at
LAX with a tub of sunscreen." (And possibly Gail's fishbowl with a
mini palm tree and a teeny-tiny Hollywood sign.)

As if that's not enough on this busy morning, Donna's agog at her
huge new office, Will and Kate have a date with a train derailment, a
looming ice storm, and a jurisdictional border dispute, and it appears
one New England governor or another is about to become what the
president calls "a star player in my soon-to-be-written autobiography."
Plus, the outgoing commander in chief still has to write a few

meaningful sentences to the incoming one. What we're saying is, yes, fine, it's a reflective episode. But the world keeps spinning.

The *real* drama, of course, is the reason "Claudia Jean" is presently hovering in the Oval: the will-he-or-won't-he of Toby's presidential pardon. The FBI investigation into the White House leak of classified intel has outed her friend and former colleague as the source.

This is a far cry from the last time we saw C.J. and Toby, back in the show's penultimate episode, "Institutional Memory." Watching these two tearfully reconnect in Richard's final *West Wing* scene, witnessing the quiet, easy intimacy between them and the yearslong bond they had shared, we felt the actors speaking as much for their characters as for themselves.

                        TOBY

        I missed you.

                        C.J.

        Yeah. We had it good there for a
        while.

Now, back in "Tomorrow," the practically Shakespearean struggle President Bartlet exhibits—to pardon or not to pardon—comes to a more or less happy end. As he affixes his signature to the document with just minutes to spare, Jed Bartlet's long national nightmare is over. He'll always feel conflicted about this outcome, but at least Molly and Huck won't have to look at their father "in an orange jumpsuit across an aluminum picnic table" for the next five years.

Behind the Resolute desk, as Bartlet grapples with the pardon issue, Martin embodies a mix of frustration, betrayal, and a profound and palpable sadness. Then, from what appears to be the depths of his soul, his Bartlet exhales and we witness the cathartic transformation that comes with the decision to forgive. Even if it is a complicated forgiveness. It's a stellar piece of acting that touches every part of the

Bartlet we've come to know: the politician, the leader, the father figure . . . and the man of faith. Martin, on the other hand, saw it as a simpler choice: "I couldn't imagine *not* pardoning Toby," he says, "because I don't think Richard would have ever spoken to me again!"

One more thing about that pardon letter. The bottom half of the document features this: The signature line across from the one for "Josiah Bartlet, President of the United States" has the name of the pardon attorney. It's out of focus on your screen, but—trust us, we've seen the prop—the name of that pardon attorney is "Aaron Sorkin."

And that isn't the only time the *West Wing* creator shows up in the finale. Aaron still had an office at Warner Bros. and, after he drove onto the lot that day, word went out to ask if he'd consider being in the inauguration scene. "It wasn't even something that we'd planned ahead of time," Misiano says. Production asked. He said okay. It was as low-maintenance as the show ever got. (**MELISSA:** It didn't hurt that the man writes dressed in what Malina refers to as "inauguration wear." He didn't even need a costume fitting!)

This is how it came to be that, in the middle of Keb' Mo's moving rendition of "America the Beautiful," viewers were treated to a close-up of the show's creator. There he sat, dapper in a jacket and tie and sporting what we could swear were Sam's Gage-Whitney–era wireless frames. This grace-note cameo was a piece of a stirring montage:

Starting out on production designer Ken Hardy's sweeping inauguration facade, one that overtook an entire Warner Bros. parking lot, the sequence cuts between the swearing in of the new president and the systematic dismantling of the old one's office. As the White House domestic staff expertly packs up—taking artwork off the walls, wheeling out boxes, snapping up a Zoey photo from the Resolute desk—the nation's majesty is on full display, embedded in the peaceful transfer of power. "America the Beautiful" indeed.

Naturally, in the inauguration's aftermath, there's still work to be done and power to transfer. Which brings us to soft-spoken Secret

Service agent Ron Butterfield. Misiano remembers a subtle but significant move made by actor Michael O'Neill. "There's this moment when Bartlet gets in the car after Santos is sworn in. As a Secret Service agent, Butterfield watches Bartlet until he moves away, then his attention snaps instantly back to Santos. I hadn't noticed it at the time. Michael told me later. He just completely shifts his focus, like 'That guy's my past, *this* guy's my present, I gotta watch out for this guy now.' I love that."

Between the assassination attempt at Rosslyn, the threats against C.J., and the kidnapping of Zoey Bartlet, Ron Butterfield had gotten most of his *West Wing* face time during the first four seasons of the show. But as the series drew to a close, John Wells opted to bring Agent Butterfield back into the fold. "John wanted Butterfield to hand off the transition," Michael told us. "He wanted the stability of that passage."

Talking about the series finale brought up a lot of feelings for a lot of cast members, for one reason in particular. "It's emotional for me," Michael told us, "because of Spence. I remember standing there with Martin—outside, arriving for the inauguration. I said, 'My God, I wish Spencer could be here.' Martin looked at me and said . . . 'He is.'"

From Mallory telling C.J. that "Dad loved every moment he spent here" to Will whipping Toby's pink Spaldeen against his office wall, John Wells's script managed to bring the spirit of absent characters effectively (and affectively) into the present. That includes the bit where C.J. hands Josh a rumpled Post-it with "WWLD?" written on it. "What would Leo do," she explains. Then, in a gesture of reassurance from the current chief of staff to the nervous former deputy who's about to be, she says, "You're gonna do great, Josh. You don't need me."

Even as a sense of "life goes on" simmers throughout the episode— even as we love it when President Santos hits Josh with his inaugural "What's next?"—the fact remains that this finale was primarily a series of emotional goodbyes.

That's how Melissa saw it. "That last sequence filmed, where President Bartlet bids farewell to his junior staffers, still stands out for so many of us. The chance to memorialize on film a final moment of heartfelt gratitude for and farewell to Martin, and to the show, was a gift of incalculable value. Brad said it well: 'You didn't have to act.'"

One of the most memorable in that final run of exchanges involved a back-and-forth between President Bartlet and West Wing staffer Nancy.

> **PRESIDENT BARTLET**
> Nancy, how's your mother doing?
>
> **NANCY**
> She's fine now, Mr. President.
>
> **PRESIDENT BARTLET**
> Tell her I'm looking forward to seeing her again soon, would you please?

As you'll recall, "Nancy" is played by a talented actress named Renée Estevez, who also happens to be Martin's daughter. So, when Bartlet asks Nancy to tell her mother "I'm looking forward to seeing her again soon," the sly wink to Martin finally getting to spend some quality time with his wife, Janet Sheen, was unmistakable. It was also this—improvised. "Misiano and I just laughed," Martin told us. "Both of us thought it'll never be in the final cut. And of course, it was."

Renée wasn't the only one of Martin's children in the room that night. Ramón Estevez was there too, along with one of his brothers. As their father said to us, "Charlie was over filming *Two and a Half Men* and somebody got ahold of him and said, 'Your old man's shooting his last scene,' so he rushed over and said, 'Just let me stand in the crowd.' And he did. And I saw him."

WHAT'S NEXT

Moments later—right after rushing future congressman Will Bailey (D-OR, 4th District) off the phone—President Bartlet comes face-to-face with future Georgetown law student Charlie Young. The scene between this surrogate father and the guy we hope will someday be his son-in-law is the last exchange ever shot on *The West Wing*.

In yet another moment of Misiano's innate directorial sense of less is more, Bartlet and his body man play it simple, raw, and honest. When the president hands Charlie his family's battered old copy of the US Constitution, the emotion brimming in Martin's eyes, and Dulé's, is palpable.

> PRESIDENT BARTLET
> I don't need this anymore. I
> thought maybe you could get some
> use out of it. I was trying to
> remember if my father had given it
> to me when I was in the tenth grade
> or the eleventh. Considered getting
> you a tie with the scales of
> justice on it. Figured you'd use
> this more.
>
> CHARLIE
> Thank you, Mr. President.
>
> PRESIDENT BARTLET
> Thank *you*, Charlie.

At that point in the evening, the sentimental mood on set had grown increasingly raw. On-set costumer Frankie Bruno put it to us this way: "Every time a cast member would wrap out—'That's a series wrap for Allison Janney'—I would cry just . . . ugly buckets of tears. I mean, this was like my *family*." Looking back, Frankie still marvels at the experience of that night and of all the ones that came before it. "So much life was lived in that seven years."

Of course, it wasn't all tears. The run-up to the end also included some pre-wrap celebratory drinking, and a buzzing anticipation. But what happened when Chris Misiano yelled "Cut!" after the very last take of that very last scene amounted to a collective emotional release. With cast and crew cheering and clapping and sighing and crying, Martin found himself surrounded. That was a "series wrap" on *The West Wing*.

That chaotic celebration remains one of the strongest memories Josh Malina has of his time on the show. "I remember kind of backing up and feeling—even though it was very special and I was moved—like it was other people's moment. The people who had been there from the beginning, it was *their* very special thing. I was happy to be even peripherally involved."

That's how it was for Mary too. "Looking around at Brad and Janel and Allison and Melissa . . . cast and crew who'd been there from the start . . . it was such an emotional moment to be a part of, even for me, and I was finishing up my third year on the show. It's like C.J. said in the previous episode: 'It looks different on the far side of eight.' As someone who'd come late to the *West Wing* party, I just honestly felt lucky to have been invited."

Brad Whitford recalls that last *West Wing* night as a jumble of emotions. It was the kind of moment that brings to mind his long-running bit about legacy: "No matter what any of us does next, this is the first line of our obituary." He was thrilled with what had been achieved over seven seasons; it was a happy-sad closing of a critical chapter in his life. What marked the occasion more than the sudden presence of closure, though, was the lingering absence of a friend. "I remember thinking of John," Brad says, "and having to navigate that loss, in that moment, along with . . . celebrating this wonderful thing. It was a big deal. All of it was."

What stood out to Chris Misiano that night was an overwhelming sense of gratitude. "Those emotions for the actors," he says, "it's exactly what you wanted to be doing. Having a moment with these people to say an honest goodbye . . . and thank you." Which brings us to the end, by which we mean . . . The End.

While the scene with Bartlet, Charlie, and the US Constitution was the last scene filmed, the last scene of the *episode* was a far more understated affair, at least when it came to production. It took place on an aircraft that, just like the president it was carrying home, was suddenly operating in a slightly more ex officio capacity.

The scene as written was not, as the director put it to us, "something that had to be orchestrated." Production-wise, it's short and sweet. Martin takes the gift Mallory left for him, unwraps it, meditates a moment on What It All Means, goes over to Abbey, hands it to her, sits, and looks out the window. You'd think that would be pretty easy to shoot, no?

Okay, yeah, it was. For everyone . . . but especially for the director. "I think for Martin," Misiano says, "the loss of John Spencer was obviously enormous, and taking that napkin out in the scene, which was originally a gift from Leo . . . and with the weight of that loss for both Stockard and Martin . . . as a director, what are you gonna do except just go, 'Wow . . . look at *that*!' It's not something you remember directorially," he told us. "It was more about the simple gift of being present."

"The simple gift of being present." That kind of says it all for the cast and crew of *The West Wing*. From that last night of filming, all the way back in time to the table read of the pilot (and everything in between), just being there was a gift.

Not long after *The West Wing* ended, Martin and I were driving to San Diego together for the opening of the Kroc Institute for Peace and Justice. He said, "You know, Melissa, I didn't go to college, but people always say those were the best years of their lives. They just wish they had appreciated it." Then he said, "*The West Wing*, those were the best years of our lives, but we did appreciate it. We *knew*." I said, "Martin, you're absolutely right. We all knew." You couldn't not know.

So. How do you end *The West Wing*? What words do you choose to evoke the sense of inspiration and hope that the series embodied, even as it comes to a close? Back in the pilot, Aaron found a perfect two-word phrase: "What's next?" Here in the finale, John Wells summoned that spirit and chose this simple couplet:

                    ABBEY
        What are you thinking about?

                     JED
        Tomorrow.

The series ends amid a melancholy tranquility. A plane glides over a wide expanse of glittering sea, heading off toward Jed and Abbey Bartlet's old stomping grounds. Leaving behind the political battlefields of Washington, the weight of the world, and the bustling, hallowed halls of the West Wing, they are headed north. To a place—quieter and slower-paced—in the heart of the state of New Hampshire.

GOODBYE, FAREWELL AND AMEN

I n the late twentieth century, political campaigns began to really tap into the zeitgeist, leaning on pop culture (particularly in the realm of music) to connect with young voters. If that meant embracing a gross misinterpretation of Bruce Springsteen's "Born in the U.S.A.," so be it. The candidate could live with that. But come hell or high water, middle-aged politicians were going to come across as "in touch with the youth vote," and those focus groups, dammit, were gonna spin their dials toward "wanna have a beer with."

So, they'd send this or that junior flunky/staffer backstage to cue up "Some Nights" by Fun. (Never mind that the refrain goes: "What do I stand for . . . most nights I don't know anymore.") For more overtly disaffected supporters, "We're Not Gonna Take It" by Twisted Sister might do the trick. Ditto for Tom Petty's "I Won't Back Down." Then there's the hyper-hopeful über-anthem of baby boomers, inspirationalists, and cockeyed optimists everywhere: Fleetwood Mac's "Don't Stop (Thinkin' About Tomorrow)."

I mean, sure, these songs (and countless others) make for some pretty awkward campaign-stage dancing, but they're used for a reason.

They're effective. They bring energy, send a message, and strike a chord—with their words as much as their music.

As we close out this book, the idea of "words" and "music" reminds us not just of Aaron Sorkin and John Wells and all the other *West Wing* composers, from Snuffy Walden to everyone who ever sat in the writers room. It brings to mind the notion that, while music is what humanity has often turned to when words do not suffice, words—when deployed in just the right way—can transform into a very real kind of music, with rhythm and pitch and timbre and volume. Which brings us, of course—and at last—to Josiah Bartlet. Who better, we thought, to send us off on our pursuit of life, liberty, and happiness than the Nobel Prize–winning economist, ultimate *West Wing* father figure, and klutzy rider of bikes into trees than the man Leo and Abbey call Jed. So, without further ado, ladies and gentlemen, here now . . . in (mostly) his own words—courtesy of Aaron Sorkin and seven seasons of phenomenal *West Wing* scripts—the president of the United States:

PRESIDENT BARTLET*

I can sense civic duty a mile away. It's something we pass on, something with a history, so we can say, "My father gave this to me and his father gave it to him and now I'm giving it to you . . ."

It seems more and more we've come to expect less and less from each other, and I think that should change. How do we end the cycle? Be subject to one another. If a guy's a good neighbor, if he puts in a day, if every once in a while he laughs, if every once in a while he thinks about somebody else and, above all else, if he can find his way to compassion and tolerance, then he's my brother. So, where are we going? What's next?

---

* Nearly every word of this imagined address comes from the scripts of *The West Wing*. Think of it as a remix, if you will.

What's next is: Get in the game. Make a substantive contribution. If you go down swinging, at least you took your shot. Just don't watch the pitch go by.

"Joy cometh in the morning," scripture tells us. I hope so. I don't know if life would be worth living if it didn't. Because there's evil in the world. There'll always be, and we can't do anything about that. The streets of heaven are too crowded with angels. They're our students and our teachers and our parents and our friends. Yet the true measure of a people's strength—and this is what's next—is how they rise to master that moment when it does arrive. We learn these lessons the hard way.

There's violence in our schools, too much mayhem in our culture, and we *can* do something about that. There aren't enough teachers in our classrooms. There isn't nearly enough, not nearly enough, not <u>nearly</u> enough money in our classrooms and we *can* do something about that. Run for a seat on your local school board, advocate for budget increases. Get in the game.

What will be the *next* thing that challenges us? That makes us work harder and go farther?

Global warming constitutes a clear and present danger to the health and well-being of this planet and its inhabitants. If that concerns you . . . get in the game. If you're off-the-charts tired of the gun lobby tossing around words like "personal freedom" and nobody calling them on it . . . get in the game. What's your thing about? Election security, civil rights or veterans issues, healthcare or homelessness . . . choice? Spend the next six weeks organizing a voter registration drive. Get in the game.

My great-grandfather's great-grandfather was Dr. Josiah Bartlet, who was the New Hampshire delegate representative to the Second Continental Congress, the one that sat in session in Philadelphia in the summer of 1776 and announced to the world that we were no longer subjects of King George III, but rather a self-governing people. "We hold these truths to be self-evident," they said. "That all men are created equal." Strange as it may seem, that was the first time in history that anyone had ever bothered to write that down. Decisions are made by those who show up.

They're telling me that we're out of time. So, here's your homework. At the end of the day, you really have to ask yourself: "What are you thinking about?" The answer? *Tomorrow.* That's what's next: Don't stop thinking about tomorrow.

There's a promise that I ask everyone who works here to make: Never doubt that a small group of thoughtful and committed citizens can change the world. You know why? It's the only thing that ever has. This is a time for American heroes. This is a time to do what is hard. To achieve what is great. To run into the fire—run *into* the fire—and reach for the stars.

However you reach for the stars in your corner of the universe, however you get in the game, please believe me when I tell you: It makes a difference. You're gonna open your mouth and lift houses off the ground—whole houses clear off the ground.

So, what do you say? You wanna come help us out?

Class dismissed. Thank you, everyone. God bless you. And God bless America.

UNCOMMON CAUSE

The West Wing Cast and Crew . . . and Service

The cast and crew of The West Wing *hold a variety of service organizations close to their hearts. We are pleased to be able to spotlight a handful of them here and hope you'll consider supporting these endeavors in whichever ways you can. So, please, check 'em out and spread the word. And tag us on social media when you do!*

ALLISON JANNEY (C.J. CREGG)

Amelia Air
Amelia Air is a tax-exempt rescue organization staffed by volunteers dedicated to saving animals from high-kill shelters and flying them to rescues who have the resources to find them loving families. They are a small but mighty group committed to one goal: save five hundred animals each year by flying them off death row to rescues who place them with loving forever families.
www.ameliaair.org

Planned Parenthood
Planned Parenthood's mission is to ensure all people have access to the care and resources they need to make informed decisions about

their bodies, their lives, and their futures. Founded in 1916, Planned Parenthood is a trusted healthcare provider, educator, and passionate advocate here in the US as well as a strong partner to health and rights organizations around the world. Each year, Planned Parenthood delivers vital sexual and reproductive healthcare, sex education, and information to millions of people.

www.plannedparenthood.org

ROB LOWE (SAM SEABORN)

Wounded Warrior Project

Every warrior has a next mission. We know that the transition to civilian life is a journey. And for every warrior, family member, and caregiver, that journey looks different. We are here for their first step and each step that follows, because we believe that every warrior should have a positive future to look forward to. There's always another goal to achieve, another mission to discover. We are their partner in that mission.

www.woundedwarriorproject.org

White Heart

White Heart is a nonprofit that helps our nation's post-9/11 injured warriors and is committed to serving the needs of our severely injured warriors through direct community support.

www.whiteheart.org

Susan G. Komen

In 1980, Nancy G. Brinker promised her dying sister, Susan, that she would do everything in her power to end breast cancer forever. In 1982, that promise became the Susan G. Komen organization and the beginning of a global movement. Their efforts helped reduce deaths from breast cancer by 40 percent between 1989 and 2016, and they promise that they won't stop until their promise is fulfilled.

www.komen.org

MARTIN SHEEN (PRESIDENT JOSIAH BARTLET)

The Catholic Worker Movement

Catholic Workers live a simple lifestyle in community, serve the poor, and resist war and social injustice. Most are grounded in the gospel, prayer, and the Catholic faith, although some houses are interfaith. There are 159 Catholic Worker communities across the United States and 28 Catholic Worker communities abroad.

www.catholicworker.org

All Rise

All Rise is a national nonprofit championing justice system reform for people impacted by substance use and mental health disorders by promoting treatment instead of incarceration. All Rise leads the establishment of treatment courts, the most successful intervention in our nation's history for leading people living with substance use and mental health disorders out of the justice system and into lives of recovery and stability.

www.allrise.org

DULÉ HILL (CHARLIE YOUNG)

Everybody Dance LA!

Everybody Dance LA! began as an after-school program in 2000 in an affordable housing project near downtown Los Angeles. Today, the program serves 2,400 students, ages four to twenty-one, and is the leading provider of high-quality, low-cost dance instruction in the city's impacted, underserved communities.

www.everybodydance.org

Make-A-Wish Foundation

The Make-A-Wish Foundation creates life-changing wishes for children with critical illnesses.

www.wish.org

MELISSA FITZGERALD (CAROL FITZPATRICK)

All Rise

All Rise is a national nonprofit championing justice system reform for people impacted by substance use and mental health disorders by promoting treatment instead of incarceration. All Rise leads the establishment of treatment courts, the most successful intervention in our nation's history for leading people living with substance use and mental health disorders out of the justice system and into lives of recovery and stability.

www.allrise.org

Justice for Vets

Justice for Vets is a division of All Rise that transforms the way the justice system identifies, assesses, and treats our veterans. Justice for Vets provides training and technical assistance to bring together local, state, and federal resources to directly serve justice-involved veterans including specific training and resources for veterans treatment courts. Justice for Vets keeps veterans out of jail and prison and connects them to the benefits and healthcare they have earned.

www.allrise.org/jfv

EMILY PROCTER (AINSLEY HAYES)

The Ground

The Ground is a social and emotional language awareness program designed to combat negative personal narratives and support peaceful conflict resolution. The goal of the Ground is to recognize what we share, celebrate what makes us unique, and support the ability to build healthy community everywhere.

www.emilyprocter.com/the-ground

RICHARD SCHIFF (TOBY ZIEGLER)

The ACLU

The American Civil Liberties Union was founded in 1920 and is the United States' guardian of liberty. The ACLU works in the courts, legislatures, and communities to defend and preserve the individual rights and liberties guaranteed to all people in the United States by the Constitution and laws of the United States.

www.aclu.org

Environmental Defense Fund

Guided by science and economics, and committed to climate justice, the Environmental Defense Fund works in the places, on the projects, and with the people who can make the biggest difference.

www.edf.org

JANEL MOLONEY (DONNATELLA MOSS)

International Medical Corps

The mission of the International Medical Corps, established in 1984 by volunteer doctors and nurses . . . is to improve the quality of life through health interventions and related activities that strengthen underserved communities worldwide. With the flexibility to respond rapidly to emergencies, the International Medical Corps offers medical services and training to people at the highest risk, always working to strengthen local healthcare systems and promote self-reliance.

www.internationalmedicalcorps.org

Riley's Way Foundation

Riley's Way invests in a youth-led kindness movement, providing young people with the programs, support, and inclusive community they need to thrive as change-makers. Riley's Way is committed to

supporting these young leaders to build a better world that values kindness, empathy, connection, and the voices of all youth.
www.rileysway.org

BRADLEY WHITFORD (JOSH LYMAN)

Be a Hero
Here in the richest country in the world, and everywhere, Be a Hero believes healthcare should be a human right. Everyone should have the care they need, no matter who they are, where they live, what job they have, or whether they have a job at all. The Be a Hero team takes on critical fights to transform America's healthcare system so that it guarantees all of us the care and dignity we deserve.
www.beaherofund.com

Fair Fight Action
Fair Fight Action promotes fair elections around the country, encourages voter participation in elections, and educates voters about elections and their voting rights. Fair Fight Action brings awareness to the public on election reform, advocates for election reform at all levels, and engages in other voter education programs and communications.
www.fairfight.com

JOSH MALINA (WILL BAILEY)

Americans for Peace Now
APN's mission is to educate and persuade the American public and its leadership to support and adopt policies that will lead to comprehensive, durable Israeli-Palestinian and Israeli-Arab peace, based on a two-state solution, guaranteeing both peoples' security, and consistent with US national interests. APN also works to ensure Israel's future and the viability of Israel's democracy and Jewish character through education, activism, and advocacy in the United States, and

by mobilizing American support for Shalom Achshav, APN's sister organization in Israel.

www.peacenow.org

HIAS

Welcome the stranger. Protect the refugee. Founded as the Hebrew Immigrant Aid Society in 1881 to assist Jews fleeing pogroms in Russia and Eastern Europe, HIAS has touched the life of nearly every Jewish family in America and now welcomes all who have fled persecution.

www.hias.org

MARY McCORMACK (KATE HARPER)

Justice for Vets

Justice for Vets is a division of All Rise that transforms the way the justice system identifies, assesses, and treats our veterans. Justice for Vets provides training and technical assistance to bring together local, state, and federal resources to directly serve justice-involved veterans including specific training and resources for veterans treatment courts. Justice for Vets keeps veterans out of jail and prison and connects them to the benefits and healthcare they have earned.

www.allrise.org/jfv

The Trevor Project

Our long-term vision is to build a world where we are no longer needed—where every LGBTQ+ young person is loved and accepted for who they are, and therefore not at higher risk for suicide or mental health crisis. Until then, we'll continue to meet the need sustainably and refine our efforts intentionally so that we can provide support to every LGBTQ+ young person who needs it.

www.thetrevorproject.org

Moms Demand Action

Moms Demand Action is a grassroots movement of Americans fighting for public safety measures that can protect people from gun violence.

www.momsdemandaction.org

ALAN ALDA (SENATOR ARNOLD VINICK)

The Alan Alda Center for Communicating Science

The Alda Center opened in 2009 as a result of collaboration between Alan, Stony Brook, and Stony Brook's School of Communication and Journalism, with Brookhaven National Laboratory and Cold Spring Harbor Laboratory.

www.aldacenter.org

KATHLEEN YORK (CONGRESSWOMAN ANDY WYATT)

The Feminist Majority Foundation

The Feminist Majority Foundation (FMF) was created to develop bold new strategies and programs to advance women's equality, non-violence, economic development, and, most importantly, empowerment of women and girls in all sectors of society.

www.feminist.org

MARLEE MATLIN (JOEY LUCAS)

The National Association of the Deaf

The National Association of the Deaf (NAD) is the nation's premier civil rights organization of, by, and for Deaf and Hard of Hearing individuals in the United States of America. The NAD was shaped by Deaf leaders who believed in the right of the American Deaf community to use sign language to congregate on issues important to them, and to have their interests represented at the national level.

www.nad.org

ALLISON SMITH (LEO'S DAUGHTER, MALLORY O'BRIEN)

Allison has been a public servant throughout her career, including going to Haiti with Save the Children after *The West Wing*. In more recent years, she has helped build a school for girls in Jacmel, Haiti, which continues to educate girls daily.

Save the Children

Save the Children believes every child deserves a future and works in the United States and around the world to give children a healthy start in life, the opportunity to learn, and protection from harm. When crisis strikes and children are most vulnerable, Save the Children is always among the first to respond and the last to leave, doing whatever it takes for children—every day and in times of crisis—transforming their lives and the future we share.

www.savethechildren.org

DAVE CHAMEIDES (STEADICAM OPERATOR)

Food on Foot

Food on Foot is a nonprofit dedicated to assisting our unhoused and low-income neighbors in Los Angeles with nutritious meals, clothing, and a fresh start through life-skills training, full-time employment, and permanent housing.

www.foodonfoot.org

CHRIS MISIANO (DIRECTOR, EXECUTIVE PRODUCER)

PC Project

The PC Project connects patients, researchers, physicians, and industry partners in a united and global effort to help those who suffer from the debilitating effects of this rare genetic skin disease.
www.pachyonychia.org

BILL O'BRIEN (KENNY, SIGN LANGUAGE INTERPRETER FOR JOEY LUCAS)

Deaf West Theatre

Committed to innovation, collaboration, training, and activism, Deaf West is the artistic bridge between the Deaf and hearing worlds. Deaf West engages artists and audiences in unparalleled theater and media experiences inspired by Deaf culture and the expressive power of sign language, weaving ASL with spoken English to create a seamless ballet of movement and voice.
www.deafwest.org

Theater of War Productions

Theater of War works with leading film, theater, and television actors to present dramatic readings of seminal plays—from classical Greek tragedies to modern and contemporary works—followed by town hall–style discussions designed to confront social issues by drawing out raw and personal reactions to themes highlighted in the plays.
www.theaterofwar.com

W.G. "SNUFFY" WALDEN (COMPOSER)

Alzheimer's Association

The Alzheimer's Association leads the way to end Alzheimer's and all other dementia by accelerating global research, driving risk reduction and early detection, and maximizing quality care and support. /
www.alz.org

KURT BARDELLA (POLITICAL OPERATIVE, COMMENTATOR)

Environmental Voter Project

The Environmental Voter Project identifies inactive environmentalists and transforms them into consistent voters to build the power of the environmental movement.
www.environmentalvoter.org

PETER ROTH (CHAIRMAN/CEO OF WARNER BROS. TELEVISION, 1999–2021)

Array

Founded in 2011 by filmmaker Ava DuVernay, Array is a multiplatform arts and social impact collective dedicated to narrative change. The organization catalyzes its work through a quartet of mission-driven entities: the film distribution arm ARRAY Releasing, the content company ARRAY Filmworks, the programming and production hub ARRAY CREATIVE CAMPUS and the nonprofit group ARRAY Alliance.
www.arraynow.com

JOHN WELLS (EXECUTIVE PRODUCER, SHOWRUNNER)

Motion Picture and Television Fund

The Motion Picture and Television Fund supports working and retired members of the entertainment community with a safety net of health and social services, including temporary financial assistance, case management, and residential living.

www.mptf.com

AARON SORKIN (CREATOR, SHOWRUNNER, EXECUTIVE PRODUCER)

When We All Vote

When We All Vote is a leading national, nonpartisan initiative on a mission to change the culture around voting and to increase participation in each and every election by helping to close the race and age gap. Created by Michelle Obama, When We All Vote brings together individuals, institutions, brands, and organizations to register new voters across the country and advance civic education for the entire family and voters of every age to build an informed and engaged electorate for today and generations to come.

www.whenweallvote.org

ACKNOWLEDGMENTS

We have always felt lucky to have been part of *The West Wing*. Writing this book has meant reliving every moment of those days and feeling lucky all over again. In particular, we are indebted to the myriad brilliant, helpful, good-humored, patient minds who helped us so lovingly and so often. And Josh Malina.

It would have been impossible to write this without so many of you, but special thanks must be given to the brilliant people whose names were on the front row of video village for so many years, John Wells and Tommy Schlamme. Your generosity in supporting this book has been so meaningful and has inspired us to keep striving to make this the best version of our story. Peter Roth, you have always believed in *The West Wing*. Your green light of this book was just the latest in a long line of green lights from 1999 to today, which made everything possible. And especially to Aaron Sorkin, whose unfathomable and frankly unreasonable talent made everything possible in the first place. Thank you for encouraging us. Without your kindness, without your support, without your very first "yes," there would most certainly be no book.

Our brilliant and accomplished, warm and funny castmates—and Josh Malina—thank you for walking-and-talking down memory lane with us. We've loved it, and we couldn't have done it without you. And to our wonderful, witty, and wise crew, thank you for sharing your memories with us.

Our own personal Sit Room at Dutton was helmed by our superb, positive, and blessedly patient editor, Jill Schwartzman, a national security advisor if there ever was one, and her unflappable and talented deputy, Charlotte Peters. Alongside them sat the unfailing guiding hand of John Parsley, our marketers Stephanie Cooper and Isabel DaSilva, publicist Emily Canders, cover designer Jason Booher, and the army of editors, copy editors, proofreaders, and more. If this were the real Sit Room, you would all wear rows of medals.

Thank you to our fearless agents at Javelin, Dylan Colligan and Matt Latimer, who convinced us (without much resistance) that this whole book thing would be a good idea.

Thank you to the prodigiously great John Levey for sharing with us many of your memories and some of your secrets.

Thank you to our own personal West Wing staff, our own Joshes and Tobys and C.J.s: Michael Morris, thank you for your unending support, and for wielding your scalpel with kindness. Your steadfast commitment to pitch-perfect tone, your constant steering toward quality and what is essential, are unparalleled. We are so lucky and so grateful; James Rudnick, thank you for bringing your unrivaled knowledge of all things *West Wing* to the table, time and time and time again. Theresa Bruno, queen of the hashtag, and neo-Wingnut Theo Cockrell, thank you for living and breathing all things *West Wing* for more than thirty-six months. Thank you for your incredible patience and forbearance.

And to John Cockrell, you deserve your own Oval Office. Your years-long dedication to the cause of this book, your endless sense of humor, and your blessed devotion to the five-hour phone call are all unmatched, as is your talent. Thank you, thank you, thank you from the bottom of our hearts.

There are, of course, far too many people to thank individually, but as Snuffy's music plays and the credits roll, you might glance up and see thanks to Lauren Lohman for your support and belief in us and this project, to Julie DeJoie for never screening our calls despite knowing that picking up would mean answering more and more . . . and more questions; and to one of our most essential political voices, Lawrence O'Donnell. Thank you for your endless support for our *West Wing* family, on air and off; to Tori Nevens, researcher extraordinaire, for expertly taking on whatever we sent her way; to Blanche Sindelar, property master for *The West Wing*, for taking and sharing photos of the archived props you know better than anyone; to Mindy Kanaskie, for going above and beyond as you always have; to Julie Dillard and Ned Haspel at John Wells Productions for being there for us time and time again; to our friends at the Warner Bros. Corporate Archive, archivist Mark Greenhalgh, Robert Sandoval, Matthew Truex, and Maria Cazarez; to Steve Bingen, whose excellent book *Warner Bros. Hollywood's Ultimate Backlot* provided invaluable historical context; to CNN's David Daniel: thank you for giving us permission to quote from your beautiful interview with our dear friend John Spencer. Thanks to Andrew Bernstein, Eli Attie, Michael Holland, Daniel Penchina, and Jessica Gardner for always saying yes when asked to read draft after draft; to Amy Dacey for her invaluable insights and advice, and to Kevin Walling, whose persistence and confidence in us makes him in so many ways the godfather of this book.

From **MELISSA:** To my DC family, Eric Fanning, Ben Masri-Cohen, Evie, Judi, and Maggie, for living through every minute of this process; to my All Rise family for your support throughout the writing of this book; to Shannon McMahon-Lichte for being the best cheerleader for everything, including this book; and to the rest of my GADA family, you know who you are, you know what you did. To West

Huddleston for taking a chance on me. To my family of friends, thank you for always lifting me up. And finally to my family family: Mom and Dad, Jamie, Craig, Mary, James, Russell, Mac, Joe, Luke, and Stanley for your endless support and understanding of missed dinners, games, and celebrations.

From **MARY:** Endless, undying, and forever thanks to my husband, Michael, and to Margaret, Rose, and Lillian for bingeing the series yet again with their mother, and for understanding why Mama was always busy. And thank you to my family: Bill and Judith, Norah and Gordon, Bridget, Will, for teaching me by example the meaning of the word "service." And an extra thanks to my big sister, Bridget, for being my own personal true-life *West Wing* character.

Hrishikesh Hirway, thanks to you and your brilliant production team at *The West Wing Weekly* podcast. What you accomplished continues to amaze us, and you blazed a trail for this book without which we would have been lost. And also Josh Malina.

Perhaps most importantly, thank you to the millions of *West Wing* fans from around the world, who keep coming back to the show, who keep the community alive and thriving. Without you there would exist neither seven seasons of a television show, nor this book. Wingnuts of the world, we salute you. Whether you have expressed your love for the show in incredible fan-made projects like WestWingTranscripts.com, or Fandom's *West Wing Wiki*, or simply watched, rewatched, remembered lines and details and quotes, please know that you inspired *What's Next*. We hope you have enjoyed it. It was for you.

A final thank-you to anyone and everyone who has devoted some or all of their lives to service. It is true, ultimately, that to live is to serve. Whether it is an hour a week, or a lifetime, the act of stepping outside of oneself, and making oneself available to others, is something that enriches all of us. Thank you, from the bottom of our hearts, for caring enough to make the world better.

SOURCE NOTES

All author interviews with Melissa and Mary were conducted in person or via Zoom, phone, email, or text between January 2021 and February 2024.

PROLOGUE

The prologue is based almost exclusively on Mary's and Melissa's reflections and memories.

Author interviews with Lawrence O'Donnell, Allison Janney, Bradley Whitford, and Dulé Hill.

CHAPTER 1: ORIGIN STORY: THE *WEST WING* PILOT

Author interviews with Jon Hutman, Peter Roth, Aaron Sorkin, Tommy Schlamme, John Wells, John Levey, Kevin Walling, and Kathleen York.

"The Definitive History of *The West Wing*," EmpireOnline, https://www .empireonline.com/west-wing/.

Mikey O'Connell, Marc Bernardin, and Lacey Rose, "*West Wing* Uncensored," *The Hollywood Reporter*, May 13, 2014, https://www.hollywoodreporter .com/tv/tv-news/west-wing-uncensored-aaron-sorkin-703010/.

Joshua Malina and Hrishikesh Hirway, *The West Wing Weekly*, "West Wing Reunion (Live from ATX)," Episode 0.01, June 15, 2016.

The West Wing, "Pilot," Season 1, audio commentary, DVD. Burbank, CA: Warner Bros., 2007.

CHAPTER 2: CASTING, ABOUT

John Levey, interviews with the authors.

John Rater, interview with the authors.

The West Wing, "Pilot," Season 1, audio commentary, DVD. Burbank, CA: Warner Bros., 2007.

The West Wing Weekly, "Casting the Pilot (with John Levey)," Episode 0.17, November 12, 2019.

The West Wing Weekly, "Special Interim Session (with Aaron Sorkin)," Episode 2.00, September 20, 2016.

CHAPTER 3: "THESE WOMEN . . ." AND A FEW GOOD MEN: PART I

John Levey, interviews with the authors.

The West Wing, "He Shall from Time to Time . . . ," Season 1, Episode 12 (NBC), January 12, 1999.

"The Definitive History of *The West Wing*," EmpireOnline, https://www .empireonline.com/west-wing/.

Mikey O'Connell, Marc Bernardin, and Lacey Rose, "*West Wing* Uncensored," *The Hollywood Reporter*, May 13, 2014, https://www.hollywoodreporter .com/tv/tv-news/west-wing-uncensored-aaron-sorkin-703010/.

Terri Roberts, "John Spencer: A Look Back," *Backstage*, March 25, 2013, https://www.backstage.com/magazine/article/john-spencer-look-back -31658/.

David Daniel interview with John Spencer, CNN, September 2002 featured on *The West Wing Weekly*, "Bartlet for America (with John Spencer)," Episode 3.09, June 6, 2017.

Bradley Whitford, interview with the authors.

The West Wing Weekly, "In the Shadow of Two Gunmen (with Bradley Whitford and Michael O'Neill)," Episode 2.02, September 28, 2016.

David Whitford, "The Secret Life of an Actor," *Esquire*, January 29, 2007, https://www.esquire.com/entertainment/tv/a1239/esq0501-may-whitford -rev-4/.

Allison Janney, interview with the authors.

John Levey, interview with the authors.

Kevin Scott, interview with the authors.

"The Cast of *The West Wing*," *The Ellen DeGeneres Show* (NBC), May 11, 2006.

The West Wing Weekly, "The Women of Qumar," Episode 3.08, May 31, 2017.

Sydney Bucksbaum, "Allison Janney Reveals Why C.J. Cregg on *The West Wing* Is Her Favorite Role," *Entertainment Weekly*, August 26, 2020, https:// ew.com/tv/allison-janney-the-west-wing-reunion-cj-cregg/.

The West Wing Weekly, "Tomorrow," Episode 7.22, January 28, 2020.

"See *The West Wing* Administration Reunite in EW's Exclusive Portraits," *Entertainment Weekly*, August 25, 2020, https://ew.com/tv-reunions/west -wing-reunion-portraits/.

Richard Schiff, interview with the authors.

The West Wing Weekly, "In Excelsis Deo," Episode 1.10, May 25, 2016.

Rob Lowe, interview with the authors.

The West Wing Weekly, "Casting the Pilot (with John Levey)," Episode 0.17, November 12, 2019.

The West Wing Weekly, "Someone's Going to Emergency, Someone's Going to Jail (with Rob Lowe)," Episode 2.16, January 31, 2017.

Janel Moloney, interviews with the authors.

"Six Southern Gentlemen of Tennessee," Episode 111, *Sports Night*, Daily Motion.

CHAPTER 4: MOVING MOUNTAINS AND SCRUBBING FLOORS: *THE WEST WING* AND SERVICE

Sports Night, "The Quality of Mercy at 29K," Season 1, Episode 9 (Imagine/ Touchstone), December 1, 1998.

Christopher Misiano, interview with the authors.

Dulé Hill, interview with the authors.

CHAPTER 5: A SERVICE STORY: MARTIN SHEEN

Martin Sheen, interviews with the authors.

CHAPTER 6: "THESE WOMEN . . ." AND A FEW GOOD MEN: PART II

Kevin Scott, interview with the authors.

Dulé Hill, interview with the authors.

Political Dictionary, s.v. "body man," https://politicaldictionary.com/words /body-man/.

The American President, written and directed by Aaron Sorkin (Columbia Pictures, 1995).

The West Wing Weekly, "A Proportional Response," Episode 1.03, April 6, 2016.

The West Wing Weekly, "West Wing Reunion (Live from ATX)," Episode 0.01, June 15, 2016.

Stockard Channing, interview with the authors.

The West Wing Season 4 DVD featurette: "Behind Every Good Man Is the First Lady," produced in association with Creative Domain (Warner Bros. Entertainment, 2005).

Stockard Channing, "Conversations on Broadway: Stockard Channing," SAG-Aftra Foundation, New York, March 16, 2015.

Joe Reid, David Sims, and Kevin O'Keefe, "A Definitive Ranking of Every Character on *The West Wing*," *The Atlantic*, September 12, 2014, https:// www.theatlantic.com/culture/archive/2014/09/a-definitive-ranking-of -every-character-on-the-west-wing/380098/.

Tim Davis-Reed, interview with the authors.

The West Wing Weekly, "Casting the Pilot (with John Levey)," Episode 0.17, November 12, 2019.

"Kathryn Joosten on 'The West Wing,'" EmmyTVLegends.org, https:// interviews.televisionacademy.com/interviews/kathryn-joosten.

Entertainment Weekly, "The *West Wing* Cast Remembers John Spencer & Kathryn Joosten," August 2020.

Rob Lowe, interview with the authors.

Timothy Busfield, interviews with the authors.

Blanche Sindelar, interview with the authors.

Adam B. Vary, "How 'The West Wing' Cast and Crew Pulled Off Their Groundbreaking Reunion," *Variety*, June 25, 2021, https://variety.com/2021 /tv/news/west-wing-reunion-aaron-sorkin-thomas-schlamme-1235005158/.

Mikey O'Connell, Marc Bernardin, and Lacey Rose, "*West Wing* Uncensored," *The Hollywood Reporter*, May 13, 2014, https://www.hollywoodreporter .com/tv/tv-news/west-wing-uncensored-aaron-sorkin-703010/.

Melissa Fitzgerald, interview with Mary McCormack.

Charles Isherwood, theater review of *Remembrance*, *Variety*, October 8, 1997.

Jon McDaid, "TV Guide Interview with NiCole Robinson, aka 'Margaret,'" *West Wing News Blog*, June 12, 2006, https://westwingnews.blogspot.com /2006/06/tv-guide-interview-with-nicole.html.

Emily Procter, interviews with the authors.

CHAPTER 7: FOURTH FOUNDING FATHER: THE ORIGIN STORY OF JOSIAH BARTLET

Mikey O'Connell, Marc Bernardin, and Lacey Rose, "*West Wing* Uncensored," *The Hollywood Reporter*, May 13, 2014, https://www.hollywoodreporter .com/tv/tv-news/west-wing-uncensored-aaron-sorkin-703010/.

The West Wing Weekly, "President Bartlet Special (with Martin Sheen)," Episode 4.0, October 3, 2017.

Martin Sheen, "We Day Speech 2010," YouTube, February 4, 2014.

"The Definitive History of *The West Wing*," EmpireOnline, https://www .empireonline.com/west-wing/.

Kevin Scott, interview with the authors.

The West Wing Weekly, "John Wells," Episode 0.19, December 17, 2019.

CHAPTER 8: THE TABLE READ AND *THE WAR ROOM*

Author interviews with Andrew Bernstein, Christopher Misiano, Julie DeJoie, Lauren Lohman, Devika Parikh, Richard Schiff, Allison Janney, Brad Whitford, Martin Sheen, Tommy Schlamme, and Rob Lowe.

"The Definitive History of *The West Wing*," EmpireOnline, https://www .empireonline.com/west-wing/.

CHAPTER 9: THE FIRST STEPS TOWARD TOMORROW: MAKING THE *WEST WING* PILOT

Lyn Paolo, interview with the authors.

Rob Lowe, interview with the authors.

Tommy Schlamme, interviews with the authors.

The West Wing Weekly, "Bartlet for America (with John Spencer)," Episode 3.09, June 6, 2017.

The West Wing Weekly, "Someone's Going to Emergency, Someone's Going to Jail (with Rob Lowe)," Episode 2.16, January 31, 2017.

The West Wing Weekly, "West Wing Reunion (Live from ATX)," Episode 0.01, June 15, 2016.

Brad Whitford, interview with the authors.

Richard Schiff, interview with the authors.

The West Wing Weekly, "Two Cathedrals (Part II, with Aaron Sorkin and Kristen Nelson)," Episode 2.22, March 21, 2017.

Alex Graves, interview with the authors.

The West Wing, "Pilot," Season 1, audio commentary, DVD. Burbank, CA: Warner Bros., 1999, 2000.

Dee Dee Myers, interview with the authors.

The West Wing, Season 1, Allison Janney, "The Inauguration," DVD featurette, Burbank, CA: Warner Bros., 1999, 2000.

The West Wing, Season 2, "In the Shadow of Two Gunmen: Part II," audio commentary, DVD. Burbank, CA: Warner Bros., 2000, 2001.

CHAPTER 10: AND IT'S SURELY TO THEIR CREDIT

Peter Roth, interviews with the authors.
Jennifer Littlehales, interview with the authors.

CHAPTER 11: PROCESS STORIES: WRITING *THE WEST WING*

Author interviews with Kevin Falls, Alex Graves, Lauren Schmidt Hissrich, Allison Janney, Dee Dee Myers, Kevin Walling, Deborah Cahn, Josh Singer, John Wells, Tommy Schlamme, Brad Whitford, Richard Schiff, Devika Parikh, Christopher Misiano, Kristin Chenoweth, John Wells, Rob Lowe, Timothy Busfield, Mike Hissrich, Dulé Hill, Kathleeen York, Stockard Channing, John Goodman, Alex Graves, Felicia Willson, Dave Chamedies, Tony Sepulveda, Hilary Griffiths, Tim Davis-Reed, Eli Attie, and Josh Einsohn.

The West Wing Weekly, "Game On," Episode 4.06, November 14, 2017.

The West Wing Weekly, "Bartlet for America (with John Spencer)," Episode 3.09, June 6, 2017.

The West Wing Weekly, "In Excelsis Deo," Episode 1.10, May 25, 2016.

The West Wing Weekly, "John Wells," Episode 0.19, December 17, 2019.

The West Wing Weekly, "The Women of Qumar," Episode 3.08, May 31, 2017.

The West Wing Weekly, "Posse Comitatus," Episode 3.22, September 19, 2017.

The West Wing Weekly, "18th and Potomac," Episode 2.21, March 7, 2017.

SmartLess podcast, "Jeff Daniels," October 4, 2021.

CHAPTER 12: BREAK TIME

The West Wing, "Shibboleth," Season 2, Episode 8 (NBC), November 22, 2000.

The West Wing, "Galileo," Season 2, Episode 9 (NBC), November 29, 2000.

CHAPTER 13: KEY EPISODE: "IN EXCELSIS DEO"

Richard Schiff, interviews with the authors.
Alex Graves, interview with the authors.
The West Wing Weekly, "In Excelsis Deo," Episode 1.10, May 25, 2016.
The West Wing, Season 1, "In Excelsis Deo," audio commentary, DVD. Burbank, CA: Warner Bros., 1999, 2000.

CHAPTER 14: A SERVICE STORY: RICHARD SCHIFF

Richard Schiff, interviews with the authors.

CHAPTER 15: THE GOSPEL ACCORDING TO SNUFFY

Snuffy Walden, interview with the authors.
Tommy Schlamme, interview with the authors.
Carson Fox, interview with the authors.
Judge Robert Russell, interview with the authors.

CHAPTER 16: KEY EPISODES: "WHAT KIND OF DAY HAS IT BEEN?" AND "IN THE SHADOW OF TWO GUNMEN: PARTS I AND II"

Brad Whitford, interviews with the authors.
Tommy Schlamme, interviews with the authors.
The West Wing, Season 2, "In the Shadow of Two Gunmen, Parts I and II," audio commentary, DVD. Burbank, CA: Warner Bros., 2000, 2001.
The West Wing Weekly, "In the Shadow of Two Gunmen," Episode 2.01, September 28, 2016.
The West Wing Weekly, "In the Shadow of Two Gunmen," Episode 2.02, September 28, 2016.
The West Wing Weekly, "Tomorrow," Episode 7.22, January 28, 2020.

CHAPTER 17: I CAN'T BELIEVE IT'S NOT BUTTERFIELD!

Michael O'Neill, interview with the authors.
The West Wing, "In the Shadow of Two Gunmen: Part I," Season 2, Episode 1 (NBC), October 4, 2000.

CHAPTER 18: A SERVICE STORY: JANEL MOLONEY

Janel Moloney, interviews with the authors.
Karla Nunfio, interview with the authors.

CHAPTER 19: KEY EPISODE: "NOËL"

Brad Whitford, interviews with the authors.
Tommy Schlamme, interviews with the authors.
The West Wing Weekly, "Noël," Episode 2.10, November 30, 2016.
The West Wing, Season 2, "Noël," audio commentary, DVD. Burbank, CA: Warner Bros., 2000, 2001.
The West Wing Weekly, "West Wing Reunion (Live from ATX)," Episode 0.01, June 15, 2016.
The West Wing, "Noël," Season 2, Episode 10 (NBC), December 13, 2000.

CHAPTER 20: A SERVICE STORY: BRADLEY WHITFORD

Brad Whitford, interviews with the authors.

CHAPTER 21: KEY EPISODE: "TWO CATHEDRALS"

Author interviews with Aaron Sorkin, Tommy Schlamme, Lawrence O'Donnell, and Martin Sheen.

The West Wing Weekly, "18th and Potomac," Episode 2.21, March 7, 2017.

The West Wing Weekly, "Two Cathedrals," Episode 2.22, March 14, 2017.

The West Wing DVD featurette, "Constructing Two Cathedrals," Season 2. Burbank, CA: Warner Bros., 2000, 2001.

The West Wing, "Two Cathedrals," Season 2, Episode 22 (NBC), May 16, 2001.

CHAPTER 22: WAYS AND MEANS

Alex Graves, interview with the authors.

CHAPTER 23: KEY EPISODE: "BARTLET FOR AMERICA"

Aaron Sorkin, interviews with the authors.

The West Wing Weekly, "Bartlet for America (with John Spencer)," Episode 3.09, June 6, 2017.

The West Wing, Season 3, "Bartlet for America," audio commentary, DVD. Burbank, CA: Warner Bros., 2001, 2002.

The West Wing, "Bartlet for America," Season 3, Episode 10 (NBC), December 12, 2001.

CHAPTER 24: WILL BAILEY: ORIGIN STORY

Author interviews with Brad Whitford, Josh Malina, Dylan Massin, Allison Janney, Ron Ostrow, and Christopher Misiano.

Podcrushed podcast, "Rob Lowe," August 9, 2023.

Oscar Sanchez, "Watch *The West Wing* Cast Bond Over On-Set Prankster Joshua Malina," *Entertainment Weekly*, August 27, 2020, https://ew.com/tv/west-wing-cast-joshua-malina-pranks/.

The West Wing Weekly, "In the Shadow of Two Gunmen," Episode 2.02, September 28, 2016.

The West Wing Weekly, "2162 Votes," Episode 6.22, June 18, 2019.

The West Wing Weekly, "Game On," Episode 4.06, November 14, 2017.

CHAPTER 25: KEY EPISODE: "GAME ON"

Author interviews with Alex Graves, Josh Malina, Brad Whitford, Rob Lowe, Davika Parikh, Joanna Gleason, and Kristin Chenoweth.
The West Wing Weekly, "Game On," Episode 4.06, November 14, 2017.
The West Wing Weekly, "In the Shadow of Two Gunmen," Episode 2.01, September 28, 2016.
The West Wing, "Game On," Season 4, Episode 6 (NBC), October 30, 2002.
The West Wing, Season 4, "Game On," audio commentary, DVD. Burbank, CA: Warner Bros., 2002, 2003.
David Whitford, "The Secret Life of an Actor," *Esquire*, January 29, 2007, https://www.esquire.com/entertainment/tv/a1239/esq0501-may-whitford-rev-4/.

CHAPTER 26: TRANSITION

Author interviews with Aaron Sorkin, Tommy Schlamme, John Wells, Peter Roth, Alex Graves, Bradley Whitford, Allison Janney, Dulé Hill, Josh Singer, Debora Cahn, and Martin Sheen.
The West Wing, Season 5, "The Supremes," audio commentary, DVD. Burbank, CA: Warner Bros., 2003, 2004.
The West Wing Weekly, "Season 4 Retrospective," Episode 4.24, May 15, 2018.
The West Wing Weekly, "7A WF 83429," Episode 5.01, May 29, 2018.
The West Wing Weekly, "Twenty-Five," Episode 4.23, May 9, 2018.
The West Wing Weekly, "John Wells," Episode 0.19, December 17, 2019.
The West Wing, "Election Night," Season 4, Episode 7 (NBC), November 6, 2002.

CHAPTER 27: PEACEFUL TRANSFER OF POWER

Author interviews with Josh Singer, Debora Cahn, Lauren Hissrich, and John Wells.
The West Wing Weekly, "In Excelsis Deo," Episode 1.10, May 25, 2016.
The West Wing Weekly, "John Wells," Episode 0.19, December 17, 2019.
The West Wing Weekly, "The Women of Qumar," Episode 3.08, May 31, 2017.
The West Wing Weekly, "Posse Comitatus," Episode 3.22, September 19, 2017.
The West Wing Weekly, "18th and Potomac," Episode 2.21, March 7, 2017.

CHAPTER 28: KATE HARPER: ORIGIN STORY

Mary McCormack, interview with Melissa Fitzgerald.
Moms Demand Action, www.momsdemandaction.org.
Everytown Research & Policy, https://everytownresearch.org/research/

CHAPTER 29: KEY EPISODE: "THE SUPREMES"

Debora Cahn, interviews with the authors.
The West Wing, "The Supremes," Season 5, Episode 17 (NBC), March 24, 2004.
The West Wing Weekly, "The Supremes," Episode 5.17, October 2, 2018.
The West Wing, Season 5, "The Supremes," audio commentary, DVD. Burbank, CA: Warner Bros., 2003, 2004.
Say Anything, written and directed by Cameron Crowe (20th Century Fox, 1989).

CHAPTER 30: FIRST, FAMILY

Author interviews with Martin Sheen, Richard Schiff, Allison Janney, Janel Moloney, Andrew Bernstein, Holli Strickland, Adam Ben Frank, Lauren Lohman, Julie DeJoie, Llewellyn Wells, Ramón de Ocampo, Jill Crosby, Dylan Massin, Renee Rosenfeld, Josh Malina, and Hrishikesh Hirway.
The West Wing, "The Crackpots and These Women," Season 1, Episode 5 (NBC), October 20, 1999.
The West Wing Weekly, "Season 4 Retrospective," Episode 4.24, May 15, 2018.
The West Wing Weekly, "Tomorrow," Episode 7.22, January 28, 2020.
The West Wing Weekly, "Two Cathedrals," Episode 2.22, March 14, 2017.
The West Wing Weekly, "2162 Votes," Episode 6.22, June 18, 2019.

CHAPTER 31: "WALK-AND-TALK THE VOTE"

John Cockrell, interviews with the authors.
Bridget McCormack, interview with the authors.
Aaron Sorkin, personal email correspondence.
Bridget McCormack, personal email correspondence.

CHAPTER 32: KEY EPISODE: "THE DEBATE"

Author interviews with Lawrence O'Donnell, Alan Alda, Jimmy Smits, Lauren Schmidt Hissrich, and Michael Hissrich.
The West Wing, "The Debate," Season 7, Episode 7 (NBC), November 6, 2005.
The West Wing Weekly, "The Debate," Episode 7.07, August 27, 2019.
The West Wing, Season 7, "The Debate," audio commentary, DVD. Burbank, CA: Warner Bros., 2005, 2006.
"The Definitive History of *The West Wing*," EmpireOnline, https://www.empireonline.com/west-wing/.
Alan Alda tweet, July 28, 2023.

CHAPTER 33: GONE

Author interviews with Bradley Whitford, Lee Rose, Allison Janney, Stockard
    Channing, Stephen Pfeiffer, Eli Attie, Alex Graves, Josh Singer, Martin
    Sheen, Jimmy Smits, Emily Procter, Kristin Chenoweth, Richard Schiff,
    Rob Lowe, Tommy Schlamme, Devika Parikh, Janel Moloney, Dulé Hill,
    Kathleen York, Kim Webster, Ramón De Ocampo, Lyn Paolo, John Amos,
    Josh Malina, Peter Roth, Lawrence O'Donnell, Julie DeJoie, Jill Crosby,
    Adam Ben Frank, Michael Hissrich, Aaron Sorkin, John Wells, John Levey,
    William Duffy, David Katz, Ron Ostrow, Mary-Louise Parker, Anna
    Deavere Smith, Dave Chameides, Lesli Linka Glatter, W.G. "Snuffy"
    Walden, Christopher Misiano, John Goodman, Allison Smith, Andrew
    Bernstein, and Joanna Gleason.
The West Wing Weekly, "Requiem," Episode 7.18, December 10, 2019.
Christian Holub, "The West Wing Cast Remembers John Spencer & Kathryn
    Joosten," *Entertainment Weekly*, August 26, 2020, https://ew.com/tv/the
    -west-wing-john-spencer-kathryn-joosten-tributes/.
Lynn Elber, "'West Wing' Actor John Spencer Dies of Heart Attack," Associated
    Press, December 17, 2005.
"The Definitive History of *The West Wing*," EmpireOnline, https://www
    .empireonline.com/west-wing/.
The West Wing Weekly, "Tomorrow," Episode 7.22, January 28, 2020.
"John Spencer's Emmy Win," *54th Primetime Emmy Awards*, NBC, youtube
    .com, https://www.youtube.com/watch?v=IUqsqIJrLkI.

CHAPTER 34: KEY EPISODES: "ELECTION DAY: PARTS I AND II" AND "REQUIEM"

Author interviews with Eli Attie, Bradley Whitford, Stockard Channing, Dulé
    Hill, John Wells, Josh Singer, Jimmy Smits, Alan Alda, Rob Lowe, Kristin
    Chenoweth, Richard Schiff, and Allison Janney.
The West Wing, "18th and Potomac," Season 2, Episode 21 (NBC), May 9, 2001.
The West Wing, "Election Day: Part I," Season 7, Episode 16 (NBC), April 2,
    2006.
The West Wing, "Election Day: Part II," Season 7, Episode 17 (NBC), April 9,
    2006.
The West Wing, "Requiem," Season 7, Episode 18 (NBC), April 16, 2006.
The West Wing Weekly, "Election Day: Part I," Episode 7.16, November 19, 2019.
The West Wing Weekly, "Election Day: Part II," Episode 7.17, November 26, 2019.

The West Wing Weekly, "Requiem," Episode 7.18, December 10, 2019.
"The Definitive History of *The West Wing*," EmpireOnline, https://www
.empireonline.com/west-wing/.

CHAPTER 35: MEANEST MAN IN THE WORLD

Author interviews with Christopher Misiano, Bradley Whitford, Josh Malina,
Ron Ostrow, Dylan Massin, and Jimmy Smits.
The West Wing Weekly, "2162 Votes (Live with Mary McCormack and Lawrence
O'Donnell)," Episode 6.22, June 18, 2019.
Oscar Sanchez, "Watch the *West Wing* Cast Bond Over On-Set Prankster
Joshua Malina," *Entertainment Weekly*, August 27, 2020, https://ew.com/tv
/west-wing-cast-joshua-malina-pranks/.
The West Wing, "Internal Displacement," Season 7, Episode 11 (NBC), January
15, 2006.

CHAPTER 36: MARTIN SHEEN, NUMBER ONE OF
NUMBER ONES

Author interviews with Dulé Hill, Allison Janney, Josh Einsohn, Kim Webster,
John Levey, Lawrence O'Donnell, Bradley Whitford, Llewellyn Wells,
Marlee Matlin, Annette Sousa, Josh Malina, Renee Rosenfeld, Tommy
Schlamme, John Amos, Andrew Bernstein, Lesli Linka Glatter, Rob Lowe,
Greg LaCava, Frankie Bruno, Christopher Misiano, Anna Deavere Smith,
Janel Moloney, Dave Chameides, Lyn Paolo, John Goodman, Yervant
Hagopian, Richard Schiff, Carla Ward, Jimmy Smits, Adam Ben Frank,
Debora Cahn, David Katz, Kristin Chenoweth, Mindy Kanaskie, Kevin
Falls, Stockard Channing, Tim Busfield, Holli Strickland, Alex Graves,
John Wells, Peter Roth, and Aaron Sorkin.
The West Wing Weekly, "Bartlet for America," Episode 3.09, June 6, 2017. This
podcast episode includes audio of the 2002 David Daniel CNN interview
with John Spencer.

CHAPTER 37: SIN CITY AND THE BINGO BUS

Author interviews with Martin Sheen, Dulé Hill, Carla Ward, Annette Sousa,
John Wan, David Katz, Maxine Penty, Devika Parikh, Kim Webster, Peter
James Smith, and William Duffy.
Jon McDaid, "TV Guide Interview with NiCole Robinson, aka 'Margaret,'"
West Wing News Blog, June 12, 2006, https://westwingnews.blogspot.com
/2006/06/tv-guide-interview-with-nicole.html.

CHAPTER 38: REUNITED . . . (AND IT FEELS SO GOOD): *A* WEST WING *SPECIAL TO BENEFIT "WHEN WE ALL VOTE"*

Author interviews with Aaron Sorkin, Tommy Schlamme, Bradley Whitford, Allison Janney, Janel Moloney, Rob Lowe, Dulé Hill, Richard Schiff, Martin Sheen, Chuck Noland, Anna Deavere Smith, Eli Attie, Alex Graves, and Jon Hutman.

The West Wing Weekly, Episode 0.20 ("A *West Wing Weekly* Special to Discuss A *West Wing* Special to Benefit *When We All Vote* (with Aaron Sorkin)," October 28, 2020.

Alicia Rancilio, "Sterling K. Brown on Speaking Out, Invite to 'West Wing' Reunion, Hiatus from 'This Is Us,'" Shoot Online, October 26, 2020, shootonline.com.

CHAPTER 39: STAY ALIVE: *THE WEST WING, HAMILTON* . . . AND WASHINGTON

Author interviews with Bradley Whitford, Lin-Manuel Miranda, Pete Buttigieg, Mallory McMorrow, Eden Tesfaye, Brendan Boyle, Reggie Love, Jon Lovitz, Eric Fanning, Stacey Abrams, Patrick Murphy, Sarah McBride, María Teresa Kumar, Hakeem Jeffries, Kurt Bardella, Mike Hissrich, Marlee Matlin, and Bill O'Brien. *The West Wing Weekly*, "Hamilton Special," Episode 0.06, April 3, 2018.

Video of Lin-Manuel Miranda at the White House, "An Evening of Poetry, Music & the Spoken Word," WhiteHouse.org, May 12, 2009.

Madeleine M. Joung, "Fifteen Minutes with Mayor Pete," *The Harvard Crimson*, April 11, 2019.

Mallory McMorrow, SenateDems, https://senatedems.com/mcmorrow/.

Brendan Boyle, House, https://boyle.house.gov/.

Lin-Manuel Miranda tweet, November 27, 2015.

CHAPTER 40: KEY EPISODE: "TOMORROW"

Author interviews with Christopher Misiano, Bradley Whitford, Lily Tomlin, Josh Malina, Eli Attie, Julie DeJoie, Lauren Lohman, Renée Estevez, and Martin Sheen.

The West Wing, "Institutional Memory," Season 7, Episode 21 (NBC), May 7, 2006.

The West Wing, "Tomorrow," Season 7, Episode 22 (NBC), May 14, 2006.

The West Wing Weekly, "Tomorrow," Episode 7.22, January 28, 2020.

The West Wing Weekly, "Here Today," Episode 7.05, August 13, 2019.

The West Wing Weekly, "Institutional Memory," Episode 7.21, January 21, 2020.

INDEX

ABOUT THE AUTHORS

For the entire seven-season run of *The West Wing*, MELISSA FITZGERALD played C.J. Cregg's ever-present, ever-buoyant, and dutiful assistant Carol Fitzpatrick. When the series came to a close, Melissa made the move from fictional staffer to real-world advocate, relocating to Washington, DC, where, ever since, she's worked tirelessly in the rooms where it happens. In her role with All Rise, she advocates for treatment courts and justice reform and has become a seminal voice in the movement. (Oh—also, she's a much better speller than she's given credit for.)

As Commander Kate Harper, MARY McCORMACK served as the Bartlet administration's sly, wry deputy national security advisor from season 5 through the series finale. When she's not busy on-screen, Mary's time is spent raising exactly three daughters and precisely one husband. Outside of those career and family obligations, she is honored to serve as an ambassador for Justice for Vets and the Juvenile Diabetes Research Foundation. As the proud daughter of a US Marine, Mary holds all veterans causes close to her heart, but taking part in the National Memorial Day Concert on the West Lawn of the United States Capitol Building has become an annual highlight.